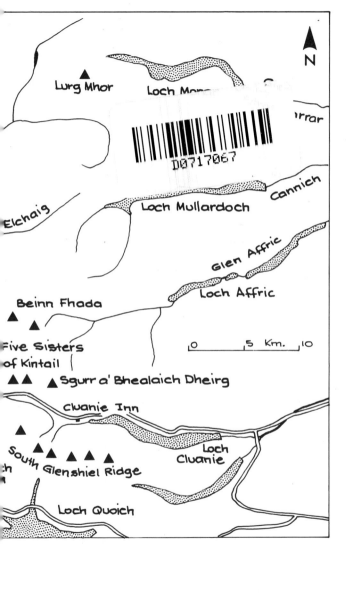

Northern Highlands

Rock and Ice Climbs

VOLUME 1

Knoydart to An Teallach

Compiled by Geoff Cohen

With contributions from Rab Anderson,
Andy Cunningham, Dougie Dinwoodie,
Andy Nisbet, Andy Tibbs, Noel Williams
and others.

Edited by Roger Everett

SCOTTISH MOUNTAINEERING CLUB
CLIMBERS' GUIDE

Published in Great Britain by the Scottish Mountaineering Trust, 1993

British Library Cataloguing in Publication Data
Cohen, G
Northern Highlands Rock and Ice Climbs
Vol. 1   2 Rev Ed
I. Title. II. Everett, R.
796.5

ISBN 0-907521-33-9

Maps drawn by Jim Renny
Diagrams drawn by Mary Benstead, Grahame Nicoll,
    Kevin Howett and Donald Bennet
Production by Peter Hodgkiss and Donald Bennet
Typeset by Elliot Robertson, Westec, North Connel
Colour separations and graphic work by Par Graphics, Kirkcaldy
Printed by St Edmundsbury Press, Bury St Edmunds
Bound by Hunter and Foulis, Edinburgh

Distributed by Cordee, 3a DeMontfort Street, Leicester, LE1 7HD

General Editor's Introduction

The northern and western highlands of Scotland include some of the most beautiful and remote mountain scenery in western Europe. The proximity of sea, loch and mountain has created a landscape which is a true pleasure to behold; the added ingredient of some of the best climbing in Britain on both summer rock and winter ice produces an environment ideal for climbers of all tastes and standards.

Until now, much of the information required to enjoy this area to the full was difficult to obtain. There was even a time when many people felt that this guide should not be published, to leave a wilderness for true exploration. Fortunately, such views have not prevailed. Over the past several years, Geoff Cohen and his helpers have been exploring both the mountains and the climbing journals to collate the information for this book. It is common knowledge that there has been some criticism of the time this has taken. A glance at the result should convince all of the unfairness of the critics. The area covered is vastly greater than that included in any other British climbers' guide and there are huge numbers of different crags and climbs. If the distances of many of the crags from the road and from the central belt of Scotland are also considered, then it is easy to appreciate the amount of work that was necessary to produce this guide.

It has been a pleasure to edit Geoff's typescript and to help to bring this guide to publication. Thumbing through the pages kindles all the excitement of looking forward to great climbing in a very special area. With the road links getting progressively better, and the advent of this book, the magic of the north is now widely accessible.

This volume describes the climbs starting from Knoydart in the south, then proceeding northwards up the western side of the Highlands as far as An Teallach. The climbing areas which are most conveniently approached from the Inverness to Braemore Junction road (including the Fannaichs), and all areas further north and east, are described in Volume 2.

Roger Everett.   October 1992

Contents

List of Illustrations

List of Diagrams and Maps

The Climber and the Mountain Environment

With increasing numbers of walkers and climbers going to the Scottish hills, it is important that all of us who do so should recognise our responsibilities to those who live and work among the hills and glens, to our fellow climbers and to the mountain environment in which we find our pleasure and recreation.

The Scottish Mountaineering Club and Trust, who jointly produce this and other guidebooks, wish to impress on all who avail themselves of the information in these books that it is essential at times to consider the sporting and proprietory rights of landowners and farmers. The description of a climbing, walking or skiing route in any of these books does not imply that a right of way exists, and it is the responsibility of all climbers to ascertain the position before setting out. In cases of doubt it is best to enquire locally.

During stalking and shooting seasons in particular, much harm can be done in deer forests and on grouse moors by people walking through them. Normally the deer stalking season is from 1st July to 20th October, when stag shooting ends. Hinds may continue to be culled until 15th February. The grouse shooting season is from 12th August until 10th December. These are not merely sporting activities, but are essential for the economy of many Highland estates. During these seasons, therefore, especial care should be taken to consult the local landowner, factor or keeper before taking to the hills.

Climbers and hillwalkers are recommended to consult the book HEADING FOR THE SCOTTISH HILLS, published by the Scottish Mountaineering Trust on behalf of the Mountaineering Council of Scotland and the Scottish Landowners Federation, which gives the names and addresses of factors and keepers who may be contacted for information regarding access to the hills.

It is important to avoid disturbance to sheep, particularly during the lambing season between March and May. Dogs should not be taken onto the hills at this time, and should always be kept under control.

Always try to follow a path or track through cultivated land and forests,and avoid causing damage to fences, dykes and gates by climbing over them carelessly. Do not leave litter anywhere, but take it down from the hill in your rucksack.

The number of walkers and climbers on the hills is leading to increased, and in some cases very unsightly erosion of footpaths and hillsides. Some of the revenue from the sale of this and other SMC guidebooks is used by the Trust to assist financially the work being carried out to repair and maintain hill paths in Scotland. However, it is important for all of us to recognise our responsibility to minimise the erosive effect of our passage over the hills so that the enjoyment of future climbers is not spoiled by landscape damage.

As a general rule, where a path exists walkers should follow it and even where it is wet and muddy should avoid walking along its edges, the effect of which is to extend erosion sideways. Do not take short-cuts at the corners of zigzag paths. Remember that the worst effects of erosion are likely to be caused during or soon after prolonged wet weather when the ground is soft and waterlogged. A route on a stony or rocky hillside is likely to cause less erosion than on a grassy one at such times.

Although the use of bicycles can often be very helpful for reaching remote crags and hills, the erosion damage that can be caused by them when used 'off road' on soft footpaths and open hillsides is such that their use on such terrain must cause concern. It is the editorial policy of the Scottish Mountaineering Club that the use of bicycles in hill country may be recommended on hard roads such as forest roads or private roads following rights of way, but it is not recommended on footpaths or open hillsides where the environmental damage that they cause may be considerable. Readers are asked to bear these points in mind, particularly when the ground is wet and soft after rain.

The proliferation of cairns on hills detracts from the feeling of wildness, and may be confusing rather than helpful as regards route-finding. The indiscriminate building of cairns on the hills is therefore discouraged.

Climbers are reminded that they should not drive along private estate roads without permission, and when parking their cars should avoid blocking access to private roads and land, and should avoid causing any hazard to other road users.

Finally, the Scottish Mountaineering Club and the Scottish Mountaineering Trust can accept no liability for damage to property nor for personal injury resulting from the use of any route described in their publications.

The Mountaineering Council of Scotland is the representative body for climbers and walkers in Scotland. One of its primary concerns is the continued free access to the hills and crags that we now enjoy. Information about bird restrictions, stalking and general access issues can be obtained from the National Officer of the MCofS. Should any climber or walker encounter problems regarding access they should contact the National Officer of the MCofS, whose current address is published in CLIMBER AND HILLWALKER magazine.

Acknowledgments

A great many people have contributed to this guide over many years. First I must thank the authors of the previous SMC climbing guides, Ian Rowe and Derwent Turnbull. These formed a sound basis for the present work, as did the the SMC Northern Highlands District Guide by Tom Strang, the winter guide by Hamish MacInnes and Kevin Howett's summer guide.

In the early stages of my undertaking I built on preparatory work by Dave Jenkins. Much of the photographic printing was done by Mungo Ross who was extremely generous with his time, and went to enormous trouble to get good results from negatives that were not always of the best. The photodiagrams by Grahame Nicoll, the crag drawings by Mary Benstead, Kev Howett, and Donald Bennet and the maps by Jim Renny deserve special mention.

Various authors have compiled or made large contributions to substantial parts of the text. Principally these were:
  Noel Williams on Knoydart, Andy Tibbs on the area from Loch Hourn to Glen Carron, Andy Cunningham on Liathach, Andy Nisbet on Beinn Eighe (Coire Mhic Fhearchair) and Diabaig, Rab Anderson on Seana Mheallan and Creag Mhor Thollaidh and Dougie Dinwoodie on Carnmore, Ghost Slabs and the Sandstone Buttresses.

Many other climbers have contributed their knowledge and advice by providing drafts, reading parts of the text, checking routes or helping with text preparation. In particular I would like to thank:
  Gordon Rothero (Flora), Alastair Matthewson and Noel Williams (Geology), Grahame Nicoll (Beinn Eighe Coire Ruadh-Staca and Jetty Crag), Steve Chadwick (Beinn Alligin, Slioch and Gairloch crags), Ginger Cain (Beinn a'Mhuinidh and Furnace crags), Kev Howett (Diabaig and Loch Maree Crags), Martin Moran (Achnashellach and Applecross), Allen Fyffe (Sgorr Ruadh), Dougie Dinwoodie (Beinn Bhan), Peter Langhorne (Meall Gorm), Dave Broadhead (Beinn Airigh Charr and Beinn Lair), Matt Shaw (Fisherfield Forest and Dundonnell), and Alastair Todd (Beinn Dearg Mor).

Finally, it is unlikely this guide would ever have appeared without the efforts of Roger Everett. His enormous energy, enthusiasm and organising ability have been invaluable.

Introduction

A personal view by Geoff Cohen

In the twenty or so years since the last SMC climbers' guide to this area was published there have been enormous changes. Numbers of climbers and hillgoers have mushroomed, attitudes to rock and ice climbing have been transformed and access to the North-west Highlands has become vastly easier. Less often commented upon has been the explosion of information regarding climbing - in books, magazines and other media. While the climbs in North-west Scotland have hitherto been relatively immune from over-exposure, it may be thought that the present guidebook will change this. If I tender apologies to those who have been impatiently waiting many years for this guide, I feel bound to say that I also sympathise with the minority who would have been only too happy to wait indefinitely. It may be self-indulgence, but perhaps some clarification of my ambivalence is required.

Much is talked about conservation, but to my mind one aspect is too little recognised, namely the conservation of the unknown. If, as I believe, the thrill of discovering a route for ourselves and the sense of achievement from overcoming unexpected difficulties constitute some of the most profound rewards of climbing, it follows that the more that is known about a prospective climb the less, on the whole, will be the sense of reward we gain from it. Naturally there are many qualifications to this. Weather and conditions can transform a 'well-known' route into an entirely new experience. For many of us, climbing at the limit of our abilities is sufficient challenge in itself. When 'knowing' the technical grade gives no guarantee we can get up a climb, the process of self-discovery in attempting it may be quite enough of an adventure, without having route-finding difficulties as well. And of course information enables us not to waste time on poor climbs, saves us getting lost on routes, and directs us to good crags. In any case my premise is questionable insofar as having read a classic account of a first ascent, or knowing that our friends had an epic on a climb, may be just why we want to climb it, or may provide the extra spice that transforms our own ascent into something memorable.

So information is undoubtedly a convenient 'commodity'. But the trend towards 'convenience mountaineering' has many aspects, some of which have been deplored even by the BMC! The effort required to reach the remote North-west of Scotland 30 years ago was incomparably greater than today; but the sense of adventure in doing so was far greater. There is obviously a spectrum of attitudes among climbers as to how 'convenient' they would like their climbing to be, from those who are content with their local climbing wall to those prepared to drive to Cape Wrath to wrestle with huge unexplored sea-cliffs. Equally obviously, individuals are not located at one point of the spectrum but vary at different times according to the other constraints on their lives. It would thus be presumptuous for any individual to attempt to demarcate a boundary between 'permitted' and 'excessive' convenience; and for that reason this guide is as comprehensive as it can be. For those who prefer to discover things for themselves, the artificial option remains of disdaining the information offered.

I will only put forward three personal observations. First, it is hypocritical to publish information extolling the beauties of a 'last unspoilt' or 'little visited' place, be it a Greek island, a Himalayan peak or a Highland crag. To the extent that I believe the remoteness and quietness of climbs in the North-west are part of the attraction, this book must fall in that category. Secondly, there is always a tension between the desire to conserve the qualities of an unspoilt or little known place or climb, and the desire to communicate, to give others the same opportunity to experience the pleasures and rewards found there. I don't know of anyone who has really resolved this paradox. Thirdly, the perennial face-saver, midges and weather will always contrive to reduce the appeal of summer climbing in the North-west, while global warming may put paid to our winter climbing. Thus the area is unlikely ever to be very intensively climbed upon. There will remain many cliffs where (weather and midges permitting) you can climb all day without seeing a soul, potter up routes that have not been climbed for 20 or 50 years or, if you wish, excavate something new from under the heather and grass.

The climbs described in this guide cover an enormous range. There are summer and winter climbs; mountain and outcrop climbs; ancient and modern climbs. Many will not have had a second ascent and only a small percentage have been climbed frequently. The style, accuracy and detail of the descriptions will be found to vary widely. In part this is the inevitable result of covering such a disparate variety of climbs and climbing areas. In part too it is the result of a conscious endeavour to let the climbers of earlier generations speak for themselves through their descriptions. In the many cases where it has been impossible to verify a description by repeating the route, the editorial pen has been wielded with some compunction, so as to allow those who so wish to engage in a kind of literary exegesis. Thus thoughtful interpretation of the descriptions, with an eye to history, will help. A description from the 1950s may refer to good rock where a climber of the 1990s will see an overabundance of vegetation. Equally the 1950s climber may have described at length steep walls, overhangs and difficult moves, perhaps on a climb graded Severe that will be very straightforward to the majority of modern climbers. On the other hand the laconic descriptions of some luminaries of the 60s and 70s may leave much to the imagination, giving little away as to where the difficulties occur. It is worth bearing in mind that what was a sapling 40 years ago may now be a more substantial tree, while cairns built at the base of routes have a tendency to disintegrate under the passage of the tiny feet of sheep over the decades. I have tried to eliminate such potentially misleading references, but don't doubt that some remain.

In general it will not surprise me if some of the descriptions are found hard to follow. Some of the crags are rather lacking in features, especially when discerned through a fine Highland mist. While the more enthusiastic route recorders love to mention 'obvious' grooves and terraces, it can be difficult at times to decide which of the many alternatives they have blessed with their passing. Excessive description of features of unspecified size leaves the guidebook writer nonplussed. So much the better for adherents of the laconic description and those prepared to tackle routes in a more exploratory manner. Descriptions of winter climbs are of course notorious for mentioning highly contingent ice pitches. An assertion that a certain pitch will 'usually' be the crux, or that a chimney is 'heavily iced', should be taken with a pinch of sodium chloride.

Finally, although it has at times seemed an awful burden, I have always found that whatever we put into the mountains they give us back many fold. Through compiling this guide I have been led to places I might never otherwise have visited, have discovered dozens of interesting climbs I might never have considered climbing and have spent many wonderful days and nights in this most precious corner of the world. I very much hope users of this guide will find the same.

Geology

Much of the special character of the climbing in the North-west Highlands is associated with the unique variety of rocks that occur there. Only five main types of rock are present, but they are all remarkably different from the igneous rocks, the granites and lavas, which are found in the classic climbing areas of Glen Coe, Glen Etive, Ben Nevis and the Cairngorms.

Lewisian Gneiss
The rock at the bottom of the pile is a coarsely crystalline metamorphic rock known as Lewisian gneiss. It is one of the oldest rocks in Europe, and can be regarded as the foundation on which the later rocks have been built. At least two major episodes of metamorphism can be recognised in the group, dated at 2800 and 1700 million years ago. The rock occurs extensively in the far North-west, and tends to be confined to the lower ground. However it is generally very rough sound rock, and where it does form crags it offers superb quality climbing. Possibly the two most notable crags of Lewisian gneiss are at Carnmore and Diabaig.

Torridonian Sandstone
Resting on the Lewisian gneiss is a very old, well-stratified sedimentary rock called Torridonian sandstone. It is one of the most distinctive rocks in the north-west because it forms much of the high ground. The rock is commonly dark red in colour and is more or less flat-lying. Its total thickness has been estimated at more than seven kilometres. Torridonian sandstone is some 800 million years old, which means that it is much too old to contain readily recognisable fossils (which did not start to appear until about 600 million years ago). It is thought that the original Torridonian sediments were deposited by rivers draining from a mountainous region which lay further north-west. The conspicuous pebbles present in some beds have been linked with rocks now found in south-east Greenland. Despite its great age, Torridonian sandstone has survived more or less unchanged since it first formed. In other words, it has not been metamorphosed and so must have remained outwith any mountain building areas.

There are not as many long mountain routes on Torridonian sandstone as might be imagined from the amount of exposed rock. This is because the bigger mountain faces tend to be broken up too frequently by terraces. However there are some fine long rock routes such as the Cioch Nose in Applecross and major winter routes in the corries of Beinn Bhan. As well as the countless short routes on the sea cliffs near Reiff there are several sea-stacks, such as the Old Man of Stoer and Am Buachaille, which offer the jaded climber something a bit out of the ordinary, and on the oldest sedimentary rock in Britain at that.

Cambrian Quartzite

Lying on top of the Torridonian sandstone is another sedimentary sequence of contrasting character. It consists largely of a pure quartz sandstone referred to as Cambrian quartzite. This forms a very distinctive capping on many Torridonian peaks, including Beinn Eighe. The rock is white or grey in colour and tends to break into sharp angular fragments. It is badly shattered in places, but where it is sound it provides first rate climbing, for example on the ramparts and buttresses of Beinn Eighe. One particular type of bed is known as Pipe Rock because of the conspicuous markings it contains. These markings represent the vertical burrows left by organisms that lived in the sediment on the sea floor.

The quartzite beds dip towards the south-east and cut across the Torridonian strata. The Cambrian quartzite must therefore have been deposited much later than the Torridonian sandstone, after that rock had been tilted and eroded. The quartzite beds are dated at about 550 million years old.

Moine Schists

The deposits which started with the Cambrian quartzite continued with the Durness limestone. Then a major mountain-building episode began that culminated in the formation of the massive Caledonian Mountain chain. This chain was formed when two 'plates' collided with each other head-on. The sediments in the ocean between the two plates were squeezed and heated during the collision, and produced a series of metamorphic rocks. As a result of the squeezing most of the metamorphic rocks were overfolded on a huge scale. In the north-west Highlands an extraordinary structure called the Moine Thrust zone developed as the pile of metamorphic rocks was pushed up and over the block of rocks that remained undeformed to the north-west. This stable block comprised the three main rock types described above, the Lewisian gneiss, Torridonian sandstone and Cambrian quartzite.

The Moine Thrust runs from Whiten Head on the north coast down to Loch Alsh on the west coast, from where it continues onto the Sleat peninsula of Skye. The Moine schists make up most of the Highlands lying to the east and south of this thrust. They originated as marine sediments, some possibly being contemporaneous with the Torridonian rocks. A great pile of schists was eventually transported several tens of kilometres north-westwards along the plane of the Moine Thrust, and came to rest on top of the younger Cambrian quartzite. Some 16 km south of Inchnadamph, at Knockan cliff, there is a Nature Trail, which visits an excellent exposure of this remarkable feature. This is a must for anyone interested in seeing this structure at first hand.

The Moine schists are a less interesting group of rocks from a climbing point of view, being rather vegetated on the whole. However, they do offer winter climbing opportunities, on Ladhar Bheinn for example.

Old Red Sandstone
Some 400 million years ago, after the Caledonian mountain building episode had passed its climax, a further group of freshwater sediments began to accumulate. These deposits are now well represented among the rocks of Caithness and Orkney. They comprise flaggy, red sandstones and contain fossil fish. Many spectacular sea-cliffs such as those on Hoy are formed from this rock. The Old Man of Hoy is set on a plinth of volcanic ash and basalt. Lesser but very scenic cliffs occur around Duncansby Head.

The final moulding of all these various rocks was brought about largely by the action of the huge ice sheets and glaciers which built up and melted down many times during the Ice Ages of the last two million years. At times the whole of Scotland was covered by ice, with the possible exception of the highest mountain summits. The last main ice-maximum occurred 17,000 years ago. In the north-west Highlands glaciers flowed both east and west, carving out the characteristic U-shaped valleys, corries and aretes, depositing moraines and sculpting the 'scarred and silent' landscapes in which we climb today.

The Flora of the North-west Highlands

The area covered by this guide is not rich in rare alpine plants and most of the interesting species can be seen, often in greater profusion, in the higher hills south of the Great Glen. The area lacks the extensive exposures of base-rich rock which many of the arctic-alpine species require and the high rainfall ensures that acid soils and areas of peat often prevail. As a result much of the vegetation is strikingly similar, even monotonous, with large areas of poor grassland dominated by Mat Grass *(Nardus stricta)* or tussocks of Purple Moorgrass *(Molinia caerulea)*, of heather moorland (often heavily punished by sheep and deer) or of 'blanket bog'. This uniformity conceals an interesting flora which is often centred on the craggy areas and the hill tops, partly as a result of grazing pressure and burning. The climber is as likely as any to see a good range of plants (whether he or she wishes to or not!).

On all of the hills, the first flowers to catch the eye will be the ubiquitous yellow Tormentil *(Potentilla erecta)* and the tiny white flowers of Heath Bedstraw *(Galium saxatile)*. Common alpine plants of poor soils such as Least Willow *(Salix herbacea)*, Moss Campion *(Silene acaulis)*, Trailing Azalea *(Loiseleuria procumbens)*, Dwarf Cudweed *(Gnaphalium supinum)*, Stiff Sedge *(Carex bigelowii)*, Crowberry *(Empetrum nigrum)* and Three-leaved Rush *(Juncus trifidus)* are usually frequent around the summits.

On some of the highest hills, in gullies where the snow lies late, rarities like Highland Saxifrage *(Saxifraga rivularis)* and Starwort Mouse-ear *(Cerastium cerastoides)* may occur with the more widespread Sibbaldia *(Sibbaldia procumbens)*. In better drained, rocky grassland there is usually a profusion of the silvery-leaved Alpine Ladies-mantle *(Alchemilla alpina)* often with Thyme *(Thymus praecox)*. By springs and small burns there can be an abundance of Yellow Saxifrage *(Saxifraga azoides)* or the white Starry Saxifrage *(Saxifraga stellaris)* in a carpet of bright green mosses.

On the crags themselves the flora will depend on the base status of the rock, the aspect and drainage. Many of the drier crags frequented by climbers, have ledges dominated by heather *(Calluna vulgaris)*, Blaeberry *(Vaccinium myrtillus)*, Cowberry *(Vaccinium* vitis-idaea) and Crowberry *(Empetrum nigrum)*, enlivened only by the yellow spikes of Golden Rod *(Solidago virgaurea)*   and occasionally by the prostrate bushes of Juniper *(Juniperus communis)*.

Where the rock is a little richer and damper, the fleshy stems of Rose-root *(Sedum rosea)* appear, often accompanied by Globe Flower *(Trollius europaeus)* and Mountain Sorrel *(Oxyria digyna)* and other tall herbs like Water Avens *(Geum rivale)* and Devil's-bit Scabious *(Succisa pratensis)*. Richer rocks that take some drainage can be festooned with the trailing stems of Purple Saxifrage *(Saxifraga oppositifolia)*, often starting to flower while most thoughts are still of winter climbing.

Ladhar Bheinn is rather poor in mountain flowers, the best area being around Stob a' Chearcaill and there is some relict pine woodland above Barrisdale. The Kintail hills have a good, if patchy, flora but the rarer plants are away from the main climbing interest. The remote hills above Loch Monar have all of the common species mentioned above and in places on summit ridges, a rich and interesting short sward of Woolly Hair-moss *(Racomitrium lanuginosum)* with Moss Campion, Thrift *(Armeria maritima)*, Alpine Bistort *(Polygonum viviparum)*, Mossy Cyphel *(Minuartia sedoides)* and the rare moss, *Aulacomium turgidum*.

The Torridonian sandstone mountains, with their large extent of bare rock and scree, are often poor botanically, and this is even more true of the capping of Cambrian quartzite. The best ledges on the crags may have Roseroot, Mountain Sorrel, Angelica *(Angelica sylvestris)*, Alpine Saw-wort *(Saussurea alpina)*, Scurvy-grass *(Cochlearia officinalis)*, Water Avens, Meadowsweet *(Filipendula ulmaria)*, Globe Flower, Thrift and Mossy Saxifrage *(Saxifraga hypnoides)*. Much less common are Arctic Mouse-ear *(Cerastium arcticum)* and Northern Rock-cress *(Arabis petraea)*; the very rare Tufted Saxifrage *(Saxifraga caespitosa)* is restricted to thin, lime-rich bands on two hills.

On Beinn Eighe the flora is richer where there are outcrops of calcareous mudstones and these also outcrop on the northern side of Loch Maree; in Glen Docherty there are limestone outcrops with a good flora and a detached limestone outcrop by Lochan Fhada flaunts the beautiful Mountain Avens *(Dryas octopetala)*. The Lewisian gneiss and schist crags on the hills of the Letterewe Forest can also be locally base-rich giving a more diverse plant life; this is notably so on Beinn Lair and Beinn Airigh Charr where most of the common montane species can be found.

The climate of the Northern Highlands means that climbing conditions are fickle but we can take some comfort from the fact that the high rainfall and humidity means that the area has an internationally important flora of 'lower plants', the mosses, liverworts and lichens! Probably the most important community occurs in north-facing corries where there is heathery block scree. Here occur a number of large leafy liverworts which individually have a remarkably disjunct global distribution; the community as a whole is strongly centred on north-west Scotland. The lower crags are often associated with some broadleaf woodland, as at Tollie Bay, and this can also be rich in rare 'lower plants', some nearing their most northerly sites in the world.

History

Protected by poor roads and the vagaries of the Scottish climate, the development of climbing in the Northern Highlands has been notably sporadic. Only in the last decade or so have improved roads and a greatly increased population of climbers promoted an avalanche of new routes - particularly on smaller outcrops which former generations might have spurned to record. The enormous variety of rock and of setting, the grandeur and isolation of the magnificent corries and wild sea-cliffs have always attracted the exploratory climbers – for here as nowhere else in Britain it is possible to climb in the authentic mountain atmosphere and to experience rock climbing as it must have felt to the pioneers of a century ago. The frequently wet and vegetatious crags demand patience and route-finding ability, but also offer scope for a more generous and spacious vision of rock climbing. Here, despite the attentions of the modern enthusiasts of the meticulous record, it is possible to escape the confined feeling of other British crags where routes are squeezed like sardines onto far too small an area of rock, and to feel instead the liberty of finding one's own way up a large buttress following 'more or less' the natural line taken 'perhaps' by the first ascensionists.

While a few of the greatest enthusiasts have ranged far and wide over the whole gamut of climbing in the Northern Highlands – one thinks of Ling and Glover, Patey and, more recently, Nisbet – it is perhaps only natural that the development of certain areas was very much the preserve of dedicated groups. Thus the Fisherfield forest will ever be associated with the Cambridge University climbers of the 1950s led by Wrangham, O'Hara and others; the 1960s exploration of Seana Bhraigh, Alladale and the Fannaichs was almost entirely the inspiration of the Corriemulzie Club driven especially by the energy of Tranter; the steady development of north-west Sutherland, both Foinaven and lesser cliffs, was for many years the preserve of a talented group of Sheffield climbers, including Paul Nunn and Clive Rowland; the exploration of the southern Fannaichs and the outcrops of Strathconon and Easter Ross in the late 70s was fired by the restless and insatiable John Mackenzie; and so on.

For these reasons it is difficult to give a synoptic history of climbing in the area as a whole. What follows is a brief and very subjective view of some of the highlights, described according to the chapter headings in the main text.

KNOYDART

The surprisingly few and rather undistinguished rock climbs in Knoydart were climbed by various teams in the late 1960s and early 1970s. The winter climbs, of much greater interest, have a much longer history, beginning with a notable ascent by Harold Raeburn and partners during the famous SMC yachting meet at Easter 1897. Bad weather had driven the party back from Loch Scavaig on Skye. Sixty five years then elapsed before a visit by another outstanding climber, Tom Patey, accounted for two more major lines, Gaberlunzie and Viking Gully.

Ewing and Sproul added Para Handy Gully in 1971, but it was not until the late 1970s that development began in earnest. A visit by two Aberdonian teams in 1978, Nisbet and Tipton, and Dinwoodie and McIvor, produced the first routes on Spider Buttress; Face Route and West Pillar. The sight of their footprints spurred Con Higgins into action. From his base in Fort William he began a quiet campaign to realise the true potential of Coire Dhorrcail. His first contribution, Tir na Og, was a major plum. It takes a compelling line directly up the centre of Spider Buttress. It is the hardest route in Knoydart and arguably one of the finest in the North-west Highlands. Three more routes fell to Higgins in 1978, his American partner being the inspiration for the naming of Thunderchicken and Transatlantic Bong. The following year Higgins closed his campaign with another direct line on Spider Buttress, East Rib.

Several new climbs were added by a variety of teams in the 1980s. It was not until 1986 that Bottleneck Gully, which Patey had described in 1962 as "well deserving a visit", was finally climbed by Jeffrey and Williams. Most of the more obvious lines in the corrie have now been climbed, although scope remains for further routes.

COULIN FOREST

As early as 1895 the crags of Fuar Tholl, An Ruadh Stac and Glas Bheinn were graphically described by Lionel Hinxman, a founding father of the SMC. Coming up from Achnashellach towards Coire Lair he remarked: "Over the lower part of the glen frown the great precipices of Fuar Tholl, of which those that hem in the corrie of that ilk are absolutely perpendicular. AP too appear to be the sides of the great buttress of terraced sandstone that hangs imminent over the little tarn of Coire Mainreachan....That these cliffs are also absolutely inaccessible I would not venture to affirm".

A decade later a dash by Raeburn in foul April weather allowed him to snatch his eponymous buttress on Sgorr Ruadh. Leaving Aviemore at 8.30am with E.B.Robertson, he arrived in Achnashellach four hours later in 'dense mist, howling sleet-laden gale and 8-10 inches of slush'. Two days later, though the gale 'blew with undiminished violence' the weather was colder and the snow better. They found the climbing on the buttress 'not very easy, but icy snow usually adhering to grassy walls gave good hitches and handholds could also be cut as required'. It sounds like a typical Raeburn *tour de force*.

Apart from a single climb on Fuar Tholl in the 1930s, nothing of real note seems to have been achieved until 1969 when the potential of the steep sandstone cliffs of Fuar Tholl was realised by the teams of Martin Boysen and Dave Alcock and Hamish MacInnes and Ian Clough. An earlier prowl by Jimmy Marshall in 1952, and a later climb by Peter Macdonald, had avoided the forbidding challenge of Mainreachan. The 1969 exploration started with Investigator, a tentative up the short upper right wall, and continued with several routes of some stature up the highest section of the wall; several easier climbs on the south-east cliff of Fuar Tholl were also completed, although the highest section of this was left unattended. Neither cliff has many natural lines and the steep sandstone is often loose, vegetated and greasy into the bargain. However the MacInnes guide of 1971 referred to the 'wonderful Coire Mainreachan', and the 1973 SMC Climbers' Guide described it as 'celebrated'. George Shields and Russell Sharp had indeed added another climb in 1972, and Boysen returned in 1974, but after this the cliffs lapsed into obscurity once more. Several parties reported disappointment with the quality - the climbs are certainly not in the modern idiom - but it remains rewarding to those whose sense of fun embraces route-finding difficulties, large dodgy blocks and all the other peculiarities of the Scottish game.

Meanwhile the late 1970s saw the start of an appreciation of the winter potential, with a difficult ascent of Fuar Folly by Rob Archbold and Dave Nicholls, sadly deflected from the true line by the onset of darkness. It remained for Mick Fowler and Phil Butler to take up the magnificent challenge of the steep ice in the centre of the south-east cliff, followed later by Martin Moran who added further routes there and also forced a major winter climb up the improbable north face of Mainreachan.

Sgorr Ruadh also had to wait until the late 1960s before the first new winter climbs were made, with Bill Brooker's ascent of Raeburn's Buttress Direct. A spate of ascents of the more obvious gullies by Hamish MacInnes and Alan Fyffe followed. A couple of slightly harder gullies were added by Andy Nisbet and then more recently Martin Moran contributed some good harder climbs on the north side of Raeburn's Buttress.

APPLECROSS

In July 1891 Hinxman visited Beinn Bhan and described it in the Journal as having 'every attribute of hell except its warmth'. He went on to paint a marvellous picture of Coire na Poite. 'Some little way above the loch (Coire na Poite) a rock terrace .... forms the lip of the inner corrie, on whose ice-worn floor lie two little Alpine tarns of green water, crystal-clear. Immediately behind the highest of these rises the mountain wall, - 1,200 feet of purple sandstone - broken here and there by narrow green ledges and seamed with dark rifts, out of which pour streams of stony debris. The talus slopes are carpeted with a luxurious growth of parsley-fern, to which succeeds a zone of delicate-fronded oak-fern; while the lower ledges, dark with dripping moisture, are lit by the bright blossoms of the globe-flower and the sea-green fleshy leaves of the rose-root.' In spite of a violent thunderstorm and the absence of companions, Hinxman managed to climb the Upper Connecting Ridge of A'Chioch. On the summit plateau, at the head of Coire nan Fhamhair, he came upon two shepherds from Applecross who 'had little of the English and were much surprised'! The fastnesses of the Karakoram are today less remote than these hills were barely a century ago.

In 1908 the redoubtable Glover and Ling visited A'Chioch of Sgurr a'Chaorachain having heard that 'an eminent mountaineer ..... is forming a collection of cabinet-stucke in the form of prominences in North Britain styled A'Chioch'. One suspects Collie, who had climbed the Applecross Chioch by a devious route two years earlier. Upon arrival Glover and Ling 'circled round it like wrestlers looking for a grip' then 'went up a succession of short chimneys which a few moments before we had waltzed up in thought .....The chimneys were lined with steep grass and loose and rounded rock'. Clearly impressed by the airiness of the situations, Glover later dreamed of the future : 'When aeroplanes become commonplace, say in three years' time, I hope to possess a 6 Sparrow-power Vol-au-Vent, or a 60 Eagle-power Soarer ... and I intend to circle around some of these towers to assure myself how really easy these cliffs would be to climb straight up.'

Nearly half a century was to elapse before these dreams were realised. It was Tom Patey and his Aberdonian comrades who first demonstrated the true climbing potential when in 1952-3 they explored the north buttresses of Sgurr a'Chaorachain and Meall Gorm. But perhaps because of the vegetation, or difficulties of access, further exploration had to wait seven years until Patey returned with Bonington to discover that the impressive nose of A'Chioch could be climbed with surprising ease. The following year Patey reported the fine Sword of Gideon on the roadside south face of Sgurr a'Chaorachain and also explored Beinn Bhan via the Upper Connecting Ridge of A'Phoit.

Strangely, another eight years were to pass before he began to exploit the obvious winter possibilities; whether this was due to the unfounded belief that the low altitude and westerly position made for infrequent good conditions or simply because he had so many other plums to pick, it is difficult now to say. At any rate the first major winter route on Beinn Bhan, March Hare's Gully, fell in 1969 and was soon followed by exploration by leaders of Hamish MacInnes's winter courses, in particular Kenny Spence's fine ascents of Blaeberry Corner on Meall Gorm and Wall of the Early Morning Light. The latter, the first route to breach the great back wall of Coire na Poite, was not rivalled until Norrie Muir and Arthur Paul's ascent of the Silver Tear icefall in 1977. Three years later Brian Sprunt and Andy Nisbet's success on Der Reisenwand, publicised with pictures of horrifying steepness in *Cold Climbs*, began a trend of increasing popularity of the area in winter. The early 1980s saw Dougie Dinwoodie contribute a number of interesting new climbs in Coire na Feola and Coire na Poite but undoubtedly the most spectacular climbs were Mick Fowler's ascents of Gully of the Gods and Great Overhanging Chimney in Coire nan Fhamhair. These lines had of course been known to Scottish enthusiasts for years, but it took Fowler's flair, skill and weather-eye to seize them. So far as is known they await repeat ascents (and first summer ascents too!) The later 1980s saw a series of good winter climbs on the north buttresses of Sgurr a'Chaorachain, and most recently, a phenomenal 'girdle' of Beinn Bhan by Martin Moran. Plenty of scope remains for new winter climbs of all grades; and the school that sees any lightly dusted rock buttress as a winter challenge will not be put off by the fickle weather of the last few years.

The rock climbing in Applecross developed rather spasmodically after Patey's initial impetus. Most of the cliffs are vegetated (the most notable exception being A'Chioch) and natural lines tend to be escapable. There was a flurry of climbs in the late 60s and early 70s (including George Shields' mysterious Big Daddy), then an interim when the 'moratorium' policy of the SMC discouraged reporting of small or indifferent new routes. Only a trickle of new routes have been reported since, no doubt for the reasons given. It remains a place for enjoyable rock climbing in the leisurely 'old style', not somewhere for tigers to sharpen their claws.

TORRIDON

Hinxman again is the first to appear in the story, with a fine photograph of the triple buttresses of Beinn Eighe and an article on the rock possibilities in the very first issue of the SMC Journal (1891). A few years later he returned and made the first ascent of the Northern Pinnacles of Liathach in the company of Douglas, Rennie and W.Macdonald, the head keeper of the estate, whose protestations ('no man in the world could go up there') appear not to have hindered the party. The rock was exceedingly loose, but they felt sure that its 'unstable condition would lessen with each ascent,' and the route proved popular. In April 1900 it received its first winter ascent by two separate parties, led by Naismith and Raeburn. 'A hitch was found, one of those rare hitches whose occurrence maketh glad the heart, as the occurrence of hitches does not always do.'

The first recorded climb on Beinn Eighe was Lawson, Ling and Glover's climb on Sail Mhor at Easter 1899, although Collie had previously attempted Central Buttress. Writing to Douglas in 1898 he revealed 'I think I have discovered the finest rock climb in the British Isles - on the precipices of Ben Eighe'. After cutting steps up West Central Gully for about 800 feet he had traversed left onto Central Buttress but been stopped by a 'perpendicular and overhanging cliff' at least 200 feet high. The next day he had descended the right-hand side of Central Buttress by a complicated route to reach the cairn he had left. In 1907 came the first ascent of the East Buttress of Coire Mhic Fhearchair by Gibbs, Backhouse and Mounsey. They inspected the bottom pitch of East Central Gully but decided against it and instead went diagonally left up to Broad Terrace. 'A direct ascent ... was out of the question for the holds were all the wrong way.' After an excursion into East Central Gully on snow they regained the buttress by a 'delightful' chimney and thereafter found 'nowhere extreme difficulty, or need for great exertion. .... No better rock had been our fortune in all Scotland.'

A strong SMC party attempted the West Buttress in March 1910, but were stopped by 'a stretch of AP rock' and finished up Far West Gully. The first ascent of this buttress had to wait until Bower and Meldrum's visit in 1919 - they declared that for the crux sandstone slab 'rubbers or stocking feet are probably essential', while they felt that the final quartzite tower 'would probably succumb to a frontal attack'. This was followed three years later by Piggott's Route on Central Buttress, by a raiding English party later to be more famous for their deeds in Wales. J.F.Hamilton, another climber more famous for his deeds elsewhere, added his route on Central Buttress in 1936, but nothing more of note was climbed until the 1950s.

Post-war exploration started with a fruitful June visit by Len Lovat and Tom Weir in 1954, then around 1960 Tom Patey made a few characteristic forays, producing Gnome Wall, The Gash and the adventurous Upper Girdle. An Edinburgh University Mountaineering Club meet in 1961 found Robin Smith the first to take the challenge of the Eastern Ramparts. His description of Boggle remains a classic admonition for guidebook writers. The steep quartzite was subsequently left alone for a decade apart from a fine day's climbing by Jim Brumfitt and Bill Sproul in 1966 when Kami-kaze and Samurai were climbed, and another single day visit by Allan Austin.

The early 1970s saw Kenny Spence make a winter ascent of Central Buttress, a notable achievement. The writing of a new Torridon Climbers' Guide by the Turnbulls sparked exploration of the quartzite cliffs of Coire Rudha-Staca, whose quality is better than it appears from a distance. A new era for the steep quartzite may be said to have begun with the ascent of the delightful Groovin' High in 1973 by John Ingram, Greg Strange and Rob Archbold. This was instantly recognised as a classic and remains one of the most satisfying climbs in the country. The Aberdonians continued their campaign with intermittent visits, one of the most significant being the weekend in 1980 when The Reaper and Pale Diedre fell to Brian Sprunt and Greg Strange. The Reaper had long been recognised as a challenge and its ascent on sight was a very bold achievement. Other useful additions in this period came from Richard McHardy on the sandstone of the West

Buttress and Arthur Paul and Norrie Muir. In the later 1980s Andrew Nisbet began a typically long and thorough development of the cliffs. With a variety of partners, a host of new climbs both summer and winter were produced. Worthy of particular mention are Ling Dynasty, easily the hardest route so far, taking a spectacular roof towards the right of the Far East Wall - a phenomenal on-sight lead by Graeme Livingston; and the magnificent Angel Face and Seeds of Destruction, which take the improbable challenge of the beautiful smooth grey wall left of The Reaper.

Meanwhile, in addition to a series of good winter routes on the Central Wall, mainly by Nisbet, the very hard winter Direttissima on the West Buttress was forced by Rab Anderson and Rob Milne in 1986, and in 1987 Mick Fowler seized the opportunity to climb the ferocious ice of West Central Gully and to follow a winter version of the Upper Girdle.

Little of any significance was climbed on Liathach before the 1970s - Bell's Buttress had fallen in 1947 and other odd rock climbs like Reflection Wall and Dru were recorded in the 1950s. The obvious straightforward snow gullies were also climbed, like the Trinity gullies in Coire na Caime. It is possible that these and some similar routes recorded later had earlier unclaimed ascents. The most significant event of the 1970s was the ascent of Poacher's Fall by Richard McHardy and Andy Nisbet, an excellent ice route 'stolen' from Clive Rowland. The early 1980s saw exploration of the north side of Alligin by Steve Chadwick, but climbers were fairly slow to take up the potential of Liathach. Some good ice routes were done in all the corries in the intervening years, but it was not until 1986 and 1987 that a real avalanche of new ice routes was recorded - no less than 23 on Liathach alone in these two winters. Partly this reflected the excellent ice conditions in these years, but at least as important was the enthusiasm of Andy Cunningham, Andy Nisbet and others. Martin Moran produced four new routes on Tom na Gruagaich of Beinn Alligin as well as two difficult solos on Toll a'Meitheach of Liathach. The pace of new ice routes slowed down in the following years, particularly as the winters were poor, but Liathach remains established as a prime destination for those in search of good pure ice routes.

Of the lesser outcrops in the Torridon area, Diabaig will probably always retain pride of place for its beautiful situation as well as the quality of its climbing. Although known about earlier, it only began to be developed in the mid-1970s by Allan Austin and Ed Grindley. Later it became a happy hunting ground for Kev Howett, Dave Cuthbertson and others, who produced a host of fine and difficult routes. For visiting climbers whose lack of patience with long walks, midges and bad weather precludes the higher crags, this will remain one of the lodestones of Torridon.

KINLOCHEWE

At the SMC Easter meet in 1899 Lawson, Ling and Glover climbed a route up the east end of Liathach on April 1st, and a gully on Sail Mhor of Beinn Eighe on the 2nd. For the third day Glover and Inglis Clark chose to investigate the Waterfall Buttress of Beinn a'Mhuinidh, probably in the company of Ling. A six-hour struggle with vegetation and steep rock ensued, including much gardening and a difficult stomach traverse, but the trio were victorious, and much satisfied with their achievement.

The 1910 Easter Meet saw Inglis Clark return to this hill and record a climb on Craig Roy (now called the Bonaid Dhonn), slightly left of the corner of Gleann Bianasdail. On this occasion they had excellent spring weather and 'the spirit of Pan seemed everywhere'. The next visitors were J.H.B. Bell and his wife in 1946, who climbed two splendid Diffs on the Bonaid Dhonn, as well as a variation to the Waterfall climb. A steady trickle of new routes followed over the next decades, the exploratory spirit overcoming any reluctance to venture onto the sometimes loose and vegetatious quartzite. The best routes were Cunningham and March's climbs, Vertigo and The Creep, which take improbable lines up the steepest section of the Bonaid Dhonn. Mention should also be made of Ginger Cain's explorations both on Waterfall Buttress and on the smaller outcrops further up Loch Maree, near Furnace. The early 1980s saw Steve Chadwick take a proprietary interest in the north face of Slioch, producing several routes to add to the classic Stepped Ridge and Main Buttress. Finally in 1984 a cold spell allowed Andy Nisbet and Phil Thornhill to seize a winter ascent of the Waterfall on Beinn a'Mhuinidh - a magnificent pure ice climb.

LETTEREWE and FISHERFIELD

The end of May 1909 saw that indomitable pair Ling and Glover take an interest in Beinn Lair and Beinn Airigh Charr. Their first foray on Beinn Lair met with 'loose shaly rock, wet earth and a lamentable lack of hitches'. The next day, on Martha's Peak, they found a more satisfying climb, so much so that they were determined to return the following year. With the aid of 'some very superior rowing' a large party crossed from the Loch Maree Hotel and made their way to the foot of the face of Martha's Peak. While Charles Inglis Clark, C.Walker and R.W.Worsdell 'elected to explore the west end - as three such fashionable bachelors might be expected to do', Ling and Glover's party took a central route on the face. Glover described the upper part of their climb : 'holds were small but always dipped the right way and one could climb at a high angle with comfort and safety, which (much as I love the extreme north-west Highlands) is an unusual luxury on most of the rounded sandstone peaks which chiefly congregate there. ... My advice to the youth of the SMC is to explore to the west of the first half of our climb, and after that to try to the east above our cairn.' This advice was taken up by Burt, Bell and Matheson who, in 1928, tackled the prominent curved buttress left of Ling and Glover's route and reported a rib of excellent clean rock with a sensational finish.

Apart from two routes recorded by Pat Baird and party in 1933 on Torr na h'Iolaire and A'Mhaighdean, no other climbs done before the Second World War are of sufficient merit to be still remembered. The real development of the extraordinary rock climbing potential of this area began with the explorations of a variety of university student teams in the early 1950s. This followed a stimulating survey of rock climbing throughout the Northern Highlands by Frank Cunningham in the 1951 SMCJ. In 1951 parties from Glasgow, Edinburgh, Aberdeen, Leeds and Cambridge universities all recorded routes on Beinn Lair, the best climbs falling to the Glasgow team who discovered Wisdom Buttress among others. There was overlap amongst these explorations, but a clear review by Dr Bell in the 1952 SMCJ reduced the confusion to an acceptable level. Following this *annus mirabilis* only two scrappy summer climbs have been recorded on Beinn Lair in the ensuing forty years, though a number of interesting winter ascents have been made. The year 1951 also saw tentative explorations on Beinn Airigh Charr, Torr na h'Iolaire and A'Mhaighdean by the team of Slesser, Dutton and Wight; followed a year later by the first climb on Carnmore - Diagonal Route by the Cambridge University climbers Wrangham and Clegg. The seed of knowledge had been sown in Cambridge, but the avalanche of new climbs awaited the arrival some years later of Mike O'Hara, George Fraser, Bob Kendell and their friends. A few days in the summer of 1955 accounted for the exploration of Maiden Buttress on Carnan Ban and the discovery of Na Bearta Buttress; 1956 saw investigation of the less awesome left wing of

Carnmore and the fine Ipswich Rib on Torr na h'Iolaire; then 1957 saw their finest hour with the discovery of Fionn Buttress, Dragon and a host more routes on Torr na h'Iolaire and other outlying crags. These university vacation trips must have had a care-free atmosphere. The Cambridge climbers would happily spend days of their holidays ferrying food into the Carnmore barn from Poolewe and leisurely exploring the secrets of their new playground. Competition, if it existed, was restricted to their small circle - out of the tiny number of British climbers (as compared with today) only a small proportion knew of the treasures hidden in the wilds of Colonel Whitbread's estate.

After the Cambridge era new climbs tended to come from isolated visits rather than sustained campaigns, but word must have got around that intimidating lines could be climbed. Gob in 1960 by Haston and Smith; Balaton in 1966 by Higgins and Gorman; and Abomination, also in 1966, by McLean, Cunningham and Currey were all routes of the highest quality. The following year saw St George fall to Geoff Cram while a fruitful few days by a Manchester team comprising Dick Isherwood, Gordon Macnair, Bob Jones and Eddie Birch produced five more first class routes, including The Sword. As this was unaccountably omitted from Ian Rowe's 1969 Climbers' Guide, it remained something of a mystery for many years, its true worth being appreciated in the 1980s. Soon after, Rab Carrington and John Jackson explored the Ghost Slabs and the Carcase Wall on Torr na h'Iolaire, and they returned a year later to pluck the much sought after plum of Carnmore Corner.

Meanwhle the first climbs at Creag Mhor Thollaidh had been done by Tom Patey and the Edinburgh Squirrels. The early 70s saw a lull in new route activity generally, although Paddy Buckley maintained an active interest, combining an immense amount of scholarly research into Carnmore's climbing history with some intricate linking of pitches to create several new routes.

The 1980s finally saw modern rock climbing standards reach Carnmore, the principal culprit being Dougie Dinwoodie. Wilderness, the imposing crack on the left of Carnmore Corner, was climbed on sight by Dougie Mullin in 1980 to give the first E3; Dinwoodie then produced the magnificent Orange Bow on the right arete of the corner in 1985, the first E5. He returned in 1986 with Graeme Livingston to climb three fine difficult routes on the Dragon Wall and the first E6, Death-Wolf, up the enormous roof left of Abomination. Further significant routes on several of the outlying crags were added by Dinwoodie and Nisbet in 1988, while Kev Howett produced some excellent hard climbs at

Thollaidh. Thus the area now has a number of challenging routes for visitors aspiring to test their capacities in the harder grades, but its particular distinction will always be the variety of middle grade climbs it provides in a mountain ambience unrivalled in Britain.

AN TEALLACH and BEINN DEARG MOR

Thomas Pennant in 1772 described An Teallach as 'a chain of rocky mountains ... with sides deep, dark and precipitous ... here Aelous may be said to make his residence, and be ever employed in fabricating blasts, squalls and hurricanes, which he scatters with no sparing hand over the subjacent vales and lochs.' The mountains of Dundonnell were popular with the early SMC and one of the first notes of exploration of Beinn Dearg Mor appeared in 1895 when Edward Greenly of the Geological Survey spent a month at Larachantivore (then a welcome little lodge often mentioned by travellers) and made observations of the corries and cliffs. A few years later Sang and Morrison made the first ascent of the south peak of Beinn Dearg Mor, and then in 1907 came a visit from the ubiquitous Ling and Glover. They climbed the precipitous buttress of Corrag Bhuidhe rising above Toll an Lochain, up steep grass and rock, then two days later attempted the gully cleaving the Central Buttress of Beinn Dearg Mor. After 450 feet they came to a chimney blocked by a big chockstone - though the 'slighter member of the party' (Ling) might have been able to crawl through, 'it was not large enough for the more massive member' (Glover). So they descended and climbed Central Gully 'by ledges, scree and snow'.

Sang returned with Morrison in 1910 to climb Hayfork Gully on Bidean a' Ghlas Thuill and his account is astonishingly dramatic. They 'kicked pigeon-holes for 50 feet, thereafter it was strenuous hewing all the way'. After two hours they were confronted by an 'evil-looking icefall' - while Sang smoked, Morrison got to grips with it. When Sang climbed, 'the raven's harsher cry betokened the expectation of human eyes for supper' .... 'the rope ... owing to the violence of my struggles had gracefully looped itself round a hundredweight block of stone which, even as I looked, started on its downward career'. Above the icefall the gully forked and they were lured onto 'as entertaining a piece of rock climbing as heart of man could desire. All that seemed obvious was perilously untrustworthy and all that was obscure was firm and difficult. All pulling in holds pulled out promptly, nor was it possible to tell if the vegetation was rooted or merely laid on the rocks for appearance' sake.' So it continued : Morrison swarmed up a crack 'large enough to admit an unencumbered man of modest proportions', and finally intending future climbers were warned that the gully 'shows signs of being a through route for falling climbers'.

Though no doubt always a popular venue, little new was accomplished on An Teallach in the inter-war years, save for Bell's ascent of Lord's Gully in 1923. However, the decade following the Second World War saw relatively more interest in the Dundonnell area. The 1946 SMC Journal had an article by E.C.Pyatt describing numerous outcrops, including Junction Buttress and Gruinard Jetty Buttress, as well as the ascents of Main Rib and the remarkable Sulphur Gully, 'Standard 3b', climbed by Barford with the aid of a jammed ice axe belay. Then in 1953 Parker climbed the Central Buttress of Beinn Dearg Mor by a route which appears from its description to have been of considerable difficulty. It may well be unrepeated. Odd new climbs, mainly in winter, continued to be added over the years up to the present, so that the main corries of An Teallach and Beinn Dearg Mor all now possess a small number of interesting winter routes.

Notes on the Use of the Guide

CLASSIFICATION OF ROUTES

Summer

The normal British grading system of Easy, Moderate, Difficult, Very Difficult, Severe, Very Severe (VS), Hard Very Severe (HVS) and Extremely Severe has been used. The Extreme grade is sub-divided into E1, E2, E3, E4, E5, and so on.

Technical grades are given for routes of VS and above where known. Much effort has been made to elicit information from active climbers about routes, some of which will have all the relevant pitches graded, while others will have only the crux pitch so described. The normal range of technical grades expected on routes of the given overall grade are as follows: VS - 4b, 4c, 5a; HVS - 4c, 5a, 5b; E1 - 5a, 5b, 5c; E2 - 5b, 5c, 6a; E3 - 5c, 6a; E4 - 5c, 6a, 6b; E5 - 6a, 6b. Routes with a technical grade at the lower end of the range will be sustained or poorly protected, while those with grades at the upper end of the expected range will have a short and generally well protected crux.

Although the British system is thought second to none by those who use it, it is known to confuse visitors from abroad. For their benefit, it can be assumed that 5a, 5b, 5c and 6a correspond approximately to the American grades of 5.9, 5.10a/b, 5.10c/d and 5.11a/b respectively. Eurocraggers should note that there is little or no fixed protection on most of the climbs, and that if they are used to cruising bolted French 6c, they may suffer some distress while attempting the corresponding 6a pitches here, with their sometimes spaced and fiddly protection. Grading information is in some cases scanty or even lacking, particularly in some of the older or more obscure routes; climbers should therefore be even more circumspect in their approach to such routes (which have been indicated by a dagger symbol). Information about these routes is always welcome.

Winter

Winter climbs have been graded from I to VI.

Grade I indicates simple snow climbs, with perhaps a corniced exit.

Grade II includes gullies with either individual or minor pitches, or high angled snow with difficult cornice exits, and the easier buttresses under winter conditions.

Grade III incorporates gullies which contain ice or mixed pitches. There will normally be at least one substantial pitch and possibly several lesser ones. Also sustained buttress climbs without great technical difficulty.

Grade IV gullies may include nearly vertical ice sections, while the buttresses will require a good repertoire of techniques.

Grade V climbs are difficult, sustained and/or serious. Some may be well protected but technically very hard.

Grade VI routes have exceptional overall difficulties.

Split grades indicate uncertainties due to the route being known to be variable in condition, or a borderline case. Routes are graded for average to good conditions. It should be borne in mind that winter grades are often an approximation, because conditions (particularly in this area) can vary rapidly.

The advent of extremely difficult buttress climbs, which differ so radically from the more traditional gullies and icefalls, has put the grading system under some strain. As an experiment, a two-tier grading system, which incorporates some of the principles of the summer technical grades, has been proposed. An explanation of this system is given at the back of the book, together with the proposed two-tier grades for the harder climbs in the area. If this system becomes accepted by the majority of active climbers, then it will be used in the main body of future guide books. If you don't like it, it will go the same way as all other failed experiments.

Equipment and Style

It is assumed that a good range of modern nuts and camming devices will be carried for the harder climbs, both summer and winter. The summer climbs described in this guide do not require the use of pegs, and they should not be carried. Likewise the use of pegs on new climbs should be extremely sparing; please keep to the Scottish tradition of bold climbs with leader-placed protection. On occasion it might be necessary to use pegs on winter climbs for belays or runners; please make all efforts to find a safe alternative before resorting to pegs, especially on winter ascents of summer climbs (on which pegs would be most unwelcome).

Most of the modern harder rock climbs that are described in this book will have been cleaned or otherwise inspected prior to an ascent.

Although every attempt is usually made to grade them for an on-sight lead, it should be borne in mind that many of them may not yet have been done in this style.

Bolts
After extensive consultation with all interested parties, the Mountaineering Council of Scotland has issued a policy statement on the use of bolts in Scotland. This policy is endorsed by the Publications Sub-Committee of the Scottish Mountaineering Club.

"The MCofS acknowledge that there is a place for bolts in the future development of Scottish climbing. However, to ensure that the highly regarded ethos of, and future development of, traditional climbing (involving the use of leader-placed and second-removed protection) is not threatened, it is felt that the use of bolts should be limited to the production of sport climbs. There should be no retrospective bolting of established climbs for protection or belays, and there should be no minimalist bolting.

The production of sport climbs with bolts is acceptable on natural rock only when all the following conditions have been satisfied:

(1) On low-lying cliffs, provided that such development is not against the wishes of the landowner. Bolts are inappropriate on mountain cliffs and sea-cliffs.

(2) On routes where natural protection is absent or is inadequate for the repeated falls that such routes necessitate.

(3) Where the rock is steep and provides climbs of a high order of difficulty, at the forefront of developments of the day.

(4) Where there is no historical or local anti-bolt ethic.

Concerning quarried rock, it is felt that any future development should be constrained only by points (2) and (4) above.

Finally, it is felt that bolts should be located to ensure minimum visual impact and should be placed according to current best practices.

It is intended that these principles are not seen as simply restrictive rules, but as a guide to promote the positive development of Scottish climbing, where sports climbing, rather than becoming a substitute for traditional climbing, grows alongside it."

In practice, these guidelines indicate that the use of bolts would be inappropriate on all of the cliffs and crags described in this guidebook. It goes without saying that the use of bolts on winter climbs would be entirely unacceptable.

Terminology

Left and right refer to a climber facing the cliff or facing downhill in descent. In cases of potential ambiguity a compass direction is also given. Pegs and other fixed gear are for protection only, except where specifically stated that they are for direct aid. Do not assume that they will either be in place or in a safe state of repair.

Pitch Lengths

Pitch lengths are given in metres, to the nearest 5m (except for very short distances). Ropes of 45m should be adequate for the vast majority or routes, though 50m ropes are useful in winter.

Diagrams

On some mountains and crags the climbs are numbered, the numbering begining at 1 for each mountain or crag. These numbers refer to diagrams which are located at appropriate places in the book, so there should be no confusion in relating any numbered climb to its relevant diagram. If a numbered climb is not shown on the diagram, it will be located in relation to the numerical order of those that are.

Recommended Routes

No list of recommended climbs is given, instead a star grading system for quality has been used. Three stars indicates a route of the highest quality. If a route has no star this does not necessarily mean that it is poor, it may also indicate that insufficient is known about that route properly to assess its quality. This is particularly true of some of the remote areas, where the star ratings may be found to be inconsistent. Certain mountains, e.g. Liathach, have been left starless although known to have quality climbs. It is hoped that climbers using this guide will inform the authors of such inconsistencies so that future editions of the guide can be improved. Routes of poor quality are normally described as such or have a limited description.

Dagger symbols printed as part of route information indicate that the route has not been checked, and that there are good reasons for believing that the description or grade may not be entirely accurate. Climbers attempting these routes should do so with caution, and should be prepared to exercise more personal initiative than normal. The dagger symbol is not a health warning; it does not necessarily indicate that the route is poor, badly under-graded or in any way worse than its neighbours. Information about these routes is always welcome.

First Ascensionists

The year of first ascent, where known, is given in the text. The full date and pioneers are listed in chronological order, area by area, at the back of the guide. Further relevant details of the first and subsequent ascents where known are also listed in this section. Whether the route was climbed in summer or winter conditions is indicated by an S or W at the left end of each line. The abbreviations used in this list are standard and self-explanatory.

Maps and other sources of information.

Place names and map references have in general been taken from the OS 1:50000 Landranger Series maps; sheet numbers 19, 24, 25, 33, 34 and 40 are required to cover the area described in this volume. Occasionally information in the 1:25000 series has been used, but these maps are not necessary to navigate to and from the climbs. The 1:250000 OS Routemaster Series Sheet 2 map of Northern Scotland is very useful to put into context the whole of the areas described in both Volumes 1 and 2 of this guide.

The meanings and pronunciations of local place names can be found in SCOTTISH HILL AND MOUNTAIN NAMES by Peter Drummond, published by the Scottish Mountaineering Trust (1991).

Due to the very large area covered in this guidebook, it is impractical to include detailed information on huts, bothies, campsites and other amenities. Much useful information can be found in the Scottish Mountaineering Club District Guide to THE NORTHWEST HIGHLANDS by Donald Bennet and Tom Strang, published by the Scottish Mountaineering Trust (1990).

Weather Forecasts

Recorded telephone weather forecasts which cover the area as far north as Torridon are available on 0898 500 441, and 0891 654 669. Note that these are extremely expensive services when public telephone booths are used.

Mountain Rescue

In case of an accident requiring rescue or medical attention, contact the Police. If a victim has to be left, be sure that the exact location is known before leaving the site of the accident, and that if possible the nature of any injuries can be reported. Try to leave someone with the victim, who should in any case be made as comfortable and as sheltered as the injuries allow. Some knowledge of rudimentary first aid is a desirable thing for a climber to have, so it is wise to consult one of the large number of suitable books on mountaineering first aid, rescue techniques and rescue helicopters.

Avalanches

Avalanche conditions are less common in the area covered by this guide than in say the Cairngorms, or even Glen Coe, but they do occur, and climbers have been caught in them. To minimise the risk of exposure to avalanche it is sensible to avoid icefalls and gullies during periods of thaw and immediately following a heavy snowfall. The buttress climbs can provide alternatives in these conditions.

Avalanches occur most often following heavy snowfall or during thaw. All gullies and most slopes between 22 and 60 degrees should then be suspect. The greater the amount of fresh snow, the higher the risk. Fresh snow can include wind-blown deposits, so that stormy weather can maintain an avalanche risk for prolonged spells. Past and present weather conditions are very important. Climbers preparing for winter climbing should familiarise themselves with basic avalanche theory, using one or more of several useful books available on the subject. In the field, much can be learned by digging a hole and examing the snow profile, looking especially for different layers of snow with different degrees of bonding. Slab avalanches, for example, will be caused when a weakly cohesive layer of snow collapses underfoot. Such a weak layer is usually hidden under a firmer layer, hence its great potential as a killer. The top layer will often break into slabby fragments, the first warning.

If avalanched, try and either jump free, or anchor yourself for as long as possible, depending on circumstances. If swept down protect your access to oxygen by 'swimming' to stay on the surface, by keeping your mouth closed, and by preserving a space in front of your face if buried. Wet snow avalanches harden rapidly on settling, so try and break free if possible at this point. If trapped try to stay calm, which will reduce oxygen demand.

If you witness an avalanche, it is vital to start a search immediately, given it is safe to do so. Victims will often be alive at first, but their chances of survival lessen rapidly if buried. Unless severely injured, some 80% may live if found immediately, but only 10% after a three-hour delay. Mark the burial sight if known, listen for any sound, look for any visual clue, search until help arrives if possible. Again, a working knowledge of first aid may save a life, as many victims may have stopped breathing.

Knoydart

Knoydart, the broad mountainous region opposite the Sleat peninsula of Skye, is bounded by two long, twisting sea-lochs; Loch Hourn to the north and Loch Nevis to the south. It is an unusually wild and rugged district with a unique atmosphere. Although it contains several fine mountains, including the magnificent Ladhar Bheinn, its special character is due in no small part to its relative inaccessibilty. There is no road around the coast apart from an isolated stretch on the south-west side of the peninsula by the tiny village of Inverie (the largest settlement in Knoydart). The nearest public road leads only as far as Kinloch Hourn, at the north-east boundary of the area.

Barrisdale Bay is a broad, shallow bay situated about halfway along Loch Hourn. The best climbing in Knoydart is concentrated in two corries on either side of this bay. Consequently the most popular base for visiting climbers is at Barrisdale where bothy accommodation and camping is available at a small farm. The usual approach to Barrisdale is from the A87 by a very scenic route along a 34km single track road. This runs along Glen Garry via Tomdoun, and continues past Loch Quoich to Kinloch Hourn. The last section of road leading down to Kinloch Hourn itself is steep, narrow and twisty. In winter it should be borne in mind that cars can become trapped here by heavy snowfall. A charge may be made for parking near the small group of buildings at the road head. Parking is not permitted on the very narrow final 400 metres of track where it starts to run alongside the innermost section of Loch Hourn, known as Loch Beag. Follow a path on the south side of Lochs Beag and Hourn for 8km. This splendid walk has three sections of ascent and descent, and eventually leads to a vehicular track on the east shore of Barrisdale Bay. From there it is a further 2km to the bothy (Map Ref 871 042).

Quite an attractive alternative is to canoe along Loch Hourn. It may also be possible to charter a boat from Kinloch Hourn or Arnisdale. The various access routes from the south are unlikely to be popular with heavily-laden climbers. However, it is worth knowing that there is a boat service from Mallaig to Inverie, and that a fairly good track links Inverie with Barrisdale over Mam Barrisdale, a 450m pass. The bothy at Barrisdale can accommodate about ten people. A small charge is made for its use, and this should be paid to the farmer next door. The area is becoming increasingly popular with hillwalkers, so it is unwise

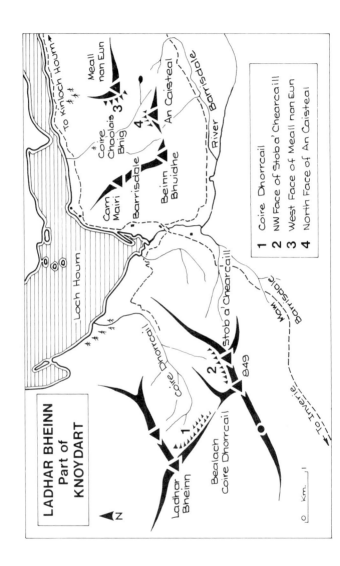

LADHAR BHEINN
Part of
KNOYDART

N

Loch Hourn

To Kinloch Hourn

Meall
nan Eun

3

Coire
Chaolais
Bhig

4

An Caisteal

Cam
Mairi

Barrisdale

Beinn
Bhuidhe

River Barrisdale

Coire Dhorrcaill

Ladhar
Bheinn

1

Bealach
Coire Dhorrcaill

Stob a' Chearcaill

2

849

Barrisdale

Mam

To Inverie

0 ___ Km. 1

1 Coire Dhorrcail
2 NW Face of Stob a' Chearcaill
3 West Face of Meall nan Eun
4 North Face of An Caisteal

to rely on there being space at the bothy, especially in summer. Parties visiting the area generally need to be self-sufficient, although bottled gas may be provided at the bothy for cooking purposes. Camping is the alternative option.

A delightful way of returning to Kinloch Hourn is to take the high-level route over the hills on the north side of Glen Barrisdale and then descend from the summit of Sgurr nan Eugallt. Those travelling a long distance will need to be reasonably well organised and determined if they are to get much climbing done in a weekend visit. The protracted approach (which is possible in the dark) and the rarity of good climbing conditions are sufficient to deter the masses. Long may this continue. Access is restricted in the stalking season.

Rescue facilities are minimal in Knoydart. There is no public telephone at Barrisdale, so it may be difficult to make contact with the police quickly in an emergency. (The farmer at Barrisdale is in daily radio contact with Arnisdale.)

There are surprisingly few rock climbs in Knoydart. Much of the rock is schist which tends to encourage vegetation and rarely forms attractive crags. However, a number of routes have been recorded in Coire Chaolais Bhig on the east side of Barrisdale Bay, where better quality gneiss and pegmatite occur. This corrie overlooks the west end of the approach path. A number of rather undistinguished routes, none harder than VS, can be found on several separate buttresses. The best of the climbing is to be found on some granite-like slabs on the north flank of An Caisteal.

The winter climbs in Knoydart are of much greater interest. They are concentrated on the faces of two spectacular schistose mountains, Ladhar Bheinn and Stob a' Chearcaill, which enclose Coire Dhorrcail on the west side of Barrisdale Bay. The majority of the lines have had few if any repeat ascents, so the grades should therefore be treated with caution.

COIRE CHAOLAIS BHIG

The four tops enclosing this north-facing corrie are, from east to west: the west top of Meall nan Eun (666m); An Caisteal (622m); Beinn Bhuidhe (569m) and Carn Mairi (513m). The climbs can be reached by ascending the hillside directly east of the bothy, and crossing Bealach a' Bho Chrubaich, the 461m pass between Carn Mairi and Beinn Bhuidhe. Alternatively, the mouth of the corrie can be approached from the north by the path along Loch Hourn.

WEST FLANK OF MEALL NAN EUN

There are several broken crags here separated by grassy gullies.
Starting from the left, the first big crag consists of numerous rock ribs
culminating in a big slab. To the right of this are two buttresses set
back slightly in a bay, and further right again is a rocky cone-shaped
hummock, which lies by the col between Meall nan Eun and An
Caisteal just north of a small stream.

Culverin   120m   Difficult   (1971)
This climbs the leftmost buttress. Start up the left-hand of the two main
ribs and finish on the left side of the terminal slab.

Cannonade   120m   Difficult   (1971)
The leftmost buttress. Start up the right-hand of the two main ribs and
finish on the right side of the terminal slab.

Sentinel   90m   Very Difficult *   (1971)
The left-hand of the two buttresses set back in a bay. Follow excellent
rock for 40m, then go up discontinuous ribs to slabs near the top.

Round House   110m   Mild Severe   (1967)
Ascends the right-hand of the two buttresses set back in a bay. Climb
the centre of a steep slab to a ledge. Traverse right to rocks on the
right of a grass gully. Then go left across the gully to grass ledge.
Continue directly to another grass ledge, then more easily to the top.

Parapet   90m   Severe   (1971)
Takes the edge facing out into the corrie on the cone-shaped hummock. Climb easily at first, then by a short vertical step to a less steep
finish.

Bastion   90m   Hard Severe *   (1971)
Climbs the south side of the cone-shaped hummock facing the stream.
Climb a crack in a steep wall, then move right to a vertical groove.
Follow this to a ledge and pass the overhang above on the left. Go
right to gain a left-leading gangway, which is followed to loose blocks
and a ledge. Climb a steep mossy wall directly to slabs and a ledge
above. A short wall leads to the top.

NORTH FACE OF AN CAISTEAL

The most attractive climbing in Coire Chaolais Bhig is found here, where there is a narrow central sweep of clean slabs, bordered by more broken wings. These slabs offer pleasant Etive-like climbing at about VS (4c). The two original routes began on opposite sides of the central slabs. Only the starts of these routes are described. A later eliminate climbed the slabs more directly.

Portcullis 205m VS   (1967)
This climb finds a way up the left edge of the central sweep of slabs. Climb a short steep crack to a rowan, and continue up a groove to a ledge under overhangs.

Direct Route 180m VS *   (1980)
This takes a fairly direct line up the centre of the slabs, passing just right of the obvious wet break in the upper overlaps.

Battlement Slab 195m VS   (1967)
Start below and right of the toe of the central sweep of slabs, (15 metres right of Portcullis), at a brown slab capped by an overhang. Climb easy rocks rightwards, then traverse left delicately to a ledge.

STOB A' CHEARCAILL

849m (Map Ref 840 027)

The winter climbs in Coire Dhorrcail are approached by a stalker's path which starts on the west side of Barrisdale Bay and goes round the shoulder of Creag Bheithe. The path descends slightly before it swings south-west into the mouth of the corrie. From this point there is a dramatic view of the cliffs some 2km away.

A prominent spur, which leads to a small top called Stob Dhorrcail, juts out from the headwall of Coire Dhorrcail and encloses a subsidiary corrie to the south called Coire na Cabaig. This corrie is dominated by the spectacular north-west face of Stob a' Chearcaill, which does not come into view until shortly after the stalker's path peters out about halfway up Coire Dhorrcail. This face is divided into several soaring buttresses by long straight gullies. It is some 250m high and has been likened in appearance to the Grandes Jorasses.

The most prominent feature of the face is the central gully; Gaberlunzie. Only the gullies have provided climbs so far. The routes are described from left to right. Possibly the quickest way back to Barrisdale from the summit is to descend the steep south flank of Stob a' Chearcaill and then head east into Coir' a' Chearcaill.

1   Para Handy Gully   240m   III   (1971)
Climbs the most prominent gully on the left-hand half of the face. Slant up leftwards from the base of the cliff to reach the start. The gully is continuously steep. The entrance and exit are likely to prove the hardest parts of the climb.

2   Bottleneck Gully   290m   IV *   (1986)
This long narrow gully starts a short distance left of the lowest point of the face. A 50m rope is recommended. Climb ice-falls directly to reach a stance at the start of a narrow chimney. Ascend the chimney, passing a constriction with difficulty. Surmount an awkward step and continue to a stance just above a jammed boulder. Climb a short steepening to reach a long section of easier gully. After a slightly steeper section, take a belay on the right arete overlooking Gaberlunzie. Return to the gully and climb it, mainly on the right side, to the summit ridge.

3   Gaberlunzie   280m   III/IV *   (1962)
This is the main central gully. It starts just right of the lowest point of the face. Above a snow fan, 30m of steep climbing leads to a snow channel. This steepens to a large cave beneath a chockstone at 55m. Surmount the chockstone on the left with difficulty to reach easier ground. The walls begin to converge again 60m from the top. The last 20m of climbing up the right-hand gully wall are perhaps the hardest on the route.

4   Marguerite   220m   IV *   (1986)
Climbs the first prominent chimney to the right of Gaberlunzie. Follow easy snow up right, then ascend mixed ground to the foot of a steep narrow chimney. Climb the chimney in two long pitches. Continue up the more open gully in two further pitches to gain the summit ridge.

A number of gully lines can be climbed on the flanks of Stob Dhorrcail, but the next worthwhile routes lie in Coire Dhorrcail proper.

STOB A' CHEARCAILL

1. Para Handy Gully
2. Bottleneck Gully
3. Gaberlunzie Gully
4. Marguerite

LADHAR BHEINN
1020m   (Map Ref 824 041)

The most obvious feature in the headwall of Coire Dhorrcail (approached from Barrisdale as described above) is a prominent gully with an enormous chockstone at half-height – Raeburn's Gully. Immediately to its right is Landlubber's Buttress. Some distance to its left is another broader and much higher buttress (with its summit at 858m) characterised by a large snowfield at one third height. This buttress is known as Spider Buttress because its snowfield is reminiscent of the White Spider on the Eiger. To the left of Spider Buttress an easy slope leading to Bealach Coire Dhorrcail offers the safest descent.

SPIDER BUTTRESS

1   Penny Wheep Gully   180m   III   (1986)
High up on the east flank of Spider Buttress there are three gullies. This route climbs the rightmost and largest gully. Climb a succession of short ice steps for 100m to an easy snow slope leading to a large chockstone. Turn this by ice on the right wall, and continue to a large amphitheatre. Exit out right to gain easy ground.

2   Eastern Chimney   270m   IV   (1979)
The left side of the Spider snowfield is bounded by the East Rib. This route follows a fault line which rises from a square-cut bay, some 90m above and left of the base of the East Rib. The fault line is extremely narrow in places, and after 120m it joins the crest of the rib. Short walls and grooves then lead in 60m to easier ground.

3   East Rib   360m   IV   (1979)
This route follows the left-hand rib of the buttress. Start at the lowest rocks and maintain a central line where possible.

4   Tir na Og   350m   V ***   (1978)
This magnificent climb takes a very direct line up the centre of Spider Buttress. Climb directly to the central snowfield (The Spider) by obvious ice grooves. Continue straight up the snowfield to the central groove system. Climb this by three pitches to finish left of the buttress summit. (After the second and crucial pitch above The Spider an easy ramp can be followed rightwards to join the final easy gully of Face Route).

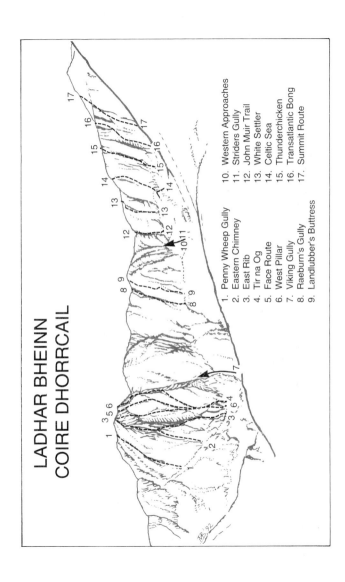

LADHAR BHEINN
COIRE DHORRCAIL

1. Penny Wheep Gully
2. Eastern Chimney
3. East Rib
4. Tir na Og
5. Face Route
6. West Pillar
7. Viking Gully
8. Raeburn's Gully
9. Landlubber's Buttress
10. Western Approaches
11. Striders Gully
12. John Muir Trail
13. White Settler
14. Celtic Sea
15. Thunderchicken
16. Transatlantic Bong
17. Summit Route

5 Face Route 360m III/IV   (1978)
This route avoids the obvious challenge taken up by Tir na Og. Gain
the central snowfield either directly or more easily from the left. Aim
for the top right-hand corner of the snowfield. Climb the right-hand of
two grooves, turning an overhang at 60m on the right by another
groove. Just short of the crest of the West Pillar take an obvious gully
on the left which leads to the buttress summit.

6 West Pillar 360m III   (1978)
Climbs the right-bounding rib of Spider Buttress. Gain the central
snowfield by a snow patch and easy grooves to the left of the direct
line. Traverse diagonally right across The Spider, and continue up a
snow ramp onto the crest of the pillar. Follow the pillar to the top.

Hidden in the angle where the right-hand side of Spider Buttress
abuts against the main line of crags is a long narrow gully. This gives
the line of the next route.

7 Viking Gully 360m III/IV **   (1962)
Climb the gully directly, or in lean conditions enter it by a slanting snow
rake on the left. Some ice pitches and a narrow snow trough lead to
a narrow twisting channel. Continue to the recessed upper portion of
the gully. A series of abrupt 15m ice pitches then follow. A long snow
fan of some 90m leads to a col between two small peaks on the main
ridge.

To the right of Viking Gully there are steep rocks, and then a broad
gully, but the next noteworthy line is the prominent gash of Raeburn's
Gully.

8 Raeburn's Gully 240m III *   (1897)
This gully is quite straightforward as far as the enormous chockstone
at half-height. Circumventing this huge monolith can prove surprisingly
difficult, involving climbing awkward slabby rocks on the left wall by
two pitches totalling some 60m. The remainder of the gully is easy.

9 Landlubber's Buttress 240m IV   (1978)
This is the obvious slabby buttress immediately right of Raeburn's
Gully. Not sustained. Climb the left side of the buttress to a rock band.
Head for a prominent flake on the right skyline. Pass it and go back

left by a snowy groove. Continue diagonally left past the next rock band to a snow ledge. A large block pinnacle above and slightly right is a *cul-de-sac,* so make a descending traverse left. Cross a crucial slab to reach an easy ramp which leads back to the crest of the buttress. Scramble to the top.

10 Western Approaches 180m III   (1984)
Climb the narrow and interesting gully on the right-hand flank of Landlubber's Buttress.

11 Strider's Gully 120m I/II   (1991)
This is the gully in the angle where the right flank of Landlubber's Buttress meets the headwall of the corrie.

12 John Muir Trail 100m I/II
This takes the shortest section of the headwall by a right-trending line to a low point on the rim of the corrie.

13 White Settler 140m III   (1991)
The prominent right-facing slabby corner, situated left of a deep twisting gully. Start just right of the line of the corner. Gain a narrow chimney which leads leftwards to a short wall at the base of the main slab. Climb the wall and follow the corner above to a final steep rockband. In good conditions it is possible to climb this direct, otherwise traverse right to find a way to the top.

14 Celtic Sea 180m III   (1984)
Start at the lowest tongue of rock to the right of Landlubber's Buttress. Gain a right-facing corner, either from the right by steep icy rock, or from the left by an easier snow ledge. Climb the corner with a steeper section part way up. Finish at a step on the ridge.

15 Thunderchicken 210m III   (1978)
This climb follows a corner situated about 50 metres right of Celtic Sea and just to the left of two prominent stepped corners.

16 Transatlantic Bong 210m IV   (1978)
Climbs the left-hand of two prominent stepped corners at the top right of the corrie.

17 Summit Route   290m   III   (1978)
Climbs the right-hand stepped corner. Ascend snow then ice to belay
left of an icefall. Traverse right, then climb to belay in a groove.
Continue in grooves until a traverse right can be made to a belay above
the icefall. Climb the snowfield and summit buttress direct to the top.

A number of lines have been climbed (mainly at grade II) on the
more broken rocks further right of Summit Route. The prominent black
rift in the most westerly recess of Coire Dhorrcail, which leads to a col
on the ridge linking Ladhar Bheinn with Stob a' Choire Odhair, is known
as **Moss Gully** (Grade II). It was climbed originally in summer conditions in 1939.

Loch Hourn to Glen Carron

The mountains of Glen Shiel and Kintail lie on either side of the A87 road between Loch Duich to the west and Loch Cluanie to the east. In general the mountains provide excellent hillwalking and some good winter climbs, but they provide little interest to the summer climber in search of clean rock. The mountains south of Glen Shiel are described first, followed by The Five Sisters of Kintail and Beinn Fhada on the north side of the glen. Beinn Sgritheall to the west, and the Loch Lochy hills to the south-east, are also included in this section.

THE LOCH LOCHY HILLS

Sron a' Choire Ghairbh (935m, Map Ref 223 945) and Meall na Teanga (917m, Map Ref 220 924) are two deeply-corried Munros on the west side of Loch Lochy. They can be approached either from forestry tracks on the Loch Lochy side or from the narrow B8005 just before it reaches the east end of Loch Arkaig. (Park at the Eas Chia-aig waterfalls and follow a track up through the trees.) One climb has been recorded in the Coire Lochain, south of the summit of Meall na Teanga.

Central Gully   120m   III   (1986)
The north-east facing crag in the upper corrie is split by an obvious gully. Climb steepening snow, with a little ice, to where the gully closes in (40m). A good long ice pitch follows with two steep sections before the gully eases and fans out (40m). The exit line will be dependent on the cornice (40m).

SOUTH GLEN SHIEL RIDGE

The South Glen Shiel Ridge links Creag a' Mhaim (947m, Map Ref 088 077) on the east and Creag nan Damh (918m, Map Ref 983 112) on the west. It includes seven Munros and is a classic hillwalking expedition. A few climbs have been recorded along this ridge.

COIRE AN T-SLUGAIN

This fine-looking corrie lies on the north side of the ridge between Druim Shionnach and Aonach air Chrith, towards the east end of the main ridge. The one climb recorded is on the eastern-most crag which lies on the west face of Druim Shionnach (Map Ref 065 085) in the south-east corner of the corrie.

The Silver Slab   100m   Severe   (1938)
Between a large gully in the centre of the crag and two large caves on the left, there are two buttresses separated by a smaller gully. This climb is on the left-hand of these two buttresses starting to the left of a small chimney and going fairly directly up slabs, cracks, and occasional short traverses. Belay as required.

SGURR A' BHAC CHAOLAIS
885m   (Map Ref 958 110)

This hill lies west of Creag nan Damh, the westernmost Munro on the ridge. One climb has been recorded on a crag on the south-west flank of the mountain roughly level with the Sgurr na Sgine col. The crag has a deep-cut gully with a well-defined buttress on its right. The following route climbs the right edge of the buttress starting near the right-hand side of the frontal face.

Mayfly   60m   VS   (1985)
1. 20m Climb a cracked slab and right-trending groove, then gain the edge above by a rising traverse left on a slab. The crest leads to a ledge.
2. 15m The corner above leads to a roof with a strenuous exit right. Short walls and ledges lead up and left onto the slabby crest.
3. 25m Ascend the gangway leftwards to climb an obvious crack. An easier crack and rib leads to the top.

THE SADDLE
1010m   (Map Ref 935 131)

The shapely mass of The Saddle is west of the main South Glen Shiel Ridge directly across the A87 road from The Five Sisters of Kintail. The best ascent of the mountain is undoubtedly by the east ridge of Sgurr nan Forcan; the Forcan Ridge. The best approach is via an obvious stalker's path leaving the road at Map Ref 968 143.

Forcan Ridge 200m of ascent Moderate or II
The ridge is an excellent scramble in summer especially if one sticks
to the crest. In winter the ridge is a more serious proposition and a
rope will be required by most parties as there is a often a short abseil
involved.

The south side of the Forcan Ridge presents a slabby face. A route
has been made leading to the bump on the Forcan Ridge which
precedes the narrow rocky section (100m, Difficult). Higher up the
corrie there is a fairly well-defined buttress which leads to the upper
part of the Forcan Ridge. It provides the following route.

Easter Buttress 100m Severe   (1961)
Stick to the crest and the standard is Severe. The climb finishes a few
metres from a horizontal knife-edge just below the summit.

COIRE UAINE

One climb has been recorded in Coire Uaine (north-west of the main
summit of The Saddle). It is a climb for a real enthusiast.

Big Gully 200m Very Difficult   (1926)
At the left or north-east end of the cliffs is a "grand gully". It includes:
"Chockstones, a sentry box, short stretches of vegetable climbing, and
a final wriggle under a rock arch. Well worth a visit by a moderately
strong party."

BEINN SGRITHEALL

974m (Map Ref 836 127)

The north side of the north top has given the only climb to date.
Looking up from Loch Bealach na h'Oidhche (Map Ref 831 138), a big
gully splits the north face. To the left is a shallower gully, and left again
is North Buttress. It has three rock steps separated by grassy ledges
and has been climbed in both winter and summer (Difficult or Grade
III).

THE FIVE SISTERS OF KINTAIL

Situated on the north side of the road, the Five Sisters provide little climbing interest in summer. Climbs have been recorded in both summer and winter, all on the north side of the ridge. Virtually all the climbs have been recorded by Edinburgh University Mountaineering Club with their convenient base at Glenlicht House, and it is likely that many climbs have gone unrecorded. Access to the climbs is by leaving the car at the road end near the camp site at Morvich (Map Ref 966 210) and walking along the good landrover track up Gleann Lichd.

SGURR NAN SAIGHEAD

929m   (Map Ref 975 178)

Sgurr nan Saighead provides two corries of interest to the climber. The corrie to the east of the summit is Coire Druim na Staidhre; it comprises several slabby buttresses separated by deep gullies, the most obvious feature being a huge rake slanting up from right to left. Forked Gully is the deep prominent gully in the centre of the face left of the rake. All routes in the corrie have been climbed in winter with the exception of **California** (80m, Severe) which climbs "an obvious S-shaped crack at the apex of the left-hand of two large scree cones". Routes are described from left to right.

Twisting Gully 120m II   (1986)
This is the leftmost gully on the face, left of Forked Gully. It contains three short pitches separated by easy snow.

Forked Gully 120m II   (1957)
The deep gully in the centre of the main face has been climbed by both forks. Its left fork gives a steep climb to finish with a short ice pitch and a spectacular exit onto the summit ridge. The right fork is Grade I.

Saighead Slot 180m I/II   (1984)
From the start of Forked Gully take the narrow steep gully to the right of the right fork. The route is obvious and finishes at The Slot, a very deep fissure, exiting onto the summit ridge. Superb rock architecture.

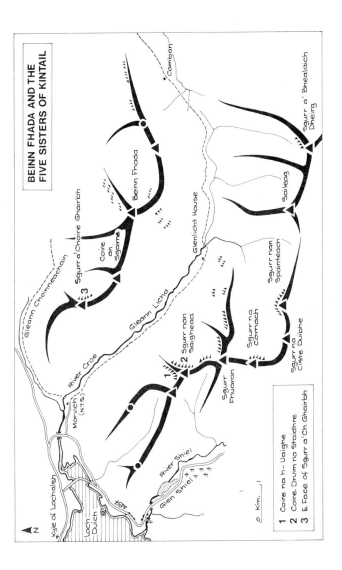

BEINN FHADA AND THE FIVE SISTERS OF KINTAIL

1 Coire na h-Uaighe
2 Coire Druim na Straidhre
3 E Face of Sgurr a'Ch Ghairbh

0 Km. 1

N

Edge of Reason 210m III/IV   (1986)
This route climbs the right arete of Forked Gully and Saighead Slot by
mossy grooves. Keep to the crest for the best climbing and finish just
right of Saighead Slot.

Hidden Gully 150m II   (1984)
Climb the prominent left-slanting rake to the second snow bay on the
right and proceed up the well-defined gully on the right above, over
chockstones of varying difficulty. A large intractable chockstone presents itself. Crawl through the tiny hole on the right into a large cave
and up a vertical shaft to a good belay. Easier ground leads to the
summit.

To the right of the rake the face becomes less steep. Easy Gully
starts well right of the foot of the rake and provides a choice of several
routes at Grade I.

Coire na h-Uaighe is the corrie to the north of the summit of Sgurr
nan Saighead. It provides the most westerly climbing on the Five
Sisters ridge and like the other areas it is far more suited to winter
climbing. Directly below the summit of Sgurr nan Saighead is an easy
gully bending right towards the top; this provides a useful means of
descent. At the back of the corrie is a compact crag split by shallow
gully lines and featuring a prominent rock fin at its base.

Left-Hand Gully 80m II/III   (1987)
Climb the left-hand gully system; variation is possible.

Grovel Gully 80m II/III   (1986)
Climb the central gully-groove system, starting just right of the rock
fin.

The rib left of Grovel Gully has been climbed in summer and is
positively not recommended. Just right of these routes, and separated
by a wide open gully (good descent), is a high broken pinnacled
buttress.

Babylon Buttress 220m Very Difficult   (1985)
This route climbs the pinnacled buttress; start at the toe of the buttress.
Climb into a cave then out left and up to a broad grassy ledge. The
first pinnacle is climbed by a groove slanting left in two pitches then

up right on grass to the pinnacle. The steep arete beyond is turned by a gully on the right. The second pinnacle is turned on the left and climbed from behind. Climb final slabs over detached blocks followed by a traverse right to finish just below the summit.

Much further right, the east-curving gully near the entrance to the corrie has been climbed and named after a well-known local landmark often visible at the local hostelry; **Brenda's Cleavage** (100m, I). The obvious deep gully between Babylon Buttress and Brenda's Cleavage which twists and narrows near the top is **Little Gully** (100m, I).

SGURR FHUARAN
1068m   (Map Ref 978 167)

The north face of Sgurr Fhuaran has a steep dark crag immediately below the summit. An obvious gully splits this crag from top to bottom with a triple fork in its upper reaches. This is **Trident Gully** and has been climbed at Grade II/III (220m). From the summit of Sgurr Fhuaran a ridge runs east towards Glenlicht House. The small top on this ridge is called A'Charraig (Map Ref 988 165). The big gully on the north flank of this ridge has been climbed in disappointingly banked-out conditions **A'Charraig Gully**, (180m, I/II).

SGURR NA CARNACH
1002m   (Map Ref 977 159)

The east face of Sgurr na Carnach is very steep and broken and has one prominent gully, **Dog's Leg Gully** (180m, II). It starts near the foot of the face and forks halfway up, the left fork finishing within a few feet of the summit.

SGURR NAN SPAINTEACH
990m   (Map Ref 992 150)

Window Gully (180m, III) is the gully splitting the north face of Sgurr nan Spainteach. A frozen ramp leads into the groove which is followed via two chockstones to the window on the summit ridge (visible from the base of the climb). Right of Window Gully is **Solo Gully** (120m, II). This is the obvious line on the left side of the corrie north of the ridge between Sgurr nan Spainteach and Sgurr na Ciste Duibhe. It finishes 200 metres east of the summit of Sgurr nan Spainteach.

SGURR A' BHEALAICH DHEIRG

1031m   (Map Ref 033 143)

This hill forms part of the easterly continuation of The Five Sisters ridge. It has a fine summit about 50 metres north of the main ridge. The following climb has been recorded in Ghlas Choire, the corrie to the north of the mountain.

Resolution Gully   120m   II/III   (1986)
This is the obvious gully in the centre of the crags at the back of the corrie. Go right at a junction above a prominent pinnacle and continue up, avoiding an icefall by an exit right onto a broken buttress which leads easily to the summit ridge. A sporting route.

BEINN FHADA

1032m   (Map Ref 018 192)

This hulk of a mountain is relatively uninteresting if approached from Gleann Lichd, but its west ridge provides an interesting means of ascent and the corries on the north side of the mountain are impressive. Most of the climbing on Beinn Fhada is concentrated on the east face of Sgurr a' Choire Ghairbh (Map Ref 994 207) where a series of slabby buttresses overlook the Choire Chaoil. Coire an Sgairne, the more easterly of the two corries is more suited to rock climbing although only one route has been recorded. For access drive up past Lienassie near Morvich to a car park just before Dorusduain House (Map Ref 980 223). Walk up the landrover track for a few hundred metres to Dorusduain House where a small path branches off rightwards and crosses the river to gain the main stalker's track leading to the Bealach an Sgairne. This excellent path is followed to the junction of two burns about one kilometre before the Bealach an Sgairne. From this point the summit buttress of Sgurr a' Choire Ghairbh is clearly visible and is the nearest buttress on the right-hand side as you look upwards.

SGURR A' CHOIRE GHAIRBH: NORTH-EAST FACE

Under the summit of Sgurr a'Choire Ghairbh there is a broad buttress split into three parts by two narrow gullies. The following routes have been climbed here:

1 Summit Buttress 200m III   (1984)
Start to the right of the right-hand gully and climb slabs to a prominent bulge at about mid-height. Continue directly to the top. The route has also been climbed in summer by traversing left across the right-hand gully at the mid-height bulge (Difficult). A disappointing climb in both summer and winter.

2 Right-Hand Gully 160m II/III   (1951)
The right-hand of the two gullies.

3 Left-Hand Gully 135m II/III   (1983)
The narrow gully immediately left of Summit Buttress. It contains numerous short steps which can often bank out making the climb considerably easier.

To the left of Summit Buttress is a broad grassy gully enclosed by steep walls. The left wall forms the edge of **Needle's Eye Buttress**, so called after a square projection half way up the buttress which is pierced by a hole. The crest of the buttress provides a poor climb of Difficult standard.

To the left of Needle's Eye Buttress is another broad grassy gully with a broad buttress to its left. The right-hand edge of this buttress is formed, in its upper half, by a steep narrow rib. This provides **Guide's Rib** (100m, Very Difficult). To the left of Guide's Rib and starting at the lowest point of the same buttress is **Porter's Climb** (130m, Difficult).

At the top of this climb and 20 metres to the right is **Continuation Climb** (30m, Difficult). At the back of the corrie are two large slabby buttresses, separate from the main mass and facing north-west. The right-hand buttress has been named **Tropical Buttress** and has been climbed in winter (120m, II). The left buttress contains the following route.

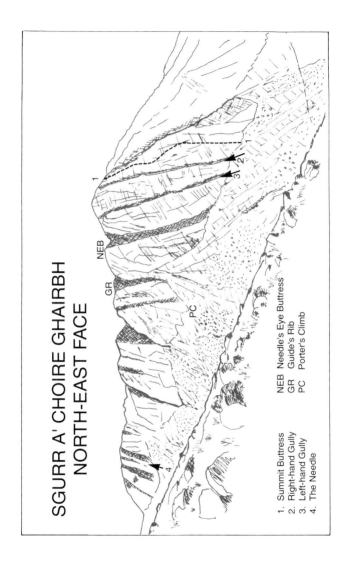

SGURR A' CHOIRE GHAIRBH
NORTH-EAST FACE

1. Summit Buttress
2. Right-hand Gully
3. Left-hand Gully
4. The Needle

NEB Needle's Eye Buttress
GR   Guide's Rib
PC   Porter's Climb

4 The Needle 110m Severe   (1952)
The route goes up the north edge of the buttress. Starting from the
lowest point, climb the groove to the edge of the slab. Traverse right
to a rib of porphyry (spike belay); the direct ascent of this slab is severe.
Climb the rib in several pitches (60m). Traverse up to the right for 10m
to a large vibrating flake and climb the wall above to the top of a
pinnacle (20m). Cross a narrow gap and scramble to the main ridge.

COIRE AN SGAIRNE

On the approach to the corrie from the Bealach an Sgairne stalker's
track, the first buttress encountered is twin-tiered and provides the
following route.

The Kintail Blanket 185m VS   (1989)
Start at the toe of the buttress a few metres right of a large embedded
boulder at a pink rock intrusion.
1. 50m 4c Climb an easy slab then the obvious broken groove above
to a prominent square cut overhang at 40m. Turn the overhang on the
right to belay on a grass ledge at the foot of a hanging groove.
2. 45m 4b Climb the groove above and cross the terrace to belay at
a 2m overhanging wall.
3. and 4. 90m 4c Climb past the right side of the overhanging wall
and up by short grooves and walls to finish up a short hard corner.
Take belays as required.

   Left of the twin-tiered buttress the cliff recedes, offering a fine
section with a large groove on the left of which is the most impressive
feature of all – a great black, blank wall, vertical and about 50m high.
No climbs have been recorded here.

GLEN CROE TO LOCH LONG

Most of the country between Glen Croe at Morvich and Loch Long
(mouth at Dornie) has numerous small bluffs and crags. Several short
climbs have been made on these and are not described. The largest
crag of note in the area is Biod an Fhithich, a west-facing buttress 2km
east of Bundalloch near Dornie.

BIOD AN FHITHICH   *(Map Ref 915 274)*

The approach to this crag is along the path south of the River Glennan with a steep climb up grass to the foot of the buttress. Features of Biod an Fhithich are the very steep, in places overhanging, left side of the cliff which is rather vegetatious, the clean slabby right half, and the easy-angled ridge which bounds it on the right. Immediately to the right of this ridge is a narrow grassy gully, useful for descent, and beyond it a smaller vegetatious crag. A grassy rake rises to the right below the crag and gives access to the foot of the steep wall below the slabs. The climbing on the slabs is better than it appears – sound quartzite with a plentiful supply of good flat and incut holds.

Hump   135m   Very Difficult   (1971)
Start immediately right of the undercut base of the cliff. Take a direct line in 3 pitches up a rib, wall, cracks, slabs and corners, to belay at the left end of a big obvious recess. Go right and up an undercut groove and exit left through the final roof.

Wrong Turn   110m   Very Difficult   (1971)
On right-hand side of slabs. Start near the right end of the vertical base (reached by easy ramp leading up from left). Climb walls and slabs above passing a big heather patch and then a smaller one on right to a platform near the right-bounding ridge above a heathery recess. A short chimney leads to easier climbing.

Ankle Ridge   120m   Difficult   (1971)
The right-bounding ridge of the main crag just left of the obvious gully. There is considerable scope for variation.

PLOCKTON CRAGS

Creagan Duilisg (Map Ref 834 333) is a north-facing 90m crag situated across the bay from Plockton. It can be reached by a minor road leading west off the A890 Stromeferry road, north of Kyle of Lochalsh. A number of routes were climbed here in the early 1970s; reliable details are not available. More recently, a number of bolt-protected routes have appeared for which detailed descriptions are unnecessary.

Achnashellach

The mountains between Glen Carron and Loch Monar, which are most easily reached from Achnashellach, are remote and have seen little climbing development. Access to most of the climbs is arduous from all directions and the climbing has an expedition flavour which is likely to involve an isolated camp.

MAOILE LUNNDAIDH; TOLL A' CHOIN
1007m   (Map Ref 133 454)

The left wall of the corrie is steep and vegetated. **Mica Ridge** (100m, Difficult) is the only climb recorded here. It follows the first definite ridge to the right of the vegetated wall, staying close to the crest and traversing by steps and ledges on the right. The first ascent had a snow comb and a big cornice to lend atmosphere.

LURG MHOR
986m   (Map Ref 065 404)

A large crag of excellent rough quartzite lies high on the flank of Lurg Mhor, above Loch Monar (Map Ref 062 405). Although north-facing with many grooves and overlaps, the slabby rock is exceptionally clean, so it dries very quickly. There are excellent campsites at the head of Loch Monar.

Munroist's Reward   90m   VS **   (1988)
A fine climb taking the left edge of the main slabs. Start at the lowest point of the buttress 5 metres right of a long grassy corner.
1. 50m 4c Climb the slab to a small steepening, then move right to the foot of a prominent V-groove at 10m. Climb the wall to the right (crux) to reach the slab above and right. Climb the slabs and two further overlaps above, moving slightly left to a pedestal stance on the edge of the buttress. An excellent pitch.
2. 40m 4b Climb the groove above, then the exposed wall to its left to easier ground. Scramble to the top.

Monar Magic   140m   VS **   (1988)
This excellent climb takes a direct line up the centre of the slabs. Start
just left of a fault which slants from left to right (most easily seen from
below) near the middle of the crag. There is a shallow inverted
U-shaped overlap just to the right of the start at the foot of the crag.
1. 45m 4b Climb straight up slabs, then thin cracks to the right of a
grassy corner to a slight steepening at 30m. Move up then diagonally
left to a tiny ledge in a short open corner. A poorly protected pitch.
2. 20m 4c Climb straight up to an obvious V-niche in the main overlap.
Climb this on good holds, then the slab above to belay in a small
overhung niche.
3. 45m 4c Move up and right into a corner in the next overlap. Swing
out onto the right arete, then climb directly up the slabs.
4. 30m 4a Pleasant slabs above lead to the top.

MORUISG; COIRE TOLL NAM BIAN
928m   (Map Ref 101 499)

Unlike the other areas described in this section, this corrie is readily
accessible from the main road through Glen Carron. Low down at the
east entrance of the corrie is a prominent buttress split by a gully (Map
Ref 090 501). **Short and Silly** (90m, II/III) climbs this gully in several
short pitches and is the only climb recorded here.

SGURR NAN CEANNAICHEAN
915m   (Map Ref 087 481)

North Gully   420m   III/IV   (1987)
This is on the west face. Several interesting pitches lead to a huge
chockstone, which has a remarkable through-route. The exit window
frames a superb panorama stretching from Liathach round to the
Applecross peaks. The upper part of the gully is straightforward.

In summer the ascent is moderate.

GLAS BHEINN

711m   (Map Ref 901 436)

This attractive crag of gneiss is easily approached from Tullich, 2km north-east of Lochcarron. The main climbing is on the cliff directly overlooking the Bealach a'Glas-chnoic. The views are very fine. The climbs are described from right to left.

Slab and Groove   150m   Severe   (1984)
At the right side of the crag is a slabby corner just left of a gully. Climb this for 90m (Moderate) to a grassy terrace. The slabby corner continues to the top of the cliff. To its left is a deep groove, entrance to which is barred by a wall with overhangs. Follow the slabby corner for about 5m until above the first overhang then traverse left across the wall and climb through the second overhang to reach the groove. Follow the groove to the top.

The wall of the main crag left of Slab and Groove has a large flake. A route has been climbed, but not properly recorded, which takes walls up to the flake on the left, then goes right and up the flake.

Black House   175m   HVS   (1972)
Start below the centre of the crag.
1. 30m From a pinnacle go right up a crack.
2. 35m Go left round a rib and up a wide scoop.
3. 40m Climb directly, sometimes grassily, to a stance below overhangs and a small white slab.
4. 25m Climb the slab on the left, traverse right, and exit steeply on the right to a ledge at the left end of a terrace.
5. 45m Finish directly up steep walls.

Clean Compromise   170m   E1 *   (1984)
Start at the centre of the crag below a groove with an overhang at 10m.
1. 40m 4c Climb the groove to below the overhang, then go right and up easily for 10m. Climb a steep shallow groove on good holds to a small stance.
2. 40m 4c Move right along a ledge, climb up slabs, a steep wall and then a rib to a slanting grass terrace.

3. 25m 4b Go up the terrace to the white slab of Black House. Climb this on the left and continue up to a ledge below a steep wall. (A more direct variation is possible on this pitch.)
4. 35m 5b Climb a steep wall to gain a short groove on the right. Climb this and the overhang above on the right (strenuous). Continue up short walls and grassy ledges.
5. 30m Continue to the top.

Adul Suh   165m   HVS   (1974)
Start about 30 metres left of Black House. (This start may be common with Clean Compromise).
1. 35m Climb a large groove, an overhang and luminous green moss above. Escape right below the overhang.
2. and 3. 65m Continue directly to below the steep grooves on the nose of the crag (taken by Clean Compromise), just left of the white slab on Black House.
4. and 5. 65m Go left and finish by shallow chimneys.

Left-hand Route   120m   VS   (1984)
This lies on the left-hand section of the crag.
1. 25m Climb a chimney past a flake to a large terrace.
2. and 3. 95m Go up a steep wall for 10m, and trend left above an overhang onto black slabs. Climb black walls to the top.

FUAR THOLL
907m   (Map Ref 975 489)

This fine mountain has two major cliffs, a large number of smaller crags and good scope for winter climbing. The major cliffs are the south-east cliff, which overlooks a small corrie just south-east of the summit, and Mainreachan Buttress, which rises from a north-facing corrie and abuts the north-west ridge. The south-east cliff, visible from the road at Achnashellach, should not be confused with a lower band of small crags which line the south-east face of the mountain. At the upper end of this band, as seen from the Achnashellach approach, is a clean nose which falls from the south-east ridge of the mountain. Further round on the north-east side of the mountain, facing the grand Coire Lair, are more broken crags and gullies, suitable for winter climbing.

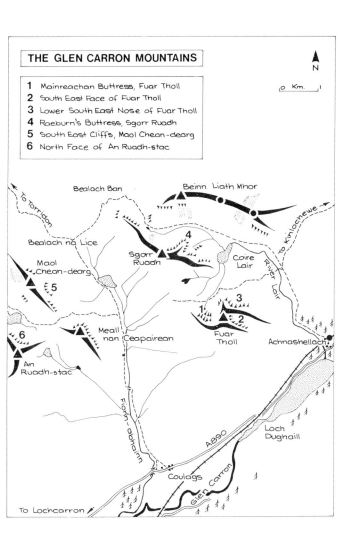

THE GLEN CARRON MOUNTAINS

1 Mainreachan Buttress, Fuar Tholl
2 South East Face of Fuar Tholl
3 Lower South East Nose of Fuar Tholl
4 Raeburn's Buttress, Sgorr Ruadh
5 South East Cliffs, Maol Chean-dearg
6 North Face of An Ruadh-stac

0   Km.   1

N

To Torridon

Bealach Ban

Beinn Liath Mhor

To Kinlochewe

Bealach na Lice

Sgorr Ruadh

Coire Lair

River Lair

Maol Chean-dearg

5

4

3

1

2

Fuar Tholl

6

An Ruadh-stac

Meall nan Ceapairean

Achnashellach

Fionn-abhainn

Loch Dughaill

A890

Coulags

Glen Carron

To Lochcarron

Access

a) South-East Cliff (Map Ref 978 488). Follow the railway for 400m west of Achnashellach station, thus crossing the River Lair, then strike off right and up steep rough slopes to a plateau at 420m. Here the burn issuing from the corrie is joined. Climb either bank of the burn, passing a small lochan, to gain the corrie (about 2 hours).

b) Mainreachan Buttress (Map Ref 973 489). Follow the very scenic stalker's path from Achnashellach to a height of 360m in Coire Lair where a second path branches left, crossing the River Lair (difficult in spate) and climbing up to the Bealach Mhor between Fuar Tholl and Sgorr Ruadh. Just below the bealach branch off left to reach the base of the buttress (about two and a half hours). Alternatively start from Balnacra in Glen Carron (Map Ref 983 463), climb to the summit of Fuar Tholl and descend either the west or east flank of the buttress to its base.

c) Lower South-East Nose and North-East flanks (Map Ref 980 493). Cross the River Lair by the railway then go right just above the forest where a fair path traverses 100m above the river. The path climbs the side valley close under the Nose to debouch on the plateau beneath the north-east flanks at 450m. This approach can be used to reach Mainreachan Buttress when the River Lair is in spate.

LOWER SOUTH-EAST NOSE

These cliffs give a good selection of routes for short days or wild weather. The climbs come into condition after a low snowfall and a couple of days of frost. About 20 metres left of The Nose (see below) there is a big turfy ramp which slants slightly left. The first route starts some 10 metres right of this.

Luck Of The Irish   175m   III   (1992)
This takes a steep groove line about 7 metres left of Newton's Law.
1. 45m Climb icy ground trending slightly left, then a steeper iced chimney to a small ledge.
2. 35m Steep moves lead into the main groove line. Follow this to a small terrace.
3. 25m Continue up the groove to a steep exit, then belay on the terrace above.
4. and 5. 70m Climb a little chimney, then surmount easier steps and grooves to reach the top.

Newton's Law   170m   III/IV   (1992)
This is the obvious chimney-groove line just left of The Nose.
1. 40m A wandering line on icy ground leads to a ledge and stance where the rock steepens.
2. 30m Climb turfy iced grooves direct to the base of an obvious hanging chimney.
3. 20m Climb the chimney, then exit right to a recess.
4. 45m Follow the continuing fault line to easy ground.
5. 35m Climb the easy final steps.

1   Nose Direct   150m   VS   (1961/1973)
The lower tier of cliffs facing the River Lair has a number of features. The Nose Direct lies up the cleanest area of rock, more or less where the line of cliff begins to face north. It was first climbed solo by Tom Patey in 1961, but a more direct route was climbed in 1973.

1a   Lair Wall   145m   IV   (1992)
This route climbs the left-slanting fault immediately right of The Nose.
1. 40m Climb the fault to a good stance below steeper ground.
2. 45m Continuously interesting climbing in the same line leads to a large terrace.
3. and 4. 60m Easy ground leads to the top.

2   Olfactory   150m   IV   (1986)
A little right of the Nose Direct is a deeply recessed easy gully. To the left of this gully are first, a short chimney with a chockstone (climbed at Grade III), and then a narrow gully running up the right side of the buttress containing the Nose Direct. The narrow gully gives a good climb in four pitches, of which the second is a steep, narrow chimney followed by steep ice on the left, and the fourth is another short steep chimney.

To the right of the Lower Nose a line of broken cliffs seamed by gullies stretches for over a kilometre around the north-east flank of the mountain. Beyond the recessed gully right of the Nose lies a craggy spur, then an obvious shallow corrie with a fine gully leading onto the upper south-east ridge of the mountain (300m, I). Further right are three parallel gullies split by narrow spurs. The rib on the left of the left-most gully is **The Pile** (150m, II). Many other good winter routes in the lower grades (I to III) may be made in this area, between 200m and 400m in length and finishing close to the summit.

SOUTH-EAST CLIFF

This is a very extensive north-facing cliff. Many variations are possible on the summer routes, but good climbing is to be had, particularly in the left-hand section. In winter it provides several long and exacting climbs, among the hardest in the area. The climbs are described from left to right. Descent is on the left.

3 Blue Finger 150m Severe   (1969)
Start 30 metres from the left end of the cliff.
1. 40m Climb up easily left, follow a short groove and hand-traverse up to a higher ledge. Move back up right and follow a groove to belay in a corner.
2. 15m Climb a crack to an overhanging block on the left, then move left and follow a groove to a terrace.
3. 95m Continue easily to the top.

4 Cold Sweat 130m VS *   (1969)
This is the line of the definite black chimney rather left of the centre of the wall.
1. 35m Climb up to the chimney making a few excursions to the right.
2. 15m 5a Climb up right past an old peg and on to the wall. Move back left into the chimney above the overhang and so to a ledge. This is more pleasant than struggling up the chimney, which may be slimy.
3. 80m Continue up easier chimneys to the top.
Winter: V   (1986)
A back-roped solo ascent was made over two days, the rope being left in place and the high point regained by jumaring. There was sustained mixed climbing in the lower section, the crux chimney being verglassed and very strenuous.

5 Boat Tundra 150m Severe *   (1969)
Start at a cairn near the centre of the wall between the obvious black chimney (Cold Sweat) and the line of a big corner which starts halfway up the cliff.
1. 45m Climb up for 7m, traverse left for 6m, then climb up and right to a small grassy bay. Continue up then diagonally right to the base of the big corner.
2. 45m The corner is vegetated and unattractive; the cliff is more broken here and variations are possible. Climb up and left, passing a

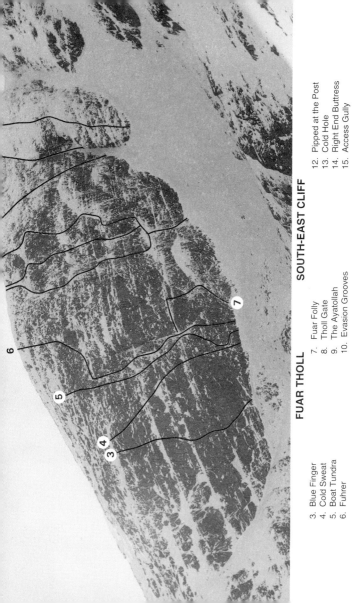

FUAR THOLL

3. Blue Finger
4. Cold Sweat
5. Boat Tundra
6. Fuhrer

SOUTH-EAST CLIFF

7. Fuar Folly
8. Tholl Gate
9. The Ayatollah
10. Evasion Grooves

12. Pipped at the Post
13. Cold Hole
14. Right End Buttress
15. Access Gully

pleasant smooth slab at about 25m, to belay on a terrace by a large pinnacle.
3. 60m There is a clean headwall above a short black corner left of the big vegetated corner which gives a good finish to the climb. From the pinnacle belay continue up broken ground to the headwall and climb it using a fine layback crack to start.

6 Fuhrer 190m V ***   (1986)
This fine route takes the big corner up the left-hand side of the cliff, mentioned in Boat Tundra. It is a straighter version of an earlier route, Fuar Folly, which escaped left from the corner under threat of darkness. Start at the obvious mixed line trending right to the foot of the hanging corner.
1. 45m Start in a short corner and trend up right to belay just below the start of the big corner.
2. 35m Gain the corner and follow it over ice bulges to a good flake on the right. Take to ice streaks on the slabs on the left and belay 8m below and left of the overhang which caps the groove.
3. 25m Just left of the stance thin ice leads through a steep wall to a belay below an ice-choked chimney.
4. 25m The ice chimney gives access to the left end of a ledge which is followed 15m rightwards to a right-trending break in the wall above.
5. 60m Take the break in the wall above and tricky ground to the top.

7 Fuar Folly 55m IV   (1978)
This is an alternative start to Fuhrer. Start a little right of Fuhrer and trend up right by a groove-ramp to the start of a snow shelf (25m). Climb straight up and step right to the foot of the great rock bastion (15m). Traverse left round the nose to the foot of the corner, and junction with Fuhrer (15m).

8 Tholl Gate 180m V/VI ***   (1984)
This takes the magnificent icy line in the centre of the cliff, 50 metres right of Fuhrer. Start slightly right of the line in a shallow bay.
1. 35m Mixed climbing trending left then right leads to a ledge line. Traverse left for 10m to belay below the ice streak.
2. 35m Mixed climbing leads to an overhanging wall which may or may not be iced. On the first ascent this was covered with organ-pipe icicles which collapsed, necessitating a peg for aid to gain the ice above. Steep thin ice for 15m then leads to a good ledge.
3. 35m The steep and fine icy corners on the right lead to a ledge.

4. 30m   Ascend diagonally right on deceptively hard ground (not obvious from the foot of the route).
5. 45m   Continue right (easy after the initial steep step) until it is possible to ascend direct to the top.

9   The Ayatollah   190m   VI ***   (1989)
Takes an uncompromising line right of Tholl Gate, following an obvious steep slab corner in the second tier, and then a series of icy grooves directly above. This is a superb route. Start, as for Tholl Gate, at a shallow bay beneath the highest part of the cliff.
1. 50m   Climb as for Tholl Gate, tricky icy grooves to a snow terrace, then a right traverse to a spike belay beneath the slab corner.
2. 30m   Make some radical moves up the smooth corner until usable ice can be gained on the slab on the left. Follow the ice smears to a narrow terrace, traverse right under an icicle, then up a rocky groove for 4m to belay at a cracked block.
3. 35m   Bridge across left to gain the icicle, then up directly. A short groove, an easier snow bay and a further iced groove lead to belays at a wedged block below a steeper icefall.
4. 45m   Climb the icefall, then go left and back right in easier angled mixed grooves to gain a terrace below the final rock wall.
5. 30m   Traverse 5m left, then go up steep snow and a runnel to the cornice.

10   Evasion Grooves   220m   V **   (1988)
This is a mixed alternative to Tholl Gate, up the big buttress to its right. It is more frequently in climbable condition than its neighbours. The line is similar to the summer line of The Fuar. An excellent climb. Start, as for The Ayatollah and Tholl Gate, at a shallow bay below the highest part of the cliff.
1. 50m   Climb tricky ice grooves, as for The Ayatollah and Tholl Gate, to a snowy terrace, and go right along this to belay beneath a prominent steep corner.
2. 45m   Traverse right for 4m to a very steep groove. Climb this direct to a hard exit, then continue to giant spike belays.
3. 45m   Go down right onto a big easy snow ramp. Follow this for 25m to a left-sloping break in the tier above. Struggle up this to reach another terrace directly beneath a fine ramp.
4. 40m   Climb the ramp to belay in an overhung corner.
5. 40m   Traverse left for 15m, then trend left up snowfields and rocky grooves to the top. Beware of the monster cornice.

11 The Fuar 185m Severe   (1969)
Start at an arrow at a line of weakness on the right of face.
1. 40m Trend slightly right to the higher of two ledges.
2. 40m Traverse right and climb a shallow groove.
3. 45m Climb up grooves and a nose slightly right to a ledge.
4. 50m Climb directly up then left to a line of weakness (loose) leading
to a ledge. Continue easily to the top.

11a Original Route 190m Very Difficult †   (1933)
An indirect line, probably similar but inferior to The Fuar. Start below
and right of an obvious, large 'semi-lunar' green shelf near the right
end of the cliff.
1. 15m Climb to the right end of the shelf.
2. 25m From the left end of the shelf climb steep easy rock, trending
right to a good ledge.
3. 15m Climb up and right to a smooth chimney.
4. 10m Climb round the nose on the right, then take an exposed
traverse to a steep shallow chimney.
5. 25m Climb the chimney, moving onto the right wall at the top.
6. 35m Climb easily to a large ledge.
7. and 8. 65m Climb two successive chimneys to rotten rock, then
continue easily to the top.

   A prominent gully ending in a *cul-de-sac*, the Cold Hole, separates
the right side of the cliff from an easier, narrower buttress.

12 Pipped at the Post 100m V   (1987)
About 30 metres lower down the gully from Cold Hole is a continuous
ice streak on the left wall.
1. 45m Climb the ice to a thinly covered wall at 15m (crux) and go up
to ledges.
2. 35m Continue in the same line up a steep corner at 20m to gain
ledges.
3. 20m Finish directly on mixed ground.

13 Cold Hole 50m V ***   (1987)
The gully is easy up to the *cul-de-sac* which forms a very steep 45m
step. This climb takes the ice sheet forming the left corner of the step.
Though short it is highly recommended.
1. 25m Climb the ice corner to belay on a small ledge on the right wall,
10m below where the groove curls left and overhangs.

2. 25m   Climb very steep ice round the left edge of the overhang to easier ground.

13a Tubular Bells 40m V   (1991)
Takes the obvious icicle-ridden corner just right of Cold Hole. Short but noteworthy.
1. 25m   Battle up through overhanging Damoclean icicles to a belay in a cave beneath the final overhangs.
2. 15m   Break left through the icicle fringe, round the overhang and gain easy slopes leading to the cornice.

14 Right End Buttress 140m III   (1976)
This is the separate buttress on the right of the gully at the right end of the cliff. Ledges and short pitches followed by an easier section lead to a steep middle band. Above this easy climbing continues to the top. The buttress has also been climbed in summer (Very Difficult).

15 Access Gully 100m I
The obvious gully to the right of Right End Buttress has a steep exit, often dangerously corniced. A steeper right fork gives an alternative finish of 50m at Grade II. The climb is not recommended in summer.

16 Right-Hand Gully 50m I
The right-hand gully in the corrie gives an easy uncorniced exit to the summit.

MAINREACHAN BUTTRESS

This cliff has lost much of its earlier popularity after a period of enthusiastic exploration in 1969/70. There is a good deal of loose rock and the climbs are serious. The buttress presents a steep north face with a scree slope below it rising sharply from left to right. Several gangways slant up leftwards from the scree marking the starts of the routes. The longest climbs follow the north-east facet of the buttress which rises from the lowest point of the cliff, and also offers the best chance of winter climbing. The upper right side of the buttress is so steep and exposed to wind that it rarely accumulates much snow. The climbs are described from right to left. Descent is on the right.

1 Investigator 140m   Hard Severe   (1969)
Start at an obvious slab gangway near the right-hand end of the cliff.
Climb the gangway for 75m. Go left around a nose and climb up a
broken groove, then traverse right to belay, (25m). Climb up and right
to gain an overhanging nose, pull up the overhang and continue to the
top, (40m).
Winter: V **   (1991)
Follow the summer line. A spectacular outing.

2 All The Way 150m   HVS †   (1972)
This climb starts from a shelf below the gangway of Investigator and
takes a direct line to the big nose of Investigator at the top of the cliff.
Go left along the shelf to a narrow corner. Climb the steep wall then
the corner to the gangway of Investigator. Go left on this to below a
groove, gain this via a wall and roof, and continue to a recess. Move
right below a nose then left across a bulge onto a slab. Finish, as for
Investigator, by pulling onto the overhanging nose on the right.

3 Private Eye 150m   HVS †   (1974)
This route climbs the buttress in the centre, through the obvious black
cave at half-height. The most obvious gangway in the centre of the
face marks the start of Snoopy; this climb starts at the next gangway
above.
1. 45m Climb the gangway with some awkward moves.
2. 30m Continue slightly right to belay in the back of the cave.
3. 30m Exit over the roof of the cave past a thread runner to a belay
above (difficult and wet).
4. 45m Continue up cracks and steep loose walls to the top.

4 Snoopy 190m   HVS *   (1969)
Start at the obvious gangway near the middle of the face.
1. 35m Go left up the gangway.
2. 40m Climb back right up a slabby ramp until below an obvious black
corner.
3. 15m 4c Traverse right to below a shallow brown groove and climb
on the right of this to a ledge.
4. 40m 5a Trend right to below a steep mossy groove; traverse hard
right on steep rock to gain another groove (belay on right if required);
follow the groove, moving left at the top to reach a large grass ledge.
5. 60m 4c Traverse left round an edge to a chimney with a pinnacle
forming its left side. Climb this and the groove above to the top.

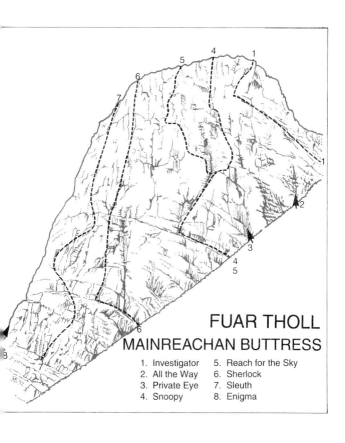

FUAR THOLL
MAINREACHAN BUTTRESS

1. Investigator
2. All the Way
3. Private Eye
4. Snoopy
5. Reach for the Sky
6. Sherlock
7. Sleuth
8. Enigma

5   Reach for the Sky   200m   VI ***   (1989)
This route follows the ramp of Snoopy before breaking out left on very steep mixed ground to gain finishing grooves. Although nowhere desperate, it is a sustained and intimidating climb with some spectacular exposure. Start as for Snoopy at a gangway leading left into the bottom of the ramp.
1. 35m Follow the terrace to a bay beneath the ramp.
2. 30m Climb the ramp corner, generally on tufts and verglas, to a terrace on the left, spike belay.
3. 40m Go back onto the ramp and via a rightward deviation on its slab gain the corner at its top. Climb this and exit left up to loose wedged blocks beneath a sheer corner. A narrow ledge leads left out of this impasse to a well-poised belay on the front of the buttress.
4. 30m Climb mixed ground trending left to an overhang. Mantleshelf over this then make a long left traverse, gaining a turfy ramp beneath iced grooves (exposed and unprotected), belay up and left at a huge cracked block.
5. 30m Step right and climb an ice column to gain easier-angled grooves which are followed first left then back right and left again to nut belays.
6. 35m Go up and right to regain the groove line which is followed through two further tiers to a sudden ending.

6   Sherlock   205m   VS   (1969)
Start at the obvious left-trending gangway below and parallel to that of Snoopy.
1. 30m Climb the gangway.
2. 20m Climb cracked blocks trending right to a good ledge.
3. 15m Go up the steep groove above the belay to a stance on the left.
4. 20m Climb the groove above to a grass ledge and continue over the bulge to another ledge.
5. 30m Climb a loose groove.
6. and 7. 90m Follow the crest on loose rock to the top.

ILLUSTRATIONS
Opposite: *Ladhar Bheinn and the cliffs of Coire Dhorrcail*
Next Page: *Munroist's Reward, Lurg Mhor (Climber, Roger Everett)*

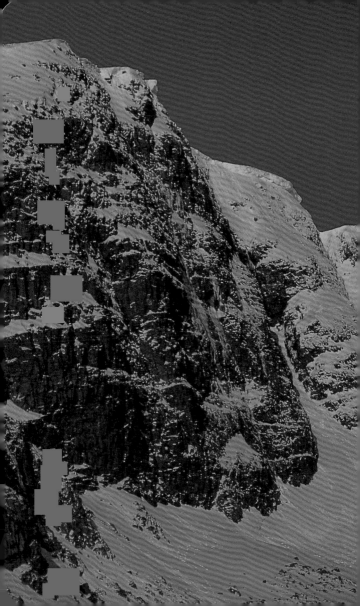

7 Sleuth 225m VS †   (1969)
Start near the right-hand end of the lowest terrace on the north-east
face. Climb the crack line until it is possible to traverse right round the
corner to easier rock leading up left to a ledge and belay. Continue up
to a broad terrace. To the right of the main barrier wall is a line of
weakness. Reach this from a ledge going up left, and go up a small
corner to a higher ledge. Traverse right to reach a damp groove; go
up this using a spike, then slightly right to near the edge and back left
to belay. Go straight up a small wall, then by easier ground to under
another wall. Go up right by overhanging blocks, then straight up to a
further ledge. Climb directly on loose rock to traverse right at a nose
with flakes above. Go round the nose to the right and up to easier
ground, reaching the top after one more pitch.

8 Enigma 200m Severe   (1952)
Start at the left end of the lowest terrace on the north-east face. Go
up the left edge on easy rock to a mossy stance, (10m). Climb the
crack on the right to a ledge, (20m). Traverse left into steep grooves
and up to a large grass platform. Go up right for 20m to a moss patch,
then up left to a big ledge. Climb a groove for 10m, then a crack to the
top of a large flake. Traverse right and climb a steep wall on good holds
to a ledge, (15m). Traverse left and climb a rib for 10m and scramble
to below a steeper rib. Climb this on small holds for 20m, then trend
left and climb short pitches and easier rock for 60m to the top.
Winter: V *   (1969)
Start as for Enigma and climb up to a broad snow terrace. Traverse
right then climb diagonally left to the left edge of the buttress. Go left
into the corner (Nimrod) and climb this to reach the big terrace about
halfway up the face. Now traverse right, go up and left and follow the
line of least resistance to the top.

   To the left of the north-east facet of the buttress are two obvious
steep corner lines, **Nimrod** (150m, Hard Severe) and **Nebula** (150m,
Severe). They are both rather dirty in summer, but provide good winter
climbs when iced up.

ILLUSTRATIONS
Previous page: Tholl Gate, Fuar Tholl   (Climber, Niall Ritchie)
Opposite: The South-East Cliff of Fuar Tholl

9 Mainline Connection 155m V   (1989)
This approximates the line of Nimrod in the lower section.
1. 50m Climb the corner over several steps to a good ledge. Beware of a large loose flake on the second step.
2. 45m Ascend the fault directly above the belay and just left of the corner, then continue in the corner to the terrace.
3. 15m Traverse left and belay below the first obvious groove.
4. 45m   Move up left and traverse right into the groove, which is climbed to smaller twin grooves, the right-hand of which leads to easy ground.

SGORR RUADH

960m   (Map Ref 959 505)

Sgorr Ruadh, the highest peak of the Coulin Forest, presents an impressive north-east and north face to the walker ascending Coire Lair from Achnashellach. The rock is sandstone throughout and rather broken, so the summer climbs are somewhat indeterminate. In winter several of the gullies and faces provide good climbs in a fine situation.

Access
The best approach is on the good path from Achnashellach station to upper Coire Lair. The alternative approaches from Torridon are considerably longer but also very scenic. Either follow the track from Annat to the Bealach na Lice and then via Bealach Ban to upper Coire Lair; or, starting from the Ling Hut (Map Ref 958 562) take the path climbing southwards. It disappears after a few kilometres, but further on the Bealach Ban track is joined.
    The climbs are described as for the Achnashellach approach. Seen from Loch Coire Lair, the furthest skyline ridge marks Raeburn's Buttress. Coming left from this is a broken south-east face, then the broad Central Couloir, and then, in front of the Couloir and partially hiding it, the long line of Academy Ridge with an easy section in the middle and a steep upper part. Left of this is another large broken area with a number of rakes running up from left to right terminating in gullies. Robertson's Gully defines the left boundary of Academy Ridge and the next buttress left is Robertson's Buttress.

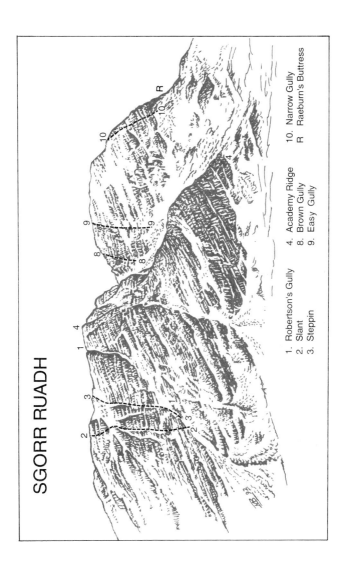

SGORR RUADH

1. Robertson's Gully
2. Slant
3. Steppin

4. Academy Ridge
8. Brown Gully
9. Easy Gully

10. Narrow Gully
R Raeburn's Buttress

1 Robertson's Gully   180m   IV   (1976)
A long snow approach climbing diagonally right leads to this steep
gully on the left of Academy Ridge. There is a deep cave just over
halfway up. Climb the gully by a series of chockstone-filled chimneys
to the cave. Traverse right and re-enter the gully by the higher of two
traverse lines above the cave.

From the diagonal snow ramp going up to Robertson's Gully, two
lines may be seen climbing vertically up to the left of Robertson's
Buttress.

2 The Slant   350m   I/II   (1969)
The left-hand line rising from the ramp. An easy climb with several
possible variations.

3 Steppin   250m   II/III   (1969)
The right-hand line rising from the ramp is an obvious corner. Follow
this for two pitches then move right and go up a small steep step.
Continue up easier ground to the top.

4 Academy Ridge   350m   Very Difficult   (1948)
The lower part of the ridge is scrambling. Above there is a discontinuity
in the crest, which re-appears on the left. Rejoin it as soon as possible
and climb the steep upper section with a fine 25m pitch.
Winter: II/III
A good mountaineering route. Follow the summer line.

5 Post Box Gully   180m   II   (1969)
This is a narrow well-defined gully in the left wall of the Central Couloir,
recognisable by a huge chockstone near its foot. Climb up to the
chockstone and continue beneath it to emerge from a slot. Continue
direct over small pitches to the top of Academy Ridge.

6 Croydon Chimney   180m   IV   (1969)
Just left of High Gully is a left-slanting chimney line. Climb this direct
with a hard slot at mid-height and a sustained upper groove. Escape
left to easy ground below the final capstone.

7 High Gully   120m   III   (1976)
High on the left wall of the Central Couloir, just below and opposite
Brown Gully, a large two-tiered icefall can form below a deep narrow
gully. Climb the icefalls trending right and enter the gully from the right.

8 Brown Gully 100m III   (1969)
This is the narrow gully on the right of and starting high up Central Couloir. Climb up right past a bend in the gully and go up an ice pitch. Climb straight up the gully to where it narrows and steepens. Follow a groove on the right and return to the gully as soon as possible. Continue easily to the top.

9 Easy Gully 180m I/II   (1969)
Halfway along the right wall of Central Couloir is an obvious long gully starting just right of an isolated pinnacle. It may have several short ice pitches.

10 Narrow Gully 150m III   (1978)
The prominent narrow gully bounding Raeburn's Buttress on the left.

11 Raeburn's Buttress 300m Difficult   (1904)
This climb follows the skyline silhouetted on the approach from Coire Lair. At the left end of the buttress the rocks are steeper and sounder than elsewhere. Start at the left end of a narrow ramp leading right across the face. Climb steep rocks up from the ramp for 25m. Alternatively climb the square-cut gully (Narrow Gully) which bounds the buttress on the left and traverse right onto the ridge. After 10m of the second pitch the climb becomes a Moderate scramble with much heather and loose rock. It is however a good, natural mountaineering route.

12 Raeburn's Buttress Direct 300m IV   (1967)
Although on the approach from Coire Lair, Raeburn's Buttress appears to have a well-defined crest, in fact as the upper corrie is reached the buttress is seen rather to have a broad frontal zone in its lower part, consisting of steep, slabby walls separated by discontinuous terraces. The winter Direct Route starts well to the right of the original route and takes a completely independent line for the first 120m. A slanting chimney divides the face just right of centre and the climb begins at a bay left of the chimney and just right of a small tongue of broken rock at the lowest rocks. Traverse up and right to the brink of the chimney. Climb the wall on the left of the chimney to a ledge and continue to another terrace. Here a steep wall rises for 30m forming an incipient tower close to the chimney. Follow a groove leftwards passing an icy section by ledges on the vertical right wall. From the narrow terrace so reached make a sensational traverse right for 15m over large detached blocks beneath an overhang to gain a recess in the chimney. Move right to reach easy ground and follow the crest to the top.

13 Raeburn's Superdirect 190m IV (1989)
This follows without deviation the prominent slanting chimney line mentioned in the Direct Route.
1. 45m Climb a short ice pitch, then a right-slanting iced groove passing a chockstone to a terrace.
2. 45m Go up the groove above to a steeper iced exit.
3. 40m Climb over short walls into an overhung *cul-de-sac* which is surmounted by tricky mixed climbing up the left wall, then up ice to easier ground. Belay on the right.
4. 40m Climb a chimney and a short step. Belay on the left.
5. 20m A final awkward step leads to easy ground.

Raeburn's Buttress gradually bends round to form the 250m north face. This is bounded on the right by a wide scree gully with a vertical left wall.

14 Fox's Face 260m III (1987)
A good mixed route up the highest part of the north face, finishing at the top of the Raeburn's Buttress. Start 5 metres right of an obvious left-slanting fault line, which leads to the top of the lower section of Raeburn's Buttress. Take a right-slanting crackline through the very steep lower tier (40m). Make a rightward deviation, then move back left into the big central depression of the face (40m). Go left at the top of the depression, then weave back right and take the final wall direct by grooves.

15 First Blood 185m IV (1988)
Start directly opposite the mouth of the gully bounding the right side of Raeburn's Buttress, about 50m above Fox's Face. A shallow bay leads to a steep corner with a prominent crack in its left wall.
1. 20m Climb the bay to belay beneath the crack.
2. 25m Follow the crack direct, finishing over a roof to good block belay, a fine hard pitch.
3. 45m Go up grooves, moving slightly left then traversing back right under roofs and up easily to belay beneath a left-slanting groove.
4. and 5. 95m Now climb the groove (awkward to start) to gain easy ground which is followed to the top of the buttress.

15a Tango in the Night 150m V † (1989)
The big chockstoned corner lying halfway up the gully on the left. The climb gives sustained crack climbing for four pitches. The last pitch, a traverse right above an overhang, is the most serious.

16 Splintery Edge 100m Very Difficult (1961)
Follow the wide scree gully for 60m to a concealed left branch which ends in a formidable *cul-de-sac*. Climb the crumbly bed of the branch gully for 15m, then follow a shelf leftwards over loose blocks to the edge. Now climb straight up for 75m on improving rock to the top.

17 Ruadh Awakening 150m V (1988)
This climb is thought to be a direct winter version of Splintery Edge. About midway up the gully are two prominent fault lines on the north face. Start in the middle of the buttress between these two lines, where a system of grooves can be seen running up the face.
1. 45m Move left along a ledge for about 5m, then climb up and right to a good ledge. Step right and continue up to a flake. Move up and right then up to a wide crack which is ascended to a ledge. Traverse left then up to a belay on blocks.
2. 25m Move right off the blocks to regain the groove line. Climb this briefly, then its right edge. Climb the bulge above and from a small recess below a steeper bulge traverse right to a ledge near the edge of the buttress.
3. 40m Continue up the groove line above. On the first ascent poor ice just short of the top necessitated a short deviation left then up the crest.
4. 40m Climb the final buttress by the right-hand of two grooves.

18 Upper Buttress, Original Route 210m Very Difficult (1955)
Upper Buttress is on the right of the wide scree gully. Start at the left edge of the buttress. Climb a 3m corner near the overhangs on the left edge and traverse 12m right to cracks on the face between these overhangs and a prominent pinnacle. Now climb more or less straight up the buttress, with slight traverses as necessary. The main difficulties end 90m up where a through route is made behind a boulder jammed in the right-hand crack. 120m of scrambling leads to the top.
Winter: III (1972)
Climb a corner at the lower left side of the buttress and escape right onto easier ground. Return back left up steep walls to gain a steep scoop. Climb the scoop, exit left, then climb steep ground directly to finish by an easier gully.

The Frivolous Pinnacle (Difficult) is the obvious pinnacle mentioned above on the right of Upper Buttress. It can be reached from the foot of the gully by ledges and a short chimney. In winter a Grade III climb goes from the back of the pinnacle straight up the buttress.

MAOL CHEAN-DEARG
933m (Map Ref 924 498)

Maol Chean-dearg and An Ruadh-stac can be approached on excellent paths either from Coulags, about 7km south-west of Achnashellach, or from Annat at the head of Loch Torridon. There is a line of quartz crags on the east side of the south-east ridge of Maol Chean-dearg leading to Meall nan Ceapairean. The two biggest buttresses are easily picked out from the east. The left-hand buttress gives a pleasant climb, **Ketchil Buttress**, (120m, Difficult). The right-hand buttress has also been climbed.

There is also some climbing on the steep north face of Maol Chean-dearg, overlooking Loch an Eoin. **Hidden Gully** (300m, II) lies at the left-hand side of the face, running from low down right up to the summit. Two climbs lie on a conspicuous light-coloured quartzite cliff about 150m above the loch, below a darker band of crags (Map Ref 923 505). The cliff has a horizontal ledge at one-third height and two big left-slanting ramps near the top. **No Birds** (100m, Very Difficult) starts below the right-hand ramp, just under some very light-coloured rock. It climbs up to the ramp in two pitches and follows it to the top. **But Midges** (110m, Severe) starts below the left-hand ramp. It reaches the horizontal ledge via a steep groove and then climbs right to a short vertical step, left into a steep recess and right to reach the ramp.

AN RUADH-STAC
890m (Map Ref 922 481)

The north face of this peak has two tiers of blocky quartzite giving climbs of up to 180m. Many variations are possible.

North Face   180m   Very Difficult   (1960)
Climb a prominent slabby rib just left of an obvious white scar on the lower tier. Above is a curving damp chimney. Go 30m left and climb diagonally left for 45m to a big recess. Continue directly to the top.

Foxtrot   180m   Mild Severe   (1967)
This route lies well to the right of North Face. There is a large black cave on the bottom terrace with an ill-defined buttress of ribs and grooves on its left. Climb the buttress up to a large amphitheatre on the right of the upper tier.

Applecross

BEINN BHAN
896m   (Map Ref 804 451)

This superb mountain offers some of the finest winter climbing in the Northern Highlands. There are five corries lining its north-east face, all easily approached from the road bridge at the head of Loch Kishorn, where a good track leads off. The first corrie, Coir' Each is somewhat open and less impressive than its neighbours. The second and third corries, Coire na Feola and Coire na Poite, each rise from an outer corrie to a high inner corrie with a magnificent back wall. Coire na Poite is enclosed by two narrow ridges with precipitous sides whose outer ends form the great castellated buttresses of A'Chioch on the left and A'Phoit on the right. Beyond A'Phoit the fourth corrie, Coire nan Fhamhair, contains on its south side one of the steepest cliffs on the Scottish mainland. There is a fifth coire, Coire Toll a'Bhein, which is unnamed on the OS map.

A straightforward descent to the road at Tornapress may be made by following the summit ridge and the south-east flank of the mountain. Descents into Coire nan Fhamhair and Coire Toll a'Bhein are also possible.

While there are a number of excellent gully climbs, the climbs on the buttresses tend to be open to traversing variations owing to the horizontal bedding of the sandstone. But this in no way lessens their appeal, for many of the climbs are almost alpine in length and exposure. Some summer climbs have been recorded but few are of great merit as the loose rock, vegetation and horizontal breaks are not generally attractive. But the routes still have length and character and pleasant shorter climbs may be found.

Contrary to opinion expressed in earlier guides, the mountain is quite often in good winter condition. Sometimes it may be worth visiting when inland mountains are swamped with unconsolidated snow. On the other hand, being low and near the sea, there are inevitably times when the climbs have little snow and ice while the higher inland mountains are in good condition. Altogether, summer or winter, the magnificent mountain scenery of these corries, with their open views east to the Coulin Forest, make them well worth a visit.

COIR' EACH

1 Deep Gully 200m IV   (1978)
The deep snow gully in the centre of the corrie. There is a large ice pitch at two-thirds height, which may bank out after heavy snow fall.

2 Skidmark Buttress 180m III   (1980)
This takes the buttress left of Deep Gully. Start at the foot of a wide groove. Follow corners and ledges for two pitches to reach the top of a right-trending ramp. Climb the steep, exposed groove above (crux) to gain a wide ledge. Traverse left for 5m and continue up grooves and corners to the top. Good protection throughout.

3 Donkey's Doobrie 160m IV   (1980)
This takes the line of an obvious narrow gully in the centre of the main face (right of Deep Gully).
1. 45m Climb the initial icefall direct for 20m, then avoid a 5m bulging section by a short corner on the left. Regain the gully and follow it to a belay.
2. 30m Continue to the base of an ice-choked chimney.
3. 40m Make a short traverse right followed by a short chimney and groove for 40m to regain the main gully just above the ice-choked chimney and a prominent chockstone.
4. 45m Climb easily to the top.

4 Hors d'Oeuvres 150m III   (1980)
This takes the rightmost gully on the main face using a direct start. An easier start is possible further right.
1. 40m Climb the obvious icefall to belay under rocks on the right.
2. 45m Follow the icefall on the left through short ice bulges and grooves to a snowfield with a spike belay on the back wall.
3. 65m The main gully is now gained which leads to easy ground.

COIRE NA FEOLA

There are some interesting features on the walls of the enclosing arms of this corrie, but the best routes are probably on or near the back wall. This curves round to the left into the prominent Easy Gully, which is split into parallel runnels by a narrow ridge with an apparent tower, and may be used as a descent route. To the left of this is Suspense

Buttress, which has the summer climb Rory-Pory in its lower part. The first two routes lie on the left, just at the entrance to the corrie, to the left of a large, black cave-like recess.

5 Couldoran Gully 170m II/III   (1986)
Start 45 metres left of the recess at the foot of an obvious Y-shaped gully. On the first ascent a 10m ice pitch was climbed at the start, and another small pitch at 45m. Above follow the right branch to the top.

6 Grey Hair Gully 170m III   (1986)
Start 10 metres left of the black cave-like recess at a steep ice-filled chimney. Climb this with a hard move right at the top (15m). Follow the gully above to the top of the buttress.

7 Rory-Pory 75m VS   (1981)
The big steep lower rock band of the triangular buttress left of Easy Gully is sub-divided into three subsidiary buttresses by two steep, wet recesses. This route takes the left rib of the left-hand buttress, just right of a grassy chimney and minor broken rib. Start at the toe of the rib and go up to climb an obvious crack-line up slabs. Surmount the bulge at the top direct (just right of a grassy recess) and gain a terrace and belay. Climb up the left side of the rib and move right into a groove system. Climb grooves to finish up the furthest left groove.

8 The Acid Queen 150m IV/V   (1984)
The slender icefall which often forms in the left recess of Suspense Buttress. It is usually accompanied by an icicle mass hanging up on the left and a twin strip of thinner ice running up just to the right. Climb the icefall in two pitches, starting up a short chimney and snow funnel. The ice at the top may be thin and this will normally be the crux. A right traverse then easier grooves lead to the top in 90m.

9 Suspense Buttress 150m II/III
The big lower wall was avoided by traversing in above it from Easy Gully. Thereafter the buttress consists of short walls broken by terraces.

10 Easy Gully 150m I
A straightforward snow climb between Suspense Buttress and the main back wall.

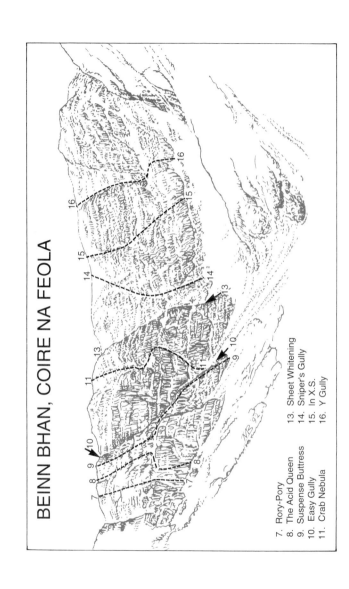

BEINN BHAN, COIRE NA FEOLA

7. Rory-Pory
8. The Acid Queen
9. Suspense Buttress
10. Easy Gully
11. Crab Nebula

13. Sheet Whitening
14. Sniper's Gully
15. In X.S.
16. Y Gully

11 Crab Nebula 275m IV **   (1980)
This takes the line of the hanging snowfield at about half-height in the
huge buttress right of Easy Gully. The two lower tiers are avoided on
the right. Start by traversing right on a snow terrace from the base of
the gully. Climb diagonally right up ramps and grooves for two pitches
then break left up a short wall to gain the snowfield. At the top of the
snowfield climb a short ice pitch to reach a higher snow patch. On the
first ascent a traverse was made from here to gain a bulging icicle
formation, and two rock pegs were then used for aid to reach easier
ground. Finish up steep snow slopes.

12 Flesheater 220m IV   (1989)
Takes a prominent diagonal fault-line in the steep cliff to the right of
Easy Gully. The line slants steeply leftwards between Sheet Whitening
and the hanging snowfields of Crab Nebula. Start at the foot of the
fault.
1. 20m Climb easy snow to steeper grooves, belay on the left.
2. 50m Go right into the grooves with a hard start. Follow the grooves,
trending slightly right then back left to a good belay at a cracked wall.
3. 40m Climb a short chimney, then continue to a deeper chimney
which is quit to a belay on the right.
4. 40m Follow grooves above directly to an entertaining exit onto a
good terrace.
5. 45m Go up a shallow chimney behind the belay, then follow the
rocky buttress crest in a fine position to easy ground.
6. 25m An easy arete leads to the top.

13 Sheet Whitening 245m IV/V   (1981)
This is the leftmost of the obvious runnels on the back wall of the corrie.
The crux is a hard ice pitch up a steep barrier rock band at 90m. The
rest of the climb is straightforward.

14 Sniper's Gully 280m IV   (1986)
The shallow gully just right of Sheet Whitening. Follow a series of icy
grooves to an easy ramp leading out right to snow slopes.

15 In X.S. 250m V *   (1986)
This route follows a continuous ice smear starting in a small basin
about 45 metres left of Y-Gully and not visible until under that route.
On the first ascent the climb gave four excellent long pitches on good
quality thin ice, with a big ice-filled corner as the highlight.

16   Y Gully   300m   IV/V *
At the right side of the back wall is a very prominent Y-shaped feature. The lowest band may be climbed slightly right of the steepest ice. After crossing some easier ground climb a long steep ice pitch in the 'stem' of the Y. Higher up either the left or the right branches of the Y may be taken, both giving pleasant climbing to the top.

COIRE NA POITE

Surely one of the most dramatic of Highland corries.

17   North Buttress of A'Chioch   150m   Severe   (1950)
This is the large, stepped buttress south-west of Lochan Coire na Poite. Start near the foot of the prominent chockstone gully bounding the buttress on the left. Trend right over walls and terraces to the top of A'Chioch.

18   North Gully of A'Chioch   120m   II   (1969)
This is the prominent chockstone gully bounding North Buttress on the left. It finishes half way up the A'Chioch spur. The climb has an easy initial cave pitch and an awkward chockstone in the upper part which is turned on the left. Finish on the left by a steep chimney. The gully has also been ascended in summer.

19   Upper Connecting Ridge of A'Chioch   150m   II   (1968)
This is the ridge from the col beyond A'Chioch to the summit plateau.

20   Dormouse Chimney   100m   IV *   (1980)
High in the centre of the north face of A'Chioch is a prominent ice-filled chimney which is often in condition. It provides two full pitches with steep and varied climbing on continuous ice. The lower section leading to the chimney may be avoided by traversing in from the right along a good ledge from the upper corrie. Above the chimney an escape right can be made on easy snow slopes.

21   Alice's Buttress   320m   III/IV   (1978)
At the left side of the upper corrie are two very fine gullies. This climb takes the buttress left of the left-hand of the two gullies (March Hare's Gully). Start to the left of the toe of the buttress. Climb diagonally right up a snow ramp to a point overlooking the gully (35m). Trend diagon-

ally left then climb more or less directly to beneath a rock band at about 225m. Traverse left around a nose then go up steeply to gain the crest on the right. Follow the crest to meet the upper connecting ridge of A'Chioch some 45m short of the plateau.

22 March Hare's Gully 300m IV *   (1969)
The first of the major winter climbs to be done on Beinn Bhan and a splendid route. It takes the obvious line on the left side of the upper corrie finishing at the point where the upper connecting ridge of A'Chioch meets the summit plateau. There are a large number of ice pitches of which the first may be the hardest; sometimes it can be avoided on the left. About 30m from the top an easier finish may be taken along a shelf to the right leading into a right fork of the gully; alternatively, finish direct. In heavy snow conditions much of this climb may bank out.

23 The Adventures of Toad 400m III *   (1983)
This takes the big buttress between March Hare's Gully and Mad Hatter's Gully and provides interesting route-finding with a 'big route' feeling. Start on the left at the foot of March Hare's Gully. Climb a steep little ice pitch, then take a zigzag line first away right then back left and up to a terrace below a formidable rock band. A traverse right along the terrace for a full pitch leads to a more broken area in the band where the terrace rises up. Above this climb direct to the easier crest of the buttress.

24 Harlequin Rib 265m IV   (1986)
This takes the right edge of the buttress between March Hare's Gully and Mad Hatter's Gully. From the start of Mad Hatter's Gully go diagonally left up a huge snow-covered slab until below the obvious steep wall. Turn this by a groove round the left edge, then continue up to a steep band which girdles the buttress at about mid-height. Gain a groove either directly or by a traverse from the left, then continue up until able to move right to easier ground. Several easier pitches lead to the top.

25 Mad Hatter's Gully 300m IV/V *   (1976)
This is the large gully in the back left corner of the corrie. The first 150m is an easy, wide snow channel. Climb the main ice pitch direct (very steep) or by left-hand variations. A belay can sometimes be taken at a rock nose halfway up.

BEINN BHAN, COIRE NA POITE

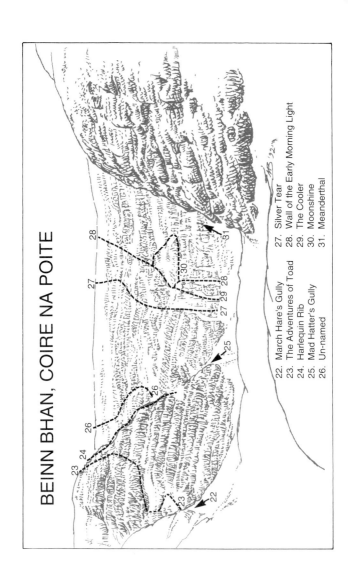

22. March Hare's Gully
23. The Adventures of Toad
24. Harlequin Rib
25. Mad Hatter's Gully
26. Un-named
27. Silver Tear
28. Wall of the Early Morning Light
29. The Cooler
30. Moonshine
31. Meanderthal

To the right of Mad Hatter's Gully is the huge back wall of Coire na Poite. The climbs here are long and impressive. In the upper part of the face traverses along the obvious snow terraces allow numerous variations, though the routes will always be serious. Several routes have been recorded but it is not possible to be sure how much they have in common. The descriptions below indicate some of the main features.

26 Unnamed 320m V   (1986)
Climb easily up Mad Hatter's Gully for 80m to the base of an icefall beside a right-facing corner on the right wall. Climb the icefall for 45m. Step out right for 5m then go up a snowfield to belay below a prominent icefall (45m). Climb the icefall (45m). Continue up a snowfield to belay below the last rock band (45m). Traverse left to find the easiest corner through the rock band (45m). Two long pitches of mixed climbing lead to the top.

27 Silver Tear 350m V ***   (1977)
In good conditions this gives a superb ice climb. The great icefall somewhat left of the centre of the wall is climbed directly for 120m to a terrace. Above this the icefall may continue, or, more likely, it may be necessary to take a more circuitous line up the bands of the upper half of the face. The easiest finish is up a right-slanting natural fault line.

28 Wall of the Early Morning Light 370m IV/V **   (1971)
Somewhat less continuous icefalls usually form in the centre of the back wall, to the right of Silver Tear and starting slightly lower. Climb these by snow and ice steps till below a steep rock band. Traverse left into an icy runnel slanting slightly right. Follow this to break through the rock band via a chimney. A natural fault line of chimneys and grooves leads up slightly right through the upper bands of the face.

29 The Cooler 350m V   (1983)
This is a direct start to Wall of the Early Morning Light. Start at the right side of the Silver Tear icefall (well left of Wall of the Early Morning Light). Climb steep ice, then a snow pitch and more ice to reach the right slanting runnel taken by Wall of the Early Morning Light. Follow this route to the top.

30 Moonshine 370m V †   (1978)
This is another variation on Wall of the Early Morning Light. Climb the
central icefalls as for that route, but where it traverses left move right
to bypass the big rock band. This leads to the left end of a large
snowfield. The steep rock barrier above may have enough ice to be
climbed further right, but on the original ascent a traverse left was
made to gain the natural fault line taken by Wall of the Early Morning
Light. This leads up rightwards by chimneys and grooves to the top.

31 Meanderthal 400m IV/V
Start up the icefall well right of the centre of the back wall. Climb the
icefall to a large snowfield at about 60m. Go up to the top of the
snowfield and climb steep ice up the next band to snow terraces about
halfway up the wall. From here the original route followed a line of
snow terraces diagonally right to finish near the top of the Upper
Connecting Ridge of A'Phoit. In good conditions a more direct finish
should be feasible.

32 Upper Connecting Ridge of A'Phoit 180m Severe (1961)
This is the ridge from the col beyond A'Phoit to the plateau. There are
three tiers of sandstone leading to a more broken upper ridge. Climb
the first tier centrally for 10m, then climb shattered blocks on the left
to a wide ledge below the third tier. From 10m left of the true nose
climb a clean crack to an overhang and step right across a loose flake
to reach the top of the tier quite suddenly.
Winter: IV *   (1971)
No details of the first winter ascent are available. On a subsequent
winter ascent the lower tiers were bare and were avoided by a long
detour to the left, giving a very fine climb at grade III.

33 Gingerbread 200m VS   (1974)
Looking towards A'Phoit from Lochan Coire na Poite one can see a
line of corners starting half way up the cleanest part of the crag. The
route gains this system of corners and follows it approximately.

COIRE NAN FHAMHAIR

Unfortunately the huge face on the left of this corrie is not often in good
winter condition. When it is, it provides some of the best routes in the
area.

34   Die Riesenwand   400m   V ***   (1980)
This outstanding and exciting route takes the line of least resistance
up the large face left of Gully of the Gods. A prominent zigzag of snow
ledges marks the line in the upper part. Good conditions are advisable
as a retreat from high up would be difficult. Start towards the left of the
face below a secondary corner. Climb steep ice for three pitches to a
niche below a huge roof, 80m. (The second pitch climbs a short barrier
wall which may be passed on the left if there is insufficient ice.)
Traverse right from the niche across steep rocky ground to gain a large
snow ledge, 30m. Continue traversing right for about 80m until another
ledge leads back up left across the wall. Follow this for 60m passing
some narrow sections and finishing with a memorable swing round a
bulge in a very exposed position. The ground is now easier and a short
traverse left leads to a shallow gully which gives a pleasant route to
the plateau, 150m.

35   Gully of the Gods   180m   V ***   (1983)
The uniquely overhanging central gully splitting the cliff gives a tremendous climb.
1. 25m A combination of back and foot with bridging on ice leads to
an excellent ledge on the right.
2. 40m Climb the back of the gully for 5m, then back and foot out to
the main ice streak and follow this into a very steep and difficult icy
groove above the main overhangs. Pass the final capstone on the
right.
3. 115m Climb easily to the top.

36   Great Overhanging Gully   180m   V/VI ***   (1984)
This is the very steep line about 45 metres right of Gully of the Gods.
1. 20m Climb tufty ground to below the overhangs.
2. 35m Climb the chimney to the overhangs; surmount these free on
ice, and continue over an awkward ice bulge to a cave stance.
3. 35m Climb to beneath the chockstone and use a threaded sling to
gain a traverse line. Continue up left to belay 5m left of the foot of a
dry overhanging pitch.
4. 12m Move left and ascend to another ledge.
5. 12m Use two pegs to reach deceptively hard turf climbing which
leads back right to the gully bed.
6. 12m Surmount the overhang to belay below the final chimneys.
7. 50m Climb grooves and chimneys to the cornice finish.

37   The Chimney 270m   III *   (1979)
The original winter line on this face takes a traverse along the sensational snow ledges on the right of the cliff for 180m to gain the upper part of Gully of the Gods.

38   Der Rise and Shine 120m   IV   (1983)
This climbs the narrow gully splitting the largest buttress on the opposite side of the corrie from the main cliff. Start left of the foot of the buttress.
1. 45m   Climb a 25m icefall at the foot of the gully. Climb small ice bulges to a belay.
2. 45m   Climb a short easy chimney, then another ice pitch.
3. 30m   Follow the gully to the top.

COIRE TOLL A'BHEIN

This is the fifth and most northerly of the Beinn Bhan corries.

39   Breach of the Peace 220m   II/III   (1984)
To the left of the main buttress is a broad easy gully (useful for descent). To its left is another buttress, split on its left side by an obvious straight narrow corridor of snow, well-defined by rock walls on either side. On the first ascent it provided some tricky steps but it could possibly bank out to Grade I.

40   Threatening Behaviour 260m   V   (1984)
The largest buttress in the corrie, on the left at the back, has an obvious pinnacle at its centre. Some way to its left there is a streak of snow and ice which trends in the upper part into a well-defined gully. Climb icy slabs for 45m, then easier ground to a steep ice pitch which provides a way up a steep rock band. Above this, steep ice for 15m leads into the upper gully. Follow this over short ice steps to the top.

41   Indecent Exposure 290m   IV   (1984)
Climb the central buttress direct heading for an obvious gully which leads to a pinnacle high on the ridge. At the top of a steep chimney traverse right across a wall to enter the upper section of the right-hand gully. Follow this to the top.

42 Das Rheingold 2800m IV ***   (1989)

A continuous girdle of the central triad of corries - Feola, Poite, and Fhamhair - using natural ledge and terrace lines. A magnificent expedition. Careful assessment of snow conditions is required as the steep ramps are prime accumulation sites for windslab and are threatened by cornices throughout. Many crucial moves depend on turf. Start at the top of Easy Gully above Coire na Feola where a horizontal terrace takes off across the corrie headwall.

Follow the ledge (generally easy apart from a few narrowings) as far as Y Gully. Climb the left branch of this for 30m, then transfer into the right branch which is followed for a further 50m until easy ground leads right onto the final crest of the Upper Ridge of A'Chioch. Continue round across the exit bay of March Hare's Gully then lose height gradually until the crest of the bounding buttress is reached. A steep rock band required a short abseil onto a broad terrace spanning the crest. Go down to the right end of the terrace, overlooking Mad Hatter's Gully. A 15m abseil and a short traverse gain the gully just below its big ice pitch. Descend a short ice groove, then down easy snow for 80m to a diagonal ramp line on the right wall. Climb this to its top, descend the far side for 10m, then go out right to gain a large snowfield where the traverse of the Coire na Poite headwall begins.

Go diagonally right across the snowfields until a snow/ice pitch gains a higher terrace. Traverse this for 300m, then follow its slightly descending continuation to gain the Upper Ridge of A'Phoit just above its steep steps. Traverse a further 100m then go up a 20m ice pitch to gain a higher ledge line. This leads out across some spectacular ground to the upper bay of the Gully of the Gods. The terrace continues beyond but diminishes to become a fault sandwiched between the overhanging cliffs of the final headwall. The fault descends slightly, crawling alternating with some moves round bulges, until the chasm of Great Overhanging Gully is reached. Descend this for 20m, then continue along steep ramps until the cliff finally runs out onto easy snow slopes 100m below the corrie rim. The final section from the Gully of the Gods reverses the line of The Chimney.

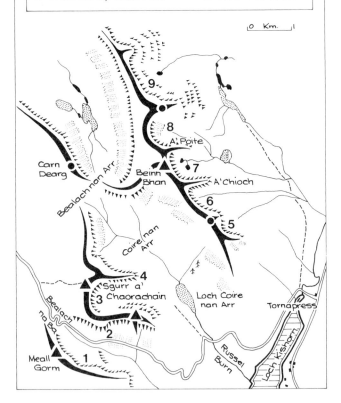

APPLECROSS HILLS

1 N Face of Meall Gorm
2 S Face of Sg. a'Chaorachain
3 Summit Buttress Sg. a'Chaorachain
4 A'Chioch, Sg. a'Chaorachain
5 Coire Each, Beinn Bhan

6 Coire na Feola
7 Coire na Poite
8 Coire nan Fhamhair
9 Coire Toll a' Bhein

N

0 Km. 1

9

8

A' Poite

7

Carn Dearg

Bealach nan Arr

Beinn Bhan

A'Chioch

6

5

Coire nan Arr

4

Sgurr a'
Chaorachain

3

2

Loch Coire
nan Arr

Tornapress

Bealach na Ba

Russel Burn

Loch Kishorn

Meall Gorm

1

SGURR A' CHAORACHAIN
792m   (Map Ref 797 417)

A'CHIOCH

This justly-famed sandstone bastion forms the end of the north-east ridge of Sgurr a'Chaorachain. It is composed in the main of excellent rough sandstone, beautifully clean on its upper frontal face, though more vegetated in the lower reaches and on the flanks. In addition to the classic Cioch Nose route, there are many good climbs in the Severe to HVS grades, while the north face provides some very worthwhile winter lines.

Access
From the bridge over the outlet of the River Kishorn follow the road to the Bealach na Ba for about two and a half kilometres to the bridge over the Russel Burn (Map Ref 814 413). The huge tower of A'Chioch is well seen from here. Walk past Loch Coire nan Arr, then slant up left towards South Gully, which flanks A'Chioch on the left. For climbs on the lower tier continue near the corrie floor.

An alternative is to start from the Bealach na Ba, climb to lower top (776m) of Sgurr a'Chaorachain (where there is a radio mast), and descend into the un-named corrie south of A'Chioch by a broad gully about 100 metres east of the mast. Coming down the corrie one passes under the steep but vegetated south flanks of the north-east ridge of the mountain until the foot of South Gully is reached.

Descent
The easiest descent from A'Chioch is via South Gully, but this requires care. The main advantage of the somewhat less pleasing alternative approach is for parties wishing to continue along the very fine east-north-east ridge of the mountain. The buttress above the flat top of A'Chioch can be climbed directly at about Severe, or more indirectly at about Difficult. From its top the ridge continues as a narrow crest with several rocky gaps, which may be quite awkward in winter, up to the 776m top, whence a short easy descent leads to the Bealach na Ba.

The buttress of A'Chioch is divided into two tiers by Middle Ledge - an obvious heathery terrace that runs right from the bottom of South Gully, gradually narrowing to a rocky ledge as it comes onto the front of the buttress. Most of the rock climbs are on the south-east and east faces of the upper tier although there are climbs on the vegetated lower tier which can be combined with those on the upper. In general the climbing is easier than it appears, with a generous supply of holds, and escape is frequently possible. The excellent quality of the climbing and the superb views make this a most attractive crag.

1 Anonymous Gully 230m III   (1980)
From the bottom of South Gully this rises directly to the end of the east-north-east ridge, some 100m above A'Cioch. On the first ascent there was an initial ice pitch, followed by a long easy section ending in a rock *cul-de-sac*. Owing to the paucity of ice, recourse was made to the rocks of the ridge on the right.

THE UPPER TIER OF A'CHIOCH
Following Middle Ledge along from South Gully, one passes success-ively two grassy bays. Then the ledge becomes narrower and there is a conspicuous long low roof only about 3m above it. Beyond this the ledge continues with rather more broken ground above until the steep clean rocks of the 'Nose' are reached. Here the ledge becomes very narrow and rocky but continues right round the front of the buttress. Climbs in the area just right of South Gully were made in the early days of the SMC by Collie, Ling, Glover and others. In particular, **Glover's Route** (Very Difficult; grade III in winter) climbs a series of chimneys starting from the first grassy bay right of South Gully.

2 Sideburn 80m Severe   (1968)
Start from the second grassy bay up the buttress on the right.
1. 35m Climb the rather ill-defined buttress, to the right of a corner, to reach a grassy ledge from which the corner can be reached without difficulty.
2. 45m Climb the corner. Exit left to easy ground.

3 Parting 95m Severe   (1970)
Start 5m left of the left end of the low roof overhanging Middle Ledge.
1. 35m Climb an obvious steep right-angled corner for 30m, then traverse up and right for 5m across a grass ledge to gain the bottom of the diedre proper.
2. 25m Climb the left wall of the diedre. Belay beneath overhangs.
3. 35m Avoid the overhangs on the left via a steep wall, after which the angle relents and easy scrambling leads to the top.

SGURR A'CHAORACHAIN   SOUTH-EAST FACE OF A'CHIOCH

SG South Gully
UL Upper Ledge
ML Middle Ledge

3. Parting
4. Gritstone Grooves
5. African Waltz

6. Forgotten Corner
7. Snothard
8   Cioch Nose

4   Gritstone Grooves   110m   VS   (1969)
Start at a clean corner just left of the low roof overhanging Middle Ledge.
1. 25m 4c Climb the corner and groove above to a grass ledge.
2. 20m 4c Continue up and climb a steep corner crack with a slab on the left.
3. 20m 4b Go up the steep corner above.
4. 45m More easily to the top.

The next three climbs start from Upper Ledge, a grass ledge about 25m above Middle Ledge, which runs across from the top of the first pitches of the last two routes to the top of the first pitch of Cioch Nose. It may be reached by scrambling up vegetated ground or by climbing the first pitch of Cioch Nose, which runs up the steep and cleaner rock about 20 metres right of the low roof. Cioch Nose then continues from Upper Ledge by a conspicuous V-chimney, which provides a useful marker.

5   African Waltz   90m   VS   (1969)
Start from Upper Ledge 35 metres left of the chimney of Cioch Nose and 10 metres right of where Gritstone Grooves crosses the ledge.
1. 20m 4b From a small niche climb up for 15m and traverse right to a grass ledge on the left of an obvious corner.
2. 15m 4b Follow a left-trending crack through a niche to a ledge.
3. 15m 4c Go right and up the wall to another niche left of the main corner, which is climbed with difficulty.
4. 40m Continue more easily in the same line to the top.

6   Forgotten Corner   90m   VS *   (1975)
Start from Upper Ledge about 10 metres left of the chimney of Cioch Nose, below an obvious corner. Climb up into the corner line, which is followed in three pitches to the top.

7   Snothard   90m   Hard Severe *   (1969)
Start at the foot of a groove 5 metres left of the chimney of Cioch Nose.
1. 35m 4b Climb the groove until it is possible to move left onto a slab on the lip of a conspicuous overhang. Climb the slab to a ledge and continue up a steep corner to belay.
2. 25m 4b Move left and climb a crack past three overhangs. Easier climbing to the top.

8 Cioch Nose 135m Very Difficult *** (1960)
This is the classic of the area, a most enjoyable climb. Start from Middle Ledge about 20m right of the low roof where the rocks become cleaner.
1. 25m The first pitch to Upper Ledge is harder than it looks and allows several variations, generally easier to the left.
2. 20m Go right to the foot of a short deep V-chimney. Climb the chimney and exit on the right, continuing up right over clean easy rock to a splendid ledge and belay.
3. 20m Go right for a few metres then up on excellent holds bearing left to a stance directly above the previous one.
4. 25m Continue up, going left of an overhang and then back right above it, finishing straight up to a grass ledge.
5. 45m Climb more easily to the top of A'Chioch.
Winter: IV
Though rarely in winter condition, Cioch Nose gives a good climb, with the third pitch the crux, as in summer.

Many will wish to continue to the top of the mountain instead of descending South Gully. If so, cross the neck connecting A'Chioch to the ridge behind and scramble up vegetation and short rock steps to reach a steep wall girdling the nose of the ridge. Climb this in the centre (Mild Severe) or, more easily, up a groove at the extreme left-hand side, followed by a traverse back right.

The ridge soon levels out and continues over several rocky tops, (which form the summits of the north buttresses), and across quite steep gaps between them, to eventually reach the lower 776m top of Sgurr a'Chaorachain.

9 Cioch Nose, Direct Start 50m Severe ** (1968)
From the ordinary start continue walking along Middle Ledge, where it becomes narrower, underneath steep rock with overhangs, until a large dark diedre is reached.
1. 40m Climb up 5m then traverse left on steep rock to gain a short vertical crack. Climb this to reach the rib on the left edge of the diedre. Follow the rib and wall above on good holds to a ledge and belay.
2. 10m Go left and up to the second stance of the normal route.

Other harder variations have been made between the ordinary and direct starts to Cioch Nose. However the rock is somewhat loose.

10   Cioch Corner   125m   VS **   (1969)
This climb is perhaps best combined with Cioch Corner Superdirect, on the lower tier (described below). Start at the large dark diedre as for Cioch Nose Direct.
1. 35m 5a Climb directly up the diedre to the roof, step right to a ledge and go straight up to a grassy recess.
2. 40m 4c Follow the line of grooves over a bulge. Climb a pleasant slab on the right of the corner, then return to the corner line. Climb a chimney-groove to a grassy bay.
3. 40m 4a Climb more easily, with a final steep corner.
4. 10m Scramble to the top.

The next three climbs lie on the steep area of rock between Cioch Corner and North Wall which lies about 40 metres further right. Numerous variations are possible as the rock is climbable almost anywhere at a sufficiently high standard. This is true also for the routes already described. It must be admitted that some of the features mentioned in the descriptions may be hard to identify; however the rock is generally so good that any route here will be found rewarding.

11   The Maxilla   130m   VS   (1968)
Start at the first break right of Cioch Corner.
1. 20m Climb the break through the overhangs, passing a small tree, to a triangular ledge below a corner capped by a large overhang.
2. 20m Traverse 5m left and climb the left edge of the corner.
3. 25m Above are four parallel grooves. Climb over a small roof into the leftmost groove and follow it and the exposed slab above to belay below a large corner.
4. 20m Climb the corner.
5. 50m Easier rocks lead to the top.

12   Mantissa   130m   VS   (1975)
Start as for The Maxilla.
1. 20m The Maxilla, pitch 1.
2. 10m Climb the crack just right of the stance and cross the rib rightwards into a large recess.
3. 35m Leave on the right and traverse right about 12m below a steep concave wall. Start up a faint rib with cracks and continue, making a move right near the top of the wall. Move left to belay.
4. 25m Trend diagonally left through overlaps to the skyline.
5. 40m Climb easily to the top.

13 Lost Wall 130m HVS   (1984)
About 30 metres right of The Maxilla a narrow slab slanting up right
can be seen, the start of North Wall. Another groove breaking through
the overhangs starts just to the left.
1. 30m Climb the groove and the wall above to a small stance below
a corner capped by an overhang.
2. 30m 5a Climb the corner passing the overhang on the left. Or, if
wet, traverse left 8m at the level of the stance and climb easier rock
up and back right to above the overhang. Now climb the steep wall
slightly left to a break.
3. and 4. 70m Continue straight to the top.

14 North Wall 140m Severe   (1952)
Start about 30 metres right of The Maxilla where a narrow slab,
undercut at its base, slants up to the right.
1. 15m Gain the slab and climb to a ledge at its top.
2. 15m Climb up and right to a terrace.
3. 40m Move right past the foot of a deep-cut rock funnel crowned by
overhangs until below a prominent layback crack. Climb the crack,
then the groove on its left to a ledge. Continue up the groove, or the
rib on its left, to large terraces.
4. 30m The ground is more broken above. The left skyline forms a
tower. Move left from the belay, start up a chimney on the right of the
tower then traverse left onto its front and climb up, with a delightful
airy move.
5. 40m Continue easily to the top of A'Chioch.

15 Lap of the Gods 150m VS   (1969)
Well right of North Wall this route finds a way up the steep overlapping
slabs on the left of the North Gully of A'Chioch. The start is best
reached by scrambling in an exposed position along the continuation
of Middle Ledge, then climbing up the gully to the point where it
becomes a steep, open chimney. Alternatively, go right round the lower
tier and scramble up 170m of vegetated ground and broken rocks left
of the lower reaches of North Gully.
1. 10m Climb a steep grey rib just right of the chimney.
2. 20m Traverse left across the slab to a fine airy stance on the far
lip.

3. 15m Go straight up the 5m wall above to a good ledge. A steep groove above is barred by overhangs, so traverse left to flakes below an overhanging nose.

4. 15m Pass just left of the nose to a shallow corner which leads to easier ground. (It is now possible to traverse left onto North Wall, or right into the upper part of North Gully.)

5. 45m Scramble up 20m to the prominent rib above. Climb it to the base of the steep final wall.

6. 10m Go slightly right up a black slabby wall to a ledge.

7. 35m Continue steeply leftwards past a poised pinnacle into a groove leading strenuously through a break left of the overhangs. Step back right and climb straight up to the top of A'Chioch.

THE LOWER TIER OF A'CHIOCH

16 Cioch Corner Superdirect 160m HVS *   (1970)
The climb takes the obvious line of grooves which runs the full length of the lower tier below Cioch Corner. It is best combined with the latter to give an excellent, sustained climb of seven long pitches. Although there is some vegetation and loose rock on the lower tier, the climb has a lot of interest and can be recommended in dry conditions. Start at the foot of the grooves by a huge pinnacle. Climb directly up the groove line all the way in 4 pitches (5a, 5a, 4c, 4b) to reach Middle Ledge.

17 Cleavage 160m VS   (1968)
This route climbs the next corner right of the Superdirect. The corner starts about 30m above a slabby spur at the foot of the face, and has a prominent overhanging beak on its left.

1. 30m Climb a right-slanting slab and heather to a ledge at the foot of the corner.

2. 12m Climb the corner to a small stance below a slight overhang, between the offset continuation of the corner on the right and a steep layback crack on the left.

3. 25m Climb the layback crack for 3m, pull across the left wall onto a small ledge, and climb up and right to a ledge and belay above the corner.

4, 5. and 6. 90m Trend right to a rib and climb directly up to Middle Ledge, reaching it below the start of The Maxilla.

THE NORTH BUTTRESSES

Beyond North Gully there is a row of five buttresses supporting the north side of the long east-north-east ridge of Sgurr a' Chaorachain. They have been called the north-west buttresses although they appear to face more or less due north. They are numbered 1 to 5 from left to right, numbers 1 and 2 being the largest. In summer they offer somewhat grassy routes, but both buttresses and gullies give good climbs in winter. In winter the best way off the top will often be to continue along the east-north-east ridge to the 776m top of Sgurr a'Chaorachain. From the top it is a long walk back down via Bealach na Ba if the cars have been left at Russel Bridge.

18 Voyager 350m IV/V **   (1986)
A fine corner line on the left of No.1 Buttress. Gain the base of the corner by climbing up and left for two pitches towards North Gully and then traversing easily right. First ascent details were as follows. After a start up the corner, a deviation left and back right led to the base of an icefall. The ice was thin and the steepest section was avoided by a difficult bulge in the corner on the right. The ice led to a roof in the corner, split by a very co-operative chimney. Two pitches in the same line, the second a deceptively awkward chimney, led to the top of the buttress.

19 Jupiter 300m Mild Severe   (1952)
This is a good summer climb up the centre of No.1 Buttress. From the lowest rocks climb indeterminate ground to the base of the first big tier (60m). Start to the right of a recessed chimney which is right of some mossy overhangs. Diverging from the chimney, go up 20m to a platform. Here a thin ledge under an overhang leads back left above the top of the main chimney. At its end a 3m chimney leads to easier ground. The middle tier of the buttress rises in front. Climb a deep 5m chimney, a 5m flake crack and an 8m groove on the left. From here a perched spillikin can be seen on the right in an exposed situation. Balance round this then go straight up to a terrace (25m). Go a few metres right then climb another 20m with one awkward move. The buttress now falls back somewhat, but a steep 20m band circles it, barring the way. Follow a thin crack; at 3m there are some awkward jammed blocks and the crack remains hard for 6m above. After another 15m serious difficulty ends. Climb easy rock for 60m, then a narrow arete sweeping up for 60m gives a good finish.

Winter: IV/V   (1991)
Frozen turf is unusual but close to essential. Start from the toe of the buttress about 50 metres right of Voyager.

1. 40m Climb a turfy groove.
2. 40m Climb a steep chimney.
3. 50m Go up to the base of the largest tier.
4. 45m Take a heavily vegetated trough left of the crest.
5. 45m Go diagonally right passing a tree to a ledge. Climb a vertical wall with a good crack, passing a roof on its right.
6. 60m Go up to the next tier and a corner on the left.
7. 50m Climb the wall left of the corner on big flakes, then take a slabby wall on the right up to the next tier.
8. 50m Climb the central corner, then a right slanting line of flakes to easier ground.
9. 60m Blocky ground leads to the top of the buttress.

20   White Dwarf 300m III   (1984)
Towards the right side of No.1 Buttress is a narrow gully ending at a steep band of rock (not to be confused with a slabby corner further right, ending at the same height in a big overhang). Climb the gully with some deviations on the right, and when stopped by the steep band of rock crawl right along a ledge past a tree to a V-groove. Climb the groove until it is possible to step awkwardly onto some jammed blocks on the right wall. Trend slightly right for 70m until past the steep part of the buttress. Return easily left to the crest and follow it over short walls and blocks to the top.

21   No.1 Gully (Lang Tam's Gully) 150m III
The gully on the right of No.1 Buttress. Climb to an obvious cave, which is turned on the right by an icy curtain. Near the top take the right fork to gain the ridge.

22   Sinister 150m III   (1984)
Climb the left edge of No.2 Buttress to a small rock tower facing No.1 Buttress. Climb with difficulty for 10m above this, then continue more easily to the top. This route has been climbed in summer at Very Difficult, but is not recommended.

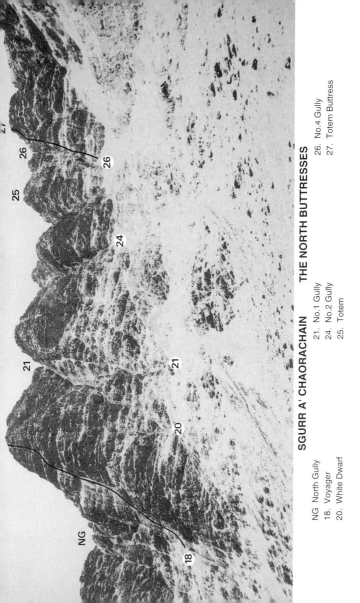

SGURR A' CHAORACHAIN   THE NORTH BUTTRESSES

NG North Gully
18. Voyager
20. White Dwarf

21. No.1 Gully
24. No.2 Gully
25. Totem

26. No.4 Gully
27. Totem Buttress

23 Dexter 150m Difficult   (1953)
Scramble up the right side of No.2 Buttress for 90m to a partly
detached tower. Pass the tower by a dark chimney on the right. Step
off a flake to a ledge and go round a corner to the right to a large
platform. Climb a slab with small holds (20m) and continue easily to
the top.
Winter: III/IV   (1991)
Follow the summer line, except avoid the dark chimney by the wall on
its right, which leads to a short icefall at the right side of the slab.

24 No.2 Gully (London Welsh Gully) 180m III
This is the gully between No.2 Buttress and No.3 Buttress. No details
are available.

   No.3 Buttress and Gully are shorter than the others and no climbs
have been recorded.

25 Totem 135m Difficult   (1953)
A curious rock pillar, seen on the skyline near the top of No.4 Buttress,
gives this climb its name. Start on the right flank of the buttress below
an obvious 5m chimney. Climb the chimney and make an awkward
exit to a grassy depression which leads to a terrace. Follow the terrace
to the left side of the buttress then return right as soon as possible to
the crest. Surmount a small rocky nose to reach a steep tower above.
On the left climb a deep chimney to ledges. Ascend a short pitch over
huge blocks to a ledge below the final rampart. Finish by a steep
chimney on the right.

26 No.4 Gully 150m IV   (1977)
Between No.4 and No.5 Buttresses is a narrow gully. After an initial
ice pitch a huge cave is reached at 60m. Climb the steep pillar on the
right to easy slopes. Continue to where the gully forks. Take the left
fork leading to two short awkward pitches and a final snow slope.

27 Turret Buttress 200m Severe   (1952)
This is No.5 Buttress, which is right at the back of the corrie, facing
Beinn Bhan. Seen from below it appears to culminate in a pinnacle
50m below the top, but this is just a promontory linked by a narrow
ridge to the upper cliff. Start on the left, at the foot of No 4 Gully. Climb
mixed rock and grass to the first tier (30m). Climb this about 8m from
the edge of the gully at a short steep corner. Follow easier rocks to

the second tier, which is climbed up the left edge by a short slab. The third and steepest tier is gained and the only line of weakness is in the centre. Surmount a steep, narrow slab by a layback crack on the right (10m). Another 60m of interesting climbing leads to the narrow arete behind the promontory. On the first ascent the final 45m of the upper cliff looked wet and unpleasant and was avoided by a gully on the left.
Winter: IV   (1986)
Follow the summer line approximately. On this ascent the first tier was the crux. The final cliff was avoided on the left, but not in the gully.

SUMMIT BUTTRESS

This is the large, usually wet buttress at the head of the corrie between the south-east and east-north-east spurs of the mountain. It is most easily reached by climbing from Bealach na Ba to the 776m top of Sgurr a'Chaorachain and descending the broad gully about 100m east of the radio mast, where the plateau takes an obvious sharp turn.

1 Big Daddy 120m HVS †   (1972)
At the left end of the cliff is a gully. Start 30 metres right of the gully, below an undercut groove. Climb through the bottom overhang to a shallow undercut corner. Climb the corner (1 peg for aid) to a small stance. Move hard right across an overhung slab to gain a ledge, then go diagonally right across the wall to a narrow corner. Go up this and finish up a wider corner.

In winter two prominent icefalls form on this cliff giving the following routes:

2 Excitable Boy 120m IV/V   (1986)
This is the left-hand icefall.
1. 30m From the terrace at the foot of the cliff climb steepening snow to a good block belay.
2. 45m Climb very steep ice to a small snow bay.
3. 45m Leave the bay by a short chimney on the left and trend right over short snow steps to the top.

3 Blade Runner 105m IV   (1986)
The right-hand icefall.
1. 30m Climb steep ice to belay below a chimney.
2. and 3. 75m Climb the right-slanting chimney to easier ground, which leads via one short step to the top.

4 Synergy 80m HVS   (1989)
The right side of the crag (right of Blade Runner) is a long steep wall.
Towards the left end of this wall is a big right-facing corner, initially very
vegetated, which leads up to the big terrace at two-thirds height.
1. 25m 4c Climb the vegetated corner using the right wall for entry
before a hollow flake gives access to a good belay ledge.
2. 25m 5a Follow the steep corner above to a bulge, which provides
the crux, then take an excursion to the right to a wide terrace.
3. 30m 5a On the left an obvious crackline leads to a final overhang
which is climbed on the right by exciting moves. Care is required with
the last few moves. Belay well back.

SOUTH FACE

This is the crag that rises steeply on the right of the road to Bealach
na Ba at a point opposite the waterfalls in the floor of the corrie (Map
Ref 790 412). It offers very pleasant, clean sandstone climbing, near
the road, and is often warm and dry.
   The crag consists of six buttresses numbered from left to right. No.1
is the best, having a broad 40m wall of excellent clean rock in its
middle section. No.2 is more broken and is separated from No.3 by a
square-cut, mossy gully. Nos.3 and 4 are narrow pillars separated by
a narrow gully with caves. No.5 is a much larger buttress coming down
almost to the road, while No.6 is the broken buttress beyond the broad
gully to the right of No.5.
   The lower section of No.1 Buttress gives delightful, easy climbing
up to a terrace at the base of the steep middle section which forms a
clean reddish wall. The first three climbs are described from there.

1 Ganglion 70m VS   (1971)
On the left of the wall is an obvious chimney leading to a large black
recess below an overhanging groove.
1. 20m Climb the crack to belay in the recess.
2. 25m 4c Climb the recess and the groove above onto the face on
the left and continue directly to a belay.
3. 25m Climb easily to the top.

SGURR A' CHAORACHAIN
SOUTH FACE

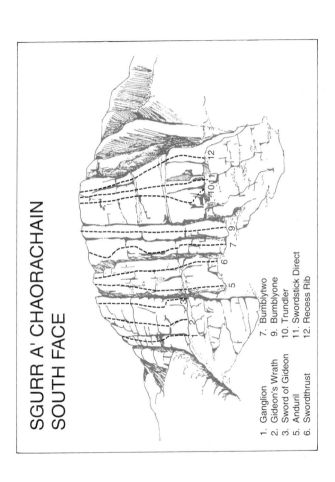

1. Ganglion
2. Gideon's Wrath
3. Sword of Gideon
5. Anduril
6. Swordthrust

7. Bumblytwo
9. Bumblyone
10. Trundler
11. Swordstick Direct
12. Recess Rib

2 Gideon's Wrath   70m   HVS **   (1971)
Start from the terrace below the reddish wall at a thin crack leading
to a triangular niche.
1. 15m 4c Climb the thin crack to the niche and traverse 3m left to
belay below an overhang.
2. 25m 5b Climb the overhang above and follow a line trending right
to reach a short wide crack. Continue up and right to finish just right
of the biggest bulge.
3. 30m Climb short walls and corners to the top.

3 Sword of Gideon   70m   VS **   (1961)
This is the original route of the crag, and very enjoyable.
1. 35m 4c Starting from the right end of the terrace, climb a groove
in the right edge of the buttress for 15m, then traverse left for 4m to
beneath the prominent crack in the right-hand part of the buttress.
Climb the crack, which eases after 5m, to a belay.
2. 35m Continue in the same line to the top.
Direct Start: 20m E1 **
Climb the thin groove directly to the prominent crack in the upper part
of Sword of Gideon.

4 North Circular   65m   HVS   (1973)
This is a girdle traverse of No.1 Buttress from left to right. A description
is given in SMCJ 1976.

5 Anduril   100m   VS *   (1970)
This route follows a line of cracks towards the left side of No.2 Buttress.
Start just right of the gully separating buttresses 1 and 2. The first three
short pitches are avoidable.
1. 15m 4a Climb the left edge of clean slabs to a grass ledge.
2. 20m 5a The wall on the right has a thin groove going slightly left.
Climb this awkwardly, then continue up a short rock step and grass to
the next clean wall.
3. 10m 4c Climb the left edge of the clean wall to a good hold and
continue easily to the Terrace.
4. 20m 4b Climb the crack in the wall above to a small terrace, then
continue to a larger terrace.
5. 35m 4b Move right to a bay below a clean overhanging crack in a
corner. Climb this direct, then continue up a conspicuous deep corner
to easier climbing and the top.

6 Swordthrust 100m VS   (1971)
This may have taken the same line as Anduril for the last two pitches, but the line shown here assumes that it takes the prominent straight grassy crackline directly above the square-cut corner. Start at a square-cut corner near the right edge of No.2 Buttress.
1. 30m Climb the corner and break out left onto the grass ledge crossing the buttress.
2. and 3. 70m Traverse left to a prominent crack splitting the middle of the buttress. Climb the crack to the top.

7 Bumblytwo 135m Severe   (1970)
Start at the foot of No.3 Buttress.
1. 45m The first pitch is climbed just right of centre.
2. 25m Continue straight up and avoid a steep wall by going left up a ramp to a ledge.
3. 25m Traverse right to a crack, climb this, then go back left to the centre of the face and up to a large block.
4. 40m Turn a wall above on the left and finish up a cracked slab, a groove and easier rocks to the top.

8 Bee Gully 120m IV   (1987)
The gully between Nos.3 and 4 Buttresses. The highlight is the last pitch, a fine narrow ice-smeared chimney.

9 Bumblyone 125m Severe   (1970)
Start at the foot of No.4 Buttress at an obvious crack. Go straight up in four pitches to the top.

10 Trundler 120m Hard Severe   (1970)
Scramble easily up to the left side of the steeper continuous part of No.5 buttress.
1. 45m The diedre on the left of the buttress above is protected by overhangs at its base. Climb up to the overhangs, turn them on the left by a delicate traverse, and climb the diedre to the next big ledge.
2. 30m Climb the wall and overhang on the right of the chimney ahead.
3. 45m Follow easier rock to the top.

11 Swordstick Direct 125m VS   (1968)
This takes a central line on No.5 Buttress, starting at a deep, and often black, groove on the left of a big overhanging prow in the steep section of the buttress (about 15 metres left of the recess of Recess Rib). The

original route (Hard Severe) trended left to easier ground from about halfway up the first pitch, and then climbed up to the terrace. The overhangs on pitch 2 were avoided by a chimney on the right. Start by scrambling easily to the base of the steep section.

1. 35m 4c Climb the right wall of the central groove for 6m to a ledge. Step left and climb the left wall, passing the overhang. Continue straight up the groove and surmount a small overhang to reach another ledge.

2. 30m 4c From the big terrace, climb directly through the overhangs above, moving slightly right at the top.

3. and 4. 60m Easy climbing leads to the top.

12 Recess Rib 125m   Hard Severe   (1969)
This route lies on the right side of No.5 Buttress. Directly above the passing place on the road and to the left of an obvious steep corner there is a steep recess with a thin crack in its right-hand rib. Start by climbing easy slabs up to a ledge below the recess.

1. 40m Traverse right to a large, prominent square ledge. Climb up the thin crack in the right-hand rib of the recess and pull over a nose. Climb the V-groove above on the right and continue to a terrace.

2. 35m Climb up to a prominent square chimney, climb this and belay below a long corner.

3. 50m Climb the corner and scramble to the top.

13 Broken Buttress 90m   Severe   (1970)
This route lies on No.6 Buttress. Much variation is possible. Start at the right foot of the buttress. Climb the right edge on easy rocks for 30m and scramble up the next tier to the foot of a steep wall. From a good belay below the wall climb the slab above to the overhang and turn it on the right. Continue on good holds to the top.

SOUTH-EAST CLIFF

This cliff is above and right of the six buttresses forming the South Face. It presents a steep face above a gully which runs down to the road about a mile below the layby for Sword of Gideon, but the cliff is, in fact, best approached from No.1 Buttress. The cliff is well seen in the distance when driving up from Loch Kishorn, just after a right-hand bend at Map Ref 808 405.

14 Pommel 60m VS (1984)
At the left end of the cliff is a steep clean wall with a very prominent deep diedre above two corners (left of an enormous block).
1. 25m 5a Take the crack into the right-hand corner and climb it.
2. 35m 4b Climb the slab and arete on the right to easier ground.

15 Rig-Veda 105m HVS * (1984)
Start at a line of corners directly beneath the upper wall of the cliff at a grassy corner which bounds the right side of the steepest section of the lower wall. About halfway up the upper wall a small undercut nose can be seen with a short wide crack on its right. The line goes directly up corners and grooves to this.
1. 20m 4c Climb grassy corners to a terrace.
2. 20m 5a Continue up black cracks just left of a corner to belay on the grass terrace beneath the upper wall.
3. 40m 5a Climb cracks and a corner to reach the left side of the undercut nose. Step right, go up a right-facing corner and continue up cracks to the terrace.
4. 25m 4a Finish up the corner on the left.

16 Hotline 70m HVS (1991)
Scramble up to the ledge below the steepest section of the wall. Start midway between the Rig-Veda belay and the right end of the ledge, where there is a small ledge at head height.
1. 30m 5a Climb past the ledge and up the central of three small left-facing corners to a bulging section. Go through this trending right, then straight up to a grass ledge 5m below the terrace.
2. 40m 4b Move right then straight up to the top.

17 Sanctuary 80m E2 (1988)
Scramble up as for Hotline, and start at the right end of the ledge. This route climbs a series of flake cracks up the right side of the overhanging band at 25m before breaking left.
1. 40m 5b Follow the left slanting crackline with a hard move to gain a good ledge. Ignore the hollow flake on the left and follow the improbable crackline on good holds before moving boldly right through the hanging band to a rest. Traverse left to gain the easier continuation crack which is followed over several breaks to a good stance.
2. 40m Easier climbing leads to the top.

18 Dougie's Climb 90m Severe (1971)
This lies on the right of the cliff. See SMCJ 1973.

MEALL GORM
710m   (Map Ref 779 409)

The northern side of Meall Gorm presents a broken line of cliffs overlooking the Allt a'Chumhaing, the valley leading up to the Bealach na Ba. Although very impressive from a distance the cliffs are, in the main, too terraced and vegetated to provide good rock climbing. There are however several good winter climbs, though the low altitude means that they are not often in condition. The first major feature when travelling up the Allt a' Chumhaing is the large eastern buttress which has a prominent terrace at half-height. A shallow gully line ascends from a scree cone to the right-hand end of the terrace, and then divides into three branches. This forms the start of the Spiral Terrace and Trident Gully climbs.

Spiral Terrace   600m   II   (1986)
Ascend the shallow gully for 100m to the right end of the terrace. Follow the terrace leftwards for 300m to a deep gully. Continue for 100m to a large flat ledge in front of a short, steep wall. From the right end of the ledge ascend to a shallow gully slanting up right for 100m to the plateau.

Blue Moon   200m   III   (1991)
This route follows the crest of the buttress left of Trident Gully left branch. Start on the terrace left of the gully and climb two steep walls (crux). Follow the exposed left edge of the buttress to the top.

Trident Gully, Left Branch   350m   II   (1986)
Climb the shallow gully to the terrace (100m). Continue up the gully, keeping left where it forks, to the plateau (250m).

Trident Gully, Right Branch   380m   III   (1986)
Ascend to the terrace (100m). Continue up the gully to where it forks below twin chimneys (50m). Climb the left chimney to regain the gully (40m). Climb easily to a large roof (100m). The escape to the right of the roof would probably provide a more sustained finish, but the first ascensionists traversed left to a narrow gully, exiting right to gain the plateau (90m).

Moving west from Trident Gully there is a broad buttress, then a left-slanting gully with several indefinite branches to its right.

Wee Beastie 210m I/II   (1986)
Climb the left-slanting gully.

To the right of Wee Beastie is a broken buttress, then three easy-angled gullies separated by buttresses. The right-most gully has been used for descent. At this point there is a steep step in the valley floor and a long buttress descends into the step. To the right lies a wide gully, Easy Gully.

Way Out 210m II   (1980)
This route is the least obvious and furthest left on the long buttress. It is shallow and trends continuously left, taking in icy grooves and turfy walls to finish on the left of the ridge.

Stonner Falls 95m III/IV   (1980)
This climb lies on the buttress right of Easy Gully, and follows a right-trending gully topped by a large cascade of ice. The ice rests on a broad terrace running the width of the buttress.
1. 40m Climb a short ice step then an easy gully to a wide terrace.
2. 30m Follow ice bulges on the left; belay below the final icefall.
3. 25m Climb the icefall on the left through bulges to a broad terrace.

Moving right, there is an area of broken ground, then a three-tiered buttress, then a broken buttress followed by the prominent Cobalt Buttress with the narrow Blue Pillar on its left.

Blaeberry Corner 105m Severe   (1955)
This climbs the left side of the three-tiered buttress. It is a steep climb on good rock. Start up the gully on the left of the buttress. After 15m traverse right over a block and up a wall to a terrace. Climb up the steep wall ahead for 25m to the top of the first tier. Climb the second tier by the vertical wall straight ahead, over some flakes, ending by a traverse right. Climb the third tier by the crest.
Winter: IV   (1971)
Follow the summer line, with a difficult middle pitch.

Blue Pillar 150m Very Difficult   (1953)
This is the conspicuous, narrow pillar on the left of the massive Cobalt Buttress. Start at the foot and follow the crest. At mid-height a vertical step is climbed by a crack on the right with a precarious jammed flake at the top. Surmount the final tower by a deep chimney on the right.

Winter: IV   (1958)
The first 60m can be climbed in the gully on the right; thereafter the
summer route is followed.

Lobster Gully   160m   IV   (1987)
This is the gully separating Blue Pillar from Cobalt Buttress. Several
short, steep steps in the first 80m lead to two fine chimney pitches in
the upper section.

Cobalt Buttress   150m   III   (1970)
Start about 30m up to the right from the toe of the buttress, just above
the toe of Wedge Buttress and below a short, steep pitch in the gully
bed. Follow a ledge to the left to a belay below a short corner.
1. 15m Climb the corner with difficulty and make an awkward traverse
left to easier ground.
2. 20m A short wall above leads to the first terrace.
3. 25m Go up trending slightly right to a higher terrace about halfway
up the buttress.
4. 25m Climb up left towards a block on the skyline, but before
reaching it move slightly right onto a pedestal and over the bulge
above. Easier climbing leads to a terrace.
5. 35m Move up right to the right edge of another ledge.
6. 30m Climb the wall on the left and go diagonally right to a ledge.
Easy climbing leads to the top.

   The original summer route on this buttress is Moderate and rather
featureless.

Rattlesnake   135m   Severe   (1965)
This route follows the obvious line of corners running up the centre of
Cobalt Buttress.
1. 35m Scramble up to the first unavoidable tier and climb directly
below the line of corners some distance left of a large black patch.
2. 35m Follow grass to the foot of the first and most impressive corner.
Climb a smaller corner to the right until a right-slanting crack leads
more easily to a grass ledge.
3. 35m Traverse left into the line of corners and climb to the top of the
third tier.
4. 30m Climb the last set of corners directly.

The Smooth Creep 90m VS   (1971)
This route lies on the wall between Rattlesnake and Blue Pillar.
Scramble up preliminary tiers to the foot of a smooth vertical corner
about halfway along the wall.
1. 20m Start up the corner, trend right and climb a crack to belay below
a steep wall.
2. 20m Step right and climb to a stance below the left-hand of two
corners.
3. 10m Climb the corner to a ledge below a small overhang.
4. 35m Go left along the ledge and climb steep cracked slabs then
two huge poised flakes to a good ledge.
5. 5m Finish by a short overhanging chimney.

Wedge Buttress is the triangular buttress to the right of Cobalt
Buttress. To the right of Wedge Buttress is a broad, easy gully, then a
terraced buttress divided by a narrow gully, which gives the following
route.

The Six-track Mono Blues 210m II   (1978)
Climb the narrow gully, which has two short pitches.

MINOR CRAGS

CAMUSTEEL SEA-CLIFFS
The hamlet of Camusteel lies just south of Applecross village. The 10m
sandstone sea-cliffs are regularly used by the local Fairbridge Drake
Centre for top-roping from the wooden stakes at the tops of the climbs.
The finishes are vegetated and protection is generally poor, so although a visit may salvage something from a showery day, it is
probably not worth a special excursion. The Camusteel cliffs are 100
metres south-west of the hamlet and have 13 routes, mostly from Very
Difficult to VS in standard. The Tracking Station Cliffs are 200 metres
further west with 8 routes varying from 5a to 5c (up to E3). The
Margarette Cliffs are 400 metres further north, just beyond a dry stone
wall, and have 20 routes in the 5a to 5c range.

North of Applecross village, just north of the Allt Tasabhaig, is a
south-west facing slab on the sea-cliff. The slab has been climbed by
two routes, HVS and E2, with metal belay stakes in place at the top.

LOCH NA CREIGE CRAG   (Map Ref 769 557)

This small compact crag in north Applecross lies two minutes from the coast road and faces west across the loch. The four routes recorded were all climbed by P. Potter and M. Welch in the spring of 1988.

Corner Route   20m   HVS 5a
Climb the obvious left-facing corner nearest the roadside.

Little Plum   25m   E1 5b
Start 5m right of Corner Route. Follow a vague crack to reach the slabby wall, which gives good fingery climbing.

Diagonal   30m   HVS 5a
Follow the left-slanting diagonal break to the left side of the large left-curving overhang in the centre of the crag, then climb the corner on the left.

Slab Route   25m   VS 4c
Start at the right end of the crag, right of the overhung section, and take a direct line up the steep slab.

ARDHESLAIG   (Map Ref 784 558)

This is a clean slabby gneiss crag with eight 25m to 40m routes of Difficult to VS standard which are ideal for beginners. There is also some good bouldering on the outcrop below the main crag.

SHEILDAIG

There are a numerous gneiss outcrops scattered above the village on either side of the road. These give good short climbs and bouldering.

Torridon

LIATHACH
1054m   (Map Ref 929 579)

Liathach comprises a range of seven tops forming an 8km chain running east to west on the north side of Glen Torridon, towering directly above the road. The highest point on Liathach is Spidean a' Choire Leith at 1054m, midway between Stuc a'Choire Dhuibh Bhig, 913m, guarding the east end of the chain, and Mullach an Rathain, 1023m, at the west end above Torridon village. A broad shoulder extends west for 2km from Mullach an Rathain rising slightly to Sgorr a' Chadail before dropping steeply, but easily, down to Coire Mhic Nobuil and the footpath.

Since most of the rock on Liathach consists of broken vegetatious Torridonian sandstone terraces, usually wet streaked, only a handful of rock climbs have been recorded. However, in winter the mountain is transformed to produce some of the best icefall climbing in Britain. The traverse of the mountain in both summer and winter gives one of the classic ridge expeditions of the mainland, with sensationally exposed views onto the surrounding prehistoric-looking hills of the Torridon area.

In the past, winter climbing conditions on Liathach were renowned for being rather fickle. However, with more information available from recent activity, it seems that good ice forms regularly every season, for limited periods at any time between January and April. A warm weather system may strip the buttresses and thin icefalls, but the ice will re-form quickly on a return to colder conditions. The most reliable climbs will be found in Coireag Dubh Mor and high up in Coire na Caime. With heavy snowfalls, or late in the season, most of the bigger gullies will bank out with snow.

Main ridge descents
Since Liathach is a complex ridge mostly circled by steep sandstone tiers, the following are recommended winter descent routes. Obviously local snow conditions should be taken into account. All directions given are facing out. All names have been taken from the 1:25000 *'The Cuillin and Torridon Hills'* OS map.

Stuc a' Choire Dhuibh Bhig. Descend the north-east ridge to the top of a steep rock band. Scramble down to the left (north) and traverse back right along a wide terrace hard under the rock band to easy snow slopes running south-east out of Stringless Gully.

Spot Height 833m. At the first col on the ridge west of top Bidean Toll a'Mhuic, which in turn is the subsidiary top west of Stuc a' Choire Dhuibh Bhig, descend south down a narrow but easy gully for 200m to a wide open snow slope. Either turn right and traverse into Coire Liath Mhor to descend by the stream bed, or, turn left and traverse across to the open slopes of the Allt nan Gobhar. The descent north from the same col leads into Coireag Dubh Beag via Access Gully, grade I.

Coire Liath Mhor (Toll a' Meitheach). The quickest descent from the summit of Spidean a'Choire Leith, or after a route in Coireag Dubh Mor, is to gain the first col east of Spidean. Now descend south down a wide gully leading leftwards onto a large flat area. From near the left end (cairn), descend a short tier onto a wide terrace. Traverse this leftwards until able to break through the next tier down the line of a stream leading into the Allt an Doire Ghairbh. Follow the path down the left bank. The descent north from the same col on the main ridge leads into Coireag Dubh Mor via Way Up, grade I.

Mullach an Rathain. The descent due south from the summit leads down steep uniform slopes into drainage lines funnelling into the Allt an Tuill Bhain.

Torridon Stone Shoot. This is a wide scree and boulder-filled couloir descending due south into the Allt Slugach and Torridon village. From Mullach an Rathain, follow the wide shoulder west for 800 metres (line of cairns) to the head of the couloir.

Sgorr a' Chadail. Descend slopes north-west to the Coire Mhic Nobuil path.

Liathach Main Ridge Traverse   4km   II

A superb expedition with continually interesting walking and spectacular mountain and loch scenery. It is usually traversed from east to west. Ascend Stuc a' Choire Dhuibh Bhig via Stringless Gully (I/II), or by its north-east ridge. The hardest part is the traverse of the Fasarinen Pinnacles which, when taken direct, warrants grade II. (A low traverse of the pinnacles on the south side, in summer a path, can be more difficult than the direct, especially in bad snow conditions). The main ridge finishes at Mullach an Rathain.

Approaches

The climbs on the north side of Liathach are described from east to west, approaching via the Coire Dubh Mor footpath, starting from the National Trust car park in Glen Torridon (Map Ref 958 568). The path rises under the east buttress of Stuc a' Choire Dhuibh Bhig and round the back to give access to the three northern corries of Coireag Dubh Beag, Coireag Dubh Mor (the north-east corrie of Spidean) and the larger spectacular Coire na Caime.

Routes on the south side of Liathach are described last, from west to east, finishing with those on the south-east slopes of Stuc a' Choire Dhuibh Bhig.

The first routes are visible from the path high up on a short band of rock ringing the east buttress of Stuc a' Choire Dhuibh Bhig.

1 Stringless Gully 150m I/II   (1976)

This is the first obvious steep-sided deep gully approximately 200 metres left of the right-bounding ridge.

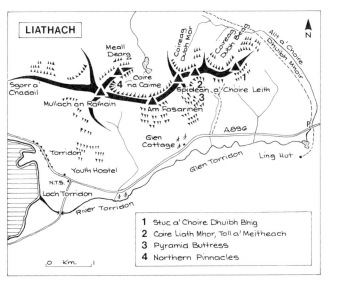

1 Stuc a' Choire Dhuibh Bhig
2 Coire Liath Mhor, Toll a' Meitheach
3 Pyramid Buttress
4 Northern Pinnacles

2 Triceratops 90m Very Difficult   (1970)
This route follows the right ridge of Stringless Gully. Start at the lowest
point of the ridge, turn the first of three pinnacles on the right and climb
the other two direct to the top.

3 Fairy Queen 80m IV   (1987)
An obvious icefall forms in a bay some 30m right of Stringless Gully.
It is climbed in two fine steep pitches; the first an ice-cased corner and
the second with devious climbing up an icicle clinging to the headwall.
Move right to finish.

  Descend by walking right above the band of cliffs and down the
ridge.

4 East Buttress (Stuc a' Choire Dhuibh Bhig) Difficult   (1899)
Recorded for posterity. To quote: 'This is the black, broken, unwhole-
some-looking cliff low down on the main east ridge of the mountain,
overlooking the Coire Dubh track'. It was originally climbed by Lawson,
Ling and Glover on an SMC Easter Meet in wet and windy conditions.
The first tier had some steep little pitches, the second was passed by
a grassy gully on the left, and the third was climbed by steep rock and
a small chimney.

5 Chi Squared 450m III/IV   (1968)
This takes the watercourse descending the north flank of Stuc a'
Choire Dhuibh Bhig, before the entrance to Coireag Dubh Beag.
Consistent climbing on water-ice leads to the crux at a band of crags
high up. Take the left fork to finish.

COIREAG DUBH BEAG

This is the first of the northern corries. The best approach is to follow
the burn draining from the corrie, which is a classic bowl with an easy
snow gully on its back left side and broad steep terraces sweeping
round to the right. From a distance, the cascades of ice look discontinuous, but the lines become more apparent on closer inspection.

  Between the Chi Squared watercourse and Beag Pardon, cutting
the hillside on the east of the corrie, are obvious gully lines with various
branches offering a variety of pleasant grade I/II routes to the summit
of Stuc a' Choire Dhuibh Bhig. One better line has been recorded:

6 Left Gully 200m III   (1977)
Two gully lines run leftwards from the diagonal snow slope start of
Beag Pardon, converging at a snow bowl below the summit of Stuc a'
Choire Dhuibh Bhig. Left Gully starts steeply on ice leading to a snow
slope. Take the gully above with a steep left wall and normally a short
pitch.

7 Beag Pardon 200m II
On the left side of the corrie is a right diagonal snow slope leading into
a narrow cleft. From the top of the narrows, a short step on the left
leads into a left-trending couloir line.

8 The Snotter 30m V   (1986)
The very steep icicle that drools down the left wall at the start of Beag
Pardon. Descend by abseil, or continue very easily to the summit.

9 Access Gully 120m I
The obvious snow gully tucked into the left side at the back of the
corrie. It gives a pleasant route onto the main ridge and may also be
used as a descent.

10 Hidden Gully 210m II
This climb sneaks up left from the lower reaches of Access Gully,
breaking into a gully directly above.

   When in condition, the back and east-facing walls of the corrie
literally dribble with ice down every rock terrace. The following fine
routes have been recorded:

11 Footless Gully 150m IV   (1977)
The obvious line on the back wall, where it bends round into the
east-facing wall. Start up an awkward narrow vertical chimney on the
first tier (crux). Continue in the same line up the tiers above.

12 Thumbscrew 200m IV/V   (1989)
This climb links a series of icefalls to the left of Footless Gully. Start
some 8 metres left of the Footless chimney and take a short leftward
slanting groove to the foot of a very steep narrow icefall. Climb this to
a large terrace and continue up and left to climb a large icefall leading
to a second terrace. Mixed ground leads to an obvious deep chimney
cleaving the final tier.

13   Thumbscrew Direct   60m   V   (1989)
A two-pitch steep icefall start straightens the line. Start about 40 metres
left of Thumbsrew. Climb a very steep right-facing icy corner up the
first tier. Follow the same line in the second tier then move 5m right
into Thumbscrew.

14   Headless Gully   150m   IV/V   (1984)
The main line on the right (east-facing) wall and the route most likely
to form regularly. Start by the highest point of snow under the middle
of the wall. Climb an initial short steep icefall to the first terrace. Move
left into the main icefall which is steep for 25m (crux) before easing
onto more terraced ground. Finish via an ice-filled corner through the
top tier onto the summit snowfield. (The main icefall forms down a
chimney line and, under lean conditions, this may prove technically
easier.)

15   The Executioner   140m   IV/V   (1986)
A large snow ramp leads right from under the line of Headless Gully,
to finish at an overhang at the base of a shallow gully. The Executioner
gains the gully higher up, avoiding the overhang on the left. Start
halfway up the ramp and follow a very steep ice-filled corner, vertical
to start, to a pinnacle belay on the right. The icefall continues right of
the pinnacle in two steps to a big snow ledge. Move right into the main
gully which leads to the top.

16   Rambler's Rib   350m   II/III   (1987)
This route follows the rib bounding the left side of a narrow curving
gully (Hillwalk) and bounding the west of Coireag Dubh Beag itself.
Start in the gully and climb out onto the rib at the earliest opportunity.
Climb a series of walls and steps by grooves and corners, avoiding
the final rock tower on the left or right.

17   Hillwalk   300m   II   (1966)
The fine curving narrow gully immediately right of Rambler's Rib, which
finishes up the same open slopes at the top. It normally gives several
short pitches through interesting scenery, but may bank out.

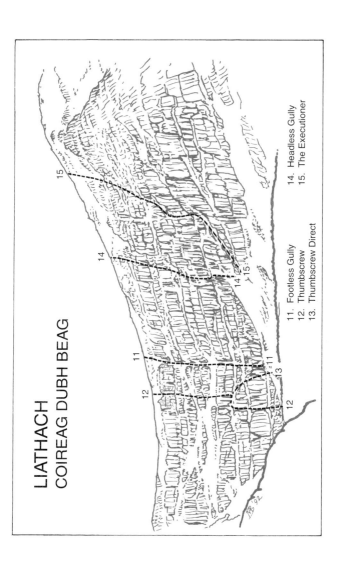

LIATHACH
COIREAG DUBH BEAG

11. Footless Gully
12. Thumbscrew
13. Thumbscrew Direct

14. Headless Gully
15. The Executioner

COIREAG DUBH MOR

This corrie is topped by Spidean a' Choire Leith, the highest peak of Liathach, and provides the best concentration of ice climbs on the mountain. The corrie faces north, with huge rambling buttresses on the left cut by two obvious gullies, West Gully and Spidean Way, followed by a deep snow gully, Way Up, bordering the left end of the steep back wall. Way Up leads to a bealach on the main ridge. The 200m back wall extends rightwards to a left-curving gash, George, before merging into the north ridge of Spidean. In the centre of the back wall, and obvious from a great distance, is the magnificent ice cascade of Poacher's Fall, the line that forms most readily.

Access into the corrie is from the Coire Dubh Mor footpath, leaving it at the watershed and angling up to join the burn draining from the corrie itself. The routes are described from left to right.

18 West Gully 300m III   (1978)
This is the first obvious gully line in the mouth of the corrie, with a steep right wall and bounding the left side of a huge rambling terraced buttress. Normally banked up, it can form a steep icefall at the narrows.

19 Spidean Way 250m III   (1977)
The next gully line, left slanting and bounding the right side of the huge terraced buttress. Again, the difficult steps may bank out.

20 Way Up 250m I
The straightforward snow gully leading to the bealach on the main ridge. It is also a way down!

The following routes are described in relation to Poacher's Fall, first left towards Way Up, then right to the gash of George.

21 Poacher's Fall 180m V   (1978)
Take the right side of the obvious steep wide icefall draining the middle of the back wall.

22 The Salmon Leap 200m V   (1986)
This is the left side of Poacher's Fall, separated in the top half by a rock rib. Finish through the top tier by a narrow chimney into the easier gully above.

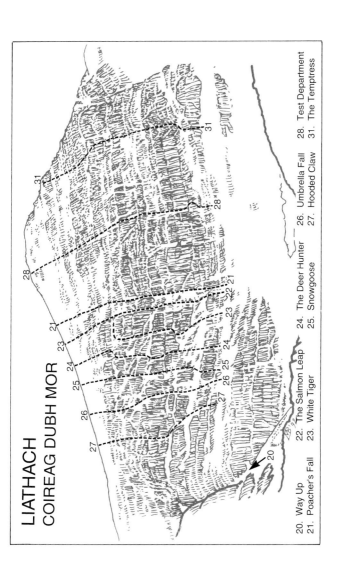

LIATHACH
COIREAG DUBH MOR

20. Way Up
21. Poacher's Fall
22. The Salmon Leap
23. White Tiger
24. The Deer Hunter
25. Snowgoose
26. Umbrella Fall
27. Hooded Claw
28. Test Department
31. The Temptress

23 White Tiger 220m V   (1987)
The first of three thinner ice lines left of The Salmon Leap. The first
main tier is avoided by a right traverse from an icy bay left of the main
line. Four steep tiers lead to a final rock barrier. Follow a delicate right
traverse into the final pitch of The Salmon Leap. The obvious direct
finish has also been climbed in mixed conditions; it is slightly harder.

24 The Deer Hunter 200m V   (1986)
The middle of the thin ice lines left of The Salmon Leap. The line is
obvious at mid-height as a thick ice-cased right-facing corner. The first
short bulging tier may be turned on the left. Again, the last tier is bare
of ice and a short right traverse leads to a strenuous chimney with a
difficult exit (crux).

25 Snow Goose 230m IV/V   (1986)
The left-hand thinner icefall and just right of Umbrella Fall. The line
includes a pitch up the lowest tier, which extends as far as Way Up.
The ice is continuous over six tiers; the fourth a steep iced wall of a
right-facing corner and the fifth tier (crux) a weave through two
overhangs by a corner on the right and an icicle above.

26 Umbrella Fall 230m IV   (1984)
This is the largest and most obvious icefall left of Poacher's Fall. Take
a line up the lowest tier to the terrace below the main fall. On the first
ascent, the main pitch formed a huge ice umbrella which was turned
on the right.

27 Hooded Claw 150m IV   (1987)
The next prominent ice line left of Umbrella Fall. Start from a long
traverse left along the terrace above the first tier (or climb a line on the
tier a bit to the right). The fine crux pitch follows a steep iced groove
to an ice 'hood', bypassed on the right via a short icicle.

The face between Poacher's Fall and George forms four obvious
icefalls draining down a very steep first tier, giving the crux of the
climbs. The first line right of Poacher's remains unclimbed as it bottoms
out over a roof on the lower tier. Maybe one day the icicle will reach
the ground!

28 Test Department 185m V   (1987)
The second icefall right of Poacher's. On the first ascent the lower
icicle did not reach the ground so a start was made to the right and
two pegs were used to gain the icicle. Above, climb a free-standing
column of ice and a series of steep ice bulges to below a major
steepening. Take the left-hand of two ice lines and continue easily up
to the final wall. Mixed ground, following a shallow groove almost
directly above the lower pitches, leads through a niche to easy ground.

29 Brain Strain 180m V   (1991)
This takes a series of ice streaks in line with the first pitch of Brain
Drain. Start up a shallow chimney-groove 15 metres right of Test
Department (Brain Drain). Trend slightly right to belay beneath a steep
ice-smeared corner (25m). Climb the corner and continue to the next
steep band (35m), which is climbed by an ice line just left of Brain Drain
(30m). Continue direct to a buttress forming the final step (40m), which
is passed by ice grooves on its left (50m).

30 Brain Drain 180m IV/V   (1987)
The third fall right of Poachers forms a thin bulging entry pitch. This is
avoided on the left by a hidden icy chimney-groove (crux), followed by
a traverse right to join the main line. Continually interesting and varied
climbing on ice leads in three or four piches to easier ground.

31 The Temptress 220m IV   (1988)
The rightmost icefall right of Poacher's, much less continuous than the
others. A short steep introductory pitch leads to a steep shallow
left-facing ice groove. Climb the groove (crux) and a long easier
section to belay under steep walls with obvious icy direct finishes. On
the first ascent, these were avoided by a traverse left to finish up Brain
Drain.

32 George 230m III   (1967)
The steep back wall of the corrie finishes at a deep gash immediately
left of the north ridge of Spidean; this is the line. The gully becomes
more defined in the upper section (sometimes with a through route)
and finishes by the right fork.

33 Sinister Prong 150m III/IV (1978)
This takes the left fork of George below the steep upper section. Start at the top of steepening snow, below a steep groove. Climb the groove to step left at the top and up parallel slabs to a stance by a vertical chimney-groove (old abseil sling). Take the chimney-groove, over a bulge to a *cul-de-sac*. Traverse right to the rib and easier ground.

The north ridge of Spidean a' Choire Leith gives a Moderate scramble to the summit if taken direct, and an interesting grade I/II in winter.

COIRE NA CAIME

Walking west along the Coire Dubh path, this is the third, the most appealing and largest of the northern corries. As the name may suggest, 'crooked corrie', it is more complicated than the typical bowl shape. Loch Coire na Caime lurks at the entrance, with Meall Dearg on the west and Spidean towering above to the east. The broad ridge of P.C. Buttress divides Coire na Caime leaving a small hanging bowl on the left enclosed by the Fasarinen Pinnacles and Am Fasarinen, and a larger three-stepped corrie reaching high to the right, finishing in upper Coireag Cham overshadowed by Bell's Buttress, Mullach an Rathain and the Northern Pinnacles. The best approach is to leave the path at the watershed as for Coireag Dubh Mor and skirt round to the loch under the north ridge of Spidean (2 hours).

The routes are described from left to right, (east to west), starting with the Fasarinen Pinnacles and Am Fasarinen.

THE PINNACLES

34 No.1 Gully 100m I
A straightforward snow slope running up the left side of the first pinnacle.

35 No.2 Gully 100m I
The right-trending gully between the first and second pinnacles.

36 3rd Pinnacle Gully 120m II (1955)
The gully between the second and third pinnacles. After 75m, traverse left along a snow ledge into a subsidiary gully and climb this to the main ridge. The main gully, with a steep final pitch, is grade III.

37 Dru 150m Severe   (1959)
The third pinnacle forms a rocky tower, which, with a bit of imagination,
might seem similar to the slightly bigger Chamonix mountain of the
same name!   From the lowest point of the pinnacle climb into an open
groove at 12m and move out left at 30m to a broad grassy ledge. Climb
just left of a chimney-crack to a narrower ledge (20m). (This point can
be reached by a long right traverse along the ledge from 30m up 3rd
Pinnacle Gully, making it possibe to climb the fine final arete at an
overall grade of Very Difficult). Traverse 20m right, then gain the top
of a small detached needle from the right. Follow the narrow crest
behind in a superb situation to easier ground and the top.

38 Dru Couloir 150m IV/V   (1986)
The left-slanting chimney-gully on the Dru Pinnacle. Start right of the
the foot of the pinnacle at a left-facing tapering corner, directly below
the chimney-gully. Climb the corner to a ledge at 30m. Gain the
chimney-gully and follow it for 30m to a belay on the left. Continue in
the same line to the bealach where the detached needle of the summer
line abuts the summit ridge. Take the easiest line up the ridge to the
top.

   Bordering the fourth pinnacle are two gullies which form a V.

39 4th Pinnacle Gully 120m II
The left-hand gully usually has good but short ice pitches.

40 Gully 5 120m I
A straightforward snow gully, the right-hand of the V.

   Next is the 5th pinnacle (as seen from the corrie) before the main
ridge swings west over Am Fasarinen, forming the back wall of a small
hanging corrie, which in turn is bounded on the right by P.C. Buttress.
Between 5th Pinnacle and Am Fasarinen is an easy snow slope only
defined in the top half and split by a rock rib at the top, Grade I.

AM FASARINEN
On close inspection Am Fasarinen sports five fine-looking thin ice
lines, the middle three being the most obvious chimney gullies directly
under the summit. The left one (Jerbil) is the deepest, and the middle
one (The Andes Couloir) is essentially a right-facing corner. The right
one is only defined in its upper part.

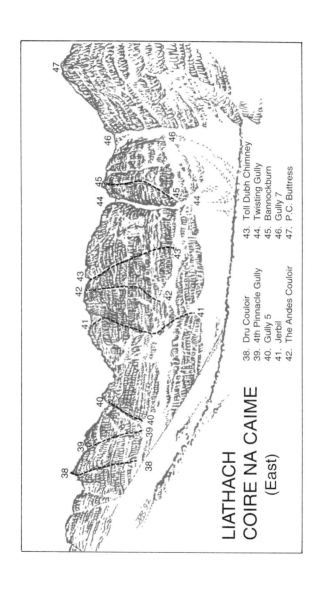

LIATHACH
COIRE NA CAIME
(East)

38. Dru Couloir
39. 4th Pinnacle Gully
40. Gully 5
41. Jerbil
42. The Andes Couloir

43. Toll Dubh Chimney
44. Twisting Gully
45. Bannockburn
46. Gully 7
47. P.C. Buttress

41 Jerbil 120m IV   (1985)
Start in a high snow bay shared by a left-slanting gully. Climb a steep
ice pitch leading to a small snow amphitheatre in the deep gully (45m).
Continue in the same line avoiding difficult obstacles on the left or right
as necessary to an easy bay leading to the main ridge.

42 The Andes Couloir 180m IV   (1986)
A short ice pitch leads to a snow ledge under a steep iced corner. Pull
into the corner over a strenuous bulge (crux) and take the superb
right-facing ice corner above to an easing below the main ridge.

43 Toll Dubh Chimney 250m V   (1987)
This route follows the left-trending chimney line on the buttress
100 metres left of Twisting Gully; it is the rightmost of the five obvious
chimney lines. Climb to the foot of the deep icy chimney at one third
height in two pitches. On the first ascent, the chimney was overhung
at the base and was climbed by a dry crack in the right wall until the
ice was regained after 25m. The next pitch culminates in a short
overhang after which difficulties eased. A good route.

44 Twisting Gully 180m II   (1955)
The deep snow gully on the right of Am Fasarinen, which finishes at
a notch on the main ridge, is easy except for an ice pitch at two thirds
height. This may sometimes be avoided by a through route.

45 Bannockburn 200m IV   (1987)
Climbs the fine obvious line of icy chimneys and grooves up the middle
of the buttress between Twisting Gully and Gully 7. The steep crack
in the final rock band provides the crux.

46 Gully 7 180m I
The wide open couloir left of P.C. Buttress.

47 P.C. Buttress 210m Difficult   (1939)
This is the terraced buttress bounding the west side of the small
'Fasarinen' corrie. The lower terraces are easy, but the upper section
narrows and steepens where the route climbs to the right of centre up
a precipitous tower to a false top (some loose rock) Scrambling leads
to the top. In winter the climb is a pleasant Grade III.

48   Gully 8   120m   I/II
This easy snow gully starts high up at the top of a huge snow slope on the west side of P.C. Buttress, and goes through fine rocky scenery.

West of P.C. Buttress and Gully 8 is a high broad broken face cut by numerous shallow chimney lines. The face ends in a buttress of more compact rock, Bell's Buttress, above the entrance to upper Coire na Caime and forms a high point on the main ridge.

49   Titanium Gully   200m   IV   (1984)
At the left end of the face and starting at a snow bay just above the lowest rocks is an obvious narrow ice line running virtually the height of the face.

50   Valentine Buttress   250m   IV   (1987)
Yet another fine chimney line past the right side of a squat buttress in the middle of the face. Start 30m left of Vanadium Couloir at the top of a snow bay and take the right-hand of two chimneys close together. Climb the chimney line for about 100m, with unusual subterranean moves, until easier climbing leads out right onto the buttress. Follow a series of grooves up the rocks above leading to the ridge.

51   Vanadium Couloir   300m   IV   (1979)
The obvious steep open gully line immediately left of Bell's Buttress, starting from the highest point of the snow bay.

Bell's Buttress is a high area of steep compact rock streaked with shallow chimney-gully lines on the left side and cut by two deep gullies on the more continuous right side; the left one is a *cul-de-sac* and the right one is the line of Bell's Gully. Access in winter is easy up a shelf running right from the start of Vanadium Couloir to a snow terrace at the base of the routes.

52   Bell's Buttress, Left Chimney   230m   IV/V   (1987)
A fine route taking the furthest left chimney line on Bell's Buttress. Start up the left of a pair of chimneys and step into the right-hand one at 10m. Where it overhangs, climb out right and up the gully above to a huge block belay on the left (30m). Continue up the chimney line to snow ledges, turning two blocking overhangs on the right (30m). Follow the gully on the right through several narrowings past a rightwards ramp at 45m, and continue in the same line to finish.

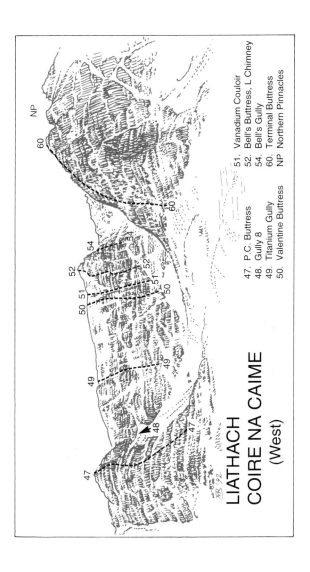

LIATHACH
COIRE NA CAIME
(West)

47. P.C. Buttress
48. Gully 8
49. Titanium Gully
50. Valentine Buttress

51. Vanadium Couloir
52. Bell's Buttress, L Chimney
54. Bell's Gully
60. Terminal Buttress
NP Northern Pinnacles

53 Bell's Buttress 150m Severe   (1947)
Climb the left-hand narrow buttress in the middle of the face in three
pitches. Scrambling then leads to the top. It may be made easier by
moving left.

54 Bell's Gully 230m IV   (1986)
The right-hand and most obvious of the two gully lines on the right side
of Bell's Buttress. Follow the increasingly difficult gully over two
steepenings to a *cul-de-sac* at 125m. Move left and take the shallow
gully above to easy ground.

The upper corrie of Coire na Caime, Coireag Cham, feels almost
alpine. It is guarded on the left by Bell's Buttress and on the right by
the spectacular Northern Pinnacles of Mullach an Rathain, rising from
the outrider of Meall Dearg. Mullach an Rathain itself tops the back of
the corrie. Since this corrie is high and sheltered it comes into condition
sooner and holds snow longer than elsewhere on the mountain.

The wide snow slope leading up to the bealachs between Bell's
Buttress and Mullach an Rathain may be used as an easy descent or
ascent to the main ridge.

55 Gully 1K 120m I/II   (1928)
The snow gully leading to the main ridge east of the summit of Mullach
an Rathain. Start from the highest point of snow at the back of the
corrie.

THE NORTHERN PINNACLES
These are numbered ascending from right to left, One to Five. The
gullies between the top pinnacles provide good winter routes.

56 Left-Hand Trinity Gully 90m III   (1928)
The wide icy gully between the fifth pinnacle and Mullach an Rathain.

57 Central Trinity Gully 105m II   (1955)
The gully between the fourth and fifth pinnacles normally gives two ice
pitches.

ILLUSTRATIONS
Opposite: Sword of Gideon, Sgurr a'Chaorachain (Climber, Trevor Jones)
Next Page: Salmon Leap, Liathach (Climber, Andy Cunningham)

58 Right-Hand Trinity Gully 120m III   (1955)
This lies between the third and fourth pinnacles. It is usually the best
and most difficult of the Trinity gullies.

59 Holy Trinity 150m IV   (1990)
The obvious chimney-flake and left-slanting ramp line up the front face
of the Third Pinnacle. Start in the middle of the buttress and climb the
chimney line for 90m to the edge overlooking Right-Hand Trinity Gully.
Climb the crest, turning a steepening on the left.

   Meall Dearg, the right-hand 'gatepost' to the entrance of Coire na
Caime, has two recorded winter routes.

60 Terminal Buttress 180m III   (1986)
This is the line of least resistance up the steep conical buttress at the
base of the east ridge of Meall Dearg. Start in a bay on the left side of
the east-facing buttress. Climb a snowy depression up and left until a
line can be taken back right to a shoulder on the ridge (100m).
Interesting climbing, not unlike Tower Ridge of Ben Nevis, leads up
walls, towers and terraces to the top.

61 North Buttress 200m II
This route follows a right-slanting diagonal shelf crossing the north
face of Meall Dearg onto the skyline north ridge.

62 North Flank 180m Moderate
A scramble to the top of Meall Dearg. Start in the middle of the north
face, just right of a small watercourse, and climb a steep, narrow
slanting shelf.

63 The Northern Pinnacles 130m II   (1900)
Short and sharp, the Northern Pinnacles guard the north ridge of
Mullach an Rathain. Combined with a west to east traverse of Lia-
thach's main ridge, this gives one of Scotland's finest winter round
trips. It is possible to approach via the Coire Dubh Mor path from the
National Trust car park to the base of Meall Dearg (2 hours), with grand

ILLUSTRATIONS
Previous page: *Test Department, Liathach (Climber, Chris Watts)*
Opposite: *Seeds of Destruction and The Reaper, Beinn Eighe*
                   (Climbers, Roger Everett et al)

views into the northern corries. However, the approach from the foot of Coire Mhic Nobuill is rather shorter. Nowadays an ascent of Meall Dearg by one of the above routes would seem appropriate, but a hidden wide couloir on the north-west flank of Meall Dearg leads into an easy narrow gully and so to the base of the first pinnacle. There are five pinnacles in all; the first two are small, the third has the longest ascent and the fourth is the crux. Turn any difficulty on the right.

In summer, the Northern Pinnacles offer a pleasant scramble, although on somewhat shattered rock (Moderate, 1894). The fourth pinnacle is taken direct with a traverse across a little slab just below the top.

THE SOUTH SIDE OF LIATHACH

In comparison to the northern corries, the south side of Liathach offers only a few climbs. The Glen Torridon glacier has scraped and plucked the south side relatively smooth, leaving only one small hanging corrie, Coire Liath Mhor east of Spidean a' Choire Leith, and very little in the form of continuous gullies. The rock tends to be terraced and vegetatious. In winter, the sun will quickly affect the few icefalls that regularly form, particularly later in the season.

The climbs are described from west to east, from Sgorr a' Chadail to Stuc a' Choire Dhuibh Bhig.

SGORR A'CHADAIL

64 Reflection Wall   75m   Very Difficult   (1952)
This is on the high south-facing crag below the summit of Sgorr a' Chadail. Start at the right end of the crag at a cairn below the highest point. Climb the overhang (hard), or avoid it by a little wall to the right, then move straight up to a thread belay at 15m. Continue direct to the top.

PYRAMID BUTTRESS OF SPIDEAN A' CHOIRE LEITH.

This is the shapely buttress, easily seen from the road, that terminates the short south-east ridge of Spidean. To reach it, follow the path on the right of the Allt an Doire Ghairbh and make a rising leftward traverse over awkward ground. When in condition, the buttress oozes with ice to give several fine climbs. There are basically two obvious icefalls split by a tapering rocky rib.

65 Pyramid Left Icefall   180m   IV   (1986)
Climb the icefall to where it steepens and move out right to the rocky
rib. Follow this and a narrow gully above to the top. On the first ascent,
the effects of the sun prevented a direct finish.

66 Pyramid Direct   180m   V   (1987)
Basically a hard counter-route to Pyramid Left Icefall. Climb the
dividing rocky rib until moves out left lead onto the steep top section
of the left-hand icefall. Climb this to finish.

67 Pyramid Buttress   180m   IV   (1977)
The right-hand icefall. Climb the initial ice and the depression above
for 30m until the easiest line forces out left eventually onto the rib.
Climb the rib for one pitch until a line leads diagonally right to the big
couloir directly above the start. Snow slopes lead to the top.

68 Pyramid Right Edge   180m   III   (Early 1980s)
Follow the right ridge of the buttress until near the top, then move left
into the finishing gully to avoid steepening rock.

COIRE LIATH MHOR: TOLL A' MEITHEACH
The backwall of this hanging corrie east of Pyramid Buttress comprises
steep tiers sporting cascades of ice in numerous short steep drops.
The lowest tier is about 50m high. On either side of the backwall is a
prominent gully.

69 Toll Gate West   200m   II
The left-hand of the deep gullies splitting the backwall.

70 Soul-Searcher   210m   IV   (1987)
Climb the central scoop line in the bottom tier, trending slightly right,
then go diagonally right on easy-angled ice for 25m to an icy groove-
chimney in the next tier. A good steep pitch up the chimney leads to
easier climbing in the same chimney line and onto snowfields below
the main ridge.

71 Salvation   55m   V/VI   (1987)
Left of Soul-Searcher an impressive icefall can form down the lower
tier, rarely if ever reaching ground level. Levitate past the gap onto the
steep ice screen above, which leads right to a stepped corner line

(25m) Climb the corner and the icefall left of a cave above, leftwards onto the big terrace above the first tier. Abseil descent.

72 Toll Gate East 200m II
The right-hand of the prominent gullies bordering the steepest part of the backwall, and the deeper of the two.

BIDEAN TOLL A'MHUIC
On the south-east flank of the small top Bidean Toll a' Mhuic, just west of Stuc a' Choire Dhuibh Bhig, are two obvious gullies.

73 Gully 1A 180m IV   (1979)
The westerly of the two obvious gullies, with a dog-leg to the right at mid-height. Innocuous looking, but concentrated difficulties in the first 60m when not banked out!

74 Hidden Buttress 160m II/III   (1985)
Climb the buttress left of Gully 1A, following a shallow depression over numerous icy steps.

75 Gully 2A 180m III   (1963)
The right-hand of the two prominent gullies usually has one long steep ice pitch low down.

   The terraced buttress right of Gully 2A maintains its height circling Stuc a' Choire Dhuibh Bhig, until it reaches a wide easy gully broadening at the top. Right of this again, the crag shortens towards Stringless Gully and Triceratops.

76 Snow White 200m III/IV   (1987)
The major icefall between Gully 2A and the easy gully to the right. Starting from the lowest tier, the icefall widens and steepens at mid-height. It is clearly visible from the National Trust car park.

BEINN EIGHE

1010m   (Map Ref 952 612)

COIRE MHIC FHEARCHAIR   *(Map Ref 945 605)*

Coire Mhic Fhearchair, on the north side of Beinn Eighe, is one of the finest corries in Scotland and is justly famous for its magnificent triple buttresses. Secluded from the road by a relatively long approach, they dominate the lonely corrie and offer routes of great length and character. Some of the climbs here, both summer and winter, compare with the best available anywhere in Britain.

In winter the corrie is a paradise for modern-style mixed climbing, and comes into condition very quickly. The steep blocky quartzite provides good axe placements, reliable protection and sensational lines. There is less reliance on frozen turf than, for example, in the Cairngorms, and the corrie usually holds more snow than one might imagine from the view from the car park. Good ice conditions are rarer, but the easier gullies of Sail Mhor fill readily. When in condition, two of the most spectacular ice routes in Scotland are to be found in the corrie.

Access

The best approach is to follow the well-made Coire Dubh Mor track between Liathach and Beinn Eighe starting from the National Trust car park in Glen Torridon (Map Ref 959 569). Fork right at a cairn about 2km beyond some stepping stones and follow a path contouring below Sail Mhor and rising gradually to the lip of the corrie. This takes about 2 hours and a further 30-40 minutes to the foot of the Triple Buttresses. For the more technical routes on the upper walls (Far East Wall, Eastern Ramparts, Central and West Central Walls), an approach over the top is quicker and rucksacs can be left at the top. This is not recommended for first-time visitors as the panorama of the cliff from the loch is not to be missed.

There are several variations on the high-level approach according to season and snow conditions. In winter the preferred approach is to follow the Coire Dubh Mor path for about 2km until it starts to flatten out, then go up the hillside on the right until a ramp cuts off left to reach the col west of Spidean Coire nan Clach. This slope also provides a convenient means of descent in winter, but in summer it is filled with scree so a variant further right (both in ascent and descent) may be better. This variant, possibly slightly quicker, starts at the ruin on the right of the Coire Dubh burn and follows a narrow path. When this peters out, climb straight up the blunt grassy nose that falls south from Spidean Coire nan Clach to reach the main ridge.

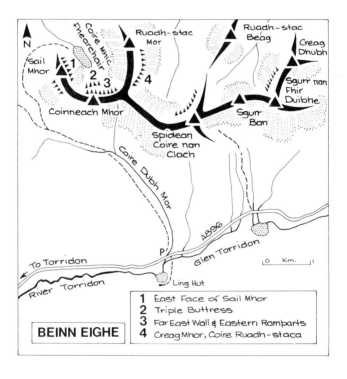

1 East Face of Sail Mhor
2 Triple Buttress
3 Far East Wall & Eastern Ramparts
4 Creag Mhor, Coire Ruadh-staca

BEINN EIGHE

These approaches meet at the col between Spidean Coire nan Clach and Coinneach Mhor. The ridge is then followed to the east cairn of Coinneach Mhor, then descended to the col leading to Ruadh-stac Mor. From here, descend the gully into the corrie (scree or easy snow). After a climb on the Eastern Ramparts or the Far East Wall, it is possible to descend in two abseils if a second climb is contemplated.

For climbs on the West Central Wall it is quicker (especially in summer) to leave the Coire Dubh Mor path later and climb steep ground right of the big gully on Coinneach Mhor's south-west slope, then follow the same line to the west cairn of Coinneach Mhor. This is virtually at the top of West Buttress, and routes can be approached by abseil after spying the line from a viewpoint near the top of Central Buttress. In winter or in mist, descend into the corrie west of West Buttress via the col leading to Sail Mhor.

Topography and Character

Seen from Loch Coire Mhic Fhearchair, the wall in the top left of the corrie is the Far East Wall. To its right is Far East Gully and then the steep left flank of the East Buttress, known as the Eastern Ramparts. Because the crests of the Triple Buttresses incline to the west, each buttress has an extensive left wall of steep quartzite facing north-east and a much narrower right wall tucked into the flanking gully. The left walls of Central Buttress and West Buttress are known as Central Wall and West Central Wall respectively, and the gullies have the obvious nomenclature East Central Gully, West Central Gully and Far West Gully.

The buttresses are composed of three tiers, the upper tiers of quartzite standing on a plinth of sandstone. The terrace above the sandstone tier, Broad Terrace, rises from left to right, so that the sandstone of the West Buttress offers much longer and better climbs than that of the East. Two further fault lines cross the buttresses. The middle fault starts on the left at the base of the Eastern Ramparts proper, continues across the top of the lower quartzite tier of East Buttress and marks the level where more continuous climbing on the left walls of Central and West buttresses begins. The highest fault is the line of the Upper Girdle, a sensational 700m climb across all three buttresses. It crosses the Eastern Ramparts about one third of the way up and on the crests of the Central and West buttresses it marks the level where the steep climbing on the final towers begins.

Although the Far East Wall and the steep left walls of the Triple Buttresses offer good lines, the nature of the climbing on the crests of the buttresses is such that numerous variations are possible, different climbs on successive tiers being easily combined. In summer both the quartzite and the sandstone are treacherous when wet and the cliffs do not dry quickly. Vegetation on the sandstone and big loose blocks on the quartzite are further problems that will be encountered. Lest this should sound discouraging, it should be added that the climbing is very satisfying and the situations are outstanding. On the quartzite very steep walls may sometimes be climbed with surprising ease using big, flat holds. Some of these climbs must be amongst the best and most sensational in Scotland. The sandstone climbing is more technical and can be deceptively hard at times.

FAR EAST WALL
Although somewhat slow to dry, this wall has some excellent routes on sensationally steep quartzite. Descent at either side is feasible, though the left-hand scree gully from the col below Ruadh-stac Mor is more convenient. The main wall catches the sun in the afternoon and evening, consequently drying out faster than much of the Eastern Ramparts which get the sun only in the morning.

1   Nightcap Groove   45m   HVS 5b   (1980)
Climb the short prominent groove on the extreme left of the wall.

2   Morning Wall   60m   VS 4c   (1983)
This route climbs the little grey wall between Nightcap Groove and Sidewinder. Start in an easy broken groove up and left of Sidewinder.
1. 40m Scramble up the groove, then continue straight up to reach the right-hand end of a grass ledge. Step round right, go up a crack and back up left to belay on a ledge above a square-cut overhang.
2. 20m Climb above the ledge, traverse left into a short corner, then go up and slightly right to a bulge. Mantleshelf over this and continue to the next terrace and easy ground above.

3   Sidewinder   90m   Severe   (1966)
This route takes the obvious line of weakness slanting slightly right in the left end of the cliff. Start 6m left of the left end of the grass terrace that runs along under the steep grey wall. Climb a fault into a niche, then up to a grass platform. Continue straight up by steep walls and grooves to the foot of a right-slanting crack and follow this to its end. Step left and follow a fault over some dubious rock to the top.

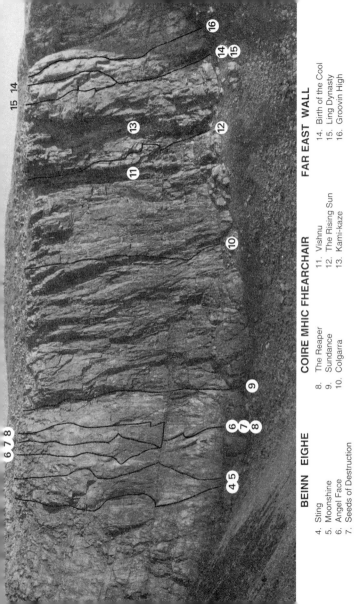

BEINN EIGHE

4. Sting
5. Moonshine
6. Angel Face
7. Seeds of Destruction

COIRE MHIC FHEARCHAIR

8. The Reaper
9. Sundance
10. Colgarra

11. Vishnu
12. The Rising Sun
13. Kami-kaze

FAR EAST WALL

14. Birth of the Cool
15. Ling Dynasty
16. Groovin High

3a   Glow Worm 80m V   (1990)
A winter ascent of a line based on Sidewinder, but taking a parallel line
below the right-slanting crack to belay near Sting, then crossing
Sidewinder to finish on its left.

On the left side of the Far East Wall is an impressively compact,
steep grey wall with a white-streaked bulging nose towards its left side.
Just left of the nose is a shallow overhanging groove, the line of
Moonshine. Left again the wall is bounded by a much more prominent
groove, with the first belay of Sting at its foot. Three routes climb the
main wall between the nose and the right-bounding big corner of
Sundance. The three have a common start, reaching the horizontal
fault by a fine left-slanting corner. Thereafter, The Reaper takes a
crackline on the right, Seeds of Destruction goes directly up, and Angel
Face goes diagonally left above the bulging nose.

4   Sting 90m HVS *   (1974)
This takes a prominent crack on the left side of the steep grey wall that
lies to the right of Sidewinder. Start a few metres right of the end of
the grass terrace running under the grey wall.
1. 40m 4b Climb an obvious left-trending groove to a grass ledge,
traverse right and gain a niche at the base of the prominent groove.
2. 15m 5a Step off a large flake on the left and follow a steep crack
to a peg runner. Move left to ledges.
3. 35m 4c Climb a short wall and a bulge, then up the prominent
hanging chimney to easy ground.

5   Moonshine 95m E4 ***   (1988)
The main pitch takes the shallow overhanging groove left of the
bulging nose of the buttress. Sustained technical climbing. Start on
the long grassy ledge under the buttress, about 10 metres from the
left end, by a small rock scar.
1. 25m 5b Go straight up the wall, then move right into a flake line
and follow this to belay by the horizontal break.
2. 35m 6a Go diagonally left to gain the base of the groove. Climb the
groove with increasing difficulty to a foothold on the left arete. Climb
straight up until level with a huge overhang on the left, then move right
and up to a ledge.
3. 35m 5b Climb the short awkward corner above, then move left and
up a long easy wall to finish.

6   Angel Face   95m   E2 ***   (1988)
A highly recommended route taking a sensational and improbable line above the bulging nose of the wall. Protection is good apart from bold moves to gain the tiny ramp on pitch 2. Take plenty of RPs. Start at the left end of a long flake which is embedded against the right side of the lower wall on the long grass terrace.
1. 15m 5a Climb a narrow ramp leftwards, move right into a shallow groove and climb it to a grass ledge at the base of a bigger groove on the right.
2. 35m 5c Take the left-leaning groove to the horizontal ledge. Traverse left about 5m along the fault to a small pedestal. Climb the wall above, then move left to gain a tiny ramp. Up this to a crack, then make a long step left into the base of a thinner crack. Climb the crack to a small roof. Traverse delicately left under the roof to the edge of nowhere, then return unexpectedly right to a belay above the right end of the ledge.
3. 45m 5b Climb the crack, and when it becomes unfriendly move slightly right and up to a large flake-ledge. Go on up the wall above to a smaller flake-ledge. Traverse left to a large block. Now trend rightwards across slabbier ground to a steep blocky finish.

7   Seeds of Destruction   95m   E3 ***   (1988)
A superb route with very sustained climbing up the wall left of The Reaper. A double set of medium-sized RPs is required for pitch 2. Start as for The Reaper and Angel Face, at a large detached flake.
1. 15m 5a As for Angel Face.
2. 20m 5c Climb the left-leaning groove to the horizontal fault and traverse left to the pedestal of Angel Face. Move right past a poor peg runner and pull over a bulge into a shallow corner. Belay on the right under a smooth groove.
3. 30m 5c Climb the groove to a big ledge on the right. Step down and traverse left until a left-facing corner can be gained. Climb the corner to the right end of the large flake-ledge of Angel Face. Climb the wall above to the next ledge.
4. 30m 5c Go up to a small rock scar, then steeply up and left to a rest at a horizontal break. Traverse right, then go up into a curving groove on the right. Above this go straight up steep blocky ground to finish.

8 The Reaper 95m E2 **   (1980)
The original route on this wall takes a bold line up the vertical crack towards the right side. Its first two pitches up to the horizontal fault were subsequently used by Angel Face and Seeds of Destruction.
1. 15m 5a As for Angel Face.
2. 25m 5c Climb the left-leaning groove to reach the prominent horizontal fault (as for Angel Face). Traverse right until below the left side of the large recess above. Climb steeply to reach a crack (which is not visible from the fault) in the left side of the recess. Climb the crack and belay in a niche.
3. 25m 5b Continue up the crack to a ledge on the left.
4. 30m 5a Go up right into a shallow corner, move further right then zigzag to finish up an obvious chimney.

9 Sundance 95m E1 *   (1974)
To the right of the grey wall is an obvious steep corner-crack cutting through several overhangs in the upper part of the crag. Start directly beneath.
1. 25m Climb up steep but grassy rocks to the horizontal fault.
2. 25m 5b Climb a crack in a wall over a bulge and up to a bigger bulge. Enter a hanging chimney which leads to a good ledge.
3. 20m 5a Climb the wall on the left to the next overhang which is climbed on good holds.
4. 25m 5a The final overhang is turned via a grass ledge on the impending right wall. Continue up mossy walls to the top.

9a Meccano 95m E3 **   (1992)
A fine sustained route which climbs a slabby ramp on the wall left of the big corner of Colgarra. Pitch 3 was led with a peg for aid, but seconded free.
1. 20m 4c Colgarra, pitch 1.
2. 25m 5b Step up and traverse 6m left to a left-slanting left-facing shallow corner, then climb this to the horizontal fault. Hand traverse right then pull up to a short corner. Climb the corner, and another above, then use an *in situ* sling to gain a slab (6a if climbed free). Belay just on the left, at the base of the ramp.
3. 50m 5c Climb the ramp to its top, then move right and follow a series of shallow grooves (left of the corner of Rudolf) to the top.

9b Rudolf 95m E2   (1992)
This takes the big left-facing corner up which Colgarra starts; it is slow
to dry and vegetated at the top. Start immediately left of the slit cave
of Colgarra.
1. 25m 5a Climb a shallow crack line, then take a direct line up the
wall (touching Colgarra), then a steep left-leaning corner to the horizontal fault. Belay at the base of a groove which leads up to the big
groove.
2. 25m 5c Climb the groove to a roof, then move left to a small ledge.
3. 45m 5b Climb up on the right, then move into the main corner.
Follow this to the top.

10 Colgarra 105m E3 ***   (1976)
This very steep route goes up the centre of the cliff, starting at a deep
slit cave. In its upper reaches it takes a hanging chimney visible from
below immediately right of a big left-curving corner. Another route of
great character.
1. 20m 4c Climb the left side of the cave and up diagonally left to a
grass ledge.
2. 20m 5b Traverse right beyond the line of the groove of Rudolf, then
go up past the horizontal fault and pull into the main corner. Follow
this to a step right and belay at a large jammed flake.
3. 10m 5a From just above the belay swing right onto the steep wall
and go up a flake crack to a smaller flake.
4. 20m 6a Climb the thin groove above to reach good holds leading
up and left into the hanging chimney, which is climbed to a grass ledge.
5. 35m 5b Climb up and slightly left to a small overhang, over this and
follow a crack (not the ramp on the left) to easy ground.

10a King of the Swingers 95m E3 **   (1992)
A route up the big corners left of Vishnu. It was led free, but a short
pendulum move reduces the grade to a consistent E1.
1. 25m 4b Climb unpleasantly to the base of the big corner left of
Vishnu, which starts at the level of the horizontal fault.
2. 20m 6b Climb the corner to a roof. Place high runners and one out
left in a crack through the roof, then traverse just below a small overlap
3m below (or pendulum, which reduces the grade to 5b) to gain a crack
which leads to a ledge below another big corner.
3. 50m 5a Climb the corner, then move left below an overhang to a
ledge. Climb a vegetated groove and finish up the rib on the right.

11 Vishnu   105m   VI ***   (1988)
A fierce winter route up the major fault line left of The Rising Son.
Protection is generally poor.
1. 15m Starting on the right, an introductory pitch leads up left to a
belay below the initial groove.
2. 20m Climb the groove on deceptively steep ice to a belay in a deep
recess below big icicles.
3. 20m An overhanging chimney leads out right to a small ledge from
where a mixed line up an overhanging groove leads to another small
ledge and good belay.
4. 50m Climb the vertical corner above until the ice can be regained
above its steepest section. Now a deep gully leads over two steep
sections to easier ground and the final snow slopes.

12 The Rising Son   100m   E2 **   (1986)
Start at the recess of Kami-kaze.
1. 25m 4c Climb up and left to belay on a grass ledge.
2. 30m 5b From the right end of the ledge go right and up over a bulge
(loose block) to a position immediately under a line of overhangs (seen
from below). Traverse left under the overhangs for about 5m, then go
up steeply for about 10m until able to make a delicate move left to a
small stance below an overhung niche.
3. 15m 5b Climb through the niche and past a ledge to belay.
4. 30m 4c Continue trending slightly left to gain a major fault which
leads to the top.

13 Kami-kaze   100m   VS **   (1966)
This follows the big fault line on the left of the large protruding buttress
which forms the right-hand section of the cliff. Start at a damp,
overhung recess about 30 metres left of a deep slit cave.
1. 30m Climb up the recess until it is possible to traverse right to a
shallow groove. Go up this, then right to belay below a chimney crack
in the obvious fault line.
2. 25m Climb the chimney to belay in the base of a deeper wider
chimney.
3. 25m Climb this overhanging chimney until it becomes a cave under
the huge beak. Traverse sensationally out left and up a groove to
easier ground.
4. 20m Finish up the groove above.

Winter: V/VI **   (1988)
Outrageous situations, but highly amenable rock, make this one of the best mixed climbs in the area. Chimneying features prominently, so sacks should not be carried. Follow the summer line.

14 Birth of the Cool   100m E1 *   (1976)
To the right of Kami-kaze the steep grey pillar is cleft by an obvious chimney line in the lower part. The climb follows this line then breaks right through a belt of overhangs and finishes up a prominent corner. Start at the wet slit cave at the base of the chimney.
1. 25m 4c Climb loose rock on the left side of the cave.
2. 15m 5a Continue up the steep chimney-crack to a ledge.
3. 15m 5b Climb a steep crack and the wall on the right to a good ledge.
4. 20m 5b Go right along the ledge, climb a narrowing groove and exit to the right with difficulty.
5. 25m 4b Climb the corner to the top.

15 Ling Dynasty   110m E5 **   (1987)
This route starts up Birth of the Cool and continues straight up a magnificent crack and through the big roof above. Follow Birth of the Cool for three pitches to the ledge where it goes right.
4. 25m 6b Step left into the crack and climb it to a roof. Pull out rightwards into the continuation of the crack and climb it to the big roof (very sustained). Traverse right to a belay (which is more comfortable than it looks) at the right end of the roof.
5. 15m 6a Return left and climb the wide crack in the roof. Go leftwards up the thin ramp above to belay.
6. 15m 4c Move right and up a corner to the top.

16 Groovin' High   90m E1 ***   (1973)
A superb route on the right side of the clean grey pillar. Start 6 metres right of the slit cave of Birth of the Cool.
1. 30m 4c Climb short walls and corners to a large ledge.
2. and 3. 60m At the left end of the ledge climb a very steep corner (5a), then move right (5b) and continue in steep grooves all the way to the top.

17 Sumo 85m E2 *   (1987)
This takes the vertical crack line and wall just right of Groovin' High,
with an excellent crux pitch. Start 2 metres right of Groovin' High.
1. 30m 4c Climb corners and short walls to the large ledge 3m right
of Groovin' High. Crawl right to belay.
2. 30m 5c Climb a steep corner, then the crack line to enter a groove
below a roof. Move left to good holds and re-enter the groove beside
the roof. A strenuous bulge leads to a belay.
3. 25m 5a Take the shallow groove above to horizontal cracks.
Traverse right into a corner, climb it and return diagonally left until
above the belay at a small roof. Finish rightwards up a slight ramp and
back left on big holds to the top.

17a Karaoke Wall 45m HVS   (1992)
Right of the pillar of Groovin' High is a gully, then a shorter wall which
tapers off rightwards. This route takes the obvious line just right of the
gully.
1. 20m 5a Climb the crack, which gradually increases in width, to a
ledge at its top.
2. 25m 4b Continue in the same line up the groove above.

THE EASTERN RAMPARTS

This is the left flanking wall of the East Buttress. It is long and complex
and the climbs are not easy to find on first aquaintance. The ledge of
the Upper Girdle runs across it at about one third height, except at the
left where the lower section is much shorter; eventually the ledge runs
into the hillside. This point, and the big corner of Claustrophobic Corner
above are good location features. Also useful is the initial right-facing
corner of Eastern Promise, about 35 metres right of the Upper Girdle
start. The Pale Diedre, a left-facing corner at the right boundary of pale
rock above the Upper Girdle, is a prominent feature in the centre of
the face. At the base of the diedre a grassy shelf, Bottom Shelf, runs
rightwards above a small lower tier of quartzite. This is the start of the
middle fault of the Triple Buttresses. The best descent is down the
easy gully left of the Far East Wall.

18a The Trundler 45m HVS 5a   (1992)
Start beside Cornice Groove, on the left. Climb an easy corner, then
move left into a second corner and follow this to roofs. Pull out right
then climb fine cracks in the wall left of Cornice Groove to finish.

18 Cornice Groove 50m VS   (1969)
At the left end of the cliff, just before it falls back towards Far East Gully, there is a slim V-groove with an overhang at 30m.
1. 35m 5a Climb the groove turning the overhang on the left.
2. 15m Continue more easily to the top.

19 Corniced Arete 55m VS   (1980)
1. 25m 4c Start as for Cornice Groove, but climb the arete on the right for 10m. Make a short traverse right and continue up and right to a good stance below and just right of a small roof.
2. 30m 4c Climb the crack on the left side of the roof and go straight up to a larger roof composed of huge blocks. Climb this on large jugs to finish.

19a The Modern Idiot 55m E1   (1992)
Between Corniced Arete and Olympus is an arch of roofs low down. Start below its left end.
1. 25m 5b Go diagonally right and pull through the roof at the second small corner from the right end. Go straight up cracks, then traverse 2m left and belay as for Corniced Arete.
2. 30m 5b Climb the right-slanting corner above until forced to traverse right below an overhang. Pass it on the right, then finish straight up.

20 Olympus 70m HVS   (1980)
This takes a line up the middle of the imposing wall right of Corniced Arete making for a vague depression about three-quarters of the way up the cliff. Start near the beginning of the Upper Girdle just left of a large right-facing corner (Claustrophobic Corner).
1. 4c Move right and back left above the initial roofs to reach ledges. Go left onto pale rock, then climb up and right to reach a small flakey ledge below a steepening in the wall.
2. 4b Climb the wall and a shallow corner on the right before swinging up left onto a ledge beneath an obvious 6m flake crack. Climb the crack, move 3m right and finish up the wall.

21 Claustrophobic Corner 70m E1   (1988)
Scramble up to start below the large right-facing corner which lies above the start of The Upper Girdle.
1. 35m 5a Climb up onto a pedestal in the corner proper. Climb the corner for about 5m to an overhang. Make bold moves out across the

BEINN EIGHE

21. Claustrophobic
22. The Ho Chi Min Trail
23. Heavy Flak
24. Turkish Delight

25. Eastern Promise
27. Pale Rider
28. Paleface Wall
29. The Pale Diedre

EASTERN RAMPARTS

Tainted Galahad
Rampage
Samurai
Shang-High

36. Fear of the Dark
37. The Tower of Darkness
38. Fairytale Groove
UG Upper Girdle

left wall and pull into a subsidiary corner. Climb this to regain the main corner. Traverse left and climb the left rib of the corner to a ledge.
2. 35m 5b Go diagonally right and break through the band of over-hangs at a jutting block on the right. Climb the wall above slightly leftwards.

22   The Ho Chi Min Trail   70m   E2 *   (1988)
A good route with a sensational first pitch. Scramble up to start in the centre of a usually wet recess right of Claustrophobic Corner.
1. 35m 5c Climb the bulging wall on good holds, then move right into the right corner of the recess. Climb this to the roof and pull over using an unusual wedged block (crux). Traverse left by a flake crack which bends upwards into a shallow groove. Go up the groove until a short left traverse leads to a tiny square belay ledge.
2. 35m 5b Return to the groove and climb it steeply until it peters out under the roofs. Go diagonally right under the roofs and pass them at their end. Climb the wall above to an easier groove leading to a short corner and roof, passed on the right.

23   Heavy Flak   80m   E1 *   (1978)
Scramble up easy ground for 10m to belay at the right side of the wet recess.
1. 20m 5a Step right and up, then traverse left to a vertical crack which is climbed to a belay in a recess.
2. 10m Climb up the fault to belay behind the huge flake.
3. 20m 5b Step left and climb the groove to belay under a roof on the left.
4. 30m 5a Traverse right for 5m and climb large flakes leftwards until a groove leads to the top.

24   Turkish Delight   95m   E3 **   (1987)
This takes a crack line up the vague buttress between Heavy Flak and a big left-facing roofed corner system on the right. Sustained and well protected. Start below the right end of a short ledge below the Upper Girdle.
1. 35m 4c Climb a shallow corner to the ledge. Continue slightly rightwards to the Upper Girdle. Climb onto big blocks under the roofed fault, then traverse left to a block under a shallow crack line just left of the more obvious right-facing double roofed corner of Feast of the East.

2. 25m 5c Climb the crack, which bends right over a bulge, then immediately move left up the wall away from the fault and up to a block belay below a thin crack.
3. 10m 5c Climb the crack to an awkward belay in a red corner.
4. 25m 5b Climb the overhanging crack above, then go straight up to finish at the left end of the fault.

24a Feast of the East 90m E1 * (1992)
This takes the diagonal crack line which cuts through the prominent left-facing roofed corner system. Start about 8 metres left of the obvious corner of Eastern Promise.
1. 30m 5a Climb a shallow corner, go right and left to pass a roof, then continue to the Upper Girdle. Belay at a huge block below the roof at the base of the corner system.
2. 15m 5c Climb onto the block, then go up the clean-cut corner with two overhangs (strenuous but well protected) to a small ledge.
3. 25m 5b Continue in the same line, now a wide crack in places, passing through the corner system.
4. 20m 4c Go up left to a big ledge, pull out left up an overhanging wall then finish easily above.

25 Eastern Promise 95m VS (1969)
About 35 metres right of the wet recess there is a clean, pale, right-facing corner in the lower tier. Start below this.
1. 30m 4b Climb the corner to mid-height, traverse left and continue up the wall to belay on the Upper Girdle.
2. 25m 4c There is a huge roof some 15m above. Climb up to its right, then step left to gain and climb a narrow chimney to a ledge and block belay.
3. 40m 4c Climb the steep wall and grooves above to the top.
Winter: V ** (1991)
Follow the summer line, except pass the roof of pitch 2 on its left. Intimidatingly steep, but co-operative and well protected.

26 Rampart Wall 115m HVS (1969)
Below and a little to the left of the pale diedre which features prominently in the middle of the upper cliff there is a left-facing corner in the lower tier (taken by Pale Rider). This is some 50 metres right of Eastern Promise. Start below this corner, about 5 metres left of the start of Bottom Shelf. The climb takes a slanting leftwards line from this point, passing some prominent square-cut overhangs at half-height.

1. 25m 4c Start up a small rectangular grey rib and climb trending left for 20m to a bulge. Move right and back up left over a flake to a belay ledge level with the base of the left-facing corner of Pale Rider.
2. 20m 4c Climb a flake crack for 6m, then traverse left into the next crack. Go up to a pinnacle belay on the Upper Girdle just left of a large shallow cave.
3. 40m 5a Climb a bulging crack to the top of a pointed pinnacle. Climb a large hanging block, then move diagonally left across a slab and follow a groove to a belay.
4. 30m 4c Climb a narrow slab on the right to a ledge and continue up short walls to the top.

27 Pale Rider   125m E1 *   (1986)
This takes the most prominent crack line on the wall left of The Pale Diedre. The crack line is characterised by two projecting blocks just at the point where its angle eases. Start below a left-facing corner, as for Rampart Wall.
1. 45m 4c Climb directly up to the base of the corner. Immediate entry is barred by a detached block, so go up left and enter above the block by delicate moves across pale rock. Follow the corner to the Upper Girdle and belay 10m further left just below and left of the crack line, about 20 metres left of The Pale Diedre.
2. 40m 5b Climb the crack to a small ledge beside the projecting blocks. Go easily up right to belay on a large ledge.
3. 30m 4c Return left to the original line, which has a blank section below a bulge. Instead go left round an edge and straight up the wall above to belay below a short chimney on the left.
4. 10m 5a Climb the wall on the right to finish.

28 Paleface Wall   100m E2 **   (1988)
A direct line up the pale wall left of Pale Diedre. Somewhat eliminate in nature, but a series of fine technical pitches on the best rock. Start at a 6m pinnacle below a rib, in whose left side is set the initial corner of Pale Rider.
1. 45m 5b Climb the front face of the pinnacle. Go up the wall above, then right and back left into a shallow corner on the crest of the rib. Go up this to The Upper Girdle.
2. 20m 5b Some 10 metres left of The Pale Diedre is a clean right facing corner. Gain this from the left and climb it to a ledge.
3. 10m 5c Climb the shallow corner above the right end of the ledges to jugs. Move left and go up to a ledge.

4. 15m 5c Climb the crack above the right end of the ledge. Move left round a roof and make a thin move left before going straight up to a big ledge.
5. 10m 5b Climb the horizontally faulted wall directly above (strenuous). A rattling flake is a crucial hold.

29 The Pale Diedre 105m E2 ***   (1980)
This is the obvious line in the middle of the upper part of the cliff. Start below and slightly left of this at the foot of a right-facing diedre. A most enjoyable climb.
1. 40m 5b Climb the diedre directly to overhangs at 24m. Move left then go up right to below the pale diedre.
2. 40m 5c Climb the diedre.
3. 25m Finish up the easy groove on the right.

30 Boggle 110m E1   (1961)
This devious line has an original description worthy of its creator. Start as for The Pale Diedre. "Zigzag to reach the left end of the ledge about 12m up. Climb a corner for 6m to a ledge on the left, then pull up into the pale smooth corner on the right. Climb this to below roofs, crawl left over loose blocks and go up and right to reach the Upper Girdle below the pale shallow diedre. Move right and climb by cracks, grooves, flakes, corners, hand-traverses and mantleshelves away up and right onto the crest of the pillar bounding the diedre. Step left and climb a corridor between roofs to top."

31 Tainted Galahad 110m E2 **   (1988)
A line between Boggle and Rampage, passing left of the square-cut roof.
1. 45m Start as for Rampage and belay on top of the large pinnacle.
2. 15m 5a Step right as for Rampage, then climb the obvious corner to belay 3m below the square roof.
3. 15m 5c Step down and left on to a foothold on the arete. Swing down under a bulge on the left, then surmount it (crux). Move left and climb a crack to a flake near Boggle. Return right and belay in a corner.
4. 35m 5a Climb the corner to just below its top. Traverse right onto easier ground. Go diagonally right, climb an awkward bulge by a large flake and finish by short corners and walls on the left. A more direct line will be better in dry conditions.

32   Rampage   110m   E2   (1977)
This climb lies to the right of Boggle and features a pale-coloured wall
in its upper half, just right of a prominent square-cut roof at mid-height.
Start 6 metres right of The Pale Diedre.
1. 45m 5a   Climb a right-slanting fault past a strenuous bulge to a
ledge below a large pinnacle. Climb the groove on the right of the
pinnacle and belay on the top, on the Upper Girdle.
2. 20m 4c   Climb up and right to the top of a second pinnacle.
3. 25m 5c Climb up for 6m to a small recess, step right, move up the
wall and into the groove on the right. Continue up this and over a bulge
to a good ledge on the right.
4. 20m 4b   Climb the chimney to the top.

33   Samurai   120m   HVS   (1966)
Although each pitch has some hardish moves, the climbing on this
route is not sustained. More direct variations are possible. Start
30 metres right of The Pale Diedre at the foot of a fault which slants
slightly to the right past a cave at 20m towards a square-cut notch in
the skyline.
1. 45m 5a   Climb the fault turning the cave on the left, and belay on
the Upper Girdle.
2. 40m 5a   Avoid the overhanging chimney ahead; instead traverse
left from the foot of the chimney into a vertical crack. Climb this for
12m, then move left round a nose and go up a steep wall to a ledge.
Continue up the fault to a stance at perched blocks.
3. 35m 5a Traverse right underneath a perched block for 6m and climb
the right-hand one of three faults; trend left into the middle fault to
finish at the square-cut notch.

About 15 metres right of Samurai there is a steep crack running up
the left side of a partly detached flake, starting about 6m up the cliff.
Some 3 metres to the left of this is a line of twin cracks which gives
the start of the next two climbs. There are a number of other possible
ways up the lower tier around here but this appears to be the easiest.

34   Simpleton   120m   HVS   (1980)
This somewhat unsatisfactory route follows a vague crack line just
right of Samurai. Notable features are a huge protruding block below
the Upper Girdle which is just to the right of the route; two overhangs
just above the Upper Girdle - a square overhang on the lower left and
a more triangular one on the upper right; and a steep corner with a

small roof just above the triangular overhang. Start below twin cracks 15 metres right of Samurai.

1. 45m Climb the crack line to a grassy ledge 10m below the Upper Girdle, then go diagonally right onto the huge flat-topped block and up to the Upper Girdle.

2, 3 and 4. 75m Climb between the two overhangs, passing just left of the triangular one and belay in the corner (4b). Continue up the deceptively leaning corner (5b, nut for aid at the roof). Finish by a steep, crack-seamed tower right of Samurai (4c).

35 Shang-High 120m HVS   (1976)
A feature of this route is the prominent chimney in the upper tier, some 25 metres right of Samurai. A line does in fact start from Bottom Shelf, but on the first ascent the lower chimney was avoided by climbing the wall on the left, approximately the same route subsequently taken by Simpleton.

1. 45m As for Simpleton.

2 and 3. 75m Climb the crack above for 6m then move right and up a steep wall until it is possible to move right to belay in the prominent chimney. Climb the chimney to a large slotted roof and turn this by a crack on the left. Continue up steep rock to the top.

Winter: V   (1992)
Steep and strenuous, but a good winter line. Follow the summer line, approximately, to the Upper Girdle (finishing by the left side of the flat-topped block - the best locating feature). From the Upper Girdle follow the chimney line direct, climbing through the slotted roof before moving left into another chimney.

At the right end of The Ramparts is a large white wall above The Upper Girdle. Between the white wall and the chimney line of Shang-High on the left is formed a grey tower, The Tower of Darkness. The white wall is bounded on either side by a corner system and above its right side is a huge detached flake, very obvious from the base of the cliff.

36 Fear of the Dark 100m E1   (1988)
Climbs the discontinuous corner system which bounds the white wall on its left. Start at the lower chimney of Shang-High.

1. 40m 5a Climb the right side of the chimney and the wide crack at the right side of the roof to belay on The Upper Girdle.

2. 10m Walk right and belay under the white wall.

3. 20m 4c A crack in the white rock above is the natural line but looks hard. Instead climb a reddish corner left of the two white areas and move left to belay as for The Tower of Darkness.
4. 40m 5b Traverse right round an arete. Climb the arete a metre or so, then move right into the main corner. Climb the corner to a roof. Traverse right, then go up the wall and over a bulge into a finishing groove (which is 10m left of the large detached flake and just right of a big roof).

37 The Tower of Darkness   100m   E4 *   (1988)
Climbs the impressive grey tower, with a fingery crux. Start just right of the lower chimney of Shang-High, which is a wide roofed fault, at a long thin crack line.
1. 45m 5b Climb the crack to a belay under the broad rib left of the pale wall.
2. 25m 5a Climb the rib to a block ledge under the tower. There is a reddish roofed groove above the left edge of the ledge.
3. 30m 6a Climb the thin crack above the right end of the ledge and go up to a roof. Step right under the roof and go up to another roof on the right edge of the tower. Finger traverse left, then go up the wall (crux) to an overhanging crack which leads to the top.

38 Fairytale Groove   100m   HVS *   (1988)
The route takes the big corner which bounds the right side of the white wall. Start below a narrow chimney right of the lower chimney of Shang-High (old cairn).
1. 45m 4b Climb straight up, passing the chimney on its right, to reach The Upper Girdle at the same place as Gnome Wall (which comes in from the right). Belay on the right, under the pale wall (as for Fear of the Dark).
2. 45m 5a Traverse right, then go up into a roofed recess. Pull out left from the recess into the main corner and follow it to easier ground.
3. 10m Climb a short wall to the easy crest of East Buttress.

39 Gnome Wall   150m   Hard Severe   (1959)
This route takes a line of weakness near the right-hand end of the Ramparts, and escapes onto the crest of East Buttress near a projecting gargoyle which is visible on the right skyline from the start of the route. The originator's description may indicate to connoisseurs of his routes what to expect. "Start just up and right from the right-hand end

of Bottom Shelf, where scrambling is required to continue rightwards. Work up leftwards to gain the Upper Girdle (45m). Traverse right along the Upper Girdle to where the ground above becomes more broken and belay in a recess (25m). Lunge onto a grassy ledge on the left. Climb a wet lichenous crack and a slab to reach a deep rock crevice on the right. An airy ledge to the right leads to an exposed 20m of climbing on excellent rock. Finish on easy rock just right of the gargoyle."

Winter: V   (1988)

The summer line gave interesting and unusual climbing to the belay below the gargoyle. A ferocious last pitch added a grade. There may be a less direct finish near the summer route on the right. Follow the summer line to belay below the gargoyle. Go up left to a pinnacle. Step off this and go up the wide crack immediately left of the gargoyle (30m). Continue to easy ground.

EAST BUTTRESS, SANDSTONE TIER

The original route up the buttress avoided most of the difficulties of the sandstone tier on the left and this may still be the preferred option in winter if time is short or conditions lean. Two summer routes on this tier and one winter route are described, but several alternatives are possible, both summer and winter, particularly on the left.

40 The Chimney 65m V   (1986)

This is the conspicuous chimney near the right end of the sandstone tier. It has been climbed in summer (Very Difficult) but is wet and loose. In winter it gives an excellent start to the buttress.

1. 25m Climb the steep chimney to a belay where the angle appears to ease and the chimney opens out to form a corner above.
2. 35m Continue directly up the corner till a short ramp can be followed to a flake. Move over this and up to belay at a short corner below the terrace, a few metres left of the chimney line.
3. 5m Climb the short corner to Broad Terrace.

41 Mango 70m VS   (1977)

Start 12 metres left of The Chimney at a small overhang.

1. 45m Climb up to a groove passing a loose block. Move right to a groove on the right, swing left and up to a belay ledge.
2. 25m Continue up rightwards to easier ground.

42 Bloodstone Start 210m   Mild Severe   (1972)
Start midway between The Chimney and East Central Gully. Gain a
ledge below a short, wet overhanging chimney. Go right round a rib
and back left up towards a fault, and then a steep crack, to enter a
recess with twin rock spikes above. Pass the spikes and go up right
towards East Central Gully, then back left more easily to Broad
Terrace.

EAST BUTTRESS, QUARTZITE TIER

43 The Gash 60m   Severe   (1962)
This is the bizarre, deeply-cleft chimney which runs up left from Broad
Terrace to end about 30m right of the start of Gnome Wall, to which it
makes a good introduction. Start on Broad Terrace just right of a 'bad
step'. Climb to a large dry cave, go through behind chockstones, and
finish up the clean rib on the left.

44 Ordinary Route 210m   Difficult **   (1907)
An enjoyable, classic climb straight up the crest of the buttress. Start
on Broad Terrace about 10m from its right end. This point may be
reached by traversing all the way along Broad Terrace from the left or
by climbing the sandstone tier by one of the routes described above.
Climb the steep face on good holds to a large ledge (30m). Continue
up an interesting and varied series of pitches to the top. Many
variations are possible.
Winter: III/IV **
The crest of the buttress may be followed, but if conditions are difficult
it may be preferable to avoid the initial steep section by climbing up
East Central Gully. Alternatively the steep icefall towards the left of the
lower tier may be used to give access to Broad Terrace. This is a good
grade IV.

45 East Central Gully IV *
This is not often climbed for its own sake but its lower part, which is
the crux and a fine pitch, may be used as an approach to the East
Buttress Ordinary Route or to the climbs on Central Wall. In summer
the gully is Severe and usually wet.

CENTRAL WALL

Central Wall is the name given to the north-east facing left flank of the upper part of Central Buttress. It is bounded on the left by East Central Gully and on the right by the crest of Central Buttress. The lower part of the wall is formed by what appears from below to be a tower about 45m high rising from East Central Gully at the level of Broad Terrace. The top of the 'Tower' is in fact a gently sloping terrace from which most of the summer climbs start. It can be reached most pleasantly in summer by climbing up the first 35m of East Buttress Ordinary Route and then traversing across East Central Gully.

In winter the easiest access is to traverse above the sandstone tier of East Buttress into East Central Gully and follow this until one can break out right onto the Tower (grade II). A more satisfying approach is to climb the first pitch of East Central Gully, then take the right fork between the Tower and Central Buttress, finally breaking out left onto the Tower (grade IV). The right fork can also be reached by the traverse across East Buttress if the initial chimney of East Central Gully is insufficiently iced. The winter climbs Pelican and Flight of the Condor naturally start up the right fork, and this is included in the length given.

46 East Central Ribs 105m Severe   (1954)
The climb follows the crest of three successive quartzite ribs, just right of East Central Gully. The ribs are steep and exposed and bordered on the right by a narrow cleft. Start in the cleft right of the first rib. Follow the cleft for a few metres then traverse left by a short, difficult overhang to the crest. Follow the crest for 25m and get to the right edge. Traverse onto the right flank and into a groove which leads up for 3m to a large ledge on the crest; continue up this for 15m to a narrow arete leading to the second rib. Start the second rib on the left and traverse with difficulty to the crest, which is followed to the top of the second rib (40m). The final rib is straight ahead. Start up an overhanging chimney on the left (6m), then a vertical wall to a ledge (9m) followed by easier rock to the top.

47 The Cool Cleft 120m IV *   (1983)
This takes the shallow curving fault immediately right of East Central Ribs. Climb an icy chimney for 30m. Continue up to a very steep icy section 12m high (crux). Follow the fault more easily to the top (70m). On the first ascent the crux section lacked ice and instead the rib on the left was climbed (IV), as for East Central Ribs.

48 Assegai 90m VS *   (1976)
Immediately right of East Central Ribs is a parallel rib, about 30m high,
and right again is a line of slanting and steep narrow slabs ending on
the right at a prominent corner. There is a big crack in the wall on the
right; start just left of it. Climb slabs to the horizontal fault of the Upper
Girdle, then a groove on the left to a good stance. Traverse left then
up, and cross to another stance. Climb straight up strenuously (crux)
then climb a loose block into an overhanging chimney and up to a
stance. Follow the chimney, then go right to a wall and a stance on
the edge. Finish up a wall of loose blocks.

49 East Wall 140m V *   (1989)
The route takes a big stepped corner system in the steep buttress
between Assegai and Fulmar Chimneys. The system starts at the foot
of an obvious vertical wide crack formed by a huge detached flake and
trends up right. The start of the route is just below and right of the wide
crack.
1. 30m Climb leftwards and follow a chimney just right of the back of
the corner system. At its top move right to a huge block belay below
vertical twin cracks.
2. 15m Climb the left-hand crack, but finish by the last moves of the
right crack.
3. 35m Take a short corner on the left with a jutting block. Move left,
then up to a squeeze chimney. Avoid this by a traverse left and
descend 10m into the main corner system. Follow this to a big ledge
on the left.
4. 25m Go more easily right and back left by a chimney to the crest.
5. 35m Easy ground to the top.
Summer: Severe   (1954)
This route was 'unidentifiable' in the last guide, but is thought to have
followed more or less the line of the winter route described above.

50 Fulmar Chimneys 90m Very Difficult *   (1970)
From the top of the Tower easy ground slopes up left. Go up this for
15m, then traverse 5m right to a small grass corner at the foot of a
deep-cut chimney. There is a flake embedded in the grass on the left.
Climb the chimney finishing to the right. Continue up a second chimney
and easy rock trending right to a nook below the final steep wall.
Traverse right past a curious triangular truncated block to the foot of
a steep, clean chimney and go up this to the top.

51   East Central Wall   180m   IV ***   (1981)
This is a winter version of Fulmar Chimneys, a good first excursion
away from the buttresses with a fine mountaineering atmosphere.
Climb East Central Gully through the sandstone, then take the right
fork between the Tower and Central Buttress. From the top of the gully
between the Tower and Central Buttress go up leftwards on broken
ground until about 10m below and right of a very prominent crack.
Traverse 5m right along an overhung ledge to the base of the chimney.
Climb this and a further right-slanting chimney to reach a triangular
bay with ice in the overhanging corner at its top. The ice is very steep
and may be avoided by climbing a shallow chimney to the right of the
bay which leads to easy ground.

52   Patey's Direct Route   105m   Hard Severe   (1957)
This is a steep and direct route up the right side of Central Wall, in the
line of the gully between the Tower and Central Buttress. Start where
this gully peters out, at a level a little below the top of the Tower and
under a shallow depression in the steep wall above. The route follows
a line of thin cracks on the left of the depression which continue after
mid-height as a V-groove with an overhang at the top. Climb the cracks
for 35m. A steep 10m wall then leads to an easier-angled wide chimney
with a flat 'card-table' on the right at mid-height. Avoid the start of the
V-groove by taking the crack on the left for 12m and then traversing
right. Continue up the groove and turn the top overhang on the left.
Winter: V   (1988)
Follow the summer line throughout.

53   Pelican   180m   Severe *   (1977)
To the right of Patey's Direct Route is a prominent, steep chimney-
crack line. This is climbed direct all the way.
Winter: 180m   V ***   (1987)
1. 45m Climb the gully to the right of the Tower (access to the Tower
is now on the left).
2. 25m Continue up the gully by a steep ice pitch to belay under a
prominent chimney with two sections.
3. 20m The first section of the chimney is very narrow and may be
climbed by a shallow corner on the right. The second section tapers
and forces an awkward, strenuous exit.
3. 35m Above is a large roof; avoid this by a ramp on the left, pulling
through the left end of the roof into an icy groove which leads to the
Upper Girdle. Climb the bulge above and go up a groove to a stance.

BEINN EIGHE

ER Eastern Ramparts	40. The Chimney	48. Assegai
BT Broad Terrace	44. Ordinary Route	49. East Wall
UG Upper Girdle	45. East Central Gully	50. Fulmar Chimne
T The Tower	47. The Cool Cleft	52. Patey's Direct

TRIPLE BUTTRESSES

4. 35m Continue up the groove (more like a shallow chimney) to a ledge. Move left into another groove system and up this to belay.
5. 20m Follow the groove to the top.

54 Condor Crack 75m Severe   (1986)
This lies on the wall between Pelican and Piggott's Route. Start on the terrace below the final tier of Central Buttress, well round to the east side.
1. 20m Scramble up easy rock until it steepens. Step up and go easily left along the line of the Upper Girdle to an awkward step down, then up. Climb over some blocks easily seen from the start.
2. 25m Muscle up the corner and step left then right into a crack line. Follow this to more blocks.
3. 30m Climb over the blocks and step right to a little slab which leads to a band of steeper rock. Pass this by a shallow chimney, then easier rock to the top.

55 Flight of the Condor 250m V/VI *   (1989)
The route takes a line up the right side of Central Wall, passing left of a big left-facing corner on the final tier. Start by traversing above the sandstone of East Buttress into East Central Gully and on to the base of the gully right of the Tower. Two short pitches in the gully lead to an easy ramp which goes out right towards the crest of Central Buttress. Climb straight up to the Upper Girdle. An obvious off-width flake crack can now be seen up on the left. Traverse left a short distance, then up a groove until a long step left gains the base of the crack. Climb the crack (hard, 30m). Climb the wall above, trending slightly right to a ledge. Traverse right, then descend to the right to gain the top of the big left-facing corner. Climb an easy chimney to blocky ground, (35m). Go diagonally left to a big pinnacle, then back right round an edge to a bay. The short chimney at the back leads to snow slopes.

CENTRAL BUTTRESS, SANDSTONE TIER

56a Central Reservation 70m HVS   (1992)
This climbs a set of slabs leading out left to the left edge of the tier. Start at the same point as Central Corner.
1. 25m 4b Move out left then up to the base of the first slab, which is climbed on its left side. The only belay is below the right-hand corner of the next steep slab.

2. 45m 4c Climb the corner, then the following slab by its left edge. Continue (unprotected) to the top.

56b Swinging in the Rain 70m HVS   (1992)
A good wee route up the face left of Central Corner.
1. 40m 5a Climb straight up into a left-facing corner about 5 metres left of Central Corner. Follow it to its end, then move left into a small corner (which is the continuation of a crack line from below).
2. 30m 4c Finish up the corner and the slabs above.

56 Central Corner 70m VS **   (1976)
Climb the very prominent diedre on the left flank of the tier in two pitches (4c, 4c). Sustained and recommended.

57 Puddock 70m HVS *   (1985)
This climbs the steep grooves just right of Central Corner. Start from a grass terrace and go up to belay below the grooves. Follow the left-hand groove to reach a good ledge below a short overhanging corner. Climb the corner and exit left to ledges. Continue more easily to Broad Terrace.

   On the front face of the sandstone tier is an obvious fault running diagonally up left. This marks the line of Piggott's Route. Below the grass ledge at the foot of this fault there is another grass terrace which runs almost all the way round the buttress just above the lowest rocks, and is reached most easily by scrambling up to the right. The next three routes start from this terrace.

58 Readymix 90m Severe   (1968)
This is the best way of starting up Central Buttress. Start on the grass terrace at the point where it is scree-covered for a short distance, about 15 metres left of the pinnacle-block of Piggott's Route.
1. 25m Climb 5m to the top of a small projecting rib, then up left onto a small slab to gain the foot of a groove. Climb to a small ledge at 12m, then more steeply to a large ledge.
2. 25m Regain the groove above by traversing right to avoid a bulge, then trend left to reach a good ledge and belay.
3. 40m The leftward trend continues up a short wall and then, by an exposed move, around a pillar of rocks, which is climbed. Finish up a steep wall.

59 Piggott's Route (sandstone tier) 90m   Difficult   (1922)
The obvious diagonal line running up from right to left. Start on the
grass terrace just above the lowest rocks, about one third of the way
from the right-hand end, where a pinnacle-block leans against the
face. Climb from the block to a terrace, move right and reach a black
cave clearly visible from below (30m). From the top of the cave follow
the grassy rake up left to Broad Terrace. The upper section of Piggott's
Route, up the quartzite tier, is described as route 62.
Winter: For a description of the entire normal winter route up Central
Buttress, see route 62.

60 Slab Route 80m   Difficult
An easy but pleasant route up the right-hand side of the tier. Many
variations are possible. Start at the right end of the grass terrace below
the face, where easy rocks lead up and round to the right. Climb the
easy rocks up right to the foot of a large slab leading slightly back left.
Climb the slab to easy ground. The finish is awkward if wet.

CENTRAL BUTTRESS, QUARTZITE TIER

Between Broad Terrace and the Upper Girdle the quartzite of Central
Buttress is rather broken, although it forms more continuous walls and
slabs further right. The first part, up to the line of the middle horizontal
fault, is somewhat steeper and is composed of blocks and short slabs
and walls; between the middle fault and the Upper Girdle it eases off
and can be climbed almost anywhere. Above the Upper Girdle the
buttress steepens considerably and appears quite formidable, but is
less daunting than it looks.
    Traditionally there are three summer lines: Parker's on the left,
Piggott's in the middle and Hamilton's on the right. The exact lines
followed by the first ascensionists cannot be determined in detail, so
only general directions are given. Most winter ascents appear to have
followed the same line, approximately that of Piggott's.

61 Parker's Route 180m   Very Difficult
This is a left-hand alternative to the quartzite tier of Central Buttress.
Start on Broad Terrace, not far from the top of Central Corner. Climb
by a series of blocks and cracks, trending slightly right, to the middle
horizontal fault. Continue on easy rock to the Upper Girdle. From the
base of the final tier, near the crest, climb slightly left for 20m on easy
rock to a stance below a steep 6m crack. Climb this and easier
chimneys above and continue to the top.

62 Piggott's Route 180m Mild Severe ** (1922)

Start from the highest point of the grass on Broad Terrace, in a bay just right of the vague ridge which separates the main face of the middle tier from the smaller north-east face to the left. This is just above the lower part of Piggott's Route. Climb up trending left to a stance in a corner (20m). Traverse left to the edge, round it, and up an exposed chimney on good holds. Go up easy ground to the foot of the final tier. Start this just right of a large detached block resting against the face. Climb an open groove and its upper continuation to a platform. Move left over a slab to a belay. Traverse below a nose and up to a spine of rock. Cross this to a mossy ledge. Climb a short, hard wall to the top.

Winter: V *** (1971)

As in summer there is considerable scope for variation on the middle tier and somewhat less on the final tier. The first part is a winter version of the sandstone tier of Piggot's Route (route 59).

1. 40m An initial pitch up short icy steps leads to the left-slanting diagonal line.

2. 50m Follow the diagonal line to Broad Terrace. Now move up to belay below a central corner line in the next tier.

3. 20m Move up left into the corner.

4. 30m Traverse left into a corner-chimney and climb this to a ledge. Move right, up a crack and then right to belay just below easy ground.

5. 60m Climb up easily to the foot of the final tower.

6. 20m Above is a left-facing corner and above this an obvious short narrow chimney with a crack just to its right. Gain the corner by first moving left into a groove, then up and right to the base of the corner. This leads to a belay below the narrow chimney.

7. 35m Climb the chimney with difficulty and continue up flakes on the right of an obvious crack. Step up left onto the wall and move up to a flake overlooking the crack on the left. Pull round into a groove above the crack and follow this to ledges and a belay on the right.

8. 40m Above is a corner and on its right more broken stepped ground on the edge. Move up and right to gain a ledge and then pull up onto easier ground which leads to the top.

63 Hamilton's Route 180m Severe ** (1936)

This is a right-hand alternative to the quartzite tier of Central Buttress, with better but harder climbing. Start on Broad Terrace, a good 30 metres right of Piggott's Route. Climb a crack for 20m to a corner and belay. Traverse right by a sensational movement and climb up the edge of the buttress by a series of steep corners linked by short traverses to the right. Go up a groove into the centre of the face and continue on easy ground to the base of the final tower. Start this right of centre at a large detached flake. Climb slabs up to the right on small holds until it is possible to go straight up. Continue up big open chimneys to the top, keeping always on the right side of the buttress.

64   Central Buttress, Right-Hand Finish   100m   IV   (1990)
This is an easier finish to the right of Hamilton's Route, which can also be taken as an easier summer finish.
1. 25m From the crest of the buttress below the final tier traverse right for 15m until it is possible to climb up right on turfy ledges and belay below a short wall on the right.
2. 25m Climb the short wall and continue rightwards until it is possible to go left onto easier ground.
3. 50m Go easily up into a short corner on the right and climb it awkwardly to the final crest.

65   West Central Gully   350m   VI ***   (1987)
The gully is easy except for a very steep 60m step sporting an ice-smeared overhanging chimney leading to steep, pure ice climbing. A very hard and fine climb. From the base of the step ascend the chimney forming the back of the gully and belay beneath a prominent overhang (25m). Climb into the groove-chimney on the left of the overhang, move up to another overhang and follow an ice-choked crack to small ledges on the left (20m). Take the mixed groove on the left to the overhang; step right onto icy smears and follow these to good, thick ice and easy ground 50m from the top (25m).

WEST BUTTRESS

The lowest tier of the West Buttress is easily the most formidable of the sandstone tiers on the triple buttresses, and contains some excellent climbs. The middle quartzite section is fairly broken on the crest and can be climbed almost anywhere, but the final tier rears up imposingly to provide situations as fine as any in the corrie. The steep left wall of the quartzite, rising from broken ground somewhat above the level of Broad Terrace also provides good climbs, of a similar but sterner character than Central Wall.

   As with Central Buttress, climbs on different tiers may be connected together at will, allowing numerous permutations. For the convenience of those who wish to follow a natural line throughout, the Ordinary

Route up the buttress and the winter direct are described first in their entirety. The climbs on the initial and final tiers are then described separately.

66 Ordinary Route 300m Severe   (1919)
Start near the extreme right of the buttress, close to Far West Gully. Climb an open scoop followed by an overhang to the right to a grass terrace. Go up to the right of a slight crack, traverse left across a corner to a slab and climb it to another grass ledge. Go slightly right and up a poorly defined groove to a sloping moss ledge. Climb the slab above working slightly left to reach Broad Terrace. The buttress is now quite easy-angled. Climb on the right of the buttress crest, with short walls and occasional interest, to the base of the final tower. This is charac- terised by a steep wall on the frontal face, sometimes referred to as a 'domino-shaped block'. Traverse right on scree ledges till near the edge where the buttress turns round to the right towards Far West Gully. Climb a line of weakness and traverse back left along ledges. Climb a deep chimney to the top of the 'domino-shaped block'. Continue more easily to the top.
Winter: III/IV **
The sandstone tier can be hard and it will usually be necessary to climb some way up Far West Gully. Get established on the buttress to the right of the steepest walls and follow the easiest practicable line to Broad Terrace. Climb up easier ground and short walls to the final tower. Follow the summer route to the top, the deep chimney giving some interesting climbing.

67 West Buttress Direttissima 345m VI ***   (1986)
This very direct winter line follows most of the large open corner of the summer route, Senior, on the lower tier. On the top tier it takes the left-hand finish. It is not often in condition, but when it is it provides a magnificent route. Traverse an initial shelf to start below the obvious corner line in the sandstone tier.
1. 30m Move up a short crack-groove to gain the corner, which leads to a narrow ledge. Step left to belay.
2. 20m Step back right and climb the corner direct via a steep crack with a difficult exit to a good belay.
3. 40m Move up the corner a little then right and up to gain the ledge system girdling the buttress; traverse this left to the frontal face. Belay below an obvious groove barred by a bulge, just past a narrowing of the ledge where a step has to be made over a loose block.

4. 40m   The way ahead looks difficult, but once the initial bulge is overcome the difficulties ease and the shallow groove leads to the crest of the buttress.

5. 115m Continue up the crest of the buttress, taking the easiest line to below the final tower.

6. 30m   The line taken is now by the left-hand variation finish. Climb a short wall, then another short wall with a thin crack in it; step left and continue to belay in a recess formed by a huge flake at the foot of the impressive final flake line.

7. 35m   Move up then left to gain the flake line which leads to a fine finish over the obvious projecting block.

8. 35m   Climb a short chimney and easy ground to the top.

WEST BUTTRESS, SANDSTONE TIER
The climbs are described from left to right.

68 Sideshow 80m HVS   (1976)
On the left side of the sandstone tier, overlooking West Central Gully, an obvious groove runs almost to the top of the tier. Start below and left of an obvious spike. Climb up and right past the spike into the groove, go up this to an overhang which is turned on the right and continue in the same groove to a ledge. Move up and right to a large rock ledge below a flared chimney. Climb the chimney to a grass ledge then take the rocks above to easy ground.

68a Cyclonic Westerly 90m E3 **   (1992)
A fine route at the upper limit of its grade, with a sustained balancy and unprotected section on perfect rock. It gives a three-star outing when combined with **Force Ten** (see page 360) on the quartzite tier. Start as for Junior.

1. 10m 4c Climb to the base of the Junior corner.

2. 25m 5c Move out left on juggy rock to the base of a shallow corner in Junior's left arete. Step left and climb the wall direct (crux) to a steep line of flakes, which lead to a good ledge.

3. 40m 5b Move out left under a roof onto the slabbier face. Trend right, then follow a left-slanting groove to a roof. Pull through this, then follow two more grooves (not far left of Junior) to a huge ledge.

4. 15m 4c Climb easily through the final tier.

Variation: E1   (1992)
 Instead of climbing the wall direct on pitch 2, go diagonally left across the face to belay near Sideshow (5a). Climb a short corner, then make

a long rightwards deviation to regain the direct route a few metres below the roof of pitch 3 (5b).

69 Junior 90m E1 **   (1976)
The straight steep corner midway between the big central corner and the left edge of the buttress. The lower section is usually wet.
1. 35m 5b From the lower grass ledge climb up to the corner and follow it directly to belay on a large ledge on the left.
2. 40m 5b Continue in the corner to a ledge on the left below an overhang. Step left and climb the steep wall into a groove. Follow the groove to a grass ledge terrace.
3. 15m Climb easily to the top of the sandstone tier.

70 Relayer 90m HVS †   (1976)
Start 15 metres right of Junior. Climb an easy groove to a ledge and belay. Follow the groove over a small bulge to a ledge, move up and right into a small niche and traverse right to another small niche. Climb up to a small overhang, traverse right, then go back up left to the foot of a small prominent corner. Climb a little way up the groove and go left along a ledge. Move up over a small bulge and right into a short corner; climb this and the rocks above to a grass ledge and finish up an obvious easy groove.

71 Senior 90m HVS *   (1976)
This is the big central corner in the sandstone tier, often wet. It is climbed directly throughout, taking the right-hand of two cracks at mid-height.

The slabs and walls right of Senior give excellent climbing. Two routes have been made here (VS, 90m), one of which takes a line about 30 metres right of the corner.

WEST BUTTRESS, QUARTZITE TIER

Above the sandstone the quartzite of the West Buttress is fairly broken on the crest, and not too steep, for some way until it rears up in a final imposing tier above the level of the Upper Girdle. West Central Wall is the left bounding wall of this tier, overlooking West Central Gully. It is very steep and impressive and contains some excellent climbs. Twilight Zone starts from the lowest steep rocks, but all the other summer routes start from the Second Terrace. This can be reached by two abseils down the line of Twilight Zone; the descent can be planned from the good view from the top of Central Buttress. To approach from below, traverse onto West Buttress from Far West Gully (above the sandstone) and climb the buttress easily until a steeper tier suggests a traverse left onto the face. Climb a short loose pitch (Very Difficult) to gain the Second Terrace.

71a Maelstrom   100m   V/VI   (1992)
This takes a left-facing corner system in the left side of West Central Wall, passing left of a big isolated roof near the top. The corner defines the left side of the big inset slab on pitch 2 of Earth, Wind and Fire. The climbing is very sustained, but protected with a large rack of rocks and thin pegs. Start in West Central Gully where it steepens, at approximately the height of the Girdle Traverse (Grade II to here).

Follow the Girdle right for about 10m to an icy groove. Climb this then move right along the next ledge, past a break, to a belay. Above the break is a chimney. Pull up left and enter the slightly overhanging chimney. Climb it and the subsequent corner for about 20m until a descent leftwards (high runner *in situ*) leads to small ledges and a belay. Climb up left into a parallel, often very icy, corner which passes left of the big roof. Follow this to the top.

71b Earth, Wind and Fire   90m   HVS   (1991)
Start towards the left end of the Second Terrace, left of the rockfall scar and left of a very mossy groove.
1. 30m 4b Pull through an initial overhang and go right until close to the vegetated groove. Return left under a smooth wall until a corner leads to a ledge below the Upper Girdle.
2. 25m 4c Go up to the Upper Girdle and break through the overhangs at their smallest point. Climb a big inset slab near its left arete.
3. 35m 4c Break out right to a ledge. Climb a shallow chimney, then go right to a blocky fault which leads to easy ground.

71c Shoot the Breeze   90m   E2 **   (1992)
A good route with sensational positions and a well protected crux. Start just right of the rockfall scar.
1. 30m 5a Climb up to and follow a corner crack which forms the right edge of the scar, then continue to a small ledge below the Upper Girdle.
2. 30m 5a Continue up the corner to the Girdle. Move leftwards through the capping overhangs at an obvious break. Go up about 5m,

then traverse left and climb a big arete which leads into the corner on the left. Belay where the corner slants right.

3. 30m 5b Regain the arete by a foot ledge and climb it into the top of the corner. Return to the arete, follow this to overhangs, then pull left into a short corner. Climb this with difficulty to easier, steep blocky ground which leads to the top.

71d Chop Suey 100m E1   (1992)
This follows a line of big grooves; it is dangerously loose in places. Start about 10 metres left of the pinnacle of Twilight Zone at the huge groove, the most prominent feature in this section of cliff (but partially hidden until one is below it).

1. 30m 5b Climb the groove to a ledge not far below the Upper Girdle.
2. 30m 5a Climb the right wall of the groove to the Upper Girdle, then follow the Girdle leftwards across the groove. Weave a line leftwards through overhangs to join the long upper groove.
3. 25m 5b Follow the groove to easier ground.
4. 15m 5a Climb a blocky step to the top.

72 Twilight Zone 180m E1 **   (1977)
This climbs the centre of West Central Wall, passing left of the large roofs near the top. Start in West Central Gully at the centre of a small buttress where the quartzite begins. Climb cracks and grooves to a terrace (45m). Go up an open corner to belay at a large pinnacle (15m). Climb the pinnacle and the groove behind until forced into a second groove which is followed to a belay on the Upper Girdle. Go right for 3m and climb grooves and steep slabs to a spike belay (20m). Move left and gain a groove leading to a large roof; climb this for 10m, then step left and climb a steep wall to belay at the left end of the roof. Climb the left arete to a corner and finish up this.

73 Wall of the Winds 115m E1 *   (1990)
This route is based on a continuous line of grooves 10 metres left of Mistral. Start midway between the initial corner of Mistral and the pinnacle of Twilight Zone.

1. 10m Climb an easy blocky groove.
2. 35m 5a Go up a continuation groove onto a pinnacle that looks like a flake from below, then up to the Upper Girdle.
3. 45m 5b The continuation is unattractive, so take a flake on the left which leads into a shallow groove. Climb this for about 8m. Traverse left to another groove which is followed to good runners. A short

descent allows a return traverse to the shallow groove. A right-trending line through the left of a roof system leads to a chimney not far left of the V-corner of Mistral.
4. 25m 4c Finish up the chimney.

74 Mistral 120m E1 *   (1976)
At the top right of West Central Wall is an obvious deep V-corner. The route leads fairly directly to the corner. Start at an obvious groove at the foot of the wall.
1. 20m 4b Climb the groove to a good ledge below a chimney.
2. 35m 5a Climb the chimney past a wedged flake and overhang. Continue up a steep crack moving right at the top to a stance on a ledge 10m below the Upper Girdle. (If wet, the chimney may be avoided by the wall on the right.)
3. 10m Continue up the crack to the Upper Girdle.
4. 30m 5b Climb a bulge and the steep wall above to a small block overhang (well seen from the foot of the climb). Step left onto the nose and climb steeply to enter the deep V-corner.
5. 25m 4c Climb the corner to the top.
Winter: VI ***   (1991)
Start up West Central Gully and, where it widens above the sandstone, break out right by a short ice pitch onto the base of the wall. Go out right and easily up the left side of West Buttress until a ledge leads back left to the start of Mistral (the second icy groove from the right). This is the start of the serious climbing.
1. 40m Climb the icy V-groove and the three-tiered overhanging chimney directly above. Traverse right and belay below another chimney.
2. 25m Climb the chimney (it has a wide crack in its right wall) to the Upper Girdle. Return left to belay directly above the previous pitch.
3. 30m Climb the crux (pitch 4) of Mistral.
4. 40m Traverse left and finish up the final chimney of Wall of the Winds.

75 Left-Hand Finish to West Buttress 60m Severe *   (1960)
This takes the left side of the steep frontal wall, or 'domino-shaped block' described in the Ordinary Route. From below the final tower climb a clean 9m wall strenuously on good holds. This leads to a recess on the left of the tower, whence an easy move left gives access to a flake crack slanting up right. Climb this, with a fine exposed finish behind an enormous projecting block. Climb the wall above to the top.

76   Direct Finish to West Buttress   60m   VS *   (1971)
On the right-hand side of the steep frontal wall is a clean-cut corner
topped by an overhang with a hole in it.
1. 35m Climb the corner to the overhang, passing a ledge on the right
at 25m. Climb the overhang through the hole to a big ledge on the
Ordinary Route.
2. 25m Climb the chimney of the Ordinary Route for 9m, then step
right below an overhang and traverse round to the foot of a crack in a
hanging corner. Climb this to another overhang and move left to finish.

77   Right-Hand Finish to West Buttress   35m   Very Difficult
From the base of the final tower follow the Ordinary Route right along
ledges to the edge of the buttress and then climb easy rocks to where
the Ordinary Route traverses back left. Above is a steep flake chimney.
Climb this until moves can be made left onto a ledge. Climb the
exhilarating wall above the right side of the ledge on excellent holds.
Winter: V   (1986)
Climb up to belay on a ledge left of the chimney, below a triangular
overhang. Step right into the chimney with difficulty and climb it directly
to the top.

78   Flying Fortress   60m   VS   (1989)
On the right edge of the top tier of West Buttress, just before it turns
round towards Fuselage Wall, there is a prominent square-cut corner
capped by a large roof. Start just round the edge of the buttress, on
the wall facing Far West Gully.
1. 30m 4b Climb stepped blocks up leftwards, then straight up to the
foot of the corner.
2. 30m 4c Climb the corner and turn the roof on the right to finish.

79   Fuselage Wall   90m   Severe   (1962)
Start in Far West Gully at the base of the final tower where a grassy
broken ledge runs left to the crest of the buttress. About 30m up there
is a 3m high pinnacle, more easily seen from the side than below.
Climb steep cracks to reach the neck behind the pinnacle from the left.
Cross the neck to the right and climb straight up for 9m, then traverse
left round an exposed corner into a scoop. Alternatively climb directly
to this point from the top of the pinnacle, passing a small overhang.
Trend right to a large platform and over the final eaves to easier
ground.

Winter: (Direct) 80m   V   (1987)
1. 30m Follow the summer route to the neck behind the pinnacle.
2. 20m Climb straight up a shallow corner and crack to a good belay ledge on the left.
3. 30m Climb the flake beside the belay and continue up the fault over a small roof to follow a corner leading to the top.

80 Far West Gully 400m I/II
This is the obvious gully between the West and Far West Buttresses. It gives probably the best easy gully climb in the corrie. It contains the wreckage of a Lancaster bomber which crashed in 1952.

81 Far West Buttress 60m Severe   (1954)
Start at an obvious corner left of the centre of the buttress. Climb steep rock for 12m, then traverse left for 5m on large, poor holds to a belay below a right-angled corner. Go up to the corner, climb it and finish up the left-hand edge.
Winter: IV **   (1991)
An excellent route with two technical but well-protected pitches, following the summer line.

82 The Upper Girdle 750m Severe   (1960)
The line is obvious all the way. A remarkable expedition, with at least half a dozen Severe pitches and tremendous situations. Start a short way right of the left end of the Eastern Ramparts. This section is the most entertaining, the traverse being continuously difficult and exposed for about 180m. From East Buttress things go easily all the way across to West Central Gully, apart from a single awkward pitch on Central Wall. The east face of West Buttress is by far the most impressive section, and has three serious pitches. The most appropriate finish is by the left-hand finish to West Buttress.
Winter: V/VI **   (1987)
The girdle was accomplished in two parts. The girdle of the Eastern Ramparts was done in about ten pitches and a finish made up East Central Gully. In the second part the Central and West Buttresses were crossed. The lower of two possible traverse lines on the east face of West Buttress was taken, giving spectacular positions.

SAIL MHOR
981m   (Map Ref 938 606)

When entering Coire Mhic Fhearchair from the north-west, the beetling crags and terraces of Sail Mhor on the right cannot fail to impress. Unfortunately they are too broken and vegetated to give good rock climbs. However the gullies give sporting winter climbs. The routes are described from right to left as this is the way one would normally approach them.

83 Morrison's Gully (No.1 Gully) 300m I
The big gully on the north face of Sail Mhor, obvious before reaching the corrie. No difficulty.

84 Lawson, Ling and Glover's Route 300m II   (1899)
The next obvious gully, starting above the north-west end of the lochan, is No.2 Gully. Climb the gully till it turns sharply left then break out up easy slopes on the right to gain the crest. This is followed to the top over rocky steps and pinnacles. A scenic route.

85 Overkill 230m HVS   (1968)
This climb lies on the steep left wall of No.2 Gully. A prominent groove cuts into the bulging area at the base of the cliff, where the gully wall turns east to form the main face. Start near the foot of the gully, below the groove which rises towards a line of rounded ribs.
1. 40m Climb the groove on its left wall to a steep, black section and go up this moving right to finish.
2. 30m Climb short walls and ledges to below and slightly right of prominent overhung snouts.
3. 30m Pass the snouts by a groove on the right to a ledge below a sharp right-angled corner.
4. 40m Climb the corner and then its left wall to a good ledge. A groove left of an overhang then leads to a terrace.
5. 90m Climb four short walls and intermediate terraces to easier ground.

86 Achilles 250m IV/V   (1986)
About halfway along the lochan a steep narrow cleft on the right sometimes gives rise to a splendid icefall. After an easy snow intro-duction, climb four pitches mainly on ice, including a free-standing ice pillar, to the first substantial terrace (120m). The next band is taken by

a groove on the left. Above this a deep chimney on the right may offer a good finish; however, on the first ascent darkness forced a traverse left into White's Gully from where the easiest line was taken to the top.

87   White's Gully (No.3 Gully)   120m   II   (1910)
A broad gully running up from the head of the lochan is joined a third of the way up by a narrow gully whose foot is a quarter of the way down the lochan. The route follows this narrow gully and is easy up to the final 30m, which is a chimney with three chockstones.

88   Smears for Fears   100m   IV   (1986)
This route may be used as a finish for Achilles or White's Gully. Take the first break left above the narrowing in White's Gully. Climb an ice-cased corner to a difficult cornice finish.

RUADH-STAC MOR

1010m (Map Ref 952 612)

CREAG MHOR *(Map Ref 954 608)*

This cliff lies in Coire Ruadh-staca, the central of the three great northern corries of Beinn Eighe on the east flank of Ruadh-stac Mor. It is composed of good quartzite. The climbs are varied and full of character, but not as serious as on the greater cliffs.

Access
From the bealach at the south end of the Ruadh-stac Mor ridge (above the south-east corner of Coire Mhic Fhearchair) descend 75m to the east and follow a faint path horizontally north for about 1km to the base of the cliff. A series of ridges and towers slant down the hillside. The two main ridges descend further than the rest. Both have large walls on their left sides, and the ridge on the right has a huge stepped pinnacle leaning against it (The Independent Pineapple), which is not easily seen from below. The climbs are described from left to right.

Sidestep   75m   Very Difficult
This is the tower to the left of the two main ridges mentioned above. Climb the ridge direct for 45m to a ledge. From the right-hand end of the ledge climb the right flank and back to the crest (loose rock) to

another ledge, (15m). From the right-hand end of this ledge again climb the right flank to the crest and reach easy ground.

Spog aig Giomach 100m VS   (1971)
This is the left of the two main ridges. Large comfortable stances are separated by short steep pitches. Start 6 metres left of the lowest point of the ridge by climbing a steep, reddish wall for 12m to a grassy stance. Climb the 15m corner above with an overhang to be avoided at 10m, then a short chimney. Move 5m left and follow a steep crack and chimneys to the halfway terrace. Walk a few metres right, climb back up left, and follow an easy crest to the top of the cliff, 45m.
Winter: IV   (1991)
Follow the summer line, except at the top of pitch 1 where a deviation left into a chimney followed by a traverse right across the initial corner leads to the stance.

Three Tier Chimney 150m III/IV   (1991)
The gully parallel to and left of Thin Man's Ridge. This is mostly easy but has one strenuous pitch of three piled chockstones. The last short chimney pitch is common with The Independent Pineapple.

Thin Man's Ridge 150m Hard Severe *   (1971)
Very large people will encounter peculiar difficulties on this climb. Start at the lowest point of the right-hand of the two main ridges. Climb 45m to a large terrace in front of an impressive tower. Traverse right into a very narrow chimney and climb this for 6m. It is now possible to pass right through the tower inside the chimney, to emerge at an airy stance on its far side. A 10m groove and a few metres of horizontal ridge lead to the halfway terrace. The route continues up the pillar of rock on the right. Climb it slightly round to the right by a steep diedre for 15m, then trending right for another 15m to a detached block and belay. Traverse delicately left for 6m across the front of the pillar. Scramble for 30m to a final 5m wall which leads to the top.

The Independent Pineapple 120m Severe   (1972)
A huge stepped pinnacle leans against the right wall of Thin Man's Ridge. This route takes a fine natural line up this wall via the pinnacle. Start at a right-angled corner about 20m left of Chockstone Gully. Climb the double cracks in the back of the corner and continue left to reach a shelf running up the face (40m). Climb the shelf past two

mossy chimneys to the top of the Independent Pineapple. To escape from the pinnacle return down the shelf for 12m, make a delicate traverse left for 6m and climb two chimneys to the top of the cliff.

Winter: IV/V *   (1991)
Follow the summer route, a short but well protected natural line.

The Pineapple Chimney   100m   VS *   (1977)
A magnificent chimney separates the right-hand side of the Independent Pineapple from the wall. Start by climbing Chockstone Gully until a narrow ledge leads left to the foot of the chimney. This gives excellent climbing to the top of the pinnacle. Climb the wall above for 6m, then an awkward move right leads round a corner to easier ground.

Chockstone Gully   100m   III   (1984)
This is the straight gully to the right of Thin Man's Ridge, unmistakable by the huge chockstone near its foot.

Midge Ridge   100m   Very Difficult   (1971)
The right bounding ridge of Chockstone Gully provides a rather broken climb, better in winter. Start 15 metres right of the gully. Ascend to the ledge above then climb an obvious narrow wall and corner. Continue up the line of least resistance. The ridge narrows at the top.
Winter: IV   (1987)
Start just right of Chockstone Gully near the toe of the buttress. Climb a groove then another groove beside the chockstone, turn the next steep wall by a chimney on the right and follow a groove to the crest of the ridge. Climb easily up and right to the finishing chimneys.

Autumn Rib   90m   Severe   (1977)
At the northern end of the cliff are three chimneys, the right-hand one having a deep cave at its foot. This route climbs the rib separating the two left-hand chimneys. The deep narrow chimney on the left (loose) leads to a platform at 15m. The rib becomes well-defined above and although short is sustained and on good rock.

RUADH-STAC BEAG

896m (Map Ref 973 614)

This is the outlying, seldom visited hill guarding the north-east side of Coire Ruadh-staca. Flanking its east end is a 100m quartzite slab with **The Long Stroll** (Very Difficult).

MEALL a'GHIUBHAIS

886m (Map Ref 977 635)

This is the hill north of Ruadh-stac Beag. On its south-west flank there is a cliff consisting of two tiers of clean quartzite, with a number of routes. **Traveller** (150m, Very Difficult) takes a prominent corner in the upper tier. The north side of the hill is split by a single gully which gives a winter climb: **Outrider** (III).

BEINN ALLIGIN
985m   (Map Ref 860 602)

Beinn Alligin, the most westerly of the three great mountains of the
Torridon Forest, has fewer ice climbs than its neighbours and is less
often in good winter condition. Although it has some steep sandstone
faces they are rather vegetated and crossed by ledges; no summer
climbs have been recorded. Despite these comparisons it is a noble
mountain, worth a visit for its winter climbs, or the traverse of its tops.

Access

Leave the road from Torridon to Diabaig at a large car park by the
bridge over the Coire Mhic Nobuil burn and follow the good path on
the east side of the burn through beautiful Caledonian forest. The first
corrie to be seen high on the left is Coire nan Laogh, which offers some
sporting winter possibilities but has no recorded climbs. The next
corrie, Toll a' Mhadaidh Mor, between Tom na Gruagaich and Sgurr
Mhor is much more impressive and offers several good ice routes on
the north-east face of Tom na Gruagaich. There are further winter
climbs on the north side of the 'Horns' of Alligin and in Toll nam Biast.

TOM NA GRUAGAICH, NORTH-EAST FACE

West Coast Boomer   300m   IV   (1973)
This is the obvious gully on the left of the face. It can be recommended
as a sustained and scenic route. There are numerous short pitches in
the lower part and a continuous steep section in the upper part.

Ice Gem   150m   IV/V   (1986)
On the left of the tier below West Coast Boomer a prominent icefall
forms on right-trending ramps. Trend left into the ramp corner, then
climb direct to the top.

The upper face right of West Coast Boomer has four lines of
weakness which can hold good snow and ice.

Crown Jewel   350m   V   (1986)
This is the left-hand line. Climb steep iced tiers, then a 50m mixed
pitch to gain an upper gully. This has many icy steps and finishes just
right of the summit trig point.

The Moonstone 300m IV/V   (1986)
The central line is gained by thinly iced ramps and leads to a steep finishing corner.

Koh-i-Noor 270m IV   (1986)
A well-iced stepped scoop further right. Follow the scoop, moving slightly left, then head directly up by mixed climbing in steeper grooves to the top.

Bilas 300m III/IV   (1987)
A thinner icefall right of Koh-i-Noor. After three pitches go left, up a further 15m and then left again to join the easy upper part of Koh-i-Noor.

Light of Bengal 270m III/IV   (1989)
The first icefall right of Bilas, directly in line with a large V-notch on the summit ridge. Start close to Bilas and climb a succession of short steep ice pitches leading to a deep gully splitting the upper rocks. Finish up the gully in two pitches.

Shezan 255m IV   (1989)
Climbs the icefall right of the previous route which leads into an obvious narrow chimney in the upper part of the face. Climb the chimney in two pitches (crux) and finish up a short gully.

On the north side of the corrie under Sgurr Mhor is a very impressive vertical wall with an easy gully running up beneath it. This is **The Great Cleft** (I).

THE HORNS OF ALLIGIN

To the north of the Horns of Alligin are several further climbs. The first lies on the north-east face of the Horns and finishes between the first (lowest) and second Horn.

Deep South Gully 250m I
This is the first gully seen on the approach towards the col between Beinn Dearg and Beinn Alligin. It curves from left to right.

Errors Cleft   250m   II   (1987)
To the right of Deep South Gully are two obvious lines of weakness. This climb gains the left-hand line by traversing up from the right. Follow the line to the top.

Diamond Cleft   260m   IV   (1988)
This is the right-hand line of weakness. Approach from the right to the start of the gully formed by a buttress on the right and a huge sandstone monolith on the left. Climb an initial steep section, then more easily into the cleft. After an interesting 45m, the climbing eases.

Deep North Gully   250m   II
The gully which finishes between the second and third Horn.

Backfire Ridge   200m   II   (1981)
This takes the most northerly of the ridges which form the north-east face of the Horns. It runs left of the triangular north-west face above Toll nam Biast. Climb the ridge direct. It has three short rock steps.

Diamond Fire   225m   IV   (1985)
This climbs a deep cleft on the north-west face above Toll nam Biast. It often has good ice even when the surrounding buttresses have little snow.
1. 35m Climb ice steps to a shelf below a corner.
2. 35m Climb the short corner on the left and go up easier ground to below a short icefall.
3. 35m Climb the icefall and go up to a deep, wide cleft.
4. 45m The icefall above is avoided. Climb the left wall, traverse left to a snow slope and climb the narrow gully above.
5. 30m Follow a snowfield to the back wall.
6. 45m Climb the final corner to the main ridge.

Backyard Gully   150m   I/II   (1984)
In the corrie above Loch Toll nam Biast there are two gullies going up to the col between the northern Horn and Sgurr Mhor. The right-hand gully is short and uninteresting. The left branch is longer and entertaining in early season but later banks out.

Backyard Buttress   110m   III   (1986)
The short buttress immediately right of Backyard Gully.

DIABAIG
(Map Ref 801 596)

Diabaig is one of the finest outcrops in Scotland. The setting is exquisite, above a picturesque inlet and village at the end of the road north of Loch Torridon (through Torridon village and passing Beinn Alligin).

The rock is excellent gneiss, usually rough, clean and slabby but occasionally overhanging and juggy. Protection is often excellent. The only disadvantages are the long approach drive and bad midges in the summer. The rock is quick to dry after showers, but there is drainage and many routes seep for a day after heavy rain.

Access
Park just before the pier at Lower Diabaig. From here the craggy hillside is obvious, but the Main Cliff and the Domes face away from the village. Walk to the end of the road and follow the right of way path towards Inveralligin (signposted through a garden). Walk up the wooded hillside and follow the path through a gate - access to Diabaig Pillar is by descent to the right. Further up, the path reaches an open gully, at the top of which is The Red Wall. The path crosses the gully and turns south, gradually descending until the steep slabs of the Main Cliff are visible up on the left. To reach the parallel cliffs of the Condome and Charlie's Tower, continue a little further along the path and cut up left.

DIABAIG PILLAR

Diabaig Pillar, the most prominent section of cliff visible from the village, is an impressive steep wall fairly low on the hillside which faces out to sea. The approach path to the Main Cliff initially runs up near its left side. Access to its base is by scrambling down and right through bracken. From below, a large inset slab is obvious at its top left. Between this and the pillar is a sharp arete, the line of Dire Wall.

1   Diabaig Corner   20m   E1 5b   (1991)
The corner left of The Pillar, which overlooks the village. An easy shelf leads right into the corner from just above the fence.

2 Dire Wall   35m   E2 *   (1984)
A fine route, but not as pure a line nor as well-protected as The Pillar.
Start about 3 metres left of The Pillar on cleaner rock.
1. 20m 5a Go up and left into the shallow groove. Climb it to join The
Pillar, but continue direct to the base of the arete.
2. 15m 5b Climb the arete.
Slab Finish: After pitch one, continue out left across the slab. This is
easier, HVS overall.

3 The Pillar   35m   E2 5b ***   (1983)
A superb quick-drying route up the continuous wall of the pillar. Despite
its intimidatingly smooth appearance, there are good holds and runners, and it provides a good sustained pitch at the lowest limit of its
grade. Climb the wall just right of a crack in the centre of the wall
(mossy but big holds) until it is possible to step left to the top of a
shallow groove which comes up from ground level. Trend right into the
centre of the wall and climb straight up.

4 Dire Straights   35m   E1 5b **   (1991)
A parallel line up the wall about 5m right of the Pillar. Start as for the
Pillar, but instead of moving left continue up a bulging crack, then an
easy ramp, and then thin cracks in the upper wall to finish at a V-notch.

LITTLE BIG WALL
Immediately down and right from Diabaig Pillar is a shorter overhanging wall, Little Big Wall, which looks insignificant from the village
because its lower half is hidden. Access is from Diabaig Pillar. The
highest section of cliff is bounded on the left by an obvious rightward
slanting unclimbed corner line. The routes on this wall seem to have
aquired a reputation for being rather fierce for their grades.

5 An Eyeful   10m   E3 5c   (1987)
The left end of the Wall is a short steep wall with a vertical crack in its
centre. Start 2m left of the crack. Strenuous and serious. Climb the
wall to half-height passing a small spike. Traverse to the crack and
climb it. Finish on the left.

The wall gains height to the right and is split by a right-slanting fault.
The next routes are on the steep wall right of this fault. The best
descent is by abseil.

6 Final Demand   25m   E3 6a   (1988)
Climb the crack in the left side of the steep wall, gained direct round bulges. The crux is at the top.

7 Local Hero   30m   E5 6a **   (1987)
Superb, bold climbing up the highest section of the crag, to the left of a system of cracks and grooves (Rubblesplitskin). Start just to the left of the crack. Climb up to the 'block' in the centre of the wall. Turn it on the left, then go up and right to a good resting place. Using two pockets move up to the bulge with a hard move. Reach left over the lip to good holds and a runner placement. Pull over the bulge rightwards gaining a good semi-rest below the obvious red streak in the headwall. Climb up the wall trending left to pull over on to a slab. Finish up and right around a rib to a tree belay. Several RP1s are required.

8 Rubblesplitskin   25m   E3 5c *   (1987)
Just left of the undercut right arete is a twin crack line. Climb the right-hand crack (sustained and steep) to an awkward exit into an open niche. Move up to a good rest, then pull over the roof to easier ground.

9 Edgewood Whymper   25m   E3 5c **   (1987)
Start just right of Rubblesplitskin at the undercut right arete. Pull onto the wall, then follow the edge rightwards to a groove. Go up this to pull out right onto a good ledge. Keep following the edge all the way.

THE RED WALL
The Red Wall lies higher up the gully where the path turns south and flattens out. It is directly above the gate on the path.

10 An Offensive Man   20m   E1 5a   (1990)
The left blunt arete, starting just on its left and staying on the right side thereafter.

11 Animal Magic   20m   E2 5b   (1990)
The thin crack line just right of An Offensive Man.

12 Porpoise Pun   20m   E3 5c   (1990)
The best route on this wall. Sustained. Climb the centre of the wall via a series of obvious pockets.

13 Batwing 20m E3 5c   (1990)
Climb the right arete of the wall with difficult initial moves.

14 The Mynch 30m HVS 5b   (1990)
The obvious overhung cleft at the far west end of the crags, directly
overlooking the village and car park and below The Red Wall.

THE MAIN CLIFF

The main cliff is a south-facing 70m wall of steep rough slab bounded
on the right by a wet gully set in a big corner, and split just below half
height by a less steep section with patches of vegetation. The routes
have two pitches with belays at this halfway point. The best descent
is by two abseils down the face; the slings may be in place. From right
(gully) to left (downhill) are the following features on the lower cliff:
slabby rock capped by a roof (Foil); a right-facing corner which leads
into the roof and sprouts a holly tree (Route One); a thin crack 3m left
of the corner (Black Streak); a smooth wall down to ground level (Wall
of Flame); a short left-facing corner (Northumberland Wall) and a
heathery ledge 5 to 10m up (Route Two touches its right end and Route
Three and Gamhnachain's Crack cross it).

The upper wall has continuation crack lines, the best defined being
The Black Streak and Route Three. The routes are well protected and
on near perfect rock, occasionally with a gritty surface which will
disappear with popularity. Being less than vertical, good footwork is
the key to success.

The descent is intricate and often muddy scrambling. Traverse right
from the clifftop and cross the gully to gain a vague ridge. Descend a
shallow gully just beyond the ridge (the upper section of the gully right
of Condome) until the ridge can be crossed rightwards and finished
steeply next to the start of Evasion. It is better to abseil down the line
of The Black Streak, or to walk over the top and down past Charlie's
Tower.

15 Foil 70m VS   (1982)
1. 25m 5a Climb the wall right of Route One to its capping roof. Go
through the roof by a right-slanting crack to a ledge.
2. 45m 4b Go up a crack beside a black streak until 1m short of grass,
then go diagonally left to the base of a steep crack. Climb this to a
ledge, then easier slabs.

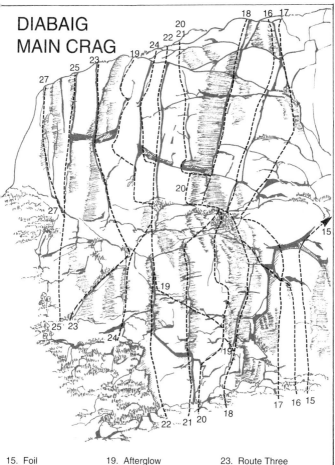

DIABAIG
MAIN CRAG

15. Foil	19. Afterglow	23. Route Three
16. Route One	20. Wall of Flame	24. Route Three Dir. Vars.
17. Going Home	21. Northumberland Wall	25. Gamhnachan's Crack
18. The Black Streak	22. Route Two	27. Dead Mouse Crack

16   Route One   70m   HVS *   (1975)
Start right of the big right-facing corner.
1. 30m 5a Climb the wall until it is possible to traverse left to the holly.
Step left onto the face and climb it trending left to a grassy ledge and
block belay beside a tree.
2. 40m 5a Climb the thin crack which starts just right of the tree. It is
easier but less satisfying to avoid a hard section at 10m on the right.
There is an easier (4c) alternative pitch further right.

17   Going Home   70m   E1   (1988)
Start between Route One and the big corner.
1. 25m 5b Go up the slab, cross the left traverse of Route One and
go up to the roof. Pull over above an obvious block and up to the belay.
2. 45m 4c Climb a series of cracks right of Route One.

18   The Black Streak   70m   E1 ***   (1976)
An excellent route. Start just left of the big corner.
1. 30m 5c Go up to and follow the thin crack (crux, overhead
protection) to join and belay as for Route One.
2. 40m 5b Climb the faint crack just left of the tree. It leads directly
into a prominent crack which forms the right boundary of a black streak.

19   Afterglow   80m   E4 *   (1988)
A left-trending diagonal line taking in the best rock and as many
independent features as possible.
1. 35m 6a Start up the Black Streak to a hollow block at 5m. Break
out left and follow a diagonal line crossing Wall of Flame and going
direct over a small overlap in the centre of the wall, before moving left
into Northumberland Wall at its bulge. Take a horizontal crack out left
and across a quartz blotch to join Route Two and belay at its grass
clump.
2. 45m 6a Go left and up slab to a jug below a blank-looking runnel.
Go up this until 2m below the overlap (the alternative finish to Northumberland Wall goes up from the overlap). Pull out left round a rib to
a flake. Go up to the right end of the roof split by Route Three and
follow a thin crack from here to its end. Make a hard move left round
a slabby rib via a thin diagonal crease to gain an easy crack and the
top.

20   Wall of Flame   70m   E4 **   (1987)
Start just right of the initial corner of Northumberland Wall.
1. 30m 6a Go up the wall just right of the arete to a faint diagonal line
running right. Follow it to its end, then pull over a bulge and a small
overlap, stepping right to reach a large flat hold (just left of the crux of
Black Streak). Go direct up a blank slab to an impasse below an
isolated overlap. Go diagonally left (crux) to gain the base of a thin
crack and up to belay as for Route One/Black Streak.
2. 40m 6a Climb the slab left of Black Streak to gain the left end of
an overlap. Climb a faint crack and subsequent cracks above.

21   Northumberland Wall   70m   E2 **   (1984)
This follows an intermittent crack line between the more continuous
cracks of The Black Streak and Route Two (nearer the latter). Fine
technical climbing.
1. 30m 5c Start up a short, left-facing corner, step left over its capping
roof then right to follow the intermittent crack to the common belay.
2. 40m 5c Go up Black Streak to the first overlap and traverse left
underneath it to join and follow Wall of Flame.

22   Route Two   75m   HVS ***   (1975)
Highly recommended and probably the best introduction to the wall.
Start below the right end of the low heathery ledge 5m up.
1. 35m 5a Climb to the right end of the ledge, then pull awkwardly up
right into the start of the crack. Follow it, then go slightly right to a large
grass clump below a thin crack.
2. 40m 5a Climb the crack.

23   Route Three   80m   E1 **   (1975)
The route follows an obvious crack line (more distinct than Route Two)
which starts from a triangular roof near the right end of the low heathery
ledge. Start 5 metres left of Route Two.
1. 15m 5b   Climb a right-facing blocky corner to belay below a
prominent holly.
2. 30m 5b Step right and climb up the wall for 3m until it is possible
to traverse right into a scoop below a turfy ramp. Follow this rightwards
to join the crack (taken throughout by the direct start). Climb the crack
line to belay below where it steepens.
3. 35m 5a Follow the crack to the top.

24   Route Three Direct Variations   75m   E2 **

An enjoyable route, with good but fiddly protection on the first pitch.
Start as for Route Two.

1. 35m 5c Gain the heathery ledge. From the apex of the triangular
roof, pull out left into the left of two thin cracks. Move up, then return
to the right and follow it to a junction with the original route. Trend over
right to the Route Two belay.

2. 40m 5c Follow Route Two until possible to go left under the overlap.
Where it ends follow a thin crack to the top.

25   Gamhnachain's Crack   75m   HVS   (1976)

A vegetated start leads to better climbing. Start as for Route Three.

1. 20m 4c Step left on to a slab, climb it then traverse left into a crack
which leads to the heathery ledge.

2. 20m 4c Climb to the holly tree. Traverse right and climb slabs just
right of heather to belay at the top right corner of a big heather patch.

3. 35m 5b Go right to a crack which takes a dog-leg to the right and
continues up as a wider crack.

26   The Grunter   70m   VS   (1991)

This is a logical combination of previously climbed pitches; perhaps it
should be re-named Monica. Start at a flake right of a heather recess
at the lower left end of the wall.

1. 20m 4c Step left, then work back right and climb a crack. Continue
to a belay at a birch (down and left of the holly belay of Gamhnachain's
Crack).

2. 20m 4c Climb the crack and slab above to a belay at a dead tree
stump.

3. 30m 4c Step right onto slabs, then trend left up cracks before
finishing straight up on easing slabs.

27   Dead Mouse Crack   25m   VS 5a   (1985)

A pink wall lies just above the path where the main cliff turns to face
the sea. Towards its right end is an obvious crack. Climb the crack with
a strenuous start. Abseil off. Alternatively, go diagonally right on rock
and heather, including a short corner, to join and finish up the last pitch
of The Grunter.

The well-defined vegetated corners left of Dead Mouse Crack are the probable line of **Upper Corner** (VS, 1975). The following routes climb the wall right of the gully and left of the scrambling descent.

28 Evasion 40m VS 4c (1990)
Start about 5m down and right from the gully at the lowest point of clean rock and climb a series of shallow scoops trending slightly left. Pull out right at the apex of a small roof system and continue to a tree. (Worrying abseil descent).

29 Bogie 40m E2 5b (1990)
Start at the base of the gully. Pull over a rounded nose on the right, then pass left of a red roof and go up cracks parallel to the gully. Pull over the small roof to reach the tree.

THE DOMES
Continuing along the path beyond the Main Cliff, an apparent dome of smooth rock becomes visible beside the top right end of the slope under the Main Cliff. This is the Condome. To the right of this is a recess beyond which the cliff turns again to form a long face parallel to the Main Cliff but of less continuous rock. Charlie's Tower is the bottom nose of this long cliff.

30 Condome 30m E4 6a * (1987)
Climbs the clean discontinuous crack. Start below the crack, just left of a large boulder at the base of the cliff. Gain and climb the lower crack, move left to ledges on the edge, then return right to climb the upper crack.

31 Instant Muscle 30m E4 6a ** (1988)
A direct variation on Condome. Start just to its right behind a small thorn bush. Climb directly up the wall to the obvious hanging crack. Climb this and, where it ends, move up left to join Condome at the ledge on the edge of the buttress.

32 The Con-Con 30m HVS 5a *
Climb the crack right of Condome to a ledge. Move right into a left-facing corner and follow it leftwards to the top.
Direct variation: E2 5c
From the ledge, continue direct past small right-facing overlaps.

33 Charlie's Tower 70m VS   (1976)
The route follows the rounded buttress right of The Condome. The line
is open to variation. Start at a short wall which forms the lower end of
the next face to the right. On this wall is a short stepped corner with
an oak tree. Start about 8m to its left. Climb the wall (5b), then a clean
crack above. Traverse down left and up a tower. Continue by a groove
and easier slabs.
Amenable Start: Hard Severe
A good start, omitting the hard initial wall. Start from the top right corner
of the slope next to the Condome (up and left from the orginal start).
Climb cracks on the left edge of a small dome. Near its top, go into
the centre and up to join the original route.

34 Boab's Corner 70m Hard Severe **   (1982)
The best of the easier climbs, taking the slabby wall right of Charlie's
Tower via an obvious right-slanting groove. Start at the stepped corner
and climb to the oak.
1. 30m Climb the wall on the right to the base of the groove.
2. 20m Up the groove.
3. 20m Scrambling to finish. Descend trending right (facing down) to
finish down the groove between this face and the Condome. The
original start (10m, 5c) climbed the undercut wall right of the stepped
corner, then a shallow corner to join the above line.

   Right of Boab's Corner, the cliff becomes more vegetated. After
about 100 metres there is a clean light-coloured pillar in its top half
(Bromide). Down to the right is a shallow left-trending slabby scoop
which leads up to an ash and holly tree below overhangs.

35 Bromide 40m HVS   (1988)
1a. 10m 4c Start up a cracked wall left of the smooth undercut cliff
base below the tree. Climb it on good holds to a ledge. Or:
1b. 15m 5a The Original Start. Move up to an overhang left of the
scoop of Plunge. Climb a crack through an overhang, past a loose
block, to the tree belay shared with Plunge. Now move up left to join
the second pitch.

ILLUSTRATIONS
Opposite: *The Triple Buttresses of Beinn Eighe*
Next page: *Diabaig Pillar   (Climber, Alan Scott)*

2. 30m 5b Climb up the overhanging nose on the right, then move right round the corner, up an overhanging groove and swing back left on to the crest above the nose. Follow the crest to the top.

36 Plunge 40m HVS   (1982)
1. 20m 5b A boulder problem start, then the scoop to the trees.
2. 20m 5b Climb the overhang directly above (3m right of Bromide groove), then follow the buttress, finishing as for Bromide.

SEANA MHEALLAN; GLAC DHORCH
(Map Ref 925 553)

This excellent sandstone crag lies in Glen Torridon about 300m above the river. It faces west-north-west and catches the afternoon and evening sun, with a superb outlook to Liathach, Beinn Eighe, and across Loch Torridon to Skye. Approach from a parking place at an obvious river bend a few hundred metres east of the trees near the foot of the glen. Cross the river and gain the crag after a 20 minute steep walk. All the routes were climbed by Rab and Chris Anderson during May and June 1990.

The climbs are on the uppermost of three tiers, and are described from right to left. At the right end of the main section of crag is an arete with a dark wall to its right. The first route starts beneath a dark corner with an overhanging right wall.

The Dark One 35m E2 *
1. 15m 5b Climb the corner and its left wall to a ledge.
2. 20m 5b Walk right then climb another corner to a ledge, then take the left of two cracks to the top.

Edge of Enlightenment 30m E3 5c **
Climb the thin crack up the left side of the arete to a ledge. Step right and climb a steep juggy wall to a slab. Move right and follow the arete to the top.

ILLUSTRATIONS
Previous page: The Torridonian, Seana Mheallan   (Climber, Rab Anderson)
Opposite: West Central Gully, Beinn Eighe   (Climber, Mike Morrison)

Path of Righteousness   30m   E2 5c **
Climb the thin crack up the centre of the slab left of the arete to a ledge.
Step right and climb the steep juggy wall (as for Edge of Enlighten-
ment) then finish up the steep corner above.

Elbow Room   30m   HVS 5b *
Climb the obvious corner then follow cracks to the top.

Dog-leg Crack   30m   HVS 5a
Climb the wide crack in the wall left of the corner to the crest, then
follow slabby ground and cracks left of Elbow Room.

Cornered   30m   Severe
A short distance left is a steep inset slab. Climb the blocky corner up
the right side of the slab.

A Touch Too Much   30m   E2 5c ***
An excellent route taking the right-slanting crack line in the right side
of the steep inset slab. Move awkwardly up a thin crack to the break
(bold) then take the crack to a shallow groove. Move up and climb the
obvious crack to the top.

Seams Obvious   30m   E1 5b **
A fine route up the crack in the centre of the slab. Gain the large
elongated pocket then reach a thin crack up on the right and follow
this to a niche. Take the right branch of the crack to a ledge then its
continuation up the final wall.

Seems The Same   30m   HVS 5a *
At the left side of the slab climb a short crack to the break, then step
right and follow a thin crack into the niche. Take the left branch of the
crack to a ledge and up the final wall.

Looks Different   30m   HVS 5a **
Climb for Seems The Same to the break, then continue straight up
until moves left lead to a prominent crack which is climbed to the top.

   At the left end of this recessed section of the crag is a corner leading
to a roof. The next two routes start up the corner.

Squeeze 'Em In   30m   E1 5b *
The wide crack in the corner leads to a ledge. Move up to a pocket, then out right to climb a thin crack into a groove and then up the left wall to finish

Wide Deceiver   30m   E1 5b *
Climb the corner, then the roof and continue up the crack above.

In The Groove   30m   HVS 5a *
Just left is an arete. Climb a shallow groove up its right side to a heathery ledge, then take the corner and its continuation crack to the top.

Around the edge to the left is a prominent crack splitting a bulge. On its left is a corner then a band of roofs. The next route takes the crack.

Fistfighter   30m   E4 6a **
Start left of the thin crack which leads to the bulge. Gain a ledge, traverse briefly right and pull blindly into the crack and move up to the break. The difficult crack above leads to the top.

Rock Around The Block   30m   E2 5c *
Climb Fistfighter to the ledge. Move up to the break, step right and climb left around a huge block into a short corner which leads to a swing out right. Go up to heather, then climb the wall on the left of the crack.

Shoot The Cuckoo   30m   HVS 5a *
On the left is a corner system. Start just left of the initial short corner and climb a short crack to gain the main corner. Follow this past a recess and finish out left.

Hunter Killer   30m   E4 6b ***
A superb route taking the thin crack and arete just left of Shoot The Cuckoo. Climb up to stand on the small undercut shelf (Rock 1 in the right of three hairline cracks). Climb to a peg runner then up the crack to the arete. Continue up the edge (small wires) to a small block in a break. Move right and up to the top.

Exterminator   30m   E2/3 5c **
The crack and groove system up the centre of the wall.

Eliminator   30m   E3 5c/6a **
Eliminate but fine climbing up the very thin crack right of the corner.
Climb easily to the break, then up the wall to the left end of a ledge.
Move left to gain then climb the crack.

The Deerstalker   30m   VS 4c **
The corner starting from a platform. There is a small rowan near the
top.

Route With a View   30m   HVS 5a *
Takes cracks in the buttress edge left of the corner to a blocky ledge.
Finish up the cracks above.

Mark of a Skyver   30m   E2 5c **
Just left is a large flake. Climb the crack up its right side then take the
thin crack in the wall.

View to a Hill   30m   E1 5b *
The corner system on the left leads to a heather ledge. Exit right to a
slab, then move up a crack to a niche and so to the top.

Crack of Ages   30m   E2 5b **
Climb the very prominent fine crack on the left.

Around the ledge to the left just before the crag bends around out
of sight there is a corner, one of the most prominent features of the
crag. The right wall contains two crack lines which share a common
start.

Sandpiper   30m   HVS 5b **
Move a short way up the crack which runs into the corner, then step
awkwardly up right to a thin crack. Now move across to the other crack
which is climbed to the top.

Sandstorm   30m   E3 6a/b **
The thin crack just right of the corner provides eliminate but excellent
climbing. Follow Sandpiper to the crack, which is climbed to the top.
Use a pocket on the left to start the upper wall.

The Torridonian   30m   E3 6a ***
The excellent corner gives a delightful technical exercise, with the crux right at the top.

Around the edge to the left is a short overhung corner with a wall above containing three parallel cracks.

Middle of the Road   30m   E3 5c **
Climb the steep corner to a ledge. Move right to climb the central crack.

Left in the Lurch   30m   E1 5b **
Climb Middle of the Road to the ledge then take the crack on the left to a niche. Step right and climb the wall to the top.

On the left is a recessed area of rock. The next route takes a hand-crack up the far left side of the left retaining rib.

Rowantree Crack   30m   E1 5b *
Climb the crack to the top, passing a small rowan.

Mackintosh Slab   30m   E1 5b *
The thin crack in the slab immediately left of Rowantree Crack leads into a corner under the obvious slanting roof. Pull out right, then continue up a crack and its thin continuation.

BEINN DAMH
902m   (Map Ref 893 502)

Creag na h-Iolaire (Map Ref 885 518) lies on the north spur of Beinn Damh and is easily reached from the head of Loch Torridon by the good stalking track which starts about 200 metres west of the hotel.

Stag Gully   150m   II/III   (1979)
The most obvious gully on the right of the main crag. It has a large chockstone and may contain three pitches.

Aetos   200m   III   (1984)
This takes the left edge of the steep part of the buttress, bounded on the left by Aquila Gully. It follows approximately the same line as the summer route Aquila. Climb the first tier by an easy chimney right of a steep wall. Climb the next band by a left-slanting ramp to easy ground. Continue up to two chimneys. Climb the right-hand chimney and then the arete on the left to finish up the top of the left-hand chimney. More easy ground leads to a steep corner-crack. Climb this and more easy ground to the final tier, climbed by an open chimney.

Aquila   110m   Severe   (1967)
This follows the light-coloured rib bounding the crag on the left. Start at a pinnacle on the lower of two terraces that cross the crag.
1. 20m Climb a chimney and the corner above to the next terrace.
2. 35m Continue up a grassy groove to the right. Exit right halfway up and climb an open chimney and overhang to a ledge.
3. 35m Climb a corner to the right, emerging on wet slabs which converge on a corner that is climbed delicately to a large terrace.
4. 20m Finish up pleasant twin cracks.

Aquila Gully   170m   III   (1979)
The gully on the left of the main crag is gained by a long ice pitch. It has several steps which can be avoided on the left.

Kinlochewe

GLEN DOCHERTY

This is the glen taken by the road from Achnasheen to Kinlochewe, on the north-west side of the bealach. One ice climb has been recorded here in particularly cold conditions. **Helter-Skelter** (240m, IV) is 'the first gully below the car park' on the west side of the bealach.

BEINN A'MHUINIDH

692m   (Map Ref 032 661)

This is the hill south-east of Slioch, divided from it by the picturesque Gleann Bianasdail. The south-west and north-west flanks have a lot of rock, providing plenty of scope for exploratory scrambling, and two crags with some worthwhile longer routes on good quartzite. Unfortunately, there is a fair amount of vegetation and loose rock, but the views up Loch Maree and across to Beinn Eighe are superb.

Access
From Kinlochewe cross the river to Incheril, and follow the path towards Loch Maree. Waterfall Buttress is seen above on the right after about 30 minutes. A broken band of rock continues slanting up across the hillside from Waterfall Buttress. This is The Lower Band, which continues round the hillside above lower Gleann Bianasdail, where it forms the best exposure of rock on the hill, the Bonaid Dhonn. To reach this it is best to stay on the Loch Maree path to the burn coming down from Waterfall Buttress, then strike diagonally up the hill following sheep tracks through bracken and heather. A good narrow goat track below the Lower Band starts near Little Buttress, the first compact mass of rock west of Waterfall Buttress. The path continues below the Bonaid Dhonn and beyond.

Above and right of Waterfall Buttress is the Upper Band, which is mainly rather broken but it does have steeper rock at its northern and southern ends. Beyond the Bonaid Dhonn the band of rock continues along the hillside, with vegetated breaks, but has so far provided no good climbing.

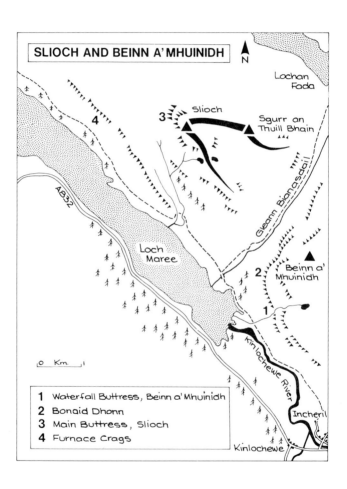

SLIOCH AND BEINN A'MHUINIDH

Lochan Fada

Slioch

Sgurr an Thuill Bhain

Gleann Bianasdail

A832

Loch Maree

Beinn a' Mhuinidh

Kinlochewe River

0   Km.   1

1 Waterfall Buttress, Beinn a'Mhuinidh
2 Bonaid Dhonn
3 Main Buttress, Slioch
4 Furnace Crags

Incheril

Kinlochewe

WATERFALL BUTTRESS

Although vegetated and loose in places, this crag has some worth-while routes. The original route, The West Climb, has a fine traditional flavour and the climbs between it and the waterfall offer excellent situations. The waterfall itself, on the rare occasions when it is frozen, gives a superb pure ice climb. Some of the original route descriptions may be of limited help. The climbs are described from right to left.

1 Prelude 45m Severe   (1951)
Start some distance right of the waterfall. From the bottom of the climb a steep corner and arete are seen on the immediate left of a gully and right of a reddish-coloured wall with a rowan tree high on the cliff to the left. Climb the wall for 12m avoiding an overhang on the left. Go up a wall to a second overhang (20m). Turn the overhang at its left edge, move back right, then straight up on small holds to a ledge with large shattered blocks (10m). Step left and climb the wall for 6m to where it ends abruptly on a ledge. Go left again to the next wall and climb 6m to the top of a small pinnacle. Continue to the top.

2 Tuit 72m Severe   (1952)
Start 20 metres right of the waterfall at the lowest point of the wall. Climb up left to a small and then a large pine tree. A chimney on the right gives access to a wall above and a ledge with a rambling pine in a corner. The narrow rib to the right of the corner leads to a final wall. Only the last pitch is Severe.

3 Chiaroscuro 100m Severe *   (1982)
Start right of the waterfall, where the black waterwashed rock is bounded by a prominent corner (10 metres left of Tuit). The route may be very similar to **Waterfall Corner**, described in SMCJ, 1973.
1. 40m Climb black rock on the left of the corner for 10m, then traverse right into the grey crack in the corner. Follow the crack on superb holds to its top then go left up a wall above to the first pine ledge.
2. 35m Go straight up behind the pine for a few metres, then left towards the foot of a rib with a detached block at its base. Step round the block into the corner beyond and follow the corner crack to a second pine ledge.
3. 25m Move up left and round a rib, then back right to finish.

4   The Waterfall   120m   V ***   (1984)
On the first winter ascent the waterfall was not completely frozen but
there was thick ice just right of the water flow. Three 20m pitches were
climbed until below a curtain of icicles. The top of the icicles was gained
via a hidden rock niche on the right, then easier ice led to the top. The
route was considered technically easy for its grade, but thawing
conditions forced the use of rock belays which were poor and hard to
set up. On a later attempt the fall was well frozen and formed a
magnificent free-standing pillar about 70m from the bottom.

5   Linea Nigra   90m   Severe *   (1972)
This follows the black rock immediately left of the waterfall. Start at a
rowan sapling.
1. 25m Traverse right 5m and follow a groove near the edge to the
foot of a prominent slab. Move left over a pinnacle and along a ledge
to an ash tree belay.
2. 40m Go back to the pinnacle, step off the top and go straight up
the wall. Move right and back left over a block, then up short walls until
an exhilarating traverse right across a final steep wall leads to ledges
which are followed up left to a corner.
3. 25m Go diagonally right and round the arete to the upper waterfall
basin, then easily up left to a ledge below a shattered crack. Climb the
crack and exit left onto a sloping ramp. Move left into an easy corner
and follow this to the top.

6   Rainbow's End   90m   Very Difficult   (1982)
Start left of the waterfall at a holly tree in a corner. The route takes the
corner towards yellow overhangs and then curves right towards the
top of the waterfall.
1. 40m Follow the chimney-crack line behind the holly, passing
various trees, to a stance in the corner below a slab.
2. 35m Climb the slab and follow it as it curves into a gangway and
ledges to the right; step across a bottomless chimney onto a hanging
rib and ledges beyond. Now go up to a stance overlooking the upper
waterfall basin.
3. 15m Take the short crack above (as for Linea Nigra), or go up below
this and exit on the right.

BEINN A' MHUINIDH

WATERFALL BUTTRESS

2. Tuit
3. Chiaroscuro
5. Linea Nigra

6. Rainbow's End
7. The Alley
8. The West Climb

9. The West Climb,
   Bell's Variation
10. Spider

7 The Alley 90m Severe   (1967)
Start 45 metres left of the waterfall at the foot of a square pillar.
1. 30m Climb the front of the pillar and two short walls above to a
large ledge and chockstone belay. (This is the large triangular ledge
mentioned in The West Climb.)
2. 30m Traverse right, then go back left by a short chimney and
continue slightly left to belay.
3. 30m Finish by a steep groove some 8m left of the large overhangs
obvious from below.

8 The West Climb 90m Severe   (1899)
This is the original route on the cliff and is remarkable for its standard
and conception at that time. The grading may be open to debate, but
if approached in the right spirit the climb will be found rewarding, with
fine situations. The following description attempts to capture the
atmosphere of the first ascent. Start at a 6m perpendicular crack to
the left of the square pillar of The Alley, 45 metres left of the waterfall.
The crack is flanked on the right by a square pinnacle and on the left
by a large buttress.
   From here, 'an unsuccessful attempt was made on the crack, but
the way proved to be for two men to get on to the top of the pinnacle,
where there was just room for the second man giving the leader a
shoulder low down, and steadying him until he reached some high
hand-holds'. Go up 3m, then left into a crack and up to the first tree
(15m). Leave the tree platform at its left-hand corner and climb a
chimney-crack on the left to a platform, a triangle with 6m sides.
   'It was agreed by all that the beautiful, both in rock scenery and
hand and foot holds, had been sought and found'. Gain a ledge 5m
above, first stepping left before ascending. Go leftwards (stomach
traverse mentioned) to an overhanging cave located in the grassy fault
on the left which leads to the top of the cliff. Climb the face on the left
of the cave to a 'comfortable platform'. Climb 'a few feet of rather rotten
work' to a ledge whence climb a small open gully at its right-hand
corner ('easy back and knee work'). Broken rocks to the top.

9 West Climb, Bell's Variation 90m Very Difficult   (1946)
Start up the buttress left of The West Climb. Moderate climbing for 9m,
then 12m of steeper rock lead to a fir tree, followed by 5m of walking.
Climb a hard pitch up a wall, then round a delicate corner to the right
until one can climb straight up the wall to a good stance. Go up the

steep face on small rounded holds for 20m, then moderate climbing for 30m leads to the top.

10 Spider 75m Difficult (1975)
Start about 15 metres left of Bell's variation, just left of a block pinnacle low on the face. Climb straight up in three steep sections, cross a grass ramp and finish easily.

11 Coloured Corner 60m Severe (1970)
Start about 30 metres left of Bell's Variation at an obvious corner with a crack at the back, a tree at 10m and a tree on a ledge at 20m. Climb the corner direct to a large platform and belay. Climb the left wall then pleasant slabs to the top.

THE UPPER BAND, NORTH BUTTRESS

Double Flake Route 75m Severe (1946)
Start at a tunnelled eye between two flakes. The lower flake, 20m up, is reached from right or left, and the wall behind the flake is climbed by a 25m pitch to a good belay. A cave ahead is avoided by slabs on the right to an exposed 3m crack which breaks through the canopy. This exit leads sensationally to a steep slab on the left, climbed by friction and vegetation. A further 30m of moderate climbing leads to the top.

Zigzag Gully 45m Difficult (1949)
On the left of the buttress start directly up a block with a prominent yellow blaze, from which an entrenched zigzag gully leads to the top.

Staircase Ridge 50m Severe (1958)
This is the steep, stepped ridge seen in profile from the foot of Double Flake Route, to the left. Go up white quartzite to a ledge. Traverse left up an overhung wall and onto the ridge. Continue direct to the top.

Stepped Chimney 50m Severe (1958)
Start right of Double Flake Route. The deep chimney on the second pitch can be seen clearly from the bottom. Go up loose blocks to a short crack on the right and up to a chockstone belay. Climb the strenuous chimney and the overhanging crack above.

Silver Slab   50m   Severe   (1958)
This takes the right edge of fine steep slabs left of a deep gully. Ascend a broken wall below the slabs on the right, (15m). Climb silver slabs and go diagonally right to a heather-filled crack at the edge, which is climbed to a stance, (25m). Climb the rib on the right to the top.

Pinnacle Gully   40m   Very Difficult   (1958)
This is the deep gully right of Silver Slab. Climb grass and loose blocks to the foot of the Pinnacle. Go up between the Pinnacle and the wall at the back and belay on top. Leap onto a broad grass ledge. Move left to the face overlooking the Pinnacle. Climb the exposed ridge above to an easier finish.

Pinnacle Face   40m   Severe   (1958)
Climb the face on the right of Pinnacle Gully, starting from a recess on the left. Ascend the Pinnacle on the right on friable holds and continue as for Pinnacle Gully.

For three other routes on this buttress, which are likely to be similar to the above, see SMCJ 1959.

THE UPPER BAND, SOUTH BUTTRESS
The central part of this buttress is steep, but loose. Towards the left there is a Severe climbed by Tom Patey (SMCJ, 1958). It takes an obvious crack set in a corner and overhanging slightly. The middle part of the crack was avoided on the left via a small tree, and regained below the top overhang, which was climbed direct. At the right of the buttress there is a pleasant slab (Difficult).

LITTLE BUTTRESS
This is the first compact mass of rock to the west of Waterfall Buttress. It is defined on the left by a wide broken gully, and is some 100 metres from the corner of the glen.

Miscellany   50m   Severe   (1959)
This route is immediately right of the gully, up a ridge, indistinct below but sharp above. Climb the ridge to a heather ledge and traverse right; go diagonally right up a yellow slab to the edge of a wide crack; climb the crack and the steep wall above. A mantleshelf leads to a ledge in 6m; turn the overhang on the right and finish by a knife edge.

Refuse Cruise   50m   VS   (1984)
This is the rib right of Miscellany. Climb easily up to a stance below
and just right of the rib (10m). Follow the rib directly to an overhang
and break through this on the left to the top.

Climax Slab   50m   Severe   (1959)
Start 15 metres right of Miscellany up the least heathery of three slabs.
Climb 18m to a heather ledge and continue to the next but one heather
ledge, below the overhang. Climb left of the overhang to a wide
chimney; take the left fork, emerging with difficulty.

THE BONAID DHONN

The path contouring round to the Bonaid Dhonn passes under a
prominent beak of rock at the 'corner' of the glen, which marks the
starts of Routes I and II. The most compact and steepest part of the
crag is a red wall about 50m further on. An obvious chimney-corner
system (Safari) defines the right side of this and right again are more
steep walls, which degenerate to more broken rock about 50 metres
to the right. The left side of the compact wall is defined by a bulging
buttress and corner crack. There is about 50m of broken rock and
heather between the path and the base of the compact section. Further
left, below the corner crack of the upper tier, the lower tier becomes
steeper and there is an overhung bay. Another 50 metres left, after
crossing a gully, the path runs below a second, more vegetated
overhung bay.

  The best descent from routes in the centre of the crag is possibly
by abseil. Alternatively, descend on the left (well beyond the second
overhung bay) or on the right, well past Route I. These descents lead
to the goat track beneath the initial 50m of scrambling. Another
possibility, although steep and exposed, is to scramble down a short
gully a little right of The Rebound and then work back diagonally left.

  The first two routes start from the goat track before the main crag
is reached.

1   Route I   120m   Difficult *   (1946)
Start from the path, under a beak of rock at the corner of the glen. After
climbing 90m up slabs move right to climb a 10m wall over a huge
square block. Continue up a series of ribs and walls. Easier ground
leads to the hardest section, an exposed 25m wall. Scramble to the
top.

2 Route II 120m Difficult ** (1946)
This is to the left of Route I. Climb 20m up the face to the right of a crack. This is very steep, with a delicate traverse to avoid an overhang. Climb 10m up a slabby rib with an overhanging wall on the left, then 10m more up a steep rounded rib with a nose at the end. Go 5m up a chimney to a ledge and climb 15m to the base of the upper cliff by an arete. Walk 15m right, climb a 12m wall right of a chimney, and then 6m in the chimney to above the overhang. Go straight up on good holds to the top (25m).

The most obvious line on the main crag is Safari, which is described first. The climbs to its right are then described, followed by those to its left. All the climbs are reached by a steep 50m scramble up rock and vegetation from the goat track.

3 Safari 95m VS (1969)
This is the chimney-corner system. From the path scramble 45m to belay by a huge perched block.
1. 30m Climb the crack until forced by vegetation onto the slab on the right; climb this and the flake above, then move back left into the chimney.
2. 30m Climb the chimney to a ledge on the left.
3. 12m Climb the difficult corner above to a niche, then mantleshelf strenuously leftwards.
4. 12m Either go straight up to a peg belay or step back right into the crack and belay in the open corner.
5. 12m Climb the open corner, passing a large flake.

4 The Tallon 80m VS * (1969)
This takes the line of a very shallow groove, undercut at its base, about 12m right of Safari.
1. 10m Climb slabs and a thin crack to a stance under overhangs.
2. 35m Go left and pull over the overhangs at the highest point. Climb up and round right to enter a steep shallow groove, which is followed for 25m, until it is possible to traverse left and go up to a small stance on the rib.
3. 20m Climb directly over two overhangs, then go up slabs to belay behind a large flake about 5m right of the main corner.
4. 15m Climb a steep wall to finish.

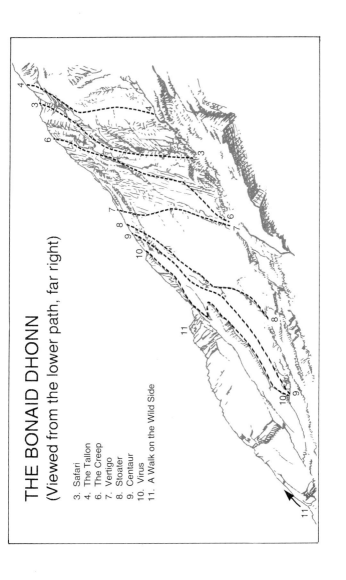

THE BONAID DHONN
(Viewed from the lower path, far right)

3. Safari
4. The Tallon
6. The Creep
7. Vertigo
8. Stoater
9. Centaur
10. Virus
11. A Walk on the Wild Side

The lower wall right of The Tallon can probably be climbed almost anywhere at about 5a/b. The line of **The Bow** (80m, VS, 1969) on this lower wall is not certain, but above it probably takes the obvious wide flake crack right of a very clean smooth wall.

5   The Rebound   60m   Hard Severe   (1968)
Start about 30m up and right of The Tallon at a 5m flake.
1. 30m 4b Climb to the top of the flake and then up right to a block. Climb a shallow right-facing groove to a ledge, then move 6m left. Climb the wall above, moving right at half-height, and continue to grass ledges.
2. 30m 4a Climb a wide crack in a shallow right-facing corner and continue up walls to the top.

Left of Safari is a steep impressive wall with a line of overhangs about 45m up. Further left is the flake crack of Vertigo.

6   The Creep   85m   HVS **   (1971)
A good climb up the wall between Vertigo and Safari; not well protected on the first pitch. Start at a large block left of a roof.
1. 45m 5a Move up and right on grass ledges, then traverse right across the wall until near the edge of the groove of Safari. Go up to a ledge (peg runner), then straight up the wall to the roof and belay on the right.
2. 40m 4c Climb the overhanging corner directly above the belay and finish up a splendid steep crack.

7   Vertigo   85m   HVS **   (1971)
This takes a fine flake crack with an overhanging base. Start as for The Creep; climb easily to the foot of the flake crack.
1. 35m 4c Climb the flake crack to a small ledge at its top and peg belay.
2. 20m 5a Traverse left and step onto a steep grey wall. Climb up and slightly left until it is possible to pull onto the steeper wall above. Climb this until an awkward move left is made into the obvious groove 5m above; climb the groove to a belay.
3. 30m 4b Climb over an overlap above, then move up and right towards an obvious easy corner. Avoid this by climbing a slab on the left to the top.

8 Stoater 90m Severe *   (1971)
This starts at a fairly wide flake crack left of Vertigo.
1. 45m Climb the flake crack then the wall above to belay on a small rock ledge beneath an overhang.
2. 45m Climb up and over the overhang then finish up the wall above on excellent holds, moving right through an overlap.

9 Centaur 100m Severe   (1967)
This takes a wide shallow groove of yellow rock slanting slightly right between the flake cracks of Stoater and Virus. Start by scrambling up left on vegetation until about 30m right of the big corner at the left side of the crag. There is a pedestal about 10m above.
1. 35m 4a Climb slabs rightwards, then climb the yellow groove to a small ledge (shared with Stoater). Poorly protected.
2. 35m 4b Continue up the slabby right wall of the groove and the steeper wall above to a small grass ledge. An alternative (more independent of Stoater) is to climb the flake crack left of the stance and continue up the wall above.
3. 30m 4b Climb slabs and surmount an overhang at its narrowest point. Finish up a prominent overhanging niche.

10 Virus 80m Mild Severe   (1967)
Start as for Centaur.
1. 35m Climb up onto the pedestal. Move up and cross below an overhang into a groove on the right. Climb the groove and exit left onto grey slabs which lead to a flaky ledge and belay.
2. 15m Ascend a shallow chimney and the wall ahead to a small ledge and peg belay.
5. 30m Move left onto slabs. Climb these to a ledge and use flakes to reach an easy corner. Follow the corner to the top, or, for a much better finish, climb straight up the vertical edge on perfect holds.

11 A Walk on the Wild Side 130m Very Difficult *   (1967)
A good steep route on sound rock following the crest of the bulging buttress left of the big corner. Start on the path to the right of the first overhung bay, where the angle relents slightly. Climb broken walls for 45m, then walk left for 45 metres on heather to reach the foot of the buttress. Climb near the crest by cracks and grooves (easier to the left). Finish by a delightfully exposed wall on the crest (12m).

An alternative, harder start is up the steep wall on the left of the first overhung bay, (40m, VS). This may be the line of **The Tappit Hen** (SMCJ 1973).

12 Aquila 150m Very Difficult   (1980)
About 50 metres left of A Walk on the Wild Side is an overhung bay above the path. This route starts below the overhang and ascends the open convex wall above.
1. 25m Exit left from the bay and ascend a large pinnacle flake.
2. 25m Climb straight up slabs.
3. and 4. 90m Ascend diagonally right to a rib bounding the left wall of a large bay. Climb the rib then the face above on rough solid rock.

Crypton Crack (55m, Severe) is about 250 metres left of the wide gully which splits the crag left of A Walk on the Wild Side, where the rock becomes more consistent again. It climbs a short wall to gain the crack, which is followed to a slab, a groove and insecure walls to finish.

FURNACE CRAGS

Above the path from Kinlochewe to Letterewe, along the north-east side of Loch Maree, are several gneiss outcrops. They are well seen from the other side of the loch at Grudie Bridge. The outcrops are bigger than they appear, have excellent rock and give pleasant climbing with a splendid outlook. The easiest approach is directly over the loch by canoe, inflatable or other waterborne means. Failing this, the path from Incheril near Kinlochewe gives a long but very scenic approach. The crags are described from left to right as seen from Grudie Bridge, which is the inverse order if coming from Kinlochewe.

Creag Mhor (Map Ref 967 703) is the clean-looking buttress about 1km east of Furnace. It can be identified by a straight grass strip running up through the heather to the foot of the cliff.

The Mad Fencer 75m Severe   (1984)
1. 15m From just right of the lowest point of the crag, move up steeply right until it is possible to move left and up to the left end of a ledge.
2. 25m Go diagonally across the face to a stance in a crack.
3. 35m Climb the crack then a little tower to the top.

Caisteal Mor (Map Ref 984 693) is the largest left-hand buttress of the Meall Riabhach group, with its main slabby face towards the east. There is a route starting on the steeper front of the buttress and following the long slab above on the right (150m, Very Difficult).

Meall Riabhach, No.1 Buttress (Map Ref 987 690) is the next crag right of Caisteal Mor. It has one route. (Note that all the buttresses are further north-west than the Meall Riabhach marked on the OS 1:50000 map.)

Riabhach Slab   120m   Severe   (1985)
1. 20m From just a few metres left of the lowest point climb steeply at first to heather ledges below slabs.
2. 40m Climb straight up the slab to a stance on the right.
3. 20m Continue up the slab to heather ledges below the final slab.
4. 40m Climb the crack on the right to an overhang, surmount this and continue to the top.

Next right is a small clean crag, No.2 Buttress, with no routes. Right again is No.3 Buttress (Map Ref 991 686), distinguished by an impending lower central area and a corner on the upper right. It has three routes all starting at the same point, a diagonal heather weakness at the right side of the crag.

Skeleton Lum   105m   VS   (1984)
1. 30m Follow the break left to a ledge with oak and aspen at the foot of a chimney corner.
2. 30m Climb the chimney, strenuous at first, to the top of the crevasse.
3. 45m The wall above leads to the top.

Norse Requiem   110m   HVS   (1985)
This takes the obvious large corner.
1. 5b Follow Skeleton Lum for about 20m, then go up right to the foot of the corner. Climb to a stance under the chockstone. Surmount this to gain the steep right wall of the corner, follow thin cracks up to the arete and go up to an exposed stance.
2. 4c Climb a pleasant slab to the base of a steep crack which is climbed to the top.

Soft Shoulder   120m   Severe   (1984)
1. 40m Go up to the foot of the big corner, around the lower block of
the corner via the chimney on the left, and traverse right to belay in a
crevasse behind a giant flake.
2. 20m Follow the flake round to the right and over a short crack to a
stance on perched flakes.
3. 40m Climb a shallow corner and slabs above to a stance on the
right.
4. 20m Take the steep slab above and scramble to the top.

Low Crag is the lowest in the Meall Riabhach group, just above the
path about 5km from the east end of the loch. It has two routes.

Indian Summer   70m   Severe   (1985)
Start in a depression near the centre of the crag, below a gnarled alder.
1. 35m Climb the wall rightwards, then directly to a pine tree.
2. 35m Follow a slanting wall rightwards to the top.

Phew   65m   Severe   (1985)
1. 25m Right of Indian Summer is a steep wall, overhanging at the
base where goats have sheltered. Climb a ramp up left into the central
depression, then back right to an oak tree.
2. 40m Move right and climb steeply to the top.

SLIOCH

980m   (Map Ref 004 691)

Driving south-east down Slattadale and along Loch Maree, the north-
west face of Slioch presents a magnificent aspect. However the length
of approach and scarcity of information has deterred most climbers.

Access
The easiest approach is to use waterborne tactics, e.g. canoes, to
cross Loch Maree. Failing this the usual approach will be from Incheril
near Kinlochewe along the north-east shore of Loch Maree. Follow
the path to Letterewe until past Meall Riabhach, about 2km beyond
Gleann Bianasdail. Follow the burn up to its source in Coire Smiorasair
(3 hours). Looking north-east, the Main Buttress now forms the skyline
on the left. An alternative approach, if staying at Carnmore, is via
Lochan Fada and Loch Garbhaig.

The entire face consists of Torridonian sandstone and the buttresses are therefore crossed by occasional terraces. The best rock is on the sheer lower section of Main Buttress, known as Atlantic Wall. There are also several good winter climbs in the gullies. On the right of Main Buttress, immediately above the boulder, is a gently-angled buttress giving some 30m of Hard Difficult climbing, followed by 220m of scrambling to the top. Dividing this from Main Buttress is **Easy Gully** (400m, Grade I).

Main Buttress   245m   Severe   (1952)
At the base of Atlantic Wall is a broad grass ledge. Start at the extreme right of the ledge, where it merges into Easy Gully. Climb the wall above the gully to a terrace (60m). Continue from there by the line of least resistance to the top.

Skyline Highway   370m   HVS   (1986)
This tackles Atlantic Wall directly. Start a few metres in from the right edge of the buttress (cairn). The initial tier is steep, but gives way to more relaxed climbing above.
1. 30m 5a Follow a shallow groove right to the base of two obvious parallel cracks. Climb these on the left, then up past a ledge and awkward finger crack to a stance.
2. 20m 4c Move left then up past a small roof and continue to the first terrace.
3. 25m Scramble up the terrace to the second tier.
4. 30m 4b Climb this tier directly, taking a blank wall at mid-height from left to right and finishing up an open corner.
5. 20m Go up the second terrace to the third tier.
6. 30m 4c Climb a flake-choked groove leading to a smooth impending corner and an off-width crack, then more easily to a stance.
7. 15m A final easy groove leads to the long summit ridge. Scramble 200m to the summit.

Starters Gully   400m   III   (1982)
This is the wide gully left of Main Buttress, between it and Stepped Ridge. Climb by any one of several runnels. The best takes the right side and a steep chimney at half-height. Where the gully crests with Stepped Ridge, traverse left for 60m and climb a gully for 100m to just short of the west summit.

Stepped Ridge   240m   Very Difficult †   (1933)
The ridge left of Starters Gully gives good individual pitches, which if
taken direct are harder than the grade given. The original route makes
detours left as necessary. It was described as fairly indefinite, 'although there is a certain amount of grass and earth work'. A summary
of the account is as follows:
    Avoid the first pitch of the first step by a gully on the right, then climb
a steep 15m pitch to the top of the first tower. Next was a 20m pitch
with a gap followed by a pitch with a severe overhang. A stomach
traverse right below the overhang led to a sensational corner and a
difficult step up to a ledge with a beak overlooking the gully on the
right. From here the route led up through a window to the top of the
second step. Above, a narrow platform led to a slabby wall climbed
diagonally left, then a steep 20m pitch with a difficult start gained the
top of the third step. The fourth step is the largest. Two thirds of the
way up a 3m vertical knife-edge forces a detour into the gully on the
left. Climb this for 45m before traversing back onto the ridge. The final
pitch to the fourth step climbs a crack on the right.

Surprise Gully   400m   II   (1984)
Left of Stepped Ridge the face opens out until another gully is reached.
After a long initial deviation right to avoid a large boulder choke, the
climb continues to a col, with a 50m drop to a hidden gully (the top
part of Starters Gully). Traverse right from the col for 40m, then take
the open face for 160m to the top.

Pinnacle Surprise   180m   Very Difficult   (1984)
The left flank of Surprise Gully below the col is made up of three
pinnacles. This is the lowest of the three. Start at the lowest rocks left
of Surprise Gully. Follow short walls and grooves to the foot of a steep
buttress. Move up and left to the buttress edge, where exposed moves
lead to a groove above. Follow the crest of the ridge for two further
pitches to reach the surprisingly abrupt and airy top of the pinnacle.
Descent is via the south side to a col, followed by an abseil down the
left (north) branch of the gully.

Gairloch

This chapter includes a number of low-level crags which are within easy reach of Gairloch, and which are suitable for a short day or for doubtful weather.

RAVEN'S CRAG
(Map Ref 795 714)

This pleasant, low level, south-facing crag provides several unserious routes. The rock is good, and it dries quickly. Just south of Gairloch take the B8056 to Badachro. After 2km, just before the Shieldaig Lodge Hotel, turn up a farm track on the left. A walk of about 2km leads to Lochan Fuar. Just before the lochan the crag will be seen in profile about 500 metres away on the right. The climbs are described from right to left.

Hydro Hek 40m Hard Severe (1982)
Start at the right end of the crag, beneath a shield of rock on the upper wall.
1. 20m Climb clean brown slabs to the base of the shield.
2. 20m From the right side traverse up left across the shield and continue to the top.

Badachro 45m Severe (1982)
Left of the shield of Hydro Hek is a wall with a diagonal crack with a slot in it. The crack continues down the lower wall as a series of thin cracks.
1. 20m Start up whitish broken rock and climb by the line of thin cracks to the heather terrace.
2. 25m Climb the diagonal crack past the slot and continue up easy walls to the top.

Lonmore 60m Severe (1983)
The middle of the wall is divided at about 15m by a heather terrace with a prominent tree, from which a diagonal fault rises up left to another tree and a recess with a small triangular overhang.
1. 15m Climb directly to the tree on the heather terrace.

2. 35m Move up left to the diagonal fault. Climb this past the tree and raven's nest. Step left round the bulge to ledges.
3. 10m Climb a short wall to the top.

Ken's Joy 55m Severe   (1982)
Start about 10 metres left of Lonmore.
1. 25m Climb by heather and rocks to the midway terrace and belay as for Lonmore.
2. 30m Climb up to a small tree on the right of the Lonmore fault and climb a parallel diagonal fault to the top.

Stage Fright 55m VS   (1985)
Takes the blank looking upper wall left of Lonmore. Start directly beneath.
1. 25m Climb slabs to the heather terrace.
2. 30m 5a Climb steeply up the wall to join the final moves of Lonmore. Continue easily to the top.

Charlestone 50m Severe   (1981)
Takes the diagonal break in the upper wall left of Stage Fright.
1. 25m Climb slabs to the terrace.
2. 25m Move left up cracks, step right to a waterworn scoop and up left to the top.

Lucy 50m Very Difficult   (1984)
Left of Charlestone there is a right-slanting diagonal weakness in the lower slabs.
1. 35m Climb directly up the line of weakness to heather ledges.
2. 15m Broken walls and ledges to the top.

At the left end of the crag there is a large grass ledge about 15m up, forming part of a left slanting rake. Below the tree on the grass ledge is a broken scoop in the lower rocks.

Entasis 50m VS   (1986)
Start just right of the broken scoop at a small ramp.
1. 25m Climb directly up slabs to reach a heather ledge at the top of a rocky ramp running up from the tree.

2. 25m 4c Climb a broken wall to a heather shelf which slopes up right from the grass ledge. Step left across the shelf into a recess and climb an awkward crack to the top.

Mountain Ash 60m Very Difficult   (1991)
Start 10m right of Entasis, directly below the topmost rowan tree on the crag. Take a direct line to the top, passing over huge blocks at 15m and continuing up a shallow depression.

Groove Climb 20m VS 5a   (1986)
This climbs the steep wall above the grass ledge. Scramble up to the grass ledge from the left and start directly behind the tree. Climb a wall, a short groove and steep cracks to finish.

Leac McCac 25m Severe   (1986)
Round the left end of the crag is a dark slab of rough rock. Climb the slab direct.

Far Post 25m Very Difficult   (1986)
Climb the rib on the left of the dark slab and finish up a groove.

Flakes 20m Very Difficult   (1991)
Climb the corner on the right of the slab rib of Far Post, passing obvious flakes on the right, then continue to the terrace.

Special K 20m Severe   (1991)
Start 1 metre right of Flakes; climb the slab by a right-slanting line, crossing Leac McCac at some point.

Jutting Blocks 20m Very Difficult   (1991)
At the right side of the dark rough slab are prominent jutting blocks. Climb to and pass the blocks on the left, then continue to the top.

Two Guns 50m Severe †   (1991)
Start under the small rounded hood of overhangs at the left end of the frontal face. Climb up to and over the overhangs, then up a whaleback to a large terrace with a birch tree. Climb the left-slanting groove system in the steep upper wall (behind the tree and at the base of a shallow grass groove).

AN GROBAN
(Map Ref 838 753)

Easily approached from Gairloch in about one hour, this crag provides a few pleasant climbs. The crag is on the north-west side of the hill and is defined by a gully on the right and grassy grooves on the left. About 15 metres right of these grooves is a large boulder which marks the start of Blackgang.

Blackgang   80m   HVS
1. 40m Start at a grassy crack 3 metres from the large boulder. Climb the crack and wall above into a corner; continue up easy rock into a corner leading to a bulge which is taken on the right.
2. 40m A short, brutal chimney (avoidable) leads to easier rocks.

The black wall 5 metres left of Blackgang has been climbed. (**Slipway**, VS; numerous variations are possible.)

Hatman   70m   VS
Start below a prominent overhang near the right side of the crag. Climb up to the first overhang, pass it on the left and go up to a second overhang. Traverse left and climb the crack above. After 40m the climbing eases.

Straker   70m   Severe
This is the obvious groove flanking the main face right of Hatman. Start at the right corner of the crag at the foot of a gully (cairn). Climb the groove steeply, step left at 7m and continue up the main groove overlooking the gully.

JETTY CRAG
(Map Ref 961 926)

This crag lies further north from Gairloch, close to Gruinard House, and is as easily reached from Dundonnell. It is a useful roadside crag with a number of routes between 15m and 30m long. The descriptions should be used with caution.

NORTH WALL

Route 1   Very Difficult
Start at a prominent V-groove 6 metres from the fence at the end of the north face of the crag. Climb the groove for a short distance, go left onto the arete and then left and up by a small tree.

Route 2   Severe
Start as for Route 1, but continue up the groove to its top. Go left onto the arete and then step across the groove to finish up the top slab, either by the left-hand crack or grooves in a slab. Alternatively, after stepping across the groove, continue up the wall.

Route Major   Hard Severe
Approximately 8 metres towards the road from the start of the fence, climb the pale-coloured rock onto a slab and continue up to a large ledge and then up a short top wall by the centre crack.

Route 4   VS
Start in the deep corner to the right of Route Major. Climb the corner crack for 4m and then go left onto the arete. Continue up the arete onto the slab and finish as for Route Major.

Buttress Crack   VS
Start at a small detached pinnacle left of black rock in a depression. Climb onto the main face awkwardly and go right to the main crack in the buttress. Climb past a small tree and continue up a groove past loose-sounding blocks at top.

Route 6   Severe
Start right of Buttress Crack by a small black cave. Climb a slanting crack trending right for 6m until opposite a large grass bank. Then trend left to the top following the left-hand crack.

Route 7   Very Difficult
Climb black streaks 6 metres right of Route 6, trending left to reach the large grass bank. Continue up the slab above.

Munroron Very Difficult
Climb the centre of the obvious bottle-shaped rib between Route 7 and Lilly The Pink.

Lilly the Pink Hard Severe
Start to the left of the north-west arete in a depression. Follow the pink-coloured rock up the centre of the depression and trend left to the top.

The edge between Lilly the Pink and Crab Crack has been climbed at HVS 5a. There is a bold lower section with no protection.

FRONT WEST WALL

Crab Crack VS
Start 5 metres to the right of the arete and fence post. Climb to a grass ledge and continue directly over a small bulge and then a thin crack. Finish as for Lilly the Pink.

Route 11 VS
Start as for Crab Crack. From the grass ledge go right up a corner past a small hollow-sounding nose and then direct to the top.

The wall left of Anthrax Flake has been climbed at E2 5c; no further details are available.

Anthrax Flake VS ***
This is the best climb on the crag. Start 5 metres from Crab Crack at the right side of a black depression. Climb pale-coloured rock up to a large detached flake. Climb the left edge of the flake, step onto the face and climb to the top of the flake, then direct to the top.

Charlie's Corner Hard Severe
Start at the obvious corner to the right of Anthrax Flake by a wall and tree. Climb the corner to a ledge on the left wall. Continue up to the left of the corner and up the left edge of pale-coloured rock above. At the top of the pale rock, step right back into main crack. Charlie's Corner Direct follows the main crack past the ivy to the top at HVS.

Right Charlie   E1 5b **
Start 8 metres to the right of Charlie's Corner. Climb the shallow corner to the top of the bulge and then traverse left past a sitting block and up to the ledge. Step right to a shallow corner directly above the start. Climb up and then left onto the face and finish by the obvious crack above.

Dave's Dilemma   VS
Start 3 metres to the left of South-West Arete. Climb the crack until level with a grass ledge on the left. Cross to this ledge and then go directly up by twin cracks.

South-West Arete   VS
Start from large boulders at the base of the arete and climb the arete direct.

FIRST SOUTH WALL
The obvious S-shaped crack 3 metres right of South-West Arete has been climbed on aid; **Bat Crack**, A1. It may be possible without aid, but it is often wet.

Limited Stop   HVS 4c
At the centre of the wall there is a large tree. Go left from the tree along a ledge and follow the edge of the rock up to an obvious crack. Follow the crack to the top.

Bus Stop   Severe
Start directly behind the tree and climb the wall and cracks.

Doddle   Very Difficult *
Start to the right of the tree and climb onto the face. Continue along a ledge for 2m and then climb an obvious crack to a large ledge and tree. Abseil off.
Alternative start: Halfway along the face between Doddle and Tick Fever there is a dark depression. Climb this to the left of a black streak to a ledge. This is a fine boulder problem that far exceeds the grade of the parent climb (5a/b).

Tick Fever   Very Difficult
Start at the right edge of the wall by a tree and the start of the fence. Climb up and left into an obvious crack and continue up this to a large ledge and tree. Abseil off.

SHORT WEST WALL

Batty   VS
Approximately half-way along the wall climb a pale slab and leftward trending crack system to a tree; pass this and climb a block to a large holly tree. Climb the back wall.

Eclipse   Hard Severe
To the right of Batty there is a prominent groove with a dark-coloured slab to the left. Climb this to a ledge and tree. Climb the back wall in the corner on loose sounding blocks.

Starwood   HVS 5a **
The next crack right from Eclipse with a small tree growing near the bottom. Climb the crack (crux) to a ledge (possible belay). Climb the back wall to a triangular block, trending right onto a large flake on the arete and then up the edge of the south wall and back onto the arete to finish in an excellent position.

SECOND SOUTH WALL

Kew   VS
Climb the wall up to the detached block on the left-hand corner. Step right onto the wall and after 10m go left onto a large flake and finish as for Starwood.

South-West Corner   Severe
Climb the corner where the Second South Wall meets the Back West Wall.

BACK WEST WALL

Gruinard Corner   HVS 5a *
Approximately halfway along the wall there is a small crack to the right of a hanging juniper bush and left of the start of the broken overhanging rock. Climb this crack to a small ledge. Continue up the crack to the left of the ledge and then go left into the corner and up this to the top.

CREAG MHOR THOLLAIDH
(Map Ref 864 776)

Overlooking the shore at the western end of Loch Maree, this rugged lump of Lewisian gneiss has numerous crags dotted about it on all sides. However, it is those which lie low down on its northern flanks that have so far been developed for rock climbing. Set amidst picturesque surroundings, the crags have an atmosphere akin to the Lake District and offer a variety of fine, easily accessible routes on excellent rock.

The area has been climbed on since the 1960s, but exploration has been slow, although over the years a number of notables have contributed to its development. Surprisingly for such an accessible crag, most routes have seen few ascents, and therefore some of the grades should be treated with caution.

There are four principal crags. Upper and Lower Tollie Crags are the nearest to the car park; Gully Crag (Map Ref 864 778) is up and to the right and Loch Maree Crag (Map Ref 880 768) is about 2km along the lochside. The crags catch the early morning sun, are fairly quick to dry and can often be climbed when the weather in the hills is poor.

Access
About 2km south of Poolewe, on the Gairloch road, a single track road (signposted Tollie Bay) branches off to run past Tollie Farm and end at a small car park close to the water's edge. There are limited spots for camping near the car park. Permission should be sought first from the farm. There is a campsite at Poolewe, with sea breezes to keep the midges at bay.

LOWER TOLLIE CRAG
Easily seen from the car park, the crag is only a few minutes walk away. On arrival a prominent short arete marks the right end of the lower right section of the crag. Descent from the climbs is either by abseil from small trees or by scrambling up right through heather to gain a small easy descent gully. The routes are described from right to left.

1 Hamilton's Groove and Arete 25m   E3 6a *   (1983)
The groove and crack in the prominent short arete.

2 Cloud Cuckoo Land 25m   HVS 5b *   (1987)
The obvious crack line through the break in the steep lower wall about
8 metres left of the arete. Climb a short corner, pull over the steepening
and follow a crack to step up left and finish by a corner crack.

3 Second Coast 30m   E2 *   (1987)
Start at a shallow cracked corner groove a short way below and left
of the previous route, where a grassy tree-lined ledge slants up left.
1. 10m 5a Climb the corner groove to a ledge.
2. 20m 5b   Move up right, climb a crack in the leaning wall and
continue up, crossing a small overlap, to finish by a short tricky slab.

4 Home Start 20m   E1 5b/c   (1988)
Start from the grassy tree-lined ledge, where a flake crack slants up
right. Climb the crack, move right then up into a niche below a steep
crack. Up this past an ancient wooden wedge.

5 Loctite 30m   E3 **   (1987)
An excellent route which starts below the tree-lined ledge at a short
undercut crack, just right of the corner of Rumple Fyke.
1. 10m 5c Gain the crack and follow it to the ledge.
2. 20m 6a Climb the flake crack as for Home Start, pull left and follow
a thin crack up the wall and move left just below the top.

6 Uhu 20m   E1 5b   (1987)
Start from the tree-lined ledge. Climb the crack left of Loctite directly,
to finish up the last few moves of Rumple Fyke.

7 Rumple Fyke 60m   VS †   (1967)
Start below the obvious, steep and often slimy corner marking the left
edge of this section of crag.
1. 15m Climb the corner to the grassy ledge and the foot of a right-
slanting flake crack.
2. 20m Climb the crack.
3. 25m Go up the slab above the belay to an overhang, then move
left to finish up steep grooves.

LOWER TOLLIE CRAG

2. Cloud Cuckoo Land
3. Second Coast
4. Home Start
5. Loctite
6. Uhu
7. Rumple Fyke
8. Friday the Thirteenth
10. Gudgeon
11. Catastasis
12. Decadent Days
13. The Trip
14. Gulf Coast Highway
15. The Hand Rail
16. Rain-in-the-Face
17. Stoney Broke
18. Each Uisge/Across the Lines
19. Shazam
20. Murray's Arete

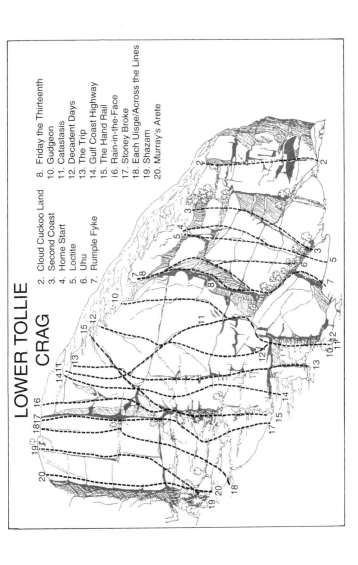

8 Friday the Thirteenth 65m HVS   (1975)
Takes the obvious corner capped by an overhang, starting as for
Rumple Fyke.
1. 20m Climb the corner and follow a grassy ramp left to the foot of
the continuation corner.
2. 45m Follow the corner to a roof, traverse out right to the lip of the
overhang and climb the large crack above to join Rumple Fyke at the
steep groove.

    Moving left, the crag now reaches its maximum height. Descent is
either by scrambling right across heather to come down on the right,
or by going up left to below the small upper buttress, making a short
abseil down a gully and scrambling down left. The next few routes
virtually share a common start.

9 North-West Orient 60m E4 *   (1990)
A good line which takes the right arete of the wall. Start to the right of
the tree start of Gudgeon beneath a short crack springing from a niche
with a holly on the left and a small tree on the right.
1. 25m 5b A flake crack leads to the niche, then climb the short crack
and so to a horizontal handrail. Traverse right for 5m, climb the wall
past a crack to reach a left-slanting ramp, then move up to belay as
for Gudgeon.
2. 35m 6a Climb the groove to a flake then step up right to a thin crack
(as for Gudgeon). Place a high runner, then traverse right to a peg and
climb the arete and cracks to the top.

10 Gudgeon 70m E2 ***   (1971/1987)
A good route with an excellent second pitch taking the thin crack up
the right edge of the crag. Start at a tree right of the obvious fault of
The Trip, at a recess.
1. 20m 5b Climb the tree and step up left to climb a short corner. Move
right, climb a groove then go right below the roofs to a stance on the
edge where a grassy ramp comes in from the right.
2. 30m 5c Step left to climb the corner crack to a horizontal break,
then step across right and climb a thin crack line in the wall to a belay
on the left of a large flake.
3. 20m 5a Climb the flake, step right then climb cracks to the top.

11 Catastasis 90m E2   (1968)
Takes the obvious diagonal crack slanting left across the face.
1. 20m 5b Pitch 1 of Gudgeon.
2. 25m 5b Climb the corner crack to the horizontal break (as for Gudgeon) then move left to gain the diagonal crack and climb this to a small stance.
3. 15m 5c Continue up the diagonal crack to a footledge. Go up and left to the upper stance on The Trip.
4. 30m 4b Move up then left and across to trees, then climb the large flake on the right to the top.
Variation to Pitch 2: **Toady** 25m
Traverse left to a rising diagonal rake blocked by a large wedged boulder. Climb the rake to where it is crossed by a vertical crack (Decadent Days) which is then followed to the small stance at the diagonal crack.

12 Decadent Days 80m E2 ***   (1983)
A superb route following a thin crackline directly up the crag. Start as for the previous routes at the tree.
1. 40m 5c Climb the tree and step up left to climb the short corner until it is possible to step left onto the lip of the roof to reach the thin crack line. Follow the crack to belay as for Catastasis at the diagonal crack.
2. 40m 5c Step up left to the diagonal crack, then move right to gain thin cracks which are climbed to the top.

13 The Trip 95m HVS *   (1967)
This route takes the obvious crack in the left section of the highest part of the crag. Start beneath the crack at a broken groove.
1. 35m Climb the groove, move left over a small overlap and follow a heathery ramp left, moving up at its end then back right to an oak tree. Climb the groove behind the tree, then continue up a small chimney to a good stance.
2. 25m Surmount the large perched blocks to the left of the stance, then step right into a groove which is followed trending up right to the base of a large flake. Move left and up for 4m, then traverse right to a constricted stance.
3. 35m Climb the cracked blocks behind the stance for 4m, step left to avoid an unpleasant heathery rake and continue up in almost a straight line, following the zigzag cracks leading to a heathery shoulder.

14   Gulf Coast Highway   75m   E3 **   (1988)
An excellent route which initially takes a line between The Trip and
The Handrail, crossing through the latter to climb a fine crack in the
headwall just right of Rain-In-The-Face. Start about 10m left of The
Trip.
1. 25m 5a   Move up and traverse right to blocks to gain an obvious
left-slanting crack, which is climbed to a tiny sapling. Step right and
climb the edge of the corner to belay beside a large flake just left of
The Trip.
2. 25m 5c   Start in the groove on the left and climb to a roof, pull round
left and move up to gain a good jug on the right. Move up left to the
edge of the buttress, then back right to surmount a roof and continue
up to a tree belay on The Handrail.
3. 25m 6a   Move up then left to gain a quartz patch, then go up to the
base of the thin right-leaning crack which is climbed to the top. An
abseil descent can be made down the corner of Stoney Broke.

15   The Hand Rail   80m   Severe **   (1966)
The left margin of the highest part of the crag is marked by the obvious
right-angled corner of Stoney Broke. Below this is a heathery depression from which a well-defined vegetated fault line slants up right
onto the main face. The route gives two fine pitches with good
exposure.

16   Rain-In-The-Face   75m   E3 ***   (1987)
A superb pitch up the obvious blunt arete right of Stoney Broke, gained
from The Handrail.
1. 40m 5a   Climb the vegetated fault of The Handrail to beneath the
roofs. Hand traverse a big jagged block to a hanging belay at the foot
of the arete.
2. 35m 6a   Make awkward moves out to the arete and up to the base
of a slim groove (hidden peg runner). Climb the groove to the roof and
move right to gain a thin crack line, which springs from the end of the
roof and is climbed in a fine position, close to the arete, to easier
ground. An abseil descent can be made down Stoney Broke.

17   Stoney Broke   70m   HVS *   (1970)
The large right-angled corner marking the left edge of the highest
section of the face. Start 12m left of The Handrail on a grassy terrace.

1. 40m 5b Climb a short wall to a heather patch, then go up diagonally right to climb a sloping ramp leading towards the corner. A small ledge is gained after a struggle with some bushes and the corner is then climbed to an overhang where a move onto the right wall and up gains a ledge and tree belays.

2. 30m 5a Continue in the corner with occasional detours onto the left wall and wide bridging to avoid some heather. An abseil descent can be made back down the line.

Variation: 40m HVS

A good alternate finish slants diagonally left across the wall from the stance at the start of pitch 2.

18 Each Uisge/Across The Lines 50m E4 **   (1987/88)

This combination of the original route and its direct start provides an excellent sustained route up the steep slab left of Stoney Broke. Scramble to a belay beneath the obvious direct entry crack to Shazam.

1. 25m 6a Immediately right of the direct entry to Shazam move up to small wedged blocks and a short thin crack, then step right and gain the horizontal break above. Continue to the next break, then climb directly to another break beneath a roof; step up left then up to holds at the next break and easier ground. Continue to a horizontal break, step up left and go up right to another break and peg belay.

2. 25m 6a Climb slabs up right then straight up to another horizontal break, peg runner. Step right and climb a thin crack with difficulty to a tree at the top. Descend by abseil.

19 Shazam 80m VS   (1969)

The wall and obvious wide crack in the steep slab left of the corner of Stoney Broke. Start by some oak trees. (The obvious direct start was climbed on the first ascent of Each Uisge, 5b).

1. 20m Break through the overhangs using the trees and climb the wall to a constricted stance.

2. 40m Traverse up and right to gain the main crack. Follow this to the ledge at the top.

3. 20m Continue up the wall above by a steep crack.

20 Murray's Arete 45m E3 5c *   (1983)

The obvious sharp arete marking the left end of the crag gives a serious pitch.

MIDDLE TOLLIE CRAG

Moving up left, two big messy gullies divide the Upper and Lower crags. The next route lies on the buttress between these gullies.

King Prawn   130m   Severe   (1969)
Start in a little grassy bay at the foot of the leftmost of the two gullies, below a slab.
1. 20m Go straight up the slab to a short heather ledge.
2. 20m Continue up the wall above to another heather ledge.
3. 10m Go up for 3m then left along the ledge to belay.
4. 15m Move up, then slant leftwards to a holly tree.
5. 20m Go left to a white birch, then continue to a ledge.
6. 20m Ascend the wall above to belay well back.
7. 25m Climb a black crack in the wall behind to finish.

UPPER TOLLIE CRAG

This lies a few minutes walk uphill from Lower Tollie Crag and has a much more open aspect. The most obvious features are the prominent tree-filled chimney fault of Knickerbocker Glory and on its right the crack of Cocaine. Descend by the easy slopes on the left.

The Ugly Duckling   130m   HVS   (1967)
Follows the right edge of the crag and is harder than it appears. Start at the lowest rocks immediately left of an obvious gully.
1. 45m Climb the black wall (crux), then go left past a small tree and up a good crack, moving left at its top to trees.
2. 40m Go left into a corner, climb the lower crack then go right to a tree and diagonally up right to mantleshelf onto the arete. Continue up thin slabs to belay.
3. 45m Climb the crack direct to the top.

Siren   70m   VS   (1968)
Takes an obvious line of cracks in a corner on the right side of the buttress to the left of The Ugly Duckling.
1. 30m Climb cracks past a tree to gain a ledge.
2. 20m The fierce corner above provides the crux and leads to a belay on the left.
3. 20m A short groove and slabs lead to easier rock and the top.

Love Is The Drug 90m   E2   (1988)
Climbs the wall right of Cocaine, starting right of that route below left-slanting twin cracks, directly below small holly and oak trees.
1. 25m 5b Climb twin cracks to a holly bush. Go up right to steep twin cracks which lead to easier climbing over huge blocks to a belay on the right.
2. 15m 5a Traverse left over the top of the blocks to a small ledge. Gain a small ledge above, then a second ledge before moving left to the line of Cocaine. Climb up for 4m and belay at the right side of the huge flake.
3. 20m 5b Leave the belay on the right and climb the obvious cracks to a roof. Pull out left and struggle up the crack above to a peg belay on a small ledge on Cocaine.
4. 30m 5a Big Toe, pitch 3.

Cocaine 80m   HVS   (1968)
The obvious crack line in the wall right of the chimney fault of Knickerbocker Glory. Although the crack is good, the remainder of the route is a bit scrappy and would benefit from some gardening. Start at the foot of the chimney fault.
1. 25m 5a Climb a right-slanting ramp, then move up to trees at the base of a huge flake. Move right to climb its right edge and squeeze through to belay on its top. Alternatively:
1a. 25m Follow Knickerbocker Glory for 10m, then go right up a crack and chimney to belay on the top of the flake.
2. 18m 5b Follow the crack above the flake to a horizontal break and step up right to belay.
3. 40m 5a/b Move right then hand traverse back left for 12m to gain a slabby ramp slanting back right to the edge.
3a. 30m 5a Alternatively and better, Big Toe, pitch 3.

Knickerbocker Glory 90m   E1   (1966)
The obvious tree-filled chimney fault with an excursion onto the left wall to avoid a bottleneck occupied by a holly tree.
1. 30m 5b Climb the loose chimney to the bottleneck. Move left, climb a thin crack to easier ground, then regain the chimney,
2. 60m Continue in the chimney to the top.

Big Toe   75m   E1 **   (1987)
A good route which cuts through Knickerbocker Glory and Cocaine.
Start immediately right of Teddy Bears Picnic.
1. 25m 5b Climb a slabby wall up and right to reach the crack of
Knickerbocker Glory. Follow this to a tree belay in the chimney.
2. 20m 5b Step down to gain and follow a right-rising crack line across
the wall to belay on Cocaine beside a perched block.
3. 30m 5a Traverse right to climb a crack leading up to the right edge,
step right and continue up easier rock to the top.

Teddy Bears' Picnic   30m   E1   (1967/88)
1. 30m 5b Climb the obvious right-slanting corner ramp over a roof
towards Knickerbocker Glory, step up left to gain a horizontal break,
then pull up to holds and climb a short crack to reach a tree belay in
the chimney. Abseil off. The original route followed the ramp all the
way into and up the chimney (HVS, 5b).

The Bug   50m   E2 5b ***   (1974)
A tremendous route taking the thin crack line in the wall left of Teddy
Bears' Picnic. To paraphrase a well-known guidebook to the area:
'similar to Diabaig Pillar, but better'. Climb the crack over a small bulge
to a ramp. Follow this rightwards, then step back left to another bulge.
Climb this on good holds to reach delightful, delicate and quite run-out
thin cracks in the slabby wall. Unfortunately, all good things come to
an end. Belay where the angle eases. Scramble up slightly right to the
top. The best descent is down heather to the left.

Heresy   50m   E4 5c
This is a serious variation on The Heretic. It takes the main feature of
the face left of The Bug, a huge right-leaning shallow scoop (The
Heretic avoids the blank lower half).

The Heretic   55m   E2/3 **   (1987)
Good though sparsely protected climbing up the wall between The
Bug and Pokey Hat.
1. 45m 5b Start as for Pokey Hat. Stand on the two blocks and step
right to a shallow slabby groove. Climb this (poor protection) to gain a
ramp (runner placement in the Bug up right). From a good hold at the
base of the ramp, move up then left to the start of a diagonal crack

which is climbed past a shallow scoop. Stand in the crack where it becomes horizontal and continue above, first right then left, to a diagonal break. Move up to another diagonal break and pull over onto a slabby ledge.
2. 10m Go easily up right, then up and off left.

Pokey Hat 70m VS   (1970)
Start 3 metres right of the obvious chimney at the left of the crag.
1. 35m Climb up right to two blocks and join a wide left-slanting flake crack. Move slightly left, then climb a thin right-slanting groove for about 9m before moving left to a wide crack which leads to heather ledges. This pitch appears to be poorly protected.
2. 35m Climb slabs and grooves crossing Knickerbocker Glory to finish.

Soft Option 75m Severe   (1969)
The right-hand of two black chimneys at the left end of the crag.
1. 30m Follow the loose chimney for 25m, then move right onto a big slab. Belay in the obvious shallow right-trending scoop.
2. 45m Do not follow the scoop. Instead, climb cracks in the steep slab above and eventually cross Knickerbocker Glory and finish up a short slab.

   Moving left level with this crag and a few minutes walk away are two ridges. **Minute**, (45m, Severe, 1975), climbs the first ridge, and **Second** (50m, Severe, 1975), the second (which is about 30 metres left of the first ridge).

THE GULLY CRAG
This lies up and right of Lower Tollie Crag. There is a smooth diamond-shaped crag on the right wall of the gully which starts from the road about 200 metres short of the car park.

Anti Gravity 65m VS   (1966)
Start in the centre of the cliff between two cracks at an arrow.
1. 35m Climb straight up, first into a groove, then on good holds to a peg belay.
2. 30m Continue up a thin crack, above and left of the belay, then left of a grassy line to trees.

WHITE WALL CRAG

This is the obvious white wall situated mid-way between Tollie Crag and Loch Maree Crag. The central fault is full of trees, and the right side is crossed by several diagonal cracks. The clean left side is split at mid-height by a diagonal crack.

The Left Arete   40m   VS 4c   (1968)
Climb the slabby left arete of the left side of the crag, keeping close to the edge all the way. The crux is at the top and is protected with RPs.

The Shimmer   30m   E4 6a **   (1992)
This gives superb face climbing, sustained and varied and with good protection, up the centre and clean left side of the wall. Start in the middle at a thin wiggly crack in a patch of black rock. Climb the crack to a small ledge. Step left, then follow the line up and right to a flake. Step right and gain the diagonal crack, then follow this left with surprising difficulty to near its end. Step back right, then go diagonally up and right (again with difficulty) to gain a thin crack to finish.

LOCH MAREE CRAG

This impressive crag lies about 2km along the lochside and is reached by following a footpath close to the water's edge then cutting up to the base of the crag. A very prominent overhanging arete is the crag's most striking feature; many of the climbs take the gently impending wall to its left. This is another place where some of the routes seem to have aquired a reputation as being rather hard for their grades. The best descent from the harder routes is by abseil, using *in situ* gear.

1   Hoax   100m   VS   (1967)
This route takes an obvious groove just right of the prominent arete. The description is that supplied by the second ascensionists, who thought the original description somewhat lacking, bearing in mind the name.
1. 30m Climb the groove up the nose for 20m, move right across a steep wall then go left and up to belay by an obvious vast nest.
2. 20m A steep wall and groove lead to a step left and loose blocks. Climb up to a ledge and tree belay.

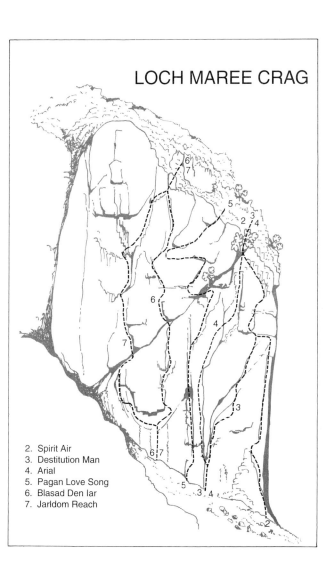

LOCH MAREE CRAG

2. Spirit Air
3. Destitution Man
4. Arial
5. Pagan Love Song
6. Blasad Den Iar
7. Jarldom Reach

3. 25m Make a remarkably ungardened traverse left across a steep wall to a groove above a grass ledge. Gain terraces above the tree belay on the right.
4. 25m Climb a fine wall on excellent rough rock diagonally left to a final short wall.

2 Spirit Air 50m E4 6a ***   (1987)
A stunning route, at the upper limit of its grade, which takes the crack up the left side of the impressive arete. Start at the base of the arete. Go up the easy groove and where this ends pull directly up the wall to gain the crack, which is followed in a mindblowing situation with continual interest until it fades out. Just above is a horizontal fault-crack which runs left then diagonally up to a large shield of white rock. Follow this, then take the right side of the shield to go up slightly right to gain large holds. Move diagonally left for 5m, then step left to obvious jugs beside the huge diagonal fault. Move up to a tree belay. Abseil off.

3 Destitution Man 50m E3 5c **   (1987)
The first crack line left of Spirit Air, steep and strenuous in its lower half. Start below the crack with a tiny sapling at 5m. Climb the crack through the bulges, trending right past blocks to follow the right-hand cracks diagonally up right, with brief excursions onto the right wall. Join Spirit Air at the white shield and finish up this.

4 Arial 50m E3 5c ***   (1992)
An excellent route which gives sustained and strenuous climbing up the fine crack line up the centre of the wall immediately below the abseil point. Start as for Destitution Man. Climb the crack through a bulge, then continue directly. The crack line becomes more defined then bends right into a jagged flake crack. Continue in the same direct line, up a shallow groove in the centre of the face to the holly tree at the top.

5 Pagan Love Song 55m E4 **   (1992)
This climbs the right-hand of the twin cracks left of Arial, then breaks out left to finish up the upper wall.
1. 30m 5c Pull into the corner and make tricky moves up and right to a small flake, which leads to a ledge. Follow the right-hand of twin cracks over several bulges to gain an obvious large niche. Continue directly up the crack above, then follow a flake bending slightly right

until above an obvious moss-covered rock boss in the fault on the left (5m below the tree). Traverse left to stand and belay on the boss.
2. 25m 6a Pull out left from the belay using an obvious horizontal line. Go up to a horizontal crack, then gain and climb the flake up and right. At its top, traverse left with increasing difficulty to join the slabby scoop of Blasad Den Iar. Climb this for 3m, until the right side bulges. Traverse out right at the level of a small slot, then move diagonally up right to the top. Belay 5m up and left.

6   Blasad Den Iar   50m   E3 5c **   (1987)
A direct line through the centre of the diagonal fault, starting about 15m up the gully from Spirit Air, where it closes to form a wide chimney. Climb a seepage of white calcite, then take the crack above to the left end of a ramp, which is followed right to below a short hanging corner. Pull steeply through an overlap on jugs to ascend the left side of the corner, then trend right to gain thin cracks leading to the large diagonal fault. Pull out of the fault via the flake and climb directly to a horizontal crack where thin climbing up an intermittent crack enables a good flat hold to be gained, runner above. A traverse right gains a shallow groove which is followed until it forms a slight ramp; break up the wall above to a large perched block on the lip and a belay on the right. Scramble left via trees to escape or abseil off.

7   Jarldom Reach   50m   E5 6b ***   (1987)
Another excellent route which starts as for Blasad Den Iar then breaks left to go directly up the wall above the diagonal fault via two scoops. Follow Blasad Den Iar to the ramp, then go up and left to cracks leading steeply to blocks at the left end of the fault. Follow the fault right just beyond a large wedged block (possible belay). Pull out of break using a flake, then follow this to another flake. Step left into a scoop, then take a slim groove on its right to a jug at its top. Pull up left with hard moves through a white bulge to a second scoop. Traverse right to a slim groove which is followed with hard moves near its top reaching right for jugs. Finish at the perched block of Blasad Den Iar.

Letterewe and Fisherfield

This area has some of the best climbing and wild walking in the Northern Highlands. The distances can be quite large; indeed, the mountain frequently cited as being the most remote Munro summit is within this area. A good approach is to plan a trip lasting a few days, thus enabling visits to several of the excellent crags. The owners of the estate have erected signs to discourage walking outwith the main paths, and also camping. However, except in the stalking season, in practice these restrictions are not enforced. It is in the interest of all climbers that good relations are maintained with the owners, so please be discreet, remove all litter, and refrain from visiting during the stalking season. The owners have recently renovated the barn at Carnmore, and there is even a sign saying "Climbers Welcome". Those wishing to stay more than one night might be well advised to contact the estate factor or stalker at Kernsary beforehand. (Tel: 044 586 215)

BEINN AIRIGH CHARR
791m   (Map Ref 931 764)

This is the most accessible of the mountains north of Loch Maree. Coming from Poolewe, the path from Kernsary to Carnmore passes close under the large north-east facing cliffs of Martha's Peak, which is the north top of the mountain. Like Beinn Lair, the cliffs are of hornblende schist, providing good incut holds but treacherous when wet. Despite their imposing appearance, the climbing on the main cliffs is primarily in the nature of Alpine scrambling, but most enjoyable all the same. There are shorter, steeper climbs towards the left (south-east) end of the cliffs, whose sensational overhanging profile is seen soon after leaving Kernsary. The climbs are described from right to left, as one would normally approach from Kernsary.

Comic Relief   250m   III   (1988)
This climbs up the face overlooking the corrie above the north-west end of Loch an Doire Crionaich, right of the main cliffs of Martha's Peak. The climbing starts at an altitude of about 500m. Follow the distinct gully-chimney line splitting the centre of the face, taking the

right fork at mid-height. Near the top it is possible to finish more easily to the right or follow the natural line up a narrow chimney.

Original Route   330m   Difficult   (1910)
The main face of Martha's Peak rises directly above Loch an Doire Crionaich. There are two lower buttresses on either side, somewhat like the parts of an arrowhead with the head formed by the main face. Go up screes and easy ground between the two lower buttresses to the foot of the main face. Thread heather ledges and easy rocks up and right until below the steep upper part of the face. Climb some way right of the steepest section, which forms a vague nose. From a platform halfway up the upper crags a wide choice of routes leads to the top. Ling's original party followed a narrow, well-defined but grassy chimney, with scant holds.

Staircase Gully   360m   Severe   (1964)
This is the gully separating the main tower of Martha's Peak from the lower cliffs to the left. The climbing is about Very Difficult except for the crux pitch. There is much loose scree between pitches. Begin by climbing the left wall of the gully. After 60m the second pitch follows a groove left of a chockstone, (20m). After another 45m climb in the right corner of another huge chockstone. Easy ground follows, then a steep, rotten section, (20m). Above this a slimy part of the gully is avoided by two pitches on the left, (45m). An overhanging chimney above gives the crux (12m), followed by 90m of easy ground to the top of the gully.

Lower Buttress   150m   Difficult   (1977)
This climbs the clean, rocky crest at the right side of the lower buttress rising above the south-east end of Loch an Doire Crionaich. There is a steep wall at 120m, breached by a 15m pitch.

Lower Buttress Direct   150m   Severe   (1951)
Start at the lowest rocks and go left up a rake on loose, flaky rock. Continue for 90m up easy grass and rock to boiler-plate slabs and then a steep 30m wall, with a crack in its upper part near the centre. Below and left is a 5m sentry-box with a grass ledge on the right. Climb with difficulty over the nose of the sentry-box and continue right on a narrow ledge with good holds, then back over slabs higher up. Easy rocks lead to the top of the Lower Buttress, from where a choice of lines may be taken up the upper face.

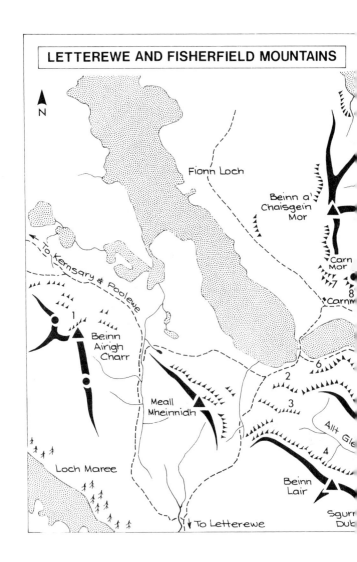

LETTEREWE AND FISHERFIELD MOUNTAINS

N

Fionn Loch

Beinn a'
Chaisgein
Mor

Carn
Mor

Carn

To Kernsary & Poolewe

To Kernsary & Poolewe

1

Beinn
Airigh
Charr

Meall
Mheinnidh

Loch Maree

2

3

6

7

8

Allt Gle

4

Beinn
Lair

Sgurr
Dub

To Letterewe

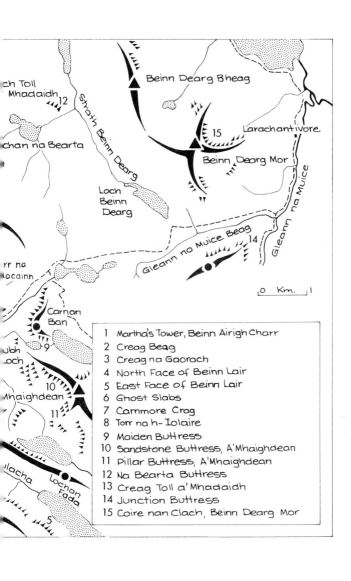

ch Toll
Mhadaidh 12

chan na Bearta

Strath Beinn Dearg

Beinn Dearg Bheag

15

Larachantivore

Beinn Dearg Mor

Loch
Beinn
Dearg

Gleann na Muice

rr na
ocainn

Gleann na Muice Beag 14

0   Km.   1

Carnan
Ban

9

ubh
och

10

Mhaighdean

11

lacha

Lochan
Fada

5

1	Martha's Tower, Beinn Airigh Charr
2	Creag Beag
3	Creag na Gaorach
4	North Face of Beinn Lair
5	East Face of Beinn Lair
6	Ghost Slabs
7	Carnmore Crag
8	Torr na h-Iolaire
9	Maiden Buttress
10	Sandstone Buttress, A'Mhaighdean
11	Pillar Buttress, A'Mhaighdean
12	Na Bearta Buttress
13	Creag Toll a'Mhadaidh
14	Junction Buttress
15	Coire nan Clach, Beinn Dearg Mor

The first climb recorded on Martha's Peak, by Glover and Ling (1909), started somewhere near the left end of Lower Buttress. After an awkward traverse they reached a heather platform near the top of Staircase Gully, whence the route went by a series of fine ledges to the top.

A little way left from Lower Buttress there is a jumble of monstrous boulders below a big wet overhanging wall, which has, as yet, no routes. Below and left of this is a very prominent clean arete with a slabby face on its right.

The Roc   90m   HVS   (1974)
Start 25 metres up and right from the base of the clean arete of The Beanstalk.
1. 40m Climb diagonally left up steep rock to overcome a lower bulge, then traverse back right to belay below a groove.
2. 35m Climb the groove to a stance on the right.
3. 15m Finish up a deep groove.

The Beanstalk   100m   HVS *   (1971)
The clean arete gives a fairly serious climb in fine position.
1. 35m Climb on the left of the arete, with an awkward move left at about 20m, and continue to a good ledge.
2. 35m Start on the left and move up and right towards the arete. An awkward move left past a bulge leads to easier climbing and a belay on the left.
3. 30m Climb the left wall to the top.

Square Buttress   120m   Difficult   (1951)
This is the next prominent buttress, well left of The Beanstalk (at Map Ref 938 705, near a small lochan unnamed on the OS map). The main feature of the buttress is on its left flank, but to the right of the buttress is an obvious black crack (50m, Very Difficult). Start at a gangway slanting left from the bottom right-hand corner, leading to a ledge which is followed right for 6m. The wall above is steep, then slabby. A further 18m pitch ends the lower half of the buttress. The upper half is easy but interesting.

MEALL MHEINNIDH
720m   (Map Ref 955 748)

This is the next hill south-east of Beinn Airigh Charr. It has one recorded route: **Glasgow Ridge** (150m, Very Difficult) takes the central rise, skirting below an obvious slanting terrace.

Below Meall Mheinnidh the Carnmore path descends towards Fionn Loch where it is joined by the path from Letterewe. The path continues below Creag Beag, past some delightful sandy strands at the head of the loch and over the causeway.

CREAG BEAG   *(Map Ref 972 753)*

This crag lies directly above the junction of the Kernsary and Letterewe paths at the south-east end of Fionn Loch. It is much larger than its name implies.

Little Big-Horn   60m   E5 *   (1988)
There is a prominent jutting roof half-way up the main left-hand dome of the crag. This route takes the obvious line of bulging grooves which skirt the great roof on the right. It is a very good climb with impressive situations. Start just left of an obvious corner flanking a tree-filled bay.
1. 15m 4c Climb straight up orange rock, where there is a quartz intrusion, to reach a curving flake-fault. Move right and up two detached flakes to traverse round right into the top of the tree-filled bay.
2. 25m 5c Move back round left and up right onto the nose. Climb the wall and bulge above into a slabby corner. Move up to the roof and traverse the slab left to belay on top of a creaking flake above the great roof.
3. 20m 6b Move up the little rib to surmount the big roof above and gain a leg-jam rest in the overhanging groove. Finish up this to a rest at a wobbly spike. Move up grassy ground past a loose tree to belay.

Temerity   85m   VS *   (1957)
A little to the right of the great central break that splits the crag is a nose, slightly undercut at its base and with a steep groove on the right. The climb is enjoyable for the first two pitches but disappointing above. Start just left of the nose at an indefinite groove.

1. 30m Go up the left wall of the groove, traverse right and pull up. Continue up for 3m and go right into a shallow groove. Ascend 3m and go right again, then climb a 5m wall and continue more easily until a left move leads to a stance below a smooth wall.
2. 20m Traverse right to a corner crack and climb this to a large terrace.
3. 35m Above the terrace the upper part of the crag is more broken. Climb a wall for 8m to a pulpit, then go right then left to an ash tree and finish up a steep wall.

A number of other climbs have been made on this crag but not recorded. **Central Groove**, (grade uncertain) is the groove leading directly up to the corner crack on the second pitch of Temerity. The rib at the right end of the crag is 75m, Very Difficult.

Following the path towards the causeway, Hanging Crag will be seen high up on the right, then the impressive Ghost Slabs and then, after the causeway, the 'jewel in the crown', Carnmore. These are described later, but first we make a detour south to describe the climbs on Creag na Gaorach and Beinn Lair.

CREAG NA GAORACH   *(Map Ref 974 747)*

These pleasant buttresses are reached by following the stream from the junction of the Kernsary and Letterewe paths at the south-east end of Fionn Loch. The stream leads into a narrow defile with three principal buttresses on the right (south) side, and another small buttress just below the col at its head.

Jealousy 200m Very Difficult   (1957)
This lies on the first (west) buttress. Start a few metres left of where the stream washes against the foot of the rocks.
1. 30m Climb a steep slab slightly left.
2. 25m Climb a slabby rib left of a wet corner crack.
3. 25m Climb up to an overhung ledge.
4. 30m Go over the lip of the overhang and straight up to a ledge; then left and up to perched blocks.
5. 25m Go diagonally right up the ledge and then up a bulbous grey slab to a small ledge.
6. and 7. 65m Follow the blunt rib and continue to the top.

The middle buttress is characterised by a large reddish slab at the bottom leading up to a prominent overhang. **Denizen** (VS, 135m) trends left up the lower slab and bypasses the steep central barrier on the left. The exact details are uncertain; see SMCJ 1980.

Zebra Slabs   135m   Very Difficult *   (1957)
This excellent climb lies on the third (east) buttress, also known as Nanny Goat Buttress. Start at the centre of the buttress behind some fallen blocks, just left of a sapling.
1. 25m Climb the steep rib, which is hard to start but soon eases, and follow it to a belay below a little lip on the left.
2. 25m Return right and gain a narrow ramp of slab leading into a crack on the left. Climb this then return to the crest of the rib at the top. Pass a small turf ledge and climb the slab above to belay in a shallow chimney on the right.
3. 35m Traverse left and climb a blunt rib to large turf ledges.
4. 15m Directly above is a block overhang on the skyline, with other overhangs on the right. Climb up to gain a slab rib which slants up left of the block overhang.
5. 35m Follow the rib to the top.

Rainbow's End   130m   VS   (1967)
This follows the rib forming the left edge of the buttress. The difficulties ease after the first two pitches. Start about 15 metres left of Zebra Slabs, just right of a gully.
1. 25m Go up the rib to a heathery stance at the foot of a corner groove below overhangs.
2. 20m Climb a short way up the steep rib and step round onto the left wall; move left and up by a crack, then back right to meet a diagonal fault going back left. Move up to a small roof and traverse blindly right round the nose above an overhang to reach easier slabs which lead to a grass ledge.
3. 40m Go up the slabby rib on the left, keeping left of a projecting block at 15m, and continue to a terrace.
4. 10m Trend left to a groove below the attractive skyline rib.
5. 25m Climb a slabby rib to a ledge and a small nose on the left to the top.

BEINN LAIR
860m (Map Ref 982 733)

The long north-east face of Beinn Lair has the greatest escarpment of hornblende schist in the country. It offers a number of interesting climbs in the lower grades, both summer and winter.

Access
The approach is usually from Carnmore or directly from Poolewe. From the path junction at the south end of Fionn Loch it is possible to climb up the Letterewe path towards Bealach Mheinnidh then strike off left and climb up to Bealach a' Chuirn, bringing one out below the cliffs at the right end of the face. A slightly more interesting variant is to go from the path junction directly up the narrow valley below Creag na Gaorach, which brings one out opposite Butterfly Buttress.

For the climbs at the south-east end of the face above Lochan Fada the Carnmore-based climber may possibly prefer an approach via Dubh Loch and Beinn Tharsuinn Chaol. Although this involves more ascent and descent, it offers a remarkable view of the face as a whole. Lochan Fada can also be reached from Kinlochewe via Gleann Bianasdail.

The greenish hornblende schist, with its sharp holds, offers an unusual and quite characteristic type of climbing. It tends to be very greasy when wet and not good for protection; however the steeper parts are less vegetated than might be expected. The climbs are described from right to left (north-west to south-east), and the individual buttresses may be identified from the diagram. The slender, cigar-shaped Wisdom Buttress is easily recognised, with the vertical slot of Bat's Gash on its left. The buttress to its right is called The Tooth, and right again is an area of indefinite cliff ending in a deep-cut gully. The first climb is on the buttress right of this.

1 Excalibur 120m Very Difficult   (1952)
This lies on the clean mass of rock right of the main crags. There is a deep gully on the left and a buttress with overhangs on the right. Start at the side of the gully. The climbing is initially moderate, becoming steeper. Negotiate some minor overhangs with good holds to reach a capacious ledge, below a steep slab ending in an overhang. Cross the slab diagonally left, then traverse right below the overhang. Climb easily to the top.

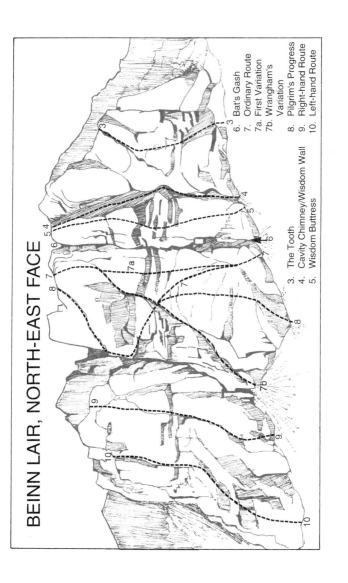

BEINN LAIR, NORTH-EAST FACE

3. The Tooth
4. Cavity Chimney/Wisdom Wall
5. Wisdom Buttress

6. Bat's Gash
7. Ordinary Route
7a. First Variation
7b. Wrangham's Variation
8. Pilgrim's Progress
9. Right-hand Route
10. Left-hand Route

2   West Chimney Route   180m   Very Difficult †   (1951)
Climbs the right side of the buttress right of The Tooth. The details may
be hard to follow. Start about 30m left of the 'nose' of the buttress.
Climb a moist groove leftwards over steep, discontinuous rock to a
large grass terrace, below a steeper wall (120m). Climb the wall by a
wet chimney in the left corner to a stance. Enter a gully leading to a
cave above. Climb a steep rib of good rock up to the right. Continue
easily to the top.

3   The Tooth   200m   Difficult   (1951)
Start near the middle of the buttress right of Wisdom Buttress. Climb
directly up until at about half-height the route joins the left crest of the
buttress. Continue to the top by a delightful series of short, exposed
pitches.

4   Cavity Chimney and Wisdom Wall   215m   Very Difficult (1951)
Cavity Chimney is the short chimney to the right of the foot of Wisdom
Buttress. This is followed by a long crack, grassy and easy, to a fork.
The buttress between the arms of the fork is The Fang, and to its left,
separated by a crack, is Wisdom Wall (on the right side of the upper
half of Wisdom Buttress). Follow the crack for 30m, then climb up and
across the exposed wall on the left (30m, poor belays). It is possible
to move left onto Wisdom Buttress, but a better finish is to traverse
back right to the crack and follow it to the top.

5   Wisdom Buttress   220m   Very Difficult *   (1951)
The obvious, slender, cigar-shaped buttress gives probably the most
popular climb on the mountain. It is exposed, sustained and of
continuous interest. Variations are possible. Start at the bottom right
corner of the buttress.
1. and 2. 75m Climb diagonally left, above a lower overhang, then up
right to a small platform. Take an obvious line of weakness to a
diminutive stance below a small overhang.
3. 25m Traverse left and evade the overhang by a slab on the left.
3. 30m Continue straight up slabs on the left, then traverse right along
a ledge to the centre of the buttress.
5. 30m Climb the nose above by an excursion on the right wall, steep
and with sloping holds, and return to the crest.
6. and 7. 60m Continue up the steep nose above, then follow the crest
of the buttress to the top.

6 Bat's Gash 220m Very Difficult **   (1951)
This is a route of maintained interest with impressive cave scenery in the middle section. Start at the foot of the deep-cut chimney immediately left of Wisdom Buttress. About 30m up there is a chimney pitch with a narrow exit, leading to a couch of blaeberries. At about 140m there is a two-tiered chimney, followed by a four-tiered one, the last of which overhangs. This is avoided on the right and the chimney rejoined above the overhang. Continue in the chimney to the top, only one pitch having any difficulty.

The buttress left of Bat's Gash is Angel Buttress. In its upper half there is an obvious bar of overhangs, split towards the right by a deep chimney which continues below as a minor gully, which divides the lower part of the buttress into separate noses.

7 Ordinary Route 240m Difficult   (1951)
Start just left of Bat's Gash. Take the line of least resistance, diagonally left following grooves across steep slabs, to gain the deep chimney. Follow the chimney through the overhangs, the most difficult section being the second chimney pitch. Continue directly to the top.
Variations: There are two possible variations. The first avoids the chimney by going up the right side of the buttress, passing the overhangs on the right. Wrangham's variation starts at the foot of the minor gully that leads to the deep chimney and follows this to join the Ordinary Route. Both are Difficult

8 Pilgrim's Progress 240m Severe *   (1951)
This is the best route on Angel's Buttress. Start from a scoop in the screes at the lowest point of the rocks, up a large triangle of slab which leads to the main slabby face on the right of the buttress. Go straight up this until the grooves of the Ordinary Route are joined just short of the deep chimney, (110m). Cross the chimney and climb the slab on the left to the foot of the great overhangs. Traverse left to the edge of the buttress, (40m). Two short pitches up the edge lead to the crux, a very exposed wall with the hardest move at the top. Follow the crest to the top of the buttress.

The broad buttress left of Angel's Buttress is Molar Buttress. The two are separated by **Y-Gully**, which encloses **Y-Buttress** between its upper arms. This has a messy and vegetated route (120m, Difficult).

Molar Buttress had five routes recorded on it in 1951, by two separate parties, but some of these are not easy to distinguish.

9 Right-hand Route   210m   Very Difficult   (1951)
Start up easy-angled slabs at the right side of the buttress, aiming left to join a system of cracks which runs up the side. Follow these for about 45m, then up steep walls slightly to the left to a scoop below an overhang of the steep band of rock which crosses the buttress in the upper half. Above and right is a break in the form of an open corner, the most westerly of the breaks in the steep band. Make an upward traverse right into the corner and climb it, with an exit left. Easier climbing to the top.

A route up the centre of the buttress was made by an Oxford party (**Damocles Cracks**, Severe), but no details are available.

10 Left-hand Route   190m   Difficult   (1951)
This follows the left edge of the buttress all the way. Start at the foot of the buttress, just left of a conspicuous short black chimney. Climb up broken rocks and vegetation, making for the foot of the chimney above. This has three pitches, the second being easier than it looks. Above, the climbing is undistinguished, keeping to the left but on the front face of the buttress. Two steeper walls intervene, the first being climbed on good holds, the second being traversed to the right. After this the angle eases.

11 Route 1   210m   Very Difficult †   (1951)
This is thought to start left of Left-hand Route and cross it higher up, but the routes may have parts in common. Start up an easy gully (with a short difficult chimney) towards the left of the buttress. From a terrace at the top of the gully traverse right towards the main mass of the buttress. Climb on the right of the crest for 30m to a large ledge. Make a hard traverse right to a sloping stance. Climb the steep wall on the right, then a shattered chimney, and finally a steep nose to regain the crest. Scramble easily to the top.

Rose Route (210m, Moderate) follows the far left side of Molar Buttress overlooking the large gully (the Amphitheatre). The gully is suitable for descent.

Left of the Amphitheatre is a large mass of rock, Butterfly Buttress, which is actually composed of four separate buttresses, the two outside ones (the wings) running the full height of the cliff, with the two smaller ones (the head and tail) inserted between them at top and bottom. To the right of the right wing, and left of the Amphitheatre, are two prominent gullies splitting the full length of the cliff.

12 Cabbage White 300m III/IV   (1978)
This is the first gully left of the Amphitheatre. A prominent, short ice step marks the start of the difficulties. Above this move right, then back left into the main line. Near the top the gully branches. On the first ascent the right fork was taken.

13 Butterfly Gully 300m II   (1978)
The long couloir left of Cabbage White; prominent from Carnmore. It forks about 150m below the plateau. On the first ascent the more interesting-looking left fork was taken.

14 Right Wing, Butterfly Buttress 300m Very Difficult (1953)
Start just right of the foot of the rocks.
1. 25m Take a ledge slanting left to the centre of the buttress and go up to a ledge with a birch tree.
2. 20m Go round the right corner of the steep wall and then up and back left. Climb about 9m to a belay under a steep wall.
3. 45m Take a shallow crack on the right which develops into a ledge curving left under an overhang. Follow this to its end, then go up the uppermost of two grass ledges.
4, etc. 200m Continue, keeping to the left for about 75m, then follow the indefinite crest to the top.

15 Left Wing, Butterfly Buttress 300m II/III   (1988)
In summer this is an undistinguished route of Moderate standard. In winter it provides an interesting climb up the crest of the buttress.

Left of Butterfly Buttress is a cone-shaped buttress of enormous bulk that falls from the summit of Beinn Lair.

16 North Summit Buttress 350m III   (1978)
In winter this gives an excellent climb with enjoyable route finding. Start up an ice runnel, then trend generally left.

Summer: Moderate   (1957)
Start at the bottom left corner of the rocks, where a stream emerges
from the left-bounding gully. Climb easily up the left edge of the
buttress for about 100m. Cross a minor gully that comes up from the
left and go across a slab to a small nick on the extreme left edge.
Continue with more difficulty for about 50m up the rib above and then
by easy ground to the foot of a steep wall with several turfy chimneys.
Pass this by a long traverse right, then climb a small ridge to easier
ground. Scramble to rejoin the left edge of the buttress, now a sharp
ridge. Follow this until it merges with the steeper upper buttress. Climb
this by a zigzag line near the edge to emerge close to the summit cairn.

Geodha Ban (350m, IV) is thought to lie to the left of North Summit
Buttress. The start is described as being 'some 200 yards left of a large
prominent standing block halfway along the main crag. Looking up
there are two obvious deeply-cut parallel gullies.' The climb follows the
left-hand gully. Short pitches lead to a chockstone, climbed on the left.
A long snow section then leads to a 90m icefall, started by a corner
on the left. Chimneys above lead to the top.

17 Marathon Ridge   390m   Difficult   (1951)
This is the long ridge which falls from the point where the spur running
east from the summit of the mountain reaches the top of the crags
(Map Ref 986 734). It sends down a long cleanish nose with a
distinctive tapering base. The ridge has a subsidiary top just below the
true top, and is joined to the summit plateau by a grassy neck. The
route is generally easy but has a short, sharp crux. Start below a 60m
nose. Climb by a succession of walls and ledges, in roughly 30m steps,
to where the ridge steepens before it joins the left-hand ridge, from
which it is separated by steep narrow chimney (240m). Climb the
chimney, which has a steep crux section (30m). Continue up to the
grassy neck on the main buttress below the final tower (60m). The
face is broad for 45m then narrows, the final climbing being by a thin
fissure on the crest. Scrambling leads to a grassy pinnacle at the top
(60m).

18 Olympus   150m   Difficult   (1953)
On the immediate left of Marathon Ridge is a rather thin buttress,
starting a good deal higher up. Scramble up this until a gully cuts

sharply across the buttress, which now steepens. Continue up, keeping as near as possible to the left edge.

Easachan (300m, III) is thought to lie left of Olympus. The start is described as follows: 'At the east end of the main crag a rounded slabby buttress borders a deep-cut bealach. The gully is on its right'. A huge chockstone is climbed on the left, and a bulging ice pitch near the top is climbed direct.

The following climbs lie on the eastern part of the Beinn Lair massif, near Lochan Fada. Stag Buttress is upstream of the loch, the remaining routes are more or less above the head of the loch.

Stag Buttress   130m   Severe   (1951)
This is the highest buttress visible from the head of Lochan Fada. It has a large steep ridge running up its left side in the upper section. Scramble easily up to the foot of the ridge (120m). Start about 30m up the gully on the left.
1. 25m Climb a corner to a moss ledge and belay.
2. 25m Follow the arete, keeping to the edge of the gully.
3. 25m Continue up the edge to a large mossy patch, then straight up to belay below steeper rock.
4. 25m Avoid the first overhang by a steep corner on the left, overlooking the gully, then move back right onto the arete and go straight up to a small stance.
5. 30m Climb a small overhang and follow the edge of the buttress to the top.

Falstaff   120m   VS *   (1951)
This is the right of the two clean buttresses near the head of Lochan Fada. Start at the lowest point of the rocks.
1. 20m Climb directly up to a ledge under a large overhang.
2. 10m Climb steep, broken rock slanting right to a ledge.
3. 20m Traverse delicately left onto the face and go straight up past a large ledge to a belay at a block in a groove on the left.
4. 20m Traverse back to the middle of the face and up to a belay in the groove on the left.
5. 20m Traverse right onto the main face and climb straight up.
6. 30m Continue up the central rib on easier rock to the top.

Sesame Buttress   140m   Severe *   (1951)
Start at the lowest point of the buttress to the left of Falstaff, to the right of a prominent crack.
1. 10m Climb the wall and move left to a heather ledge.
2. 25m From the right end of the ledge traverse left onto the arete (overlooking the crack) and climb it past a small overhang until level with a distinctive block in the crack.
3. 25m Cross the crack to a mossy ledge, then climb the arete on its left side to a prominent poised block. Continue up the arete to a grassy groove on the left.
4. 25m Move left onto an arete, then straight up to the beginning of the next arete on the left.
5. 25m Climb the arete and belay above a steep section.
6. 30m Continue straight up to easier ground.

On the hillside above and left of the last two climbs is a rock tower called The Keep. It appears as a steep-sided wedge of clean-looking rock. Its right (west) face is smaller, but cleaner and continuous and contains Rainbow Wall. Central Route goes straight up the nose. The east face is about 120m high at the centre, but tapers to about 30m and is more broken.

Rainbow Wall   105m   Severe *   (1951)
Some way up the gully on the right of The Keep there is a fork and a spring. On the left is a wall bounded by a left-trending groove and on the right an incipient crack. Start below a ledge with two poised blocks.
1. 20m Traverse left for a short distance, then climb the wall to a large sloping ledge.
2. 20m Traverse up and left to the skyline below a small overhang.
3. 20m Go straight up to a shattered ledge.
4. 10m Climb the twisting arete to a large ledge (spike belay).
5. 35m Climb another twisting arete to the top.

ILLUSTRATIONS

Opposite: *The Waterfall, Beinn a' Mhuinidh*   *(Climber, Phil Thornhill)*
Next page: *Vertigo, Bonaid Dhonn*

Central Route   220m   Severe   (1951)

Start at the lowest point of the buttress. The route stays on the central line, but variations can be made to reduce the standard to Very Difficult.

1. 25m Climb initially up to a large sloping heather ledge.

2. 20m Climb an awkward corner at the left end of the ledge, then go up a rib to another heather ledge and block belay.

3. 25m Ascend the wall above, then a groove on the right of an overhang until a left traverse can be made onto the central rib.

4. 20m Take the most central line to steeper ground.

5. 20m Climb the overhang on good holds and continue up the rib to a large ledge.

6. 20m Climb the nose above to the foot of a prominent arete.

7. 20m Climb the arete, turning the steep part on the left, and continue to a broken ledge.

8. 20m Climb the nose, then easier rock and moss to a low wall.

9. 30m Climb the wall on the left and easier rock to the top.

We now return to Fionn Loch and describe the crags at the south-east end, before moving on to Carnmore.

HANGING CRAG *(Map Ref 976 751)*

This crag, well seen from the causeway, lies high on the hillside between Ghost Slabs and Creag Beag. It can be easily recognised by its smooth slabby top. The ground below the crag is steep and broken, so it is best to approach along the ridge which extends west-north-west from the right end of the cliff towards Creag Beag. This leads to the foot of the west face, which has a steep, grey pocketed wall to the left, with corners and overhangs to the right. The largest (leftmost) over-hang is near the middle of the face, with a large right-slanting corner above and to the right. Below this overhang are two grooves. The right-hand groove leads to the foot of the aforementioned corner; the left-hand groove contains a large detached flake and peters out just below the overhang.

ILLUSTRATIONS

Previous page: Across the Lines/Each Uisge,   Upper Tollie Crag
*   (Climber, Chris Anderson)*
Opposite: Gob, Carnmore Crag

Causeway Corner 50m   Hard Severe   (1988)
This route climbs the right-hand groove and the large corner.
1. 25m Climb the groove, moving slightly right at the top into the foot
of the corner. Grassy stance and belay.
2. 25m Climb the right wall of the corner to the top.

Changing Face 70m   HVS   (1988)
An exposed and exciting climb.
1. 10m Gain a turf ledge at the foot of the left-hand groove.
2. 30m 5a Climb up the groove, passing right of the detached flake,
then traverse back left to good holds below the overhang. Follow a
rising traverse left on pockets out onto a steep undercut wall, and
around a blunt rib to easier rock. Trend up and right to a grassy stance
and small spike belay under an overhang.
3. 30m Finish leftwards up the top part of the wall towards an obvious
ledge on the skyline. Easy slabs above lead to the top.

GHOST SLABS *(Map Ref 978 755)*

These are the strikingly pale slabs running down towards the south
end of the causeway between Fionn Loch and Dubh Loch. They
descend in two distinct sweeps, overshadowed by darker headwalls.
High, wandering ramparts and dead-end terraces run underneath
these walls, overgrown with lush vegetation and stunted birches. The
slabs are of excellent white quartzitic gneiss. Easings of angle make
for more broken and easy sections in places, which is a pity because
at its steepest and most sustained the climbing is very fine.

THE LEFT WING

There are two routes on this sector, to either side of a prominent central
overlap. Both routes are broken and open to a great deal of variation,
but have some good pitches.

Left-Hand Route 270m   Mild VS   (1958)
Climbs the cleanest sheets of slab on the left side. From the high
terrace finish directly up scrappy walls, or traverse away right to finish
up an easy funnel.

Right-Hand Route 270m   Mild VS   (1958)
Nice climbing up the right side of the slabs. Finish up the easy funnel,
or take to the rocks to left or right.

THE RIGHT WING

The routes described start up the clean sheet of slab on the left side. The vertiginous headwall adds atmosphere to the location and variety to the climbing. The main part of the slab is spoiled by islands of heather and birch. At least one route has been made up the cleanest area, avoiding the islands as much as possible. The climbing is good, but poorly protected and obviously artificial. However, this area dries more quickly than the routes described hereafter. The impressive headwall is turned by traversing the terraces right and climbing a good pitch up and right round an exposed nose to escape. The 1967 routes have been given their original grades, but have not been checked and could be harder. Peg belays were used in places.

Doodle   165m   VS   (1967)
Climbs the white whaleback on the left side of the slab. The pioneers climbed up to the island with a tree belay on the right, but it is far better to start up the whaleback direct.
1. 45m 4c Scramble up to the last grass patch below the whaleback. Climb straight up the clean slab to the whaleback and on up this to belay on small wires.
2. 35m Continue directly up and right of a watercourse to climb a broken rib to a flake belay.
3. 30m Climb direct above the flake to belay on the sloping slabs to the right of an overhung recess.
4. 20m Turn the overhang on the right, then go back left and up to a ledge.
5. 35m Climb straight up the slab trending slightly left to a ledge to the right of the waterslide. Then go left under the roof and up the waterslide to finish.

Moby Dick   170m   HVS   (1988)
A long variation to Doodle, breaking left instead of right.
1. 45m 4c Doodle, pitch 1.
2. 45m 4c Start up the second pitch of Doodle, but then traverse left across the watercourse and work up left to belay at the left end of a big roof.
3. 35m 5a Climb the roof by the flakes above the belay, then go up to a grass ledge with a dead tree. From the left end of this go up onto a ramp and follow this right immediately under the next roof, to a point just below a rowan tree. To avoid the vilest vegetation, break left through the roof. Belay on the lip.

4. 45m 4c Climb directly up steep slabs, becoming scrappy, to belay on a small tree. Finish up the vegetated fault on the right. (In dry conditions it would be better to avoid this scrappy upper section and to veer right and straight up the watercourse.)

Leviathan 275m VS   (1967)
This looks an interesting route with fine situations. Start at the foot of a smooth water-streaked slab where a small burn starts. This lies below and right of the island with trees.
1. 20m Climb up the middle of the slab, passing a divot at 12m, to the left side of a grass ledge.
2. 25m From the left edge of the ledge climb straight up (peg runner used) to below a jutting flake. Traverse right and climb the slab to a good thread belay.
3. 45m Go straight up the slab above to a peg belay beneath a small triangular overhang.
4. 35m Climb the wall immediately on the right to a large ledge. Go up the rib on the right to a flake belay.
5. 30m Continue up the steep wall to birch trees below the first big overlap.
6. 20m Traverse right along the grass ledge to a prominent break in the overlap and climb this to a holly tree belay.
7. 20m Go up the corner above to gain the arete on the right. Continue up this and traverse right to a tree belay at the right edge of a big grass ledge.
8. 20m Above is a green mossy wall with an overhanging corner-crack at its left edge. Climb up the wall rightwards, then straight up to beneath a dangerous-looking flake; move right then up to a ledge, traverse right to a cracked overhang and surmount this using a nut for aid (dangerously loose above). Continue up, slightly right, to a peg belay beneath an enormous roof.
9. 25m Traverse left under the roof to a thread belay below large blocks.
10. 35m Take the obvious traverse line on the right leading to an arete above the roof. Climb this to belay well back.

CREAG DUBHDEARG

There is a big amphitheatre, or shallow corrie, left of Ghost Slabs. Creag Dubhdearg is the name suggested for the steep wall at the top of this atmospheric place. A waterfall drops down the centre of the crag, easily seen from as far away as Carnmore barn. A lengthy dry spell is needed for it to dry up, and the two existing routes take the black-stained rocks of the fall. From the cliff-top it is possible to descend by walking across to the northerly nose of the hill, then cutting back down a big diagonal terrace system.

Black Rain   105m   Hard Severe **   (1988)
Takes the main line of the waterfall. A remarkably steep and impressive route for its grade. Recommended (when dry). The lower very severe tier can be avoided on the right.
1. 25m 4c There are three grooves in the initial tier. Climb the one on the right. Above, climb a chimney behind a huge block, or avoid it by a detour right and back.
2. 15m Climb the obvious chimney line up the main wall, using the left rib.
3. 30m Continue left up a ramp to a ledge, then go straight up in the same fault line to a ledge.
4. 35m Go up the wall above, slightly right at the start, to an easy funnel. Scramble to the top.

Tannasg Dubh   85m   E2   (1988)
Climbs grooves up the right side of the fall. Not as good as Black Rain. Start about 10 metres right of Black Rain's chimney.
1. 25m Climb the wall on good holds, then move right and up a left-facing curving corner (heathery) to a ledge.
2. 25m 5b Climb a crack trending left up brown rock to a very steep groove, and up this to a ledge. Now surmount the overhang above directly (sensational, but an option to the right looks easier).
3. 35m Finish straight up juggy walls to easy ground.

BEINN A' CHAISGEIN MOR

(857m   Map Ref 983 786)

One of the least dramatic of the Fionn Loch hills, this dull plateau has little of interest for the hill walker. In contrast, its outlying shoulders drop away steeply to provide crags which offer a host of varied routes, some of which must rank amongst the best in Britain. The twin southerly knolls, Sgurr na Laocainn and Carn Mor, present an unexpected grandeur in an idyllic setting. Indeed, the very isolation of the crags adds an extra ingredient to any visit.

Torr na h'Iolaire is the huge terraced tower above Carnmore Lodge (Map Ref 980 768). Just west, and separated by a grass-sloped ravine, rises Carnmore Crag. Unimpressive from a distance, its scale and ferocity only grow apparent to the climber drawing near to the Lodge.

Access

The usual approach is from Poolewe and Kernsary, a walk of 3 to 4 hours depending on the weight carried. A much longer approach is from Kinlochewe via the north shore of Loch Maree and the Bealach Mheinnidh. (The latter can also be reached quickly by boat across Loch Maree.) Another longer but attractive approach is from Dundonnell via Shenavall. If approaching from Poolewe, permission to drive about 3km as far as a locked gate may be obtained from the Scatwell Estate. After walking about ½km past Kernsary there is a stile on the right. Descend and follow a muddy path by the Allt na Creige until past the plantation. The path continues boggily until the lochan below Beinn Airigh Charr, after which it improves.

The barn at Carnmore has recently been renovated with a new roof, and climbers are welcome to stay outwith the stalking season. Please do not abuse this considerable privilege; remove all litter and contact the stalker at Kernsary if you intend to stay for more than a night or two (Tel: 044 586 215). The situation regarding access to this whole estate is rather delicate – please read the notes at the beginning of this chapter.

CARNMORE CRAG *(Map Ref 980 775)*

This is the great crag above the barn. It is one of the few major Scottish crags to catch the sun for most of the day, and generally dries quickly after rain. The cliff is basically of solid pale gneiss – rough and gnarled, and, at its most accommodating, eroded into pockets, buckets, and letter-box slots. Nevertheless the character of the rock varies over the crag and the climber is just as likely to come across loose rock here as on most other crags.

The most popular routes are Fionn Buttress, Dragon, and Gob, and it is worth bearing in mind that all three contain very exposed traverses which are not recommended for inexperienced seconds. Most of the harder routes have had few repeats.

The crag is roughly C-shaped, the Lower Wall and Upper Wall being divided by the grassy Central Bay, with Fionn Buttress forming the left-hand upright. Descent from the crag can be made either to east or west. The west descent is probably the least knee-jarring. There will usually be short damp sections except during a dry spell. Traverse well over from the top of the crag and descend an easy gully system to grass slopes. It is important not to start descending too soon. The east descent lies down the grassy slopes of the ravine. A big gully compels a slight ascent from the top of the crag, over a couple of rocky crests, before descent of vague paths overlooking the ravine. Lower down either cut back west to the base of the crag, or continue down into the lower reaches of the ravine.

THE LEFT WING
This is the extensive, but little-frequented area of rock left of Fionn Buttress.

1 Thrutch 90m Very Difficult   (1956)
Start at the extreme left of the crag below two gullies. The route takes the one on the right, a grassy groove followed by a narrow chimney.

2 Claymore 90m HVS   (1976)
Right of Thrutch is a prominent groove capped by an overhang. Claymore takes a direct line to the foot of the groove and then climbs it. Start by traversing grassy slopes to below a steep wall and belay below the right-hand of two recesses, (or reach the same point by climbing the slabs below).
1. 25m Climb the recess and a steep corner-crack. Continue by the crack above then move right to belay.
2. 25m Climb a cracked wall, past a prominent hanging flake at 12m, then the groove above to a ledge near an embedded flake.

3. 20m Move down the ledge and round onto a rib. Follow this to belay below the final overhung groove.

4. 20m Climb the corner to the overhang, traverse right and up the groove to the top.

3 Happy Wanderer 150m   VS   (1956)
This route lies right of Claymore and avoids the final steep tier by traversing right along an obvious grass rake (the Goat Walk).

1. 30m Start up heather and slabs to gain a huge spike embedded in turf in a little recess at the foot of a prominent purple-coloured wall.

2. 15m Traverse left and up slightly into a slabby corner. Continue the traverse and gain a badly overhung recess with a little tree.

3. 20m Climb the vertical right wall by a crack, finishing at a poor stance in another slab-floored recess with steep walls.

4. 15m Escape by a left traverse below the belay, across a very steep wall. Ascend grooves and a slab beyond to turf ledges.

5. 20m Climb up to the overhang and the Goat Walk traverse.

6. 50m Continue the traverse to easier ground. A finish can also be made up the wall on the left.

4 Purple Wall 170m   HVS   (1974)
1. 30m Happy Wanderer, pitch 1.

2. 20m Climb the groove above the embedded spike to a stance where the groove widens.

3. 45m 5a Descend the groove for a few feet and traverse right onto the wall. Continuing right would lead to easy ground, so climb half-left, taking the easiest line, until roughly above the stance; go straight up to the Goat Walk. A sustained and poorly protected pitch.

4, etc. 75m Finish along the Goat Walk.

5 Tinkerbell 290m   VS   (1957)
The obvious fault bordering Fionn Buttress on the left is the Great Chimney. Lower down it peters out into vegetated grooves. Tinkerbell starts at the lowest point of the heathery slabs, left of the line of the Great Chimney, where a number of fallen blocks lie on the grass. Higher up it passes a prominent cluster of roofs on the left.

1. 40m There is a prominent block lying against the face above and slightly left of the fallen blocks. Climb easy slabs just to its right to belay to the left of its top high above a ledge.

2. 25m Climb the slab directly above the block, cross a little lip and continue until a 12m traverse left becomes desirable. Belay at a slightly overhung turf ledge well out to the left.

3. 45m Traverse left and gain a heather rake. Follow this back to the right until rocks start again.

4. 35m From some perched blocks climb directly and easily up slabs to a slab-floored corner. Climb the rib on the right, and belay above the corner at perched blocks.

5. 35m Continue up pock-marked slabs, slightly to the right after an initial crack. Belay at a bedded spike on a ledge above to the left.

6. 25m Aim for right-centre of the base of the great block of roofs. Huge flake-belay.

7. 10m A short wall behind the flake leads to an easy narrow slab which goes through the overhangs.

8. 30m Continue left over easy slabs, then follow heather to the Goat Walk. Belay in a corner at the foot of a prominent break in the overhangs above, below a minor overhang.

9. 30m Traverse about 8m left along the rake to the last likely point at which lodgement can be made on the wall above. Climb back to the right and up into a steep heathery recess below a steep corner.

10. 15m Traverse left onto the steep wall, then ascend directly to gain an obvious ledge on the left. Easy to the top.

6 Poacher's' Route 210m Very Difficult †   (1954)
Starting right of Tinkerbell, this route climbs directly up slabs to share a belay at the huge flake under the great block of roofs. Some of the climbing to this point is probably common to Tinkerbell. Poachers' Route then traverses right and up slabs and walls to join the Great Chimney which is followed to the top. Start just to the left of the fall line of the Great Chimney, and left of a 30m pinnacle leaning against the face, as seen from the right. Apparently this is a poor and vegetated climb.

FIONN BUTTRESS
This massive nose, which forms the main pillar of Carnmore Crag, is the most continuous piece of rock on the crag. It is climbed by the following route, which is one of Scotland's finest and most enjoyable classic Very Severes.

7 Fionn Buttress 240m VS *** (1957)

Although initially vegetated, this route unfolds to give an exposed and varied climb on perfect rock. Start from the highest point of the heather in a bay under the Great Chimney, at the base of a steep, clean slabby wall capped by a prominent roof.

1. 30m Start up the right of the slabby wall for a few feet. Traverse right into a corner, climb its right wall and go round onto a ledge. Climb the crack in the wall on the right for 3m then step right onto a slab. Cross this and belay at a chockstone in the chimney beyond.

2. 25m Go up the right wall and then grass trending right. Climb a flake leaning against grey slabs and belay at the top.

3. 15m Climb the slab, then left to a ledge and back right as high as possible for 2m. Then go up to an overhung ledge.

4. 25m Go left to a recess (usually wet) with large bollards. Go up the wet red corner above to a grass recess.

5. 25m Go up corners or walls above to reach the prominent overhang which is surmounted by sensational moves 3m from its right end. Move right above to stance and belays.

6. 25m Traverse right across the face to a stance and belays on the true nose of the buttress.

7. 20m Gain a flake up on the left by a steep groove above the belay. Above it move a little left then go up right to a belay.

8. 20m Follow the slabs above on the crest. Belay at a niche.

9. 20m Go up the crest to a heather ledge and perched blocks below an overhanging slab.

10. 20m Climb over the blocks and go up the slab onto a shelf. Move right to its top corner.

11. 20m Finish up the wall above and then left to the top.

8 Fionn Castle 215m VS * (1957)

A long variation finish to Fionn Buttress, climbing directly up the face of the buttress, rather than traversing to the right edge. Although the climbing is good, this line lacks the fine situations of the normal route. Start from the belay at the end of pitch 5 of Fionn Buttress.

6. 20m From the platform above the overhang climb a groove directly above the belay. Exit left to a perched block.

7. 25m Follow further grooves above.

8. 15m Continue in grooves to a narrow ledge.

9. 35m Move right a little, then go left up the wall onto a slab (hard). Go up this and a slab-ramp on the wall above, across the overhang. Follow this into a corner and climb its right wall to the top.

9 Original Route 200m VS (1956)

This is the original line up the buttress. It is vegetated and not as good as its successor, but worthwhile cleaner variations have been made. The fine upper pitches are used by Fionn Buttress. Start at a 10m plinth which lies about 20 metres left of a prominent curving fault – the Red Scar. This is well below and right from the highest heather bay where Fionn Buttress starts. The route takes the easiest looking groove above the plinth, vegetated in parts, and just left of a steep broad rib.

1. 35m Climb the plinth to a steep wall. Go up the wall to gain a deep groove to the left. Follow this to a steep section. Belay.

2. 40m Now either follow Achilles, up the steep clean rib using a shallow groove followed by slabs, or climb turfy grooves and chimneys to an overhung niche, followed by turf to the right, then up right over slabs to the foot of a steep wall. By either line head for a belay in a niche with two stairs below a short steep corner-crack.

3. 30m Climb the crack and traverse hard left and up to a grassy ramp. From here it is best to take a fairly direct line past a nose of cracked blocks, and so up steep and exposed rock to the traverse ledge and belays at a junction with Fionn Buttress. (Several variants have been made on the section. The original line goes up turf to the bottom corner of the grassy Central Bay, then directly up to an obvious traverse left to reach the same point, 75m.)

4, etc. 95m Finish as for Fionn Buttress up the crest.

10 Achilles 160m VS * (1975)

A direct version of Original Route, with some good pitches. It crosses Original at the belay niche and short, steep corner-crack. Start at the same point as Original Route at the 10m plinth. The climb heads for the steep broad rib above, on the left side of a steep black-streaked wall.

1. 40m Climb the plinth and enter the chimney on the right. Climb the chimney to a wall, past an old peg, and up to a grass ledge in a groove. (Original now continues up the vegetated groove on the left.) Step right onto the crest of the rib and climb a shallow groove to a small ledge.

2. 45m Continue directly up pleasant slabs to beneath a steep wall. Belay in a niche with two stairs below a short steep corner-crack.

3. 40m Climb the crack, traverse hard left then move back right and up to reach a grassy ramp. A few metres up the ramp climb a short crack then finger-traverse left for 6m to a grass ledge. Climb a lichenous wall to an overhung grassy bay with an abandoned eyrie.

4. 35m Leave the eyrie on the right and climb an overhung ramp to a shelf. Move left outside some perched blocks to an exposed pulpit stance. Climb up a shallow rib and under an oblique overhang emerging on the right at the end of the long traverse ledge of Fionn Buttress. Several variants have been made in the vicinity of the eagle's eyrie.

5, etc. The pioneers continued up Connie-Onnie, took a slightly descending traverse line across the left wall of Green Corner, then finished up Dragon slab, Abomination crack, and the finish of Dragon! However the natural finish is up pitches 7-11 of Fionn Buttress.

THE LOWER WALL

This is the extensive band of rock below the level of the Central Bay, and includes all the rock to the right of Fionn Buttress. The main landmarks are two broad ribs, the First and Second Ribs. Both are prominent in the morning light and both merge into slabs higher up. The First (left-hand) Rib is bounded on the left by a prominent curving red fault, The Red Scar. The Second Rib has a prominent yellow scar right of its base, bounded on the right by the very steep and obvious recess of Balaton. This has a prominent vertical black streak on its right wall.

Right of this is a more vegetated area, the location of Botanist's Boulevard, and right again the distinct shield of overlapping slab and wall is taken by Penny Lane and Strawberry Fields. The Lower Wall routes generally boast some good steep climbing, followed by pleasant slabs which peter out in the Central Bay.

11 Kaleidoscope 115m HVS *   (1967)
Left of the Red Scar fault lies a steep black-streaked wall. Kaleidoscope takes the left-bordering groove (the right side of the Achilles rib). Start on the right of the 10m plinth of Original Route, some 20m left of the Red Scar fault.

1. 35m 5b Go up slabs to a point below and left of the groove. Climb the groove via a small slab on the right, past a large jammed block. (The groove looks climbable direct, but may be wet.)

2. 35m Trend right up slabs towards an overhang on the skyline. Junction with Initiation.

3. 45m Climb the overhang on its right to finish up ribs .

12 Quagga 110m E1 *   (1988)
This is the obvious right-bordering groove of the black-streaked wall.
It angles right higher up. Like Kaleidoscope, a good main pitch. Start
at a belay just left of the grassy fault running up to the Red Scar.
1. 40m 5b Climb the brown rib just left of a recess, starting on the left
side, then move into an obvious groove on the rib's left. Climb up to
another groove slanting right, and bulging at the bottom. Climb it to a
belay above.
2. 30m Follow the rib on the right, climbing close to the Red Scar, to
join Initiation. Go up to belay under an overhang.
3. 45m Finish up ribs to grass.

On page 274/275

CARNMORE CRAG

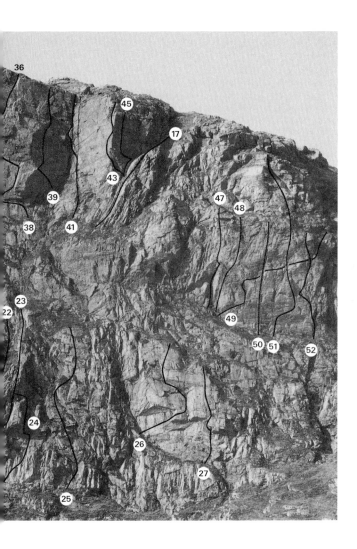

13 Initiation 185m Hard Severe   (1957)
This route starts up the approximate line of the Red Scar, then climbs
the wall and slabs directly above.
1. 40m Start up the grassy initial fault of the Red Scar, then climb right
of the Scar to a belay above a gangway on Red Scar Entry, just short
of the Red Scar.
2. 40m Go up left for a few feet, then make an ascending traverse
right across the steep red wall above to regain the crest of the rib. Go
up this then right past a detached block, and so up a groove on the
left. At its top traverse a ledge to the right, and go up to a ledge below
a steeper wall. Move left into the Red Scar. Climb the diagonal
chimney-crack to a shelf, and then to a niche and chockstone belay.
Red Scar Entry trends right here.
3. 30m Climb the wall on the left and go up to a sloping ledge, then
briefly up a steep corner. Move right and up to a heather ledge.
4. 30m Go up the boiler-plate wall on the left and traverse right to an
overhang which is passed on the left.
45m of easy climbing leads to the Central Bay.

14 Red Scar Entry 150m VS   (1956)
Starts up the First Rib, right of the fault of the Red Scar, then climbs
mainly right of the Scar. Although recommended in the past, this is not
a particularly good route. Start at the foot of the First Rib from a slightly
overhung recess.
1. 20m Climb a crack on the left for about 4m, then traverse right and
up to a slab, returning diagonally left near the top. Belay at an overhung
ledge.
2. 15m Evade the overhang by a left traverse. Go up a gangway to a
stance just short of the Red Scar.
3. 40m As for Initiation, pitch 2.
4. 15m Climb across the right wall below the overhanging scar. Belay
in a niche.
5. 30m Continue the traverse to grassy ledges. Follow these to a good
belay high on the wall.
6. 30m Climb the wall going up and left to the forest of perched blocks.

15 Black Magic 120m VS   (1982)
Between the First and Second Ribs is a recessed area of cliff with a
heathery bay. Start up the left corner of the bay.

1. 35m Ascend the left-hand short black corner. Before it finishes exit right onto a gangway. Ascend this and the parallel cracks above, passing through two bulges, to belay underneath the obvious large overhang.
2. 30m Traverse horizontally right for about 6m and climb the obvious right-trending crack system behind the vestigial tree.
3, etc. 55m Continue to the Central Bay.

16 Black Mischief   130m VS *   (1966)
An enjoyable climb and a useful preamble to Dragon. Start at the foot of an obvious black groove at the top right corner of the heather bay. This groove is capped on the right by a conspicuous square-cut overhang. An alternative, more direct, line has also been climbed above pitch 1.
1. 25m Ascend easily to the first bulge in the groove proper and surmount this on the right. Continue up the groove past another bulge and exit left to a stance.
2. 25m Climb up right where the groove steepens at 6m; good spike. Move delicately right under a bulge onto a slab. Traverse diagonally across this to a conspicuous ledge on the skyline. Climb the crack above and exit right with difficulty onto a grass ledge level with and to the right of the square-cut overhang.
3. 20m Climb the cracked wall above, (hard above a good ledge at half-height on the right). Continue more easily to large ledges.
4, etc. 60m Easier climbing leads to the Central Bay.

17 Diagonal Route   250m Severe   (1952)
The original climb on the crag. It continues out by the top right corner of the Central Bay to exit onto easy ground by a slabby gangway on the right margin of the Upper Wall. The lower half gives a pleasant approach to the Upper Wall routes. Start on the right side of the heather bay, left of the Second Rib (down and left from the Balaton recess).
1. 25m Go up and traverse right onto a line of ribs slanting right. Continue in this line to a quartzite belay.
2. 20m Step left onto a slab, climb it using a corner-crack and move right round a corner and gain a stance.
3. 10m Go straight up on good holds until it is possible to traverse left and up to a perched block.
4, etc. 195m Easier climbing leads to the slabs and heather of the Central Bay. Traverse up and right to the foot of the ramp of slabs to the right of Carnmore Corner. Climb the slabs to scrambling ground.

18 Yogi 120m HVS   (1962)
Climbs directly onto the crest of the Second Rib and then keeps to its
right side. A bit artificial above the steep lower section. Start at the left
extremity of the Balaton recess, under the Yellow Scar.
1. 35m 5b Start up two great red flakes in the left rib, then climb the
crack line straight above, avoiding a hard bit on the immediate left.
2. 45m Continue up the arete by shallow grooves.
3. 40m Finish up slabs to the Central Bay.

19 999 120m E1 *   (1984)
Climbs the corner on the left side of the Yellow Scar, just right of the
great flakes of Yogi. Above this the line is distinctly contrived, keeping
to the edge of the rib, right of Yogi, but the climbing is good.
1. 35m 5b/c Climb the corner to the large roof. Turn this on the left
and climb the crack above. Easier climbing leads to a belay.
2. 40m 4c Traverse right to a rib overlooking the Balaton recess. Climb
the rib and finish up the obvious hanging curved groove (common to
Dandelion Days).
3. 45m Continue easily to the Central Bay.

20 Dandelion Days 120m E3 *   (1982)
Takes a fierce line up the left side of the Balaton recess. Start at the
foot of the left-hand corner.
1. 35m 5b/c Climb the corner-groove for about 25m, then, when over
the band of overhangs and slightly below the second stance on
Balaton, traverse left across the wall and ascend into the obvious
niched overlap. Surmount this and go up the crack to belay on the
pinnacled arete.
2. 30m Climb the rib and pull over the overlap to finish up the obvious
hanging curved groove.
3. 50m Continue easily to the Central Bay.

21 Balaton 105m E1 ***   (1966)
Takes the very steep crack at the right side of the recess, then
traverses left under a roof to climb the obvious big corner line at the
back of the recess. This is the best line on the Lower Wall, and one of
the best routes on the crag.
1. 25m 5a Climb the crack to a belay on the right.
2. 10m 5b Descend a little, step across a crack, and traverse a steep
band of slab to belay at the foot of the large corner.

3. 35m 4c Climb the corner to a slab, traverse right, turn an overhang, then move up left to below a big roof. Break out right, then go up to a stance and belay.
4. 45m Move up and left of a rib on the skyline, then continue by slabs to the Central Bay.

22 Running Bear 95m E3 (1981/1988)
Climbs the rib right of Balaton, direct, just right of the broad black streak, then continues straight up the groove above. (The rib was originally climbed with a detour into Boo-Boo at half-height (E2 5b) but this is much inferior). Protection is poor on the lower half of the rib, but good on the hard moves higher up.
1. 25m 6a Start up a tall block (just left of Boo-Boo). Move left over a bulge and climb straight up the crest of the rib. Surmount the top bulge direct via a big jug and a fragile-looking side-pull on the left, to belay at the top of a crevasse.
2. 25m 5a Climb the bulge above and go up left into the groove. Climb this to slabs and belay.
3. 45m 5a More slabs lead to the Central Bay.

23 Boo-Boo 110m HVS (1966)
Climbs obvious grooves right of the Running Bear rib. Start just right of the tall block of Running Bear.
1. 30m 5a Climb a crack which splits a triangular overhang at 7m. The bulge is most easily climbed on the right; move up a wall slightly rightwards and climb a corner to a ledge and belay left of a larger overhang.
2. 35m Traverse left 3m then back right to a point above the belay. Climb a corner to a ledge, go up the right edge of the wall, then move left and up a slab to belay.
3. 45m Go up the slabs above to the Central Bay.

24 Naughty Alien 105m HVS (1981)
A direct line through the break in the roof right of Boo-Boo.
1. 20m 4b Start at the foot of Boo-Boo. Move right up slabs and under an overhang. Work upwards by fluted slabs to belay under the roof.
2. 15m 5a Traverse left and climb through the break in the roof to gain a groove. Climb this to vegetatious slabs.
3, etc. 70m Probably the best finish is to gain the rib of Boo-Boo on the left as soon as possible and climb this to finish.

25 Botanists' Boulevard   135m   Severe   (1956)
Lies up the recessed and vegetated area right of the Balaton recess,
leading into the lower right corner of the Central Bay. The original
description mentions belaying round a turf pinnacle at one point.
1. 30m   Start about 20 metres right of Running Bear rib, on a
heather-topped plinth. From the left edge of the plinth ascend into a
scoop, then climb up the rib on the right to the top of the scoop. Belay
below a small roof.
2. 25m Traverse right, go up a short wall and back above the small
roof to a grassy bay and belay.
3. 30m Exit over the left wall and climb up to an undercut slab. Climb
this and go left into a steep corner at 20m. Move right over a bush,
cross a steep red wall and go up a grassy rake.
4. 50m Go straight up the wall, then steep vegetation, going left when
in doubt, to an ash tree belay in the bottom right corner of the Bay.

The remaining two routes on the Lower Wall lie on a distinctive pale
shield of overlapping wall and slab. This is separated from the scrappy
Botanists' Boulevard area by a grassy rake which curves up left as a
steep fault.

26 Penny Lane   70m   HVS **   (1967)
Gain the grass rake by grassy slabs or an easy traverse from the right.
Belay up at the left end of the rake. The route traverses right along the
steep wall under a roof.
1. 30m 5a Traverse right along a big flake and continue traversing
above a lower roof to go round the corner into the central groove.
2. 25m 4b Go diagonally left under the top overlap and climb over it
into a groove.
3. 15m Finish right up slabs to the grassy Gangway.

27 Strawberry Fields   50m   HVS   (1967)
Start near the right end of the grass rake below a black corner going
up to a large roof.
1. 25m 5a Climb the wall on the left of the corner for a few metres,
traverse into the corner and climb up to the roof. Move left and go up
on quartz to a second smaller roof. Step right onto the arete and go
up to a stance.
2. 25m 4b Climb the slabs above trending left to a bulge. Climb this
into a grassy crack and go up slabs to easy ground.

THE CENTRAL BAY

The Central Bay is an area of heathery slopes and scraps of slab. Great care is needed in wet conditions. Apart from approaches via the Lower Wall routes, access or exit can be most easily made either by the Gangway (a series of exposed ledges and steps running from the right, passing above the pale shield of rock containing Penny Lane), or by broken ground to the right of the top slab of Diagonal Route. This is also exposed and rather loose (Moderate), but the best way back into the Bay from the clifftop. (It is also possible to enter or leave the Bay via the Fionn Buttress Routes).

THE UPPER WALL

This is the very steep upper band of crag, providing fine climbing with considerable exposure. Its left wall is bounded by the out-thrust nose of Fionn Buttress. To the right its height gradually dwindles. The most obvious features are:

(1) A pale easy-angled slab at bottom left. Dragon climbs the slab to the top right corner then takes cracks up the wall above, to the right of a towering corner system.

(2) A great roof roughly halfway up the central wall and descending slightly from left to right. Gob climbs up to traverse under this roof from right to left.

(3) The unmistakable Carnmore Corner, to the right. There are twin cracks in the back and it is usually wet. Its scale is diminished by a tongue of scrappy terrain extending up from the Bay. The jutting right arete is taken by The Orange Bow.

28 Connie-Onnie 100m VS (1967)
A minor climb linking the Bay with the upper part of Fionn Buttress. The left side of the slab at the foot of Dragon is bounded on the left by a big corner – Green Corner. Left of this is a smaller corner. The route climbs this and the slab above.
1. 40m 4c Climb the corner passing loose blocks at the top.
2. 15m Climb the slab to a ledge at the top of Green Corner.
3. 45m Climb slabs on the left and a steep V-chimney, then more slabs to the top. This section is the same as Fionn Buttress.

29 Green Corner 85m VS   (1963/1967)
The big corner running up to the great roof above the Dragon Slab. A
good main pitch. Start at the base of the corner.
1. 15m Up grassy rocks to a ledge.
2. 20m 4c Continue up the slab and chimney to the roof. Traverse left
under it on good holds to a big ledge.
3. 50m Move left and climb the wall above, joining and finishing up
Fionn Buttress.

30 Death-Wolf 110m E6 **   (1986)
There are two flake-gangways cutting through the great roof above
Dragon Slab. This route takes the right-hand one, then climbs the
steep wall above, trending right then left. A very strenuous climb.
1. 40m Climb the Dragon slab to its top, then traverse 10m left from
the left end of the narrow ledge to a peg belay under the gangway.
(This could be reached by a direct ascent of the slab).
2. 30m 6b There is no rest on this pitch until 10m above the roof. (The
gangway is often wet lower down but this can be avoided on the
outside). Climb the gangway out over the lip of the roof, into a little
scoop with a hidden sidepull in a crack. Go straight up the wall to a
flaky jug then move right and up onto a resting ledge. Climb the little
arete and groove above to a belay ledge close to the right arete.
3. 25m 6a From the right end of the ledge move up and across left,
then up left to gain isolated knobbles. Traverse right by a thin horizontal
crack to gain better holds and pull out right to easy ground. Move up
left to the left end of a big heather ledge.
4. 15m 5c Climb the wall above the belay (unprotected for some
distance), veering left under an obvious scooped groove and up the
wall to the top.

31 Abomination 100m HVS **   (1966)
There is a towering corner system formed where the bulging wall of
Death-Wolf thrusts out from the main wall. Abomination takes the
obvious plummeting groove in the undercut side wall. Although intimidating, it is not as hard as it looks. A fine climb.
1. 35m Climb the Dragon slab rightwards to its top.
2. 35m 5b From the ledge climb the right-hand groove for a few
metres, then step left and climb the hanging crack for 20m to a ledge.
Climb the crack on the right with increasing difficulty to a sloping ledge.

3. 30m 4c Continue up the groove to a ledge, climb a chimney to below a square-cut roof and then move right and up a slab on loose flakes to the top.

32 Dragon 95m HVS ***   (1957)
The classic original route on the Upper Wall. Superbly exposed, it takes an improbable line for its grade. Above and right of the big corner system is a huge jutting triangular roof. Dragon takes obvious cracks right of the main corners to turn the roof on the left. Start at the base of the pale grey slab.
1. 35m Climb to a grass patch then trend right up the slab to belay on a narrow ledge under the main wall. (Alternatively, the slab can be missed out by climbing a short chossy groove at the top of the right retaining wall).
2. 35m 4c Climb a groove for 5m, passing the small roof which fills it, on the right. Traverse left out of the cracks a short distance above the roof to gain easier grooves. Pedestal belay 9m up on the right.
3. 15m 5a Climb a steep short wall to reach a yellow chimney up on the left. Climb this and exit left at the top to a tiny perch under the great roof. Traverse the steep wall on the left to belay in a little bay. (Seconds falling from the traverse might have to prussik!).
4. 10m Traverse round left and up to the top.

33 Beastmaster 50m E4   (1986)
This climbs the corners just left of Dragon. Escape is possible back into Dragon in places, but the climbing is good. Start from the ledge above Dragon Slab.
1. 20m 5b Climb the obvious crack just left of the start of Dragon, going past the left side of the small roof. Go up an easy section of Dragon to belay under the bulge at the base of the corners.
2. 20m 6a Climb the awkward bulge up left to enter the first corner. Climb this and two succeeding corners direct to the belay in the little bay left of the Dragon traverse.
3. 10m 5b Finish directly up the flake-choked corner above.

There are two routes, of which Lion Rampant is the better, up the fine wall right of Dragon. They take minor breaks through the main roof on either side of the main break taken by Gob.

34 Lion Rampant 85m E5 **   (1986)
1. 20m 6b A crack in the steep right-bounding wall of the Dragon Slab
provides a good introductory pitch. Climb the strenuous crack and go
up to the ledge under the main wall.
2. 35m 6a A serious pitch. Climb the wall past a spike at 10m to an
expanding block. Pull straight over the bulge and move up right to
small ledges at the foot of a great scoop in the wall. Go up left then
right and up to an expanding flake. Move left to another flake and pull
onto the left-slanting ledge above. Continue directly up the unprotected wall above, just beside the arete overlooking the groove of The
Sword, past a poor peg runner, to gain a ledge. Go left along this to
belay at the right side of great detached blocks.
3. 15m 6a Climb the wall right of the belay to gain the traverse of Gob,
under the roof. Climb the bulge up into a small corner, then pull out
right on layaways to reach slabs and belay above.
4. 15m 5c Climb straight up to the roof above. Traverse left and pull
over the roof, using a jug to swing up and right to blocks. Veer left and
up the steep wall to an overhanging finish on big flakes.

35 Ride of the Valkyrie 65m E5   (1986)
Another serious line up the Dragon wall, rather artificial but more direct
than Lion Rampant. Start from the ledge above Dragon Slab.
1. 30m 6a Follow Lion Rampant (pitch 2) to the expanding block, then
step left to surmount the bulge at a thin crack. Climb up slightly left to
a peg runner. Step left and go up to gain a good horizontal flake running
across the wall. Step up right then back left and straight up the wall to
gain a left-pointing jug. Go up and left to ledges on Dragon and a belay
on top of the pedestal.
2. 35m 6a Climb the cracks up the wall above, then move right and
up Gob for a few metres, below the big break in the roofs. Move up
left and go rightwards up a bulge to gain undercut slabs under the
main roof. Traverse rightwards up under the roof and pull out right
using undercuts under a nose to gain easier ground. Finish obviously
as for Gob.

36 The Sword 80m E2 ***   (1967)
An atmospheric and very direct route taking the big groove above the
cave right of the Dragon Wall. One of the best natural lines at
Carnmore. Start at the right end of the ledge above Dragon Slab.

1. 35m 5c Traverse right for about 3m on the lip of the overhang, then climb up and right to gain the main groove. Climb the groove to a small stance at the Swallow's Nest of Gob. (Alternatively, use the original start (5c): Climb the wall for about 5m then traverse right to the arete. Continue delicately down and right across a steep slab, then right and up to reach the main groove)
2. 20m 5c Climb up and right through the steep break in the roof to gain the rib and go up to a stance.
3. 25m Climb the shallow groove above, the original finish of Gob.

37 St. George 90m E1 ** (1967)
This route takes the fine steep crack line in the wall right of the cave of Sword, then follows Gob through the roof.
1. 20m 5b Climb a short wall to the foot of the crack, which has an overhang at 8m. Climb the groove to the overhang. Pull round this into a sentry-box and climb the wall on the left to a superb stance on top of a big doubtful flake.
2. 40m 5a Climb the groove for 6m, then traverse left to another obvious groove. Go up this for 8m, traverse left round the arete to join The Sword, and climb up to the Swallow's Nest under the roof. Move left to a good pulpit belay.
3. 35m 4c Take the obvious break right through the roof. Finish direct up the left-slanting fault.

38 Gob 110m HVS *** (1960)
The line of least resistance on the Upper Wall, snaking left under the main roof to find its main break. A classic. Start at the right end of the main face, where the Central Bay begins to rise up into the base of Carnmore Corner.
1. 30m 4c Traverse left along an overhung ledge to a break in the overhang; go up right and climb a shallow corner to a belay.
2. 45m 4c Traverse away left by the easiest line under the great roof to negotiate an out-thrust shield of rock (the Swallow's Nest) where The Sword and St. George come up from below. Continue the traverse to a good pulpit belay not far right from Dragon's pedestal.
3. 35m 4c Take the obvious break up and right through the roof. Finish direct up the left-slanting fault, or:
3a. 45m 4c The original finish. After going right through the roof traverse away right to finish up a steep corner.

39 Wilderness 80m E3   (1980)
A diagonal crack-line (unclimbed) cuts across both walls of Carnmore
Corner. Jivaro Crack is the thinner crack running vertically above the
diagonal one on the left wall; this route climbs the wall to its left. It was
climbed on sight and has had few, if any, repeat ascents and may be
relatively loose. Start by scrambling up to an obvious diagonal break
running up left.
1. 20m 5b Climb the break, which has an awkward bulging start.
2. 35m 5c Climb a few metres up the diagonal crack, then pull out left
onto the face. Traverse left and slightly upwards for a few feet to a
recess. Move right and up to a thin crack. Move up this and continue
to join a slight groove line going up and left. Follow this to a scoop,
pull into this and climb onto the wall above. Climb twin cracks to belay
at the base of a corner.
3. 25m The original finish of Gob.

40 Jivaro Crack 60m E4   (1987)
A well protected climb apart from a bold bit leaving the diagonal crack.
Start as for Wilderness.
1. 20m 5b Wilderness, pitch 1.
2. 20m 6b Move right up the wide diagonal crack, then climb the blind
crack line to a rest at a bucket. (The crack splits before rejoining; the
thin right fork was taken on the first ascent). Pull up over the top into
an obvious slabby groove and go up this to move up right and belay
beside a detached block.
3. 20m 5c Step left from the block and go up a small hanging corner
to pull over the bulge to good holds. Join the original finish of Gob
about 10m below the top.

41 Carnmore Corner 65m E2 **   (1968)
There is a spring in the hollow at the top of this climb so a lengthy spell
of good weather is needed for it to dry up. Although relatively short,
the Corner is a route of some character; steep and intimidating. The
obvious (but unclimbed) direct start is nearly always wet and slimy so
the route starts to the right before moving left into the corner. A curving
fault with two recesses undercuts the right wall. Start below and left
of the lower one.
1. 40m 5b Climb slabby rocks up and left, then go up steeply into a
niche just up left from the second recess (old pegs). Go straight up for
a short way, then quit the crack line to follow a diagonal line, starting

as a small ramp leading up left into the corner. Belay below the big overhang.
2. 25m 5a Move left, up and delicately back right and finish up an easier crack.

42 Red Crack 65m E3 * (1988)
Climbs the right-hand crack line. It is quicker drying than the corner.
1. 20m 5a Climb Carnmore Corner to a belay in the niche.
2. 45m 6a Continue straight up the crack line to a resting place at a niche under a big bulge. Climb the bulge (crux) and follow the easier fault to the top.

43 The Orange Bow 35m E5 6a *** (1985)
The impressive arete right of Carnmore Corner. Start at ledges up on the right, 10m above the last slab of Diagonal Route. Traverse out left along a slabby shelf and negotiate a tricky bulge to move up left to big footholds under the bulging edge. Swing out left on flakes and climb a vague intermittent crack line up the overhanging wall for 10m to good runners before the crack peters out. Traverse right and up slightly for 5m to gain the edge and a rest. Climb up the edge, as the angle eases, and finish up the left-slanting crack.

44 Left-Hand Start 25m E5 6b ** (1988)
This good pitch gives the route some length, but is probably harder than the edge itself. Start below and left of the first recess of the curving fault undercutting the right wall of the Corner. Move up to the recess and swing up right onto a platform. Go up onto a bulging wall, swing left and up to a resting place. Peg runner on the right. Pull up to a good pocket, move up left to a flake, then make a hard move across right to jugs. Poor peg runner. Climb straight up the wall to gain a horizontal fault and a resting place. Traverse right and slightly down to a flake-crack and hanging belay (peg above) under the "vague crack" of the edge pitch.

45 Curare 30m E4 6a (1985)
The obvious crack line on the right wall of the Orange Bow prow. Start at the same belay ledges above the slab of Diagonal. Climb a jam-crack slanting up right, then traverse across left and up to an awkward niche under a layback crack. Climb this strenuously to a ledge and finish up the crack line over a roof.

THE GREY WALL

This is the wall right of the Central Bay, just above the Gangway approach.

46 The Kady 90m VS †   (1966)
Start from the Gangway, left from the Grey Wall proper. The route follows a break in the overhanging wall running into a hanging corner capped by an overhang which is well seen from below.
1. 45m Climb a heathery groove to beneath the overhanging wall.
2. 45m Climb the break in the wall trending right to the corner. Climb the corner until forced right onto a slab which is followed to a belay.

47 It Was Twenty Years Ago Today 50m E1   (1987)
Well right of The Kady, on the left side of the Grey Wall proper, is a prominent red diedre. This is the line.
1. 25m 4c Climb up to the diedre, then climb it to a stance.
2. 25m 5a Hand traverse a few feet left to two spikes, then up by the line of least resistance. Poorly protected at first.

48 The Cracks 40m VS †   (1967)
1. 20m Climb cracks just right of the prominent red diedre to a ledge on the right.
2. 20m Go up the crack above to ledges.

49 Avoidance 65m Hard Severe   (1957)
A devious line which goes rightwards across the Grey Wall. Start just right of the Cracks.
1. 30m 4c Traverse right along an ascending ledge for 15m, then climb a very steep crack and go up left to a ledge. Climb a short groove on the right to a ledge running right.
2. 20m Traverse right, climb up a rib in the corner and traverse right again to ledges below the steep upper wall.
3. 15m Continue traversing around the rib on the right and step across a groove to more broken ground. Scrambling to the top.

50 Crackers 70m E3   (1985)
The central parallel cracks on the Grey Wall. Start 15 metres right of the Cracks.
1. 25m 5c Climb a steep crack.
2. 45m 5a Continue up cracks. Easier to finish.

51 Trampoline 100m HVS **   (1967)
Some 12 metres left of the right-hand chimney of the Grey Wall there
is a traverse line across the steep wall. Start below a niche a few
metres along this line.
1. 25m 5a Climb into the niche and traverse right until the angle eases.
Climb the wall above by twin cracks and go up slabs to a big stance.
2. 35m 5a Climb slabs on the left to below a crack. Move right to a
short corner and step right onto the wall. Climb steeply up the crack
above and then up easy slabs to block belays.
3. 40m Finish up slabs.

52 Break-In 65m HVS *   (1984)
Start at the prominent chimney at the right end of the Grey Wall.
1. 30m 4c Climb the chimney for 7m, then break out left onto the wall
by a short hand-traverse. Climb the wall above and trend left to a good
stance below a leftward-sloping groove.
2. 35m 5a Leave the stance on the right and climb cracks to reach a
V-groove. Climb the groove, breaking out left to finish up the crack
above.

   There is one remaining route lying up the left side of the gully across
right from the Grey Wall. It is not very good, but is the only route easier
than Severe on the whole of the main crag.

53 Needle 170m Difficult   (1957)
Start just left of the gully, at the foot of some pale easy slabs a few feet
left of a detached block.
1. 35m Climb the slabs for 30m, then traverse left across a turfy
groove and up another slab to belays below a small lip.
2. 35m Climb the lip and continue directly above to belay at the foot
of a steep wall below a conspicuous overhang.
3. 20m Climb the wall to the overhang, escaping on the left.
4. 30m Continue directly above, aiming for the conspicuous 'needle's
eye' above.
4. 15m Up a blunt rib just left of the gully.
5. 20m Ignore the easier ground to the right and climb the red wall on
the left, then another short wall and finally a short slab to reach the
foot of the 'needle's eye'.
6. 15m Climb the chimney crack and surmount the eye. Easy ground
leads to the top.

THE GIRDLE TRAVERSES

There are two girdle traverses of the Upper Wall, from left to right. A third traverse, of the Lower Wall from right to left, uses Achilles/Fionn Buttress to link with either of the upper traverses to make a huge C-shaped expedition. This is Ulysses. Only key sections are described in detail, since much variation is possible, and the route-finding provides half the attraction of these adventurous wanderings.

54 Odyssey 550m HVS   (1974)
Start high up on the left of the crag under the Left Wing. Use Purple Wall to gain the Goat Walk (probably the hardest part of the girdle), or start up Happy Wanderer. Continue easily along the Goat Walk then reverse a section of Tinkerbell down right to reach a grass terrace below the great block of stepped overhangs. Climb diagonally up right in two pitches to gain the fault line of the Great Chimney. From a stance here the pioneers descended the fault for a few feet to make lodgment on the right wall. The edge above was climbed for 6m and then a diagonal traverse made up right across Fionn Castle aiming for a small col on the far side, overlooking the D-shaped slab. Descend easily over perched blocks to a stance at the top of Green Corner (6m). Reverse the main pitch of Green Corner, traverse across the slab and go up to the ledge under the main wall, as for Dragon. Climb Dragon to the Pedestal belay. A choice of lines leads across and up right to the Pulpit of Gob. Follow Gob through the overhang and take the original line of Gob away right above the great roof. Finish up the corner-line of Gob original, or continue right into Carnmore Corner, as for Ring of Bright Water.

55 Ring of Bright Water 350m HVS   (1974)
Takes a higher traverse line than Odyssey, starting up Fionn Buttress. Follow Fionn Buttress, with the option of including Connie-Onnie, to the ledge at the top of Green Corner (200m). Continue up Fionn Buttress to a shelf and move right into a corner (20m). A grassy ledge leads to a small col and thence down easily to join the top pitch of Abomination (10m). Continue up Abomination and traverse right to the top pitch of Dragon. Belay in the little bay beside the crucial traverse (10m). Reverse the Dragon traverse and descend the yellow overhanging chimney to cross right to the Pulpit on Gob (25m). Follow Gob through the overhang and away right above the great roof. Belay at loose blocks on a shattered pillar (40m). Continue traversing below a bulging wall to the stance among the overhangs of Carnmore Corner,

a pitch similar in outlook and difficulty to the Fionn Buttress traverse (25m). Continue up the second pitch of the Corner (strenuous) and delicately across the slabby upper section of the right wall (30m).

A difficult but superior alternative for both these girdles would be to reverse the Gob traverse from the pulpit and use The Sword break to pierce the great roof (E2 5c).

56 Ulysses 600m HVS   (1975)
A unique C-shaped traverse providing some 600m of continuously enjoyable climbing. The Lower Wall is traversed from right to left, the easiest start being by Botanists' Boulevard, to traverse left into Balaton at the stance above pitch 1. The pioneers continued by the second pitch of Balaton but narrowly failed to cross the left rib directly. Instead a groove with overlaps was climbed to gain the crest of the rib and a 15m descent made via Yogi/Diagonal. From Diagonal the traverse was continued and part of the second pitch of Black Mischief reversed to the stance at the top of pitch 1. A direct ascent was made for 6m to traverse across left into the Black Scar, and so to join the Red Scar. From Red Scar find a way across left and up into the eagle's eyrie of Achilles, ultimately to link up with Fionn Buttress, and one of the upper traverses.

TORR NA H'iOLAIRE *(Map Ref 985 772)*

This is the great rocky tower directly above Carnmore Lodge, leading to the summit of Sgurr na Laocainn. As with Carnmore Crag the rock is excellent and the aspect sunny. However the crag is broken by terraces into several tiers and although many climbers will prefer to join routes together to give one long climb, it is easier to describe the tiers separately. The main features are as follows:
(1) The Lower Wall, which slants down from left to right, with two prominent ribs at the left end, below a huge perched block. Well round to the right is South Gully.
(2) Harlequin Wall, which is the short steep 40m wall immediately above the perched block.
(3) Above and left of Harlequin Wall is a steep 60m wall with some prominent clean-cut corners and ribs. This is Carcase Wall, which has the hardest routes on the Torr.

(4) Above and right of Carcase Wall is an area of broken grey rock, the Lower Summit Buttress.

(5) Below the summit of the hill is a long wall of steep clean rock with twin chimneys at the left and a huge right-angled recess at the right. This is Upper Summit Buttress.

(6) Coming down and left from Upper Summit Buttress is a fine crag facing more towards the col on the north side of Sgurr na Laocainn. This is the West face of Upper Summit Buttress which has some of the best climbs on the Torr.

From most of the climbs descent on the left is easiest. However, from the east side of the terrace below Summit Buttress a goat track crosses South Gully, threads a way through very steep ground and then descends the next grassy spur to the east. This track is also useful for direct access to climbs such as Rainbow Corner.

THE LOWER WALL

1 Rose Rib 65m Very Difficult   (1957)
This route takes the left-hand of the two red ribs below the huge perched block. Start at the foot of the rib, which is undercut.
1. 30m Use a spike to gain the wall. Climb a short overhang, then the short wall to a pleasant slab leading to a narrow turf terrace. Continue up the rib to a turf ledge.
2. 35m Climb slabs and grooves just left of the crest to reach the great perched block.

2 The Long Reach 80m VS   (1957)
This takes the right-hand red rib. Start at a black greasy recess at the foot of the rib. Climb 6m to a steep grassy bay. Traverse right onto the rib and ascend 12m to a slight overhang. Step left and climb grooves to easier ground. Follow the rib easily and the rocks above to the great perched block.

3 The Eyrie 70m VS   (1978)
Start below and right of The Long Reach at a large boulder where a traverse line leads across right to a hanging corner.
1. 40m Climb right and up for 15m; traverse right and up a short groove; at the top move left onto a slab under the prominent overhang. Follow the slab and belay on the ledge to the left.
2. 30m Climb up for 3m, then left into a corner; climb this and the easy slabs above.

4 Sickle 60m VS   (1966)
Start, as for The Eyrie, at a large boulder, where a traverse line leads
across right to a hanging corner.
1. 25m Traverse diagonally right across the steep wall to a belay just
beyond the foot of the hanging corner.
2. 35m Go right for 6m across an easy ledge into another corner and
climb this to a large grass ledge. Step back left onto the steep wall and
climb it by the line of least resistance. Continue up steep rock and
grass to the top.

5 Ipswich Rib, Lower Part 70m Very Difficult   (1956)
Start at the foot of a little rib below and at the right end of the Lower
Wall. This is the lowest point of the rocks.
1. 30m Follow the crest of the rib to where it joins the steeper wall at
the foot of a crack.
2. 20m Climb a few metres, traverse right and continue into a niche
below a bulging overhang.
3. 20m Step down to a ledge below the right wall of the niche, then
up for 5m and traverse a slab into an overhanging chimney; climb this
to easy ground.

   The route can be continued by scrambling for about 250m to the
Upper Summit Buttress. Keep near the crest of the vague rib and aim
for the the great slab recess on the right of Upper Summit Buttress.
The upper part of the climb is described below.

HARLEQUIN WALL

6 Intimidation 35m HVS   (1957)
Loose rock makes this a serious climb. Start at the foot of the wall,
right of the huge perched block. An obvious crack slants up right. Gain
the top of an initial 10m pinnacle by easy grooves on its right. Follow
cracks with increasing difficulty on decreasingly stable rock, over a
bulge at 20m, to the crux at 25m. Easier ground above leads to a belay
on the the terrace.

7 Holly Tree Wall 45m VS   (1978)
This lies below and left of Harlequin Wall, on a black wall of better rock
with a holly tree. Climb up to the tree, step right and follow a crack for
5m. Traverse left across a slab and back right under a huge block into
a chimney forming the right side of the block. Climb the chimney and
belay on top of the block. Traverse right for 5m and climb the wall just
left of an unpleasant gully.

CARCASE WALL

8 Skeleton Corner 65m   VS   (1967)
The big right-angled corner with a smooth right wall at the left end of
Carcase Wall.
1. 35m Climb the steep wall directly below the start of the corner, and
follow the corner by walls and ledges to a belay beneath an overhang
where the corner steepens.
2. 30m Continue up the corner on the right to the top.

9 Skull 55m   E1 **   (1967)
This takes the rib on the right of Skeleton Corner, the prominent feature
of which is a steep red slab split by a thin crack.
1. 35m 5b Climb a groove just right of Skeleton Corner to the bottom
left edge of the steep red slab. Traverse right across the slab, and
climb its overhanging right edge to a ledge. Climb the fault above,
trending slightly right to a large ledge beneath a corner.
2. 20m Go up the corner until a move right can be made. Continue
up right to the crest and back left to finish.

10 Carnivorous Crack 45m   E2   (1988)
The large recess right of Skull contains two cracks; this takes the
left-hand one.
1. 25m 5c Climb the crack, bulging at the top, and move right into the
main recess.
2. 20m 4c Finish up the left-hand blocky fault.

TORR NA H'IOLAIRE

11 Cadaverous Crack 50m E1   (1978)
1. 30m 5b Climb the right-hand crack in the recess past three overhangs to a ledge.
2. 20m 4c Climb the dank, vegetated chimney above, then step left to finish.

12 Wishbone Rib 45m HVS   (1967)
Start at the bottom left of the rib right of Cadaverous Crack.
1. 30m Surmount a bulge. Climb up, then left, to gain a ledge which slopes up right. Go along this to the crest and then straight up to a belay in a bay.
2. 15m Climb up right, then steeply to finish.

13 Hyena Corner 40m HVS   (1988)
The corner right of Wishbone Rib (often wet).
1. 15m 4b Climb a wall by the easiest line to reach a ledge in the main recess.
2. 25m 5a Climb the right-hand crack, and so to the top of the corner. Easier rocks to the top.

LOWER SUMMIT BUTTRESS
This is the area of rock between the top of Carcase Wall and the terrace below the central part of Upper Summit Buttress. **Skyline Route** (60m, Very Difficult) follows the left side and is naturally combined with one of the routes on the Upper Buttress.

UPPER SUMMIT BUTTRESS
The obvious feature of the twin chimneys at the left of Upper Summit Buttress makes a convenient starting point for description. The climbs are described from left to right from here, then (perhaps rather illogically) the climbs on the West Face of Upper Summit Buttress are described.

14 Sarcophagus 60m VS *   (1957)
This takes the rocks left of the left twin chimney via an enormous flake. It is a good climb, steep and exposed.
1. 15m Start up a vertical wall, then an obvious chimney above to reach chockstone belays at an overhung ledge.
2. 35m 4c Move up and right to the foot of an overhung groove with a corner crack. Climb this and traverse left to the foot of more grooves

that lead to the base of the great flake. Climb the flake by the left-hand chimney (loose blocks) and go up to a large ledge.
3. 10m Ascend the slab above to a large block on the skyline.

15 Cleopatra 45m E2   (1988)
Left of Sarcophagus is a steep nose. This route takes the crack line just to the left, well seen from the top of Carnmore Crag. Start up on the right. The initial bulge is the crux (5c).

16 Frogmarch 55m Difficult   (1957)
This is the left-hand of the twin chimneys, wet and unpleasant.
1. 20m Start from the terrace below and climb steep rock and vegetation to the foot of the chimney.
2. 25m Climb the chimney to a small cave, then climb the right wall to a stance and belay on a rib.
3. 10m Move left and continue to the top.

17 Toad Hall 45m HVS   (1988)
The right-hand chimney, though dark and messy, gives a good old-fashioned route.

18 Sapros 60m VS   (1966)
To the right of the twin chimneys is a nose and then a steep corner-groove. This climb attempts to follow the wall right of the groove. The rock is doubtful.
1. 35m Start about 10m right of the groove. A line of weakness leads up left for 15m. Just short of an insecure grass ledge break right and make an ascending traverse right above the lip of an overhang.
2. 25m Ascend right across a steep slab to easy ground (junction with Tantivy Tower). Continue to the top.

19 Tantivy Tower 65m Difficult   (1951)
This takes the true nose of the Upper Summit Buttress. Start near an overhung recess at the foot of the frontal wall.
1. 15m Go up a short wall, then to the foot of a steeper wall.
2. 25m Climb the wall, moving left then up the edge to large perched blocks on the shelf above.
3. 25m Go up the blocks to the right and rightwards to a shelf below the final short tier. Reach a small recess at waist height in the wall above and climb to the top.

20 Juniper Groove 60m Severe   (1957)
Start about 20 metres right of Tantivy Tower at the bottom right-hand
corner of a large slab. On the left is a corner and a rib which juts out
a little from the face.
1. 30m Go diagonally left up the slab to gain grooves in the corner
and climb these to a platform.
2. 20m Climb the grooves to the terrace below the final tier.
3. 10m Climb this to the top.

The next few climbs start at a somewhat lower level, which can be
reached by following a lower terrace round to the right.

21 Ipswich Rib, Upper Part 60m Difficult **   (1956)
This is the continuation of the lower part of Ipswich Rib. Traditionally
the routes are combined to give a long and enjoyable climb. Start
below a rib running up the left edge of the great slab recess that lies
towards the right of Upper Summit Buttress.
1. 20m Climb a chimney just right of the rib and go up slabs to the
foot of a steep crack.
2. 15m Traverse right to a platform below the diedre in the slab recess.
Mantleshelf and traverse left to the top of the crack.
3. 25m Climb a chimney behind a flake and follow slabs to the top,
keeping close to the crest.

22 Rainbow Corner 65m VS   (1957)
This is the diedre above the great slab recess. Start a little right of a
point directly below the corner, at a shallow V-groove.
1. 40m Climb the groove and continue more or less directly by further
grooves to a small bay. Leave this at the back and gain the foot of the
main corner.
2. 25m 4c Climb the corner and finish up the easier groove.

23 Sunday Climb 60m Severe   (1957)
Start 15 metres right of Rainbow Corner, below a prominent partly
detached flake.
1. 35m Climb a series of corners and slabs to the lower right corner
of the slab recess below Rainbow Corner.
2. 25m Climb a slab to below the right end of a large roof. Traverse
right to the edge, then go up to ledges. From there traverse right into
South Gully, or climb short walls and ledges to the top.

24 Goats' Groove 85m   Very Difficult   (1957)
Start at the lowest south-west point of Upper Summit Buttress, slightly up the right-bounding gully.
1. 10m Climb a steep groove that is awkward to start.
2. 20m Cross heathery rock leftwards to perched blocks.
3. 25m Go up and left to a slabby rib, climb this and continue to a ledge with a chimney at the back.
4. 20m Climb the chimney to a ledge; belay on the left at a fallen block.
5. 10m Step from the top of the block onto the wall behind and ascend the rocks above to the top.

THE WEST FACE OF UPPER SUMMIT BUTTRESS
The climbs here are described from left to right, starting with the routes nearest the col on the north side of Sgurr na Laocainn and finishing with routes just below Sarcophagus. An obvious feature of the West Face is the large red-streaked slab of Hieroglyphics. Right of this a grassy ramp slants up to the right while left of the slab is a deep T-shaped chimney. Left again is another big striped slab, Red Admiral.

25 Wester 105m   Very Difficult   (1957)
Start near the left end of the face, about 10 metres right of a deep-cut gully, at a boulder below a striated rib.
1. 30m Go up an obvious line from the boulder, over a perched block, to the foot of the striated rib. Move left over a flake, and up to reach a small grassy ledge above the gully on the left.
2. 25m Climb behind a narrow boulder on the right, step left onto a rib, then up to a narrow ledge below an overhang. Pass this on the right and go straight up to a wide grass ledge.
3. 20m Climb a narrow wet chimney to another ledge.
4. 30m Traverse left and go up easier rocks to the top.

26 Suspension 90m Severe   (1959)
Start 2 metres right of Wester, up slabs leaning at right angles to the cliff. Follow a ledge rising to the right. Avoid an overhang on the right and climb 30m to a ledge and belay. Climb easier rock to a broad rake. Ascend a right-trending crack to a notch in the overhangs above. Climb the notch to a ledge above, just left of a prominent chimney. Climb a steep wall for 15m on the left of the chimney and finish up easier rocks.

27 Red Admiral 125m VS (1957)

Start some way left of the T-shaped chimney, at the foot of a narrow wedge of red and black striped slab.

1. 20m Go up the corner on the right of the slab.
2. 25m Continue up the slab to a belay at a turf ledge.
3. 20m Follow a little ramp to the right, then back left to gain a slanting rake.
3. 20m Climb a rib on the right of a conspicuous gully.
4. 40m Continue to the top.

28 Eryr 135m Severe (1970)

1. 20m Climb the deep T-shaped chimney to a line of overhangs.
2. 45m Traverse left along the overhung ledge for 5m to gain a bottomless groove and follow this to a belay.
3. and 4. 70m Climb right, then left along a rake and right to the foot of an open chimney, which is followed to the top.

An earlier climb, **West Face Ledge Route** (Difficult), traverses further left from the bottomless groove, and then breaks through and takes the line of least resistance, leftwards, to the top.

29 Hieroglyphics 125m VS ** (1957)

This route gives an excellent first pitch, but is much easier thereafter. Start right of the deep T-shaped chimney, at the diamond-shaped slab streaked in green and red.

1. 35m 4b Climb direct to ledges at 5m, then diagonally left to a green slab near the edge at 20m. Easier climbing leads to the ledge above and belay at the foot of a short overhanging corner.
2. 35m Climb the corner, then go directly up by a rib just right of wet grooves. Belay at the foot of a steeper wall where a prominent forefinger of rock guards the foot of a deep groove.
3. 20m Climb the groove to belays above a short overhanging section.
4. 35m Climb a rib on the left, then scramble to the top.

30 Sigma 55m VS (1957)

A grass rake runs up rightwards below the Upper Summit Buttress from Hieroglyphics. About 60 metres up this is a Cioch-like pinnacle on the right and just above this an obvious line of weakness runs across the wall on the left towards a short V-chimney.

1. 15m Follow the line of weakness and belay on top of the pinnacle forming the outside of the chimney.
2. 40m Climb the black corner above for 5m, step out left to the crest, move up and back right. Surmount an overhang on good holds, move right and climb up to easier ground.

31 Baird's Route 120m   Very Difficult   (1933)
To the right of the start of Sigma a ridge runs up to the left from the grass rake. Start just below this, where a shelf slopes up into a vertical crack. Climb the shelf and crack, avoiding the top overhang by the wall on the right. Go up the arete and into a gully flanked on the right by a steep wall. A crack in this gives a good pitch; continue easily to the top.

CARNAN BAN
652m   (Map Ref 999 764)

THE PRACTICE PRECIPICE   *(Map Ref 996 767)*

This is a small outcrop just across the stream from the Carnmore to Shenavall path, about 60m above the zigzags above the Dubh Loch. A steep wall lies to the left of three easier-angled ribs. Pleasant 40m Difficult or Very Difficult routes may be found up the ribs.
BARNDANCE SLABS *(Map Ref 998 765)*
This is the slabby mass of gneiss on the western slope of Carnan Ban. It overlooks the burn that flows out of Fuar Loch Beag. The approach from Carnmore to Maiden Buttress passes close underneath; if a climb is first undertaken on the slabs, from the top a short traverse across the hillside leads to Maiden Buttress. The main features of Barndance Slabs from below are two turfy rakes, one slanting up from left to right, the other from bottom right steeply up to cross the first. These isolate a triangle of clean grey slab between them, with a steep base and an overhanging nose at the lower right corner. Above the left rake the slabs continue upwards before becoming lost in the hillside. To the right of the right-hand rake there is a strip of steep and often wet slab.

Barndance   115m   Difficult *   (1956)
An entertaining climb. Start at the lower right corner of the triangle of slabs, below the overhanging nose.
1. 10m Climb up to the overhang, either via the slab or a corner, and belay on the right.
2. 15m Move right to the edge of the grassy chimney then up for 2m before traversing back left along an overhung ledge. From the left end move into grooves running up and left.
3, etc. 90m Follow the grooves for 60m to the left-hand rake, then continue in the same line for 30m until interest wanes.

The following two routes are on the slabs to the left of Barndance. The rock is excellent.

Strider   110m   Severe *   (1967)
Above a large pointed pinnacle in a gully is a leaning rectangular block. Start just left of the block.
1. 25m Climb slabs to a triangular recess. Go right and up to a sloping rock shelf.
2. 25m Follow the obvious gangway on the left, steepening at 10m, under an overlap. From the left end go up past a detached pinnacle to a narrow grass ledge. Move 5m left to a pinnacle.
3. 40m Step right and go up a short crack and bulges, then follow a reddish slab corner. Break out left when this becomes wet and move up to a shelf with a loose flake. Continue straight up behind the flake and climb a bulge using a right-trending crack to a shelf and belay.
4. 20m Scramble up slabs to the top.

Balrog   105m   Severe   (1967)
Start as for Strider.
1. 25m Follow the obvious right-slanting crack easily to a grass niche. Go up the curving crack above to a small heather ledge.
2. 20m Climb the crack trending left up the wall above, over the crux bulge. Belay in the fine slanting niche above.
3. 40m Follow the crack then the slabby wall to a grass ledge.
4. 20m Scrambling above.

MAIDEN BUTTRESS *(Map Ref 001 762)*

This is a small but well-formed mass of rock on the south-east side of Carnan Ban. It is visible from the Dubh Loch causeway, but is more or less concealed in the small basin that holds Fuar Loch Beag. It is well seen from the lower part of the north-west ridge of A'Mhaighdean, the path up which passes above the opposite shore of the lochan.

Access is easy from Carnmore by the Shenavall path to just beyond the zigzag, then across the ravine and up to the col, passing beneath the Barndance Slabs. The buttress is visible across the lochan from this col.

From the Shenavall direction, take the side path which leads up into the corrie of Fuar Loch Mor. Follow it for about 800 metres or so then cut over to the right to a large perched boulder on a rocky knoll. This is the top of the buttress.

Climbing on the buttress is pleasant. Most of the climbs have one or two difficult pitches at the start then become comparatively easy. The rock is good clean gneiss. The routes described were all climbed in 1955, but harder routes should be possible, taking more satisfying but eliminate lines. The climbs are described from left to right.

1 Strewth 75m VS   (1955)
Start from the grass slope at the foot of the second rib left of the bottom left of the buttress. This is about 40m above the start of Dishonour, and 10m above the start of Ecstasy.
1. 10m Climb a wall below the start of the rib and continue up the rib to a ledge.
2. 25m Climb the wall behind to gain a corner crack with a narrow slab on its left. Climb this until it begins to overhang, then take an easy crack on the left. Belay on the right.
3. 20m Continue up easy slabs on the left of the buttress, passing a big ledge on the left wall and belaying on another ledge at the foot of the steeper wall, also on the left.
4. 20m Climb the wall on the right and follow the edge of the buttress to easy ground.

2 Ecstasy 115m Severe **   (1955)
A climb of particular quality, probably the best on the crag. Start at the
foot of the first rib to the left of the bottom left corner of the buttress.
The rib widens rapidly upwards into a V-shaped slab bounded by
vertical walls.
1. 25m Go up the left edge of the V-slab for 10m then traverse
diagonally right across the slab by a finger crack. Step down under
the prominent overhang and go up right to a steep corner. Climb the
corner and exit left to a ledge.
2. 15m Go up the slab above, first right then back left to large ledges.
3. 25m Continue easily on the right of the overhangs above, then back
left to ledges below a short wall.
4. 20m Climb the wall, either by a crack on the right or cracks on the
left edge.
5. 30m Climb the clean buttress above, avoiding a blank section on
the right.

3 Dishonour 115m Very Difficult **   (1955)
A close second to Ecstasy. Start at the foot of the left edge of the front
face of the buttress.
1. 20m Climb the slab up the left edge to a steeper wall. Belay to the
right.
2. 20m Move around the edge onto a large flake, then step back right
onto the front face and climb to a small ledge in a niche. (A harder
alternative is to climb the wall direct.) Continue straight up the slab to
a ledge with a large perched block.
3. 25m Move up right into an easy chimney, climb this then go
diagonally left to a ledge under an overhang.
4. 25m Go up right then back left above the overhang, then straight
up a narrowing groove to a ledge. Take a groove on the right to reach
a large terrace.
5. 25m Climb just right of twin cracks in the wall above and up a second
wall by a crack to easy ground.

4 Tweedledum 115m Severe   (1955)
Start 5 metres right of Dishonour.
1. 20m Climb the slab between two vegetated cracks and belay on
the left below a steeper wall.
2. 10m Move right to the overhang and climb it on the right. Belay in
a niche on the left.

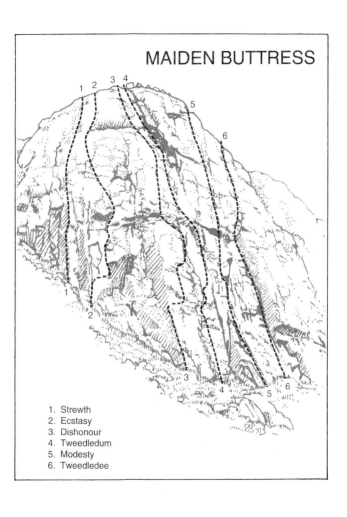

MAIDEN BUTTRESS

1. Strewth
2. Ecstasy
3. Dishonour
4. Tweedledum
5. Modesty
6. Tweedledee

3. 20m Climb the rib on the right, then a chimney on its right.
4. 20m Continue up the chimney.
5. 20m Traverse left on ledges above overhangs, then go up the broad scoop. Climb a short V-groove to a large terrace.
5. 25m Climb easily on the left of the central turfy gully, finishing up a steep 'boulder problem' wall on good holds.

5 Modesty 115m Very Difficult   (1955)
Start immediately right of a line of turfy cracks, at the centre front of the buttress, about 5 metres right of Tweedledum.
1. 15m Climb the left of the slab. The cracks in the middle are harder.
2. 25m Climb the wall on the right of the vegetated fault. Continue up the fault and step left to ledges.
3. 25m Continue up the fault and the chimney above.
4. 25m Climb easily up slabs to large terraces.
5. 25m Layback up the flake in the centre of the wall, then continue leftwards to the top.

6 Tweedledee 115m Severe   (1955)
Start towards the right of the buttress at a line of cracks which pass just left of the great overhangs as a wide shallow chimney.
1. 30m Go up the slab, or the crack, to the foot of the chimney. Climb it, passing the first bulge on the right and the others on the left.
2. 30m Follow the cracks for a short distance and then go out up the left wall to block belays on a terrace.
3. 25m Go right up a big corner crack.
4. 15m Ignore an easy escape to the right and climb the wall on the left by a diagonal crack.
5. 15m Climb the right edge of the small overhang above and continue to the top.

7 Cakewalk 80m Difficult   (1955)
Start at the base of the third narrow (red) slab right of the big overhang and immediately below a small overlap.
1. 30m Climb by cracks just right of the overlap, then follow the outside edge of the slab to belays below steeper ground.
2. 20m Follow a gangway on the right, pass loose blocks and climb a thin crack above. Belay on the shelf.
3. 30m Take the prominent crack in the wall on the left to a platform, then go easily up the slabs above.

Immediately to the right of Maiden Buttress is an easy-angled broken buttress, clmbed easily by **Doddle** (75m, Moderate).

A'MHAIGHDEAN
967m   (Map Ref 008 751)

A graceful mountain lying in the heart of this magnificent wilderness and often reckoned to be the most remote of the Munros. The bulk of the mountain is composed of Lewisian gneiss, the summit being the highest point at which this rock outcrops in Scotland. However much of the climbing is concentrated on a series of sandstone buttresses that flank the south-west side of the north-west ridge.

The rock is a coarser sandstone than in most other crags, quite akin to gritstone. The Pillar Buttress and the Gorm Loch Mor face to its east are gneissose. All the cliffs face south and south-west.

Access
The best approach to the majority of the cliffs is via the north-west ridge, easily reached from Carnmore by following the approach to Maiden Buttress as far as Fuar Loch Beag. From Shenavall the best approach is via the path to Carnmore as far as Lochan Feith Mhic-illean. Just past the lochan take the branch track that crosses the Allt Bruthach an Easain. If heading for the Sandstone Buttresses, follow this path for 800 metres or so, then cut over to the right towards the west end of the Fuar Loch Mor and thence onto the north-west ridge of A'Mhaighdean.

If aiming for the Pillar Buttress area it is best to stay on the path and to walk over the summit. On the map the path is shown as stopping underneath Ruadh Stac Mor, but in fact it continues right up to and over the saddle between the two mountains and gives good walking. The summit of A'Mhaighdean is easily reached from the col. Some of the longer climbs on the south-west face are more easily reached by walking up from the Dubh Loch.

THE SANDSTONE BUTTRESSES

The sandstone buttresses lie on the long north-west ridge. It is possible to contour below them, traversing the very steep southern slopes, leaving the ridge some distance above a big perched boulder above

Fuar Loch Beag. There are four buttresses described from left to right. The finest and most compact is number four: The Gritstone Buttress. The rock is not pure sandstone but seems to have formed an unusual blend with gneiss. It is solid and the climbing good. There are no routes on the first nondescript buttress. The second is called Breccia Buttress and has one route.

1   Conglomerate Arete   90m   Very Difficult   (1957)
Start at the bottom right corner of the buttress, at the foot of an obvious arete between the broken frontal face and the vertical right wall. Rather artificial in parts.
1. 20m   Go up a groove onto the crest of the rib and climb an overhanging nose to a little platform. Continue up the step above by a narrow crack on the edge.
2. 35m   Follow the arete over several short steps keeping near the edge.
3. 35m   Scramble up easy rocks in the same line to the top.

The third buttress is called The Red Slab. It is terminated on the right by a steep wall and the bottom right corner is badly cut away. There is a subsidiary pinnacle-like buttress on the left. An easy descent can be made down the gully between this buttress and Breccia Buttress.

2   Red Slab   110m   Difficult   (1957)
An enjoyable climb. Start in the corner between the subsidiary buttress and the slab, at the farthest right point at which an easy access to the slab is available.
1. 40m   Go up 12m to a ledge. Traverse this right to the edge. Go on up to another small ledge and up the slab above to a terrace. Belay at blocks on the left, 6m up.
2. 25m   Diagonally right is an obvious block on the edge. Gain the outer edge of the slab a few metres above this. Climb the slab above, keeping as close as possible to the edge, to a platform and belay at a large perched block.
3. 20m   Continue to a terrace.
4. 25m   Go easily to the foot of a final 9m wall. Climb the wall to the top.

A'MHAIGHDEAN, SANDSTONE BUTTRESSES

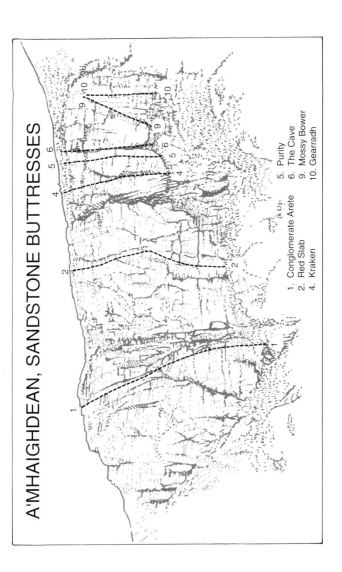

1. Conglomerate Arete
2. Red Slab
4. Kraken

5. Purity
6. The Cave
9. Mossy Bower
10. Gearradh

3 Doe Crack 80m   Very Difficult   (1957)
Takes a direct line up the slab, starting from approximately the same
position as the previous route.
1. 30m   Climb the slab, about 3 metres to the right of the corner
between it and the subsidiary buttress, to a terrace.
2. 10m   Climb a zigzag crack to the foot of a V-chimney.
3. 30m   Go up the chimney, then follow cracks to a terrace.
4. 10m   Go up the left-hand crack in the final wall.

The fourth and steepest buttress is the Gritstone Buttress. The fine
central wall is split by the deep chimney feature of the cave. This has
been climbed at its mouth and also by a through route. A third route
starts up the fine corner on the left to traverse into the chimney above
its widest section. The gully right of the buttress can be used for
descent. The routes are described from left to right.

4 Kraken 70m   Severe   (1965)
This takes a hidden internal corner round the left side of the buttress.
1. 25m   Traverse left from the central cave over broken ground, round
a corner and up to the foot of a prominent vertical corner, partially
concealed in the fault which defines the left edge of the buttress.
2.   Climb the crack in the corner, finishing in a short chimney to the
lower of two overhangs. Thread belay.
3.   Make an exposed traverse to the left for 6m to gain a short chimney
and climb this to easy ground.

5 Purity 50m   HVS   (1988)
This is the fine corner line left of the cave. An excellent pitch. Climb
the corner negotiating a bulge (crux) and so to belay on slabs. Finish
out left by big blocks.

6 The Cave 60m   Hard Severe   (1988)
An unusual subterranean climb. Go right to the back of the cave. Climb
up and out then head for the obvious narrow through route. Thread
this and follow the open chimney to the top.

7 The Cave-Mouth 50m   VS   (1988)
From inside the entrance climb out on the right wall (looking out), then
back and foot and bridge up until the chimney narrows. Climb the
chimney to the top.

8 Compensation 55m Severe   (1967)
This climb was done before the direct ascents of the Cave. Climb the corner of Purity for about 12m, then traverse right on ledges to enter the chimney. Climb the chimney to the top.

9 Mossy Bower 50m Hard Severe   (1988)
This is the obvious right-slanting fault to the right of the Cave. Dank and mossy. The fault leads to a ledge system on the right side of the buttress. Finish out right.

10 Gearradh 50m HVS 5a   (1988)
The obvious straight crack line in the column just right of the previous route. Climb it to join the ledge system.

11 Windslab 55m Severe   (1957)
Takes the slab and corner right of the Gearradh column.
1. 10m Go up blocks on the right, then traverse left into the corner to thread belays.
2. 25m Climb the vertical crack above, then take to the centre of the slab for pleasant climbing to a ledge and block belay.
3. 20m Continue up the centre of the slab to the top.

THE OCTAVE RIBS
These are obvious on the upper of the two bands of coarsely crystalline gneiss that slant across the Dubh Loch face, underneath the sandstone cliffs. Fahrenheit is the fourth rib from the left, immediately right of a very obvious red rib.

Fahrenheit 60m Mild VS   (1959)
A sustained and exposed climb. Climb the edge for 12m then traverse left into a grassy groove and climb this to a belay. Rejoin the rib crest and climb it for 30m to a stance and belay. Continue up the crest to an overhang, take this directly and finish up short slabs.

Soh What? 35m Very Difficult   (1959)
The fifth rib, just right of Fahrenheit. Follow the rib crest until a ledge is reached. Continue over a small bulge and follow the steep left wall of the groove above.

WEST FACE OF A'MHAIGHDEAN

Whitbread's Aiguille 270m Severe   (1957)
This climb is best approached by walking up from the Dubh Loch. Start at the foot of the easy-angled buttress which forms the left side of the gully below the West Face of A'Mhaighdean, the West Gully. This buttress rises from a broad base to a small pinnacle, about 60m below the north-west ridge. At the bottom left a huge pinnacle leans against the face. A detailed description was given in Vol.1 of the previous SMC Northern Highlands Climbers' Guide, but on a subsequent ascent it was found that few of the features were easily identified. Some variation is possible and quite a hard pitch may be found low down. It is a good traditional route, suitable for those who enjoy an exploratory approach.

Vole Buttress 270m Very Difficult   (1957)
This is the indefinite buttress left of Whitbread's Aiguille. Start at the foot of a prominent V-groove with a slab for its left wall, towards the left of the buttress. Climb this in a series of quite hard pitches for 120m, after which the difficulty relents.

Ermine Gully 300m III   (1978)
This is the most prominent, long gully left of West Gully, just left of Vole Buttress, and well right of the Sandstone Buttresses. On the first ascent two pitches were encountered low down.

West Face 240m Severe   (1951)
The large and indefinite West Face of A'Mhaighdean overlooks the Dubh Loch. One climb has been recorded, starting from a grass slope below the tapering southern extension of the face. The description is very vague (SMCJ Vol. 25).

PILLAR BUTTRESS

The 150m Pillar Buttress faces south just under the summit of A'Mhaighdean. The true nose of the buttress gives an enjoyable climb of Difficult standard that finishes at the summit cairn. Direct access to the base of the crag is rather laborious from the west owing to the lie of the lower cliffs. The best approach from the west is to traverse the summit and descend the nearby big grassy gully (Trident Gully) that leads towards the mouth of Gorm Loch Mor. After descending about 200m, traverse right (west) to the foot of the buttress. Alternatively the crag may be reached from Gorm Loch Mor, which is a pleasant walk from Carnmore.

Eagle Grooves 110m Severe *   (1957)
This climb lies on the west (left) face of Pillar Buttress and gives a classic climb in fine position. From further down the north-west ridge of A'Mhaighdean a prominent clean-looking rib of grey rock can be seen that starts at the same level as Pillar Buttress and immediately west of it. The start is gained by a left traverse along a turfy ledge from the boulders at the top of the first pitches of Pillar Buttress or Triple Cracks Route. Traverse the obvious ledge for 40 metres to below an indefinite rib of clean grey rock. To the left are turfy grooves and a rib culminating in overhangs.
1. 35m Climb by slabs and grooves to a tiny platform on top of a large grey flake. Some 6m above is a small niche and belay.
2. 25m Above and slanting left is a prominent crack in steeper rocks. Climb this to grooves and a spike belay beyond.
3. 30m Continue leftwards up the groove to a turfy ledge.
4. 20m Climb the slab above, then by a corner until it is possible to break out right onto easy ground near the top.

Pillar Buttress 150m Difficult   (1950)
This follows the crest of the buttress. Start at the foot of the rib. Easy rocks lead in 25m to a platform. The obvious line up grooves to the right is Triple Cracks Route. Continue up slabs and walls slanting right of the true crest of the buttress, climbing a steep slab by parallel cracks. Easy rocks, a difficult crack, then 6m of difficult slab lead to an impasse requiring an awkward traverse to a huge crack full of chockstones. Climb this to finish.

A direct start to this climb has been made, commencing from a point to the right of the original line, and joining it after three pitches (**The Leeds Variation**; SMCJ Vol.25).

A previous route recorded in 1933 (**Baird, Crofton and Leslie's Route**; SMCJ Vol.20) probably follows roughly the same line. Another variation traverses left after the first pitch and climbs grooves for two exposed pitches (Mild VS).

Triple Cracks Route   120m   Severe   (1951)
Follows the slot-like chimney several metres right of Pillar Buttress.
Climb the chimney and follow the fault directly up the buttress to finish
by the boulder-choked chimney of Pillar Buttress. Below the final
chimney is the Triple Cracks pitch, which is the crux.

GORM LOCH MOR FACE

Right (east) of Pillar Buttress is a broad gully which splits into three
branches some 150m below the top. This is Trident Gully. The west
and centre forks are easy, but the east fork rises to a damp recess
below vertical rock walls some 75m below the top. The main feature
of the flank of Pillar Buttress overlooking West Trident Gully is a blank
red wall defined on the left by the slot of Triple Cracks Route. Between
the west and central forks is a narrow rib of steep rock and grass that
nowhere rises much above the floor of the gully. A more substantial
ridge lies between the central and east forks, giving Trident Gully
Buttress. The climbs hereabouts are best approached by descending
Pinnacle Gully on the right side of the crag (see below). Goat's Ridge
can then be crossed to the left to reach the Trident Gully area.

Trident Gully Buttress   130m   VS   (1967)
The lowest rock rib is gained from the right, just above the overhanging
base. A mossy slab leads to some grass and then, following the crest
as closely as possible, pleasant climbing leads to a broad ledge below
the final tower. The main feature is a central corner-groove leading up
to an overhang at the top. An overhanging wall bars direct entry into
the groove, which is gained by climbing the detached rib on the right
of the ledge and pulling across left into the bottom of the groove. This
is climbed up to the roof, with an excursion at half-height onto the left
to climb a steep 3m wall on good holds. At the top of the groove
undercut holds under the overhang allow an escape left to the foot of
a narrow ramp which leads awkwardly up the west wall to the top.

Right of East Trident Gully is a broad ridge, Goat's Ridge, which
descends almost as low as Pillar Buttress. It has two steeper rock
sections in its lower and upper parts with an easy-angled stretch in
between (150m, Difficult).

East of Goat's Ridge is a wide, easy gully, Pinnacle Gully, leading down to an amphitheatre below a big sweep of light-coloured slabs, forming the right flank of the upper part of Goat's Ridge. A good climb starts at the lowest point of the slabs and heads for the prominent V-shaped chimney, capped by a roof, on the final tower.

Gladiator 100m Severe   (1966)
Trend slightly leftwards up the slabs to reach the grassy corner and blocks below a V-chimney in 60m. A spike belay is passed at 20m and the foot of a thin grassy groove and quartz streaks are then followed. The steep chimney-crack above is climbed to the roof, where an escape is made by a left traverse. Scramble to the top.

In Pinnacle Gully, below the level of the slabs can be found Hodge's Pinnacle. Its short upper side gives a 10m climb (Difficult). On the west face is a slightly longer and harder crack. The long south ridge gives a good Severe climb of 45m, starting up the huge boulders below. East of Pinnacle Gully is a broken ridge giving pleasant scrambling, perhaps Difficult in its lower reaches.

STAC A'CHAORRUINN   *(Map Ref 023 744)*

This 'small' crag (perhaps 150m high) is the eastern bluff of A'Mhaigh-dean. It is possibly also the bluff of the first (and probably last) persons to climb here in 1909, that unstoppable pair Ling and Glover. The pioneers were prevented from making a full investigation by the weather, but they did make a long rightwards traverse along the large lower terrace. This led them to rocks overlooking a large gully (noted for its winter potential). They then turned up leftwards, following the edge of the gully to the flat top of the bluff. The possibilities for a good direct climb were noted (SMCJ Vol.12, p.29).

NA BEARTA BUTTRESS   *(Map Ref 004 807)*

This is the considerable mass of rock which outcrops on the west side of Srath Beinn Dearg, just north of the burn that flows out of Lochan na Bearta. It lies in a remote region that is little visited and, as such, is possibly one of the few remaining habitats of that fast disappearing species, the Scottish 'VS'. The rock is Lewisian gneiss interbanded with hornblende schist, and as usual it is comparatively solid and clean. The angle is moderate and the character slabby, which gives the crag rather an unimpressive appearance that belies the quality of the climbing. A disadvantage is that the cliff faces north.

Access
The most direct approach is from Gruinard Bay, following the estate road that leads to Loch na Sealga. Leave the public road at Map Ref 961 911 (locked gate) and follow the track for 7km until it crosses the Allt Loch Ghiubhsachain. Keeping to the west side of the river, a further 5km of rough going leads to the cliff. Alternatively, from Carnmore follow the Shenavall path as far as Lochan Feith Mhic'-illean then cut north over the moor, past Lochan Cnapach, to Lochan na Bearta. From Shenavall take the Carnmore path up Gleann na Muice Beag and branch off past Loch Beinn Dearg and so down Srath Beinn Dearg.

   The structure of the crag is, firstly on the left, a large slabby buttress composed of three tiers of approximately 80m, 25m and 70m in ascending order, divided by two extensive turf ledges. The full height of this part of the cliff has yet to be climbed. On the right of this buttress is a grassy scoop, the Central Gully, to the right of which lies an extensive sheet of slabs bounded on the right by a sort of gully which has no right wall. The slabs diminish in size to the right, but there are several lines starting up the slabs from this gully. The routes are described from left to right.

Wallflower   240m   Hard Severe   (1956)
Not a very good climb, but it has some good pitches. It follows a reasonably natural line but avoids the steeper upper tier of the buttress. Start at the foot of the rocks left of the Central Gully and immediately right of a prominent gully-chimney with a cave on its right wall.
1. 30m Climb the slabs to the foot of the detached layback flake. From here an obvious line leads up right to a prominent field and trees. Ignoring this, traverse left then up to a narrow turf ledge with small trees.
2. 25m Traverse the turf ledges to the right and climb the edge of the slab on good holds. Near the top turn left, crossing a small overhang. Belay at a turfy platform with trees.

3. 15m Go up a corner on the left to a ledge and climb the slab above. This leads to broken rocks below the first big terrace.

4. 60m Scramble to the terrace.

5. 15m Opposite the point of arrival on the terrace is an obvious groove and crack in the wall above. Climb the groove awkwardly, moving left at the top into a minor groove. One aid peg was used here because of vegetation.

6. 10m An easy slab on the right leads to another terrace at a huge block.

7. 10m The steep wall above was avoided, although it looks feasible. To the right the terrace falls away into a grassy scoop, the upper part of Central Gully. Level with the terrace, but across to the right on the edge of the gully, is a tree. Traverse 'with carefully controlled breathing' along a ledge level with the tree.

8. 10m Above and on the left is a chimney. Gain its foot and belay 3m up on a ledge with blocks.

9. and 10. 60m Continue up the chimney and walls to the top.

Ricepaper   135m   VS *   (1955)
A worthwhile climb, reputedly easy for the grade. Start at the bottom right of the buttress, just right of the foot of Central Gully, where some broken slabby rocks protrude through the turf at the base of the main sheet of the slabs. Directly above the start, about 45m up, is a terrace with small trees.

1. 20m A vegetatious and rather artificial pitch leads up the broken rocks to the foot of the slabs, following a vague rib.

2. 35m Climb cracks in the indefinite scoop to the right, diagonally right at first then up to a little turfy ledge. Continue firstly up right, then direct to a traverse line. Go left along this to a crack, then up to the large terrace and belay at trees.

3. 10m Go diagonally right to the foot of a long grey groove that runs out of sight onto the slabs above.

4. 25m Climb the groove, crux. Belay above the final bulge.

5. 20m Move easily up cracks in the slab, passing to the left of a rib that rises out of the slabs. Belay on a ledge on the left.

6. 20m Climb the wall above. About 90m of easy scrambling leads to the top of the crag. Alternatively move right, continuing up rock instead of the easy scrambling.

Good Friday Slab   135m   VS   (1956)
A straight and natural line in its lower half. Difficulty is maintained thereafter by a deviation to the left, avoiding a grassy gully. Similar to Ricepaper, but harder. Start to the right of Ricepaper at the foot of the right bounding gully of the slabs.
1. 30m Climb a rib and groove past a tree to a heathery recess. Step left onto the wall and climb cracks to a scoop and belay.
2. 15m From the top of the scoop step left to a diagonal traverse leading to the right edge of the slab. Belay under the overhang.
3. 15m Traverse left to the right end of a ledge. Climb the wall above. Step left into a groove and climb to a belay.
4. 25m Continue up a crack slightly to the left.
5. 20m The crack becomes a grassy gully. Take the slab to a small belay below an undercut nose, or climb the harder right edge of the slab.
6. 15m Traverse under the nose to regain the gully at a tree.
7. 15m Finish up the gully. Alternatively return to the centre of the rib and finish up that (harder).

CREAG TOLL A'MHADAIDH   *(Map Ref 985 807)*

This is a remote but disappointing mass of slabby rock above Loch Toll a'Mhadaidh. The rock is not of a quality to really justify the long journey, except for those wishing to guarantee seclusion in a wild setting. There is only one recorded route.

Sanctuary Slabs   180m   Difficult   (1957)
Start 50 metres left of the deep grassy gully in the middle of the crag, 25 metres left of and above the lowest rocks, where a grass rake slants up right. Take the right of two short ribs.
1. 35m Go up the rib to rock platforms. Continue by slabs to a belay in a turfy corner slightly to the right.
2. 10m Climb a slabby rib on the left to an obvious break.
3. 15m Follow a gangway steeply to the left past a crack and almost into the turfy grooves beyond before climbing past a cracked block to regain the crest of the rib.
4. 30m Follow the crest of the rib above. After 10m the angle eases and slabs lead to a grass terrace. Above, 90m of easy scrambling up the rib on the left leads to the top.

Dundonnell

AN TEALLACH
1062m   (Map Ref 069 843)

This majestic mountain is one of the most sought-after in the Northern Highlands. The winter traverse of its tops ranks with Liathach as the finest in the area. The wonderful Torridonian sandstone architecture is disappointing for the rock climber as, like Liathach, it is too broken and vegetated to provide good summer climbs. Even in winter it does not equal its Torridonian rivals for quality snow and ice climbs; nevertheless it has a number of worthwhile routes.

The main ridge runs in an east-facing crescent from Sail Liath in the south over the main tops of Sgurr Fiona and Bidein a'Ghlas Thuill to Glas Mheall Mor in the north. A ridge running east from Bidein a'Ghlas Thuill separates two large east-facing corries, Toll an Lochain and A'Ghlas Thuill. Both have climbs of interest, and Toll an Lochain in particular is a magnificent sight even when, as frequently happens, winter climbing conditions are poor.

The approach leaves the road (A832) by an indistinct path through thickets of overgrown rhododendrons next to a bridge at a point opposite Dundonnell House. The path climbs up on the north side of the burn. For A'Ghlas Thuill branch off up the hillside to the east, after about half an hour, at a big waterfall; for Toll an Lochain continue up Coir' a'Ghiubhsachain and then climb the slabby hillside into the corrie.

Descents can be made at a number of places. From Bidein a'Ghlas Thuill the easiest is to follow the ridge north and then drop down the north flanks of Glas Mheall Mor to join a footpath leading to Dundonnell. Alternatively, descend into A'Ghlas Thuill from the col below Glas Mheall Mor. It is also possible (but risky) to descend steeply into Toll an Lochain from the col between Sgurr Fiona and Bidein a' Ghlas Thuill and from the cols between Corrag Bhuidhe and Sail Liath.

A'GHLAS THUILL

A prominent feature of the south side of the corrie is the bold buttress of Major Rib, with Minor Rib to the right and the clean line of The Alley in between. To the left of Major Rib are a series of parallel gullies known as the Prongs, and to the right of Minor Rib is the big Hayfork Gully leading up to an obvious notch. Right again is North Gully which leads up to the last notch left of the summit. Below and immediately right of

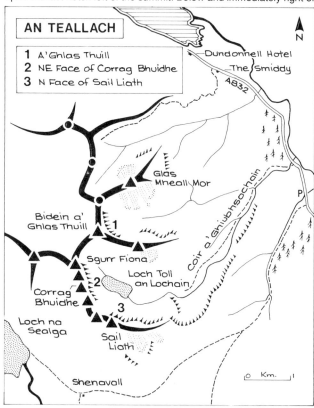

AN TEALLACH

1 A'Ghlas Thuill
2 NE Face of Corrag Bhuidhe
3 N Face of Sail Liath

N

Dundonnell Hotel
The Smiddy
A832
P

Glas
Mheall Mor

Bidein a'
Ghlas Thuill

1

Sgurr Fiona

Coir a' Ghiubhsachain

2 Loch Toll
an Lochain

Corrag
Bhuidhe

3

Loch na
Sealga

Sail
Liath

Shenavall

0 Km. 1

the summit is a rather indistinct area of buttress and snowfield, but further right there are more definite lines, the most obvious being Checkmate Chimney. The climbs are described from right to left.

1 Checkmate Chimney 250m IV   (1969)
This is the first obvious line left of the easy slopes at the back of the corrie. Climb a 10m step then 60m of snow to a fierce 30m icefall. A vertical recessed channel goes up the right side of the fall for 10m, then the cleft twists awkwardly left to end 6m higher at an overhanging canopy of icicles. A delicate step right leads off the ice and the gully is regained 6m higher. Climb a long enclosed chimney section with a number of short ice pitches, and finish up an easy 60m snow channel.

2 Stalemate 250m III/IV   (1983)
The first line left of Checkmate Chimney runs diagonally right towards it. Gain this line by a snowslope and follow it throughout, finishing over mixed ground directly above.

3 White Knight 200m III/IV   (1986)
The obvous gully left of Stalemate. The difficulties are concentrated in the lower 80m.

4 Pawn Cocktail 250m III   (1987)
This takes a line left of White Knight. Climb a 90m icefall to gain a right-slanting gully with easy-angled ice. Where this peters out go straight up to a big tongue of rock. Go left around this to gain the ridge.

5 Intermediate Face Route 450m II   (1982)
About 30m up North Gully an obvious ramp leads out right. Climb this, then follow shallow gullies and snowfields trending up right to gain an obvious line leading up right below a prominent headwall. Beyond this curve back left and climb a short gully to finish near the summit.

6 North Gully 300m I/II
This is the straightforward gully running up to the first notch left (east) of the summit of Bidein a'Ghlas Thuill.

7 Hayfork Gully 300m I   (1910)
This is the deep and straightforward gully left of North Gully running up to the second notch on the east ridge of Bidein a'Ghlas Thuill.

The buttresses left and right of Hayfork Gully were formerly called South and Central Buttress respectively, but as this does not appear to accord with their present orientation the nomenclature has been abandoned.

8 Minor Rib 300m IV   (1956)
The slabby rib left of Hayfork Gully. Climb the crest for 60m to a steep wall. Climb this in the centre by a crack and mantleshelf. Higher up pass a jutting fang of rock on the right. The rib now rears in a tower, climbed by a chimney on the right. Above this the ridge rises in easy steps to merge with the gully on the left (The Alley). Continue up the crest to a steep cracked wall, which may be passed by a gully on the right to reach the top.
Summer: Very Difficult   (1959)
A left-slanting crack in the tower mentioned in the winter description is the best feature of a rather vegetated climb.

9 The Alley 300m II/III   (1978)
The gully between Minor Rib and Major Rib gives an attractive climb with, usually, some small ice pitches in the lower section. After about 150m the gully becomes less distinct and the natural way is out right over broken rocks to the crest of Minor Rib. Continuing in the line of the gully is harder and less pleasant.

10 Major Rib 300m III/IV   (1979)
Climb an obvious break to reach a large snowfield. Climb up and trend generally left, avoiding most obstacles, to finish up a short, stiff step near the top.

11 Fourth Prong 300m II/III   (1959)
A good climb immediately left of Major Rib. There is a short pitch in the lower section. Higher up climb a narrow chimney, then trend right over rocks below a large buttress. Finish rightwards up easy snow.

The gullies left of Fourth Prong are, surprisingly, named First, Second and Third Prongs. The Second and Third give pleasant grade II climbs, while First Prong is a straightforward grade I gully.

AN TEALLACH   A'GHLAS THUILL

1. Checkmate Chimney
2. Stalemate
3. White Knight
5. Intermediate Face Route
6. Murdo's Gully
7. Hayfork Gully
8. Minor Rib
9. The Alley
10. Main Rib
11. Fourth Prong
BGT Bidein a'Ghlas Thuill

TOLL AN LOCHAIN

The climbs are described from left to right starting with the steep north-facing crags of Sail Liath on the extreme left of the corrie. A prominent ramp runs up these crags from right to left. Near the top of the ramp three deep-cut gullies cleave the steep walls on the right.

12 Sulphur Gully (Bowling Alley) 100m IV   (1945)
The central gully was climbed recently but appears to be similar to a much earlier climb. In deference to the pioneers the original name is preserved although the modern description is given. The original description mentions jammed ice-axe belays and other exotica.
1. 15m Climb a very steep iced corner to the base of the gully.
2. 40m Follow deceptively steep iced chimneys to an easier-angled section.
3. 45m Steep snow leads to a steep icy section climbing underneath a prominent chockstone. Finish up easier ground. Another 100m of easy ground leads to open slopes.

13 Bottomless Gully 135m IV/V   (1988)
This is the right-most of the three gullies. It is protected by an overhanging wall which necessitates a start 45m down the approach ramp.
1. 45m Zigzag with surprising difficulty, trending generally left, towards the base of the gully.
2. 20m Climb more easily to the gully, which is deep and narrow.
3. 30m Go up easy snow in the gully.
4. 40m A fine pitch leads out onto easy ground.

Right of Sail Liath are easy snow slopes leading up to the Cadha Gobhlach, then an indeterminate buttress and then another col, before the South Buttress of Corrag Bhuidhe, on which an early route was done by Glover and Ling as well as later summer routes of about Difficult standard (SMCJ 1936 and 1951). A long shallow couloir separates the South Buttress from the main crags of Corrag Bhuidhe, and gives the next route.

14 Constabulary Couloir 360m II
The couloir may have an avoidable icefall near the bottom. The rest is straightforward snow.

AN TEALLACH

14. Constabulary Couloir
15. Lady's Gully
16. Potala Buttress
17. 1978 Face Route

TOLL AN LOCHAIN FACE

18. Lord's Gully
18R. Lord's Gully, right branch
SF   Sgurr Fiona

The main face of Corrag Bhuidhe has near its base a large triangular snowfield above a short rock barrier. This may be used to locate the next three climbs.

15 Lady's Gully 240m II   (1974)
Gain the triangular snowfield at its lower left corner and go up to the apex. Follow the left-trending gully from there to the top.

16 Potala Buttress 240m IV   (1987)
This takes the V-shaped rock buttress between Lady's Gully and a ramp on the right taken by 1978 Face Route. Good turf conditions are advisable. Gain the triangular snowfield at any convenient point along its base, climb up to the apex and thence to the toe of the V-shaped buttress. Start 10 metres right of the toe.
1. 35m Go left, up and back right by the line of least resistance to a stance overlooking the ramp of 1978 Face Route.
2. 40m Go up slightly and traverse left to a small rock band.
3. 50m Climb the band, then up more easily.
4. 30m Continue without difficulty to a snowfield.
5. 50m Go up snow trending slightly right to a weakness.
6. 35m Climb the line of weakness to finish at a notch just left of the rightmost (north-west) tower of Corrag Bhuidhe.

17 1978 Face Route 250m III/IV   (1978)
Gain the triangular snowfield and from its apex follow a right-sloping ramp to reach the crest of the buttress overlooking Lord's Gully. Follow the crest with some difficulty to the top.

18 Lord's Gully 400m II/III   (1923,1973)
This is the long left-slanting gully between Corrag Bhuidhe and Sgurr Fiona. At its top it has two branches going either side of the huge tower of Lord Berkeley's Seat. The left branch is better defined but may be harder. Difficulties in the right branch may be circumvented by a traverse right onto the face of Sgurr Fiona.
Summer: Severe   (1958)
Follow the line of the watercourse over many short pitches, one of which, near the top, is Severe. Go up the right branch on a steep slab. If this is wet, a traverse out right from the gully may be necessary.

19 Lord Berkeley's Seat 130m V   (1991)
A spectacular route up the face of the Seat. Start just left of the toe of
the buttress.
1. 45m Climb the crest, trending slightly right until stopped by a barrier
wall.
2. 35m Traverse right and climb a short slab overlooking the right
branch of Lord's Gully. A series of walls leads to another barrier.
3. 25m Traverse left and climb corners just right of the crest.
4. 25m A short turfy ramp leads diagonally right to the final wall, which
is finished to the right of the summit.

GLAS MHEALL MOR
981m (Map Ref 076 854)

Little Glass Monkey 75m III   (1967)
The north-east shoulder of Glas Mheall Mor ends in a spur with two
buttresses divided by a miniature corrie. The north buttress, which is
easily reached from the Dundonnell path, is cleft by a Y-shaped gully.
This climb takes the left fork.

OUTLYING CLIMBS AROUND AN TEALLACH

Approaching Toll an Lochain up Coir'a'Ghiubhsachain, a west- facing
scarp of quartzite, around 60m high, offers a range of short routes.
Two severe climbs have been recorded opposite the point where the
burn from Toll an Lochain turns down the corrie. (SMCJ 1946).

On the southern continuation of this scarp another quartzite nursery
crag has been climbed on, about 2km north-north-east of Achneigie
(Map Ref 082 796). Three Very Difficult routes of about 60m were
recorded (SMCJ 1954).

The westmost bastion of An Teallach is Sgurr Ruadh (Map Ref 040
852) above the west end of Loch na Sealga. **Terminal Tower**, 120m
Difficult, starts at the lowest point of the rocks which face north-west
(SMCJ 1954).

Next to the wood of Coill' a'Bhun, on the east side of the Dundonnell
River about 3km south of Dundonnell House, (Map Ref 130 840) an
impressive icefall forms on the steep north-west face of Carn a'Bhio-
rain, a few hundred metres left of a deep obvious gully. This is **Fain
Falls**, 105m, Grade IV. Descent is via the deep gully.

BEINN DEARG MOR

908m (Map Ref 032 799)

This very attractive peak lies south-west of An Teallach overlooking Loch na Sealga. Coire nan Clach on its north-east side is well seen from the bothy at Shenavall and contains several large buttresses and gullies. The crags are disappointing for summer climbing but give worthwhile winter climbs. The climbs are described from left to right.

The rocks of the south peak on the left of the corrie were climbed by Sang and Morrison in 1899 and give an entertaining scramble. To the right of this mass of rock a narrow gully cuts into the cliff.

1 Twisting Gully 270m IV   (1980)
Climb the lower reaches, which are hidden from the corrie floor. Higher up the gully splits into three parallel right-slanting branches. Take the central branch which gives the best line.

2 Spring Maiden 250m V   (1987)
From the bottom of Twisting Gully another and easier ramp goes rightwards into the cliff. Follow this until an obvious icefall (easily seen from the corrie floor) rises up on the left wall. A convenient ledge on the left allows the ice (impending in two sections) to be climbed in two 25m pitches. Continue for a pitch up easier ground to the end of the gully. Now a short traverse to the left leads to the hidden right branch of Twisting Gully. Finish easily up this.

3 Fat Man's Folly 220m III/IV   (1987)
Below and right of the col between the south peak and the main peak is a more broken area of rock. This route starts slightly left of the lowest buttress on this face and finishes right of the col. The overhanging left wall of the third pitch means that the route is not for the stout.

Left of the massive Central Buttress (the most prominent buttress in the corrie) is the slender Flake Buttress. On its left is a gully giving the following climb.

4 Deranged 80m III   (1982)
Start to the left of Flake Buttress above a prominent spur. Climb a 6m icefall, then continue up ice for another 30m. Climb on snow and mixed ground for two pitches and finish up the left branch of the gully.

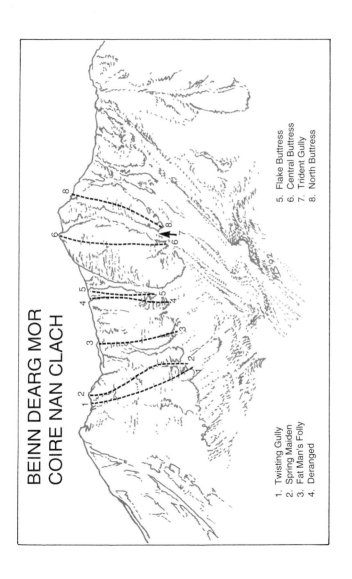

BEINN DEARG MOR
COIRE NAN CLACH

1. Twisting Gully
2. Spring Maiden
3. Fat Man's Folly
4. Deranged

5. Flake Buttress
6. Central Buttress
7. Trident Gully
8. North Buttress

5 Flake Buttress 105m Severe   (1952)
On the first ascent this was climbed in almost snow-free conditions
and was considered of sustained difficulty and interest. It is questionable whether all details of the original description will be recognisable.
1. 15m Start at the left and climb a corner for 3m, then traverse
delicately right to the extreme edge. Go up and round the edge to a
block then back left and up to a narrow ledge.
2. 20m Go right to the edge of the buttress and around it. Traverse
6m on this flank, then 5m up a steep corner and back left on to the
face of the buttress and belay.
3. 20m Go up to a platform on the left. Make a difficult step up a wall,
2m right, then go up a slanting shelf with a crack. Go round to the right,
up an exposed slab and up left to a ledge, then right to a stance below
a steep wall.
4. 10m Traverse 6m on the left flank of the buttress, then up a short,
steep groove for 3m. Traverse delicately left and go up to a belay in a
cave below a chimney.
5. 15m Climb the chimney and exit right; go up easier rock to a ledge,
then more difficult rock to another ledge and belay.
6. 25m Continue more easily to the top of the buttress which is
connected to the main mountain by a narrow ridge.

   Between Flake Buttress and Central Buttress is a straightforward
Grade I gully. The left flank of Central Buttress in winter comprises a
series of snowfields separated by short vertical walls, giving a Grade
II climb.

6 Central Buttress 240m Severe †   (1953)
The steep lower half of this buttress is bounded on the right by a gully
which separates it from the right and upper parts. The original route
took this gully, but that described here takes the right edge of the lower
buttress, overlooking the gully.
1. 20m Start on the right. A terrace gives a footing on the buttress and
a short chimney leads to the next terrace.
2. 20m Go left then back right up a deep, easy chimney.
3. 15m Slant right and up a chimney to a stance overlooking the gully.
4. 15m Climb the pillar above by chimneys on its left to a deep cleft.
5. 20m Step up a steep little wall, continue right and then left and more
easily into a chimney.
6. 20m Go up the chimney with an exit on moss, and up the right side
of a pillar to a conspicuous jammed block.

7. 20m Continue on the right to a steep corner.

8, etc. 110m Follow the same line to the level ridge at the top of the lower half of the buttress. The upper part of the buttress is easier.

7   Trident Gully   260m   II
This is the obvious gully right of Central Buttress. The lower section is straightforward snow. At 90m there is a branch to the left which goes up a chimney on the right of a prominent slender buttress. The main gully continues up the right fork until at 150m it splits into three branches of about equal size. Any branch may be taken. The left branch has a pitch just above the fork and then eases off.

8   North Buttress   260m   II
The narrow broken buttress on the right of Trident Gully has a few awkward, slabby moves low down, but most difficulties can be circumvented.

JUNCTION BUTTRESS   *(Map Ref 042 781)*

This 75m crag of Lewisian Gneiss, which is visible from Shenavall, stands at the junction of the Gleann na Muice and Gleann na Muice Beag. Seen from well round into the latter glen the buttress presents a slabby face on the left sloping down into Gleann na Muice, and on the right a bulging buttress facing Gleann na Muice Beag. These are separated by Pasture Gully sloping up to the left.

Pasture Gully   60m   Difficult   (1945)
A climb for the traditionalist. The lower chockstone-crowned chimney was avoided on the first ascent by using a groove on the right. After traversing back into the gully at 6m the climb continued on "generous heather holds with occasional rock". Half way up is a short, steep chockstone pitch. Higher up a tree had to be lassooed. The climb finished with a pitch of vertical vegetation and a short rock chimney.

The Nose   65m   Hard Severe   (1953)
This climbs the buttress left of Pasture Gully. On the left side of the buttress, about 15m up, is a large terrace covered with birch trees: The Forest. The climb gains the left end of The Forest directly. Start below a steep corner, at the foot of a fierce-looking layback crack.

1. 25m   Climb the crack and then move right along the top of a detached flake into a steep groove. Climb this past two trees to a large holly tree. From here go left up to The Forest.

2. 40m Above is a large smooth slab. Follow a line of flakes up left to the left edge above the tip of a nose. Climb the nose past a holly and a conspicuous flake crack to the skyline. Go round left and up easier ground. Scramble to the top.

Parker's Route   110m   Very Difficult   (1952)
This climb is on the crag right of Pasture Gully. Start 10 metres left of a corner, below a sweep of slabs.

1. and 2. 50m Climb to the left edge of the slabs.

2. 30m Move leftwards up the wall above, crossing the deep crack that slants right across the face (Rightward Slant) to a large grassy corner. Now move up the left wall by a quartzite staircase, finishing up a crack and a short wall onto a ledge.

3. 30m Move right over grass to a large block then step right and up the left edge of rough slabs to a ledge. Move right, then more slabs lead to the top.

Rightward Slant   120m   Very Difficult   (1964)
The obvious right-slanting line up the west (right) face of Junction Buttress.

1. 25m Start up a steep crack, then heather and two short chimneys to a tree belay.

2. 20m Continue up a vegetated groove on the right to a heather ledge and dubious flake.

3. 20m Step right round a nose to another ledge. The steep chimney on the left of the ledge appears feasible, but the route goes up steeply on the right. The initial moves up the slab lead to 6m of steep climbing (crux), then easier rock to the foot of another groove.

4. 30m Follow this groove up under a conspicuous overhang; pass this on the right and continue up to platform.

5. 25m Easier rock leads to the top.

Sapling Climb   85m   Very Difficult   (1953)
A poor route that starts 10 metres right of Pasture Gully.

1. 15m Climb the wall and move left to a tree belay.

2. 10m Go up the wall ahead using the heathery groove on the right, then left round a corner to another tree belay.

3. 25m Move up broken ground to a steeper wall.

4. 10m Move away from the gully and climb the left side of the wall by steep cracks, then slabs to another tree.
5. 10m Turn the wall above by the crack on its left.
6. 15m Climb the scoop above by cracks, then another little wall to heather and a tree.

THE SIDINGS   *(Map Ref 036 779)*

This is the next crag up Gleann na Muice Beag from Junction Buttress. The general character is slabby and uniformly steep, but there are two conspicuous features: towards the right end of the crag is a straight and narrow gully, with a well-defined rib on its left, and on the left of this is a curving chimney running almost the full height of the cliff.

The Funnel 110m Severe   (1957)
Start at the foot of the curving chimney.
1. 10m Climb the chimney to an ash tree.
2. 20m Continue up the chimney past a small tree.
3. 20m Continue up the chimney, with an awkward exit.
4. 10m Climb the groove above and up to a flake belay below a steep, black chimney.
5. 15m The exit from the chimney is holdless, so traverse out left past a detached flake into the bed of a parallel chimney.
6. 15m Start on the right and climb into the chimney at 5m, then up to a large chockstone.
7. 20m Go up on the right for 6m, then traverse back left across the chimney and up a short steep wall. Scrambling above.

Route 1 95m Severe   (1952)
Start at the rib 8 metres left of the narrow straight gully.
1. 20m Up gentle grooves and corners.
2. 15m Continue past a stance overlooking the gully. Bear left to a triangular ledge and detached boulder. Step right to a belay overlooking the gully.
3. 10m Go up left on small holds, first a groove then a crack.
4. 25m More easily above to a heather ledge, then right to the foot of a steeper wall.
5. 25m Cross the slab on the left and round to the left of the wall. Continue easily to the top.

List of First Ascents

KNOYDART

W	1897 17 Apr	Raeburn's Gully	H.Raeburn, J.H.Bell, Boyd, Brown
S	1939 Jul	Moss Gully	K.McLaren, J.Bennet
W	1962 14 Apr	Gaberlunzie	A.G.Nicol, R.W.P.Barclay, T.W.Patey

There was an unsuccessful attempt on this gully as early as May 1928

W	1962 15 Apr	Viking Gully	A.G.Nicol, T.W.Patey
S	1967 22 Jun	Round House	G.A.White, J.A.Gillcrest
S	1967 22 Jun	Battlement Slab	D.S.Nicol, P.Gunn
S	1967 22 Jun	Portcullis	I.S.Clough, B.Rex

Deteriorating weather conditions forced the FA party to follow easier ground on the left for the final 60m.

W	1971 Apr	Para Handy Gully	A.Ewing, W.Sproul
S	1971 13 Jul	Culverin	M.Horsburgh, K.Schwartz
S	1971 13 Jul	Cannonade	M.Horsburgh, K.Schwartz
S	1971 13 Jul	Sentinel	M.Horsburgh, K.Schwartz
S	1971 13 Jul	Parapet	M.Horsburgh, K.Schwartz
S	1971 13 Jul	Bastion	M.Horsburgh, K.Schwartz
W	1978 8 Feb	Face Route	A.Nisbet, P.Tipton
W	1978 8 Feb	West Pillar	D.Dinwoodie, A.McIvor
W	1978 9 Feb	Landlubbers Buttress	A.Nisbet, P.Tipton
W	1978 17 Feb	Tir na Og	A.Foster, C.Higgins
W	1978 19 Feb	Summit Route	A.Foster, C.Higgins
W	1978 Mar	Transatlantic Bong	C.Higgins, K.Sims
W	1978 Mar	Thunderchicken	C.Higgins, K.Sims
W	1979 9 Feb	East Rib	C.Higgins, R.Speiss
W	1979 24 Mar	Eastern Chimney	D.Broadhead, S.Gallacher, D.Rubens
S	1980 Aug	Direct Route	B.McMillan, G.Strange
W	1984 19 Feb	Celtic Sea	R.J.Allen, W.Jeffrey, D.N.Williams
W	1984 19 Feb	Western Approches	R.J.Allen (solo)
W	1986 2 Feb	Marguerite	R.Everett, S.Richardson
W	1986 28 Feb	Penny Wheep Gully	S.Kennedy, G.Rowbotham, S.Thirgood
W	1986 1 Mar	Bottleneck Chimney	W.Jeffrey, D.N.Williams
W	1991 Feb	Strider's Gully	P.Duggan

Probably climbed previously.

W	1991 Feb	White Settler	W.Jeffrey, D.N.Williams

Probably climbed before. Several lines are believed to have been climbed in Coire Dhorrcail by Heriot-Watt students in the early 80s, but the details have not been reported.

LOCH LOCHY HILLS

W 1986 15 Feb   Central Gully   D.A.Hetherington

KINTAIL

South Glen Shiel Ridge
S 1938 1 Aug   The Silver Slab   J.W.Haggas, S.Thompson, P.B.White
S 1985 29 May   Mayfly   J.R.Sutcliffe, N.Fletcher

The Saddle
W 1926 Easter   Big Gully   A.J.Rusk and party
    The ascent was made in "mixed" conditions. Part ice part veg.
S 1961   Easter Buttress   D.Piggot, G.S.Johnstone

Beinn Sgritheall
W 1964 14 Sep   North Buttress   H.M.Brown, A.Smith
S 1965 20 Oct   North Buttress   H.M.Brown, A.Dunsire

Sgurr a' Bhealaich Dheirg
W 1986 30 Dec   Resolution Gully   H.Irvine, A.Keith

Five Sisters of Kintail
S 1956   May   California   J.H.Barber, C.A.Simpson
W 1957 2 Jan   Forked Gully   J.H.Barber, C.A.Simpson
W 1957 2 Jan   Trident Gully   J.G.Burns, H.Kindness
W 1957 3 Jan   Solo Gully   J.G.Burns
W 1957 3 Jan   Dog's Leg Gully   J.H.Barber, G.Burns
W 1984 30 Dec   Saighead Slot   U.Jessop, P.A.Brownsort
W 1984 31 Dec   Hidden Gully   U.Jessop, P.A.Brownsort, T.Lee,
                                         F.Alexander
W 1985 1 Jan   Window Gully   J.McKeever, G.Jones
W 1985 20 Mar   Brenda's Cleavage   P.A.Brownsort, A.Keith, F.D.Munro,
                                         D.Tytler
S 1985 21 Sep   Babylon Buttress   P.A.Brownsort, R.Blackburn,
                                         F.D.Munro
W 1986 2 Jan   Edge of Reason   H.Irvine, U.Jessop
W 1986 2 Jan   Grovel Gully   A.Matthewson
W 1986 27 Mar   Twisting Gully   P.A.Brownsort
W 1986 30 Mar   A'Charraig Gully   P.A.Brownsort
W 1987 3 Jan   Little Gully   E.Barnfield, D.Johnson
W 1987   Jan   Left-Hand Gully   M.Potter

Beinn Fhada
S 1949 9 Jun   Needle's Eye Buttress   R.Grieve, R.Brown
W 1951 14 Apr   Right-Hand Gully   C.L.Donaldson, J.Russell, G.Dutton
S 1952 20 Jul   The Needle   W.J.Cole, J.R.Marshall, I.Oliver
S 1955 12 Jul   Guide's Rib   G.H.Kitchen, R.J.Porter
S 1955   Jul   Porter's Climb   G.H.Kitchen, R.J.Porter
S 1955   Jul   Continuation Climb   G.H.Kitchen, R.J.Porter
S 1961 Easter   Summit Buttress   D.Piggot, G.S.Johnstone

W 1983	19 Feb	Left-Hand Gully	S.Kennedy, N.Morrison
W 1983	19 Feb	Tropical Buttress	S.Kennedy, N.Morrison
W 1984	3 Mar	Summit Buttress	A.B.Lawson, R.Richard
S 1989	24 Jun	The Kintail Blanket	A.Matthewson, A.Tibbs

Biod an Fhithich

S 1971	Apr	Hump	R.Burnett, R.Sharp
S 1971	30 Jul	Wrong Turn	M.Horsburgh, D.Regan, K.Schwartz
S 1971	5 Sep	Ankle Ridge	M.Horsburgh, K.Schwartz

MONAR

S 1937	16 Oct	North Gully	R.B.Frere, K.Robertson, J.Wright
S 1954	15 May	Mica Ridge	A.Watson, A.Watson (senior)
W 1978	31 Dec	Short and Silly	J.R.MacKenzie
W 1987	Jan	North Gully	R.Archbold, D.Nichols
S 1988	23 Jul	Munroist's Reward	R.Everett, D.Gaffney
S 1988	24 Jul	Monar Magic	R.Everett, D.Gaffney

GLAS BHEINN

W 1972	Apr	Black House	T.Briggs, P.Nunn, C.Rowland
W 1974	Apr	Adul Suh	P.Braithwaite. P.Nunn
S 1984	26 May	Slab and Groove	G.Cohen, D.Rubens
S 1984	26 May	Clean Compromise	G.Cohen, D.Rubens
S 1984	26 May	Left-hand Route	P.Nunn, M.Richardson

FUAR THOLL

S 1933	14 Oct	Original Route	C.Ludwig, J.D.MacLennan
S 1952	25 Jul	Enigma	W.J.Cole, J.R.Marshall, I.Oliver
S 1961	7 Oct	The Nose Direct	T.W.Patey
S 1968	3 Aug	Nimrod	G.Anderson, J.R.Brumfitt, P. Macdonald
S 1969		Investigator	M.Boysen, D.Alcock
S 1969		Snoopy	D.Alcock, M.Boysen
S 1969		Sherlock	M.Boysen, D.Alcock
S 1969		Sleuth	I.Clough, H.MacInnes
S 1969		Blue Finger	I.Clough, H.MacInnes
S 1969		Cold Sweat	H.MacInnes, C.MacInnes
S 1969		Boat Tundra	I.Clough, H.MacInnes
S 1969		The Fuar	I.Clough, H.MacInnes, M.C.MacInnes
S 1969		Right End Buttress	M.Boysen
W 1969		Sleuth/Enigma	A.Fyffe, H.MacInnes, K.Spence
W 1971	24 Jan	The Pile	P.Christie, P.Macdonald
S 1971	17 Jun	Nebula	D.Barr, P.Macdonald
S 1972	Jun	Benn Gunn	G.Shields, R.Sharp
S 1972	Jun	Direct Route	G.Shields, R.Sharp
S 1972	Jun	All The Way	G.Shields, R.Sharp

S 1973		The Nose More Direct	D.Dinwoodie, B.Lawrie
S 1974	Apr	Private Eye	M.Boysen, P.Braithwaite, P.Nunn
W1976	22 Feb	Right End Buttress	W.S.McKerrow, D.M.Nichols
W1978	19 Feb	Fuar Folly	R.J.Archbold, D.M.Nichols
W1984	31 Mar	Tholl Gate	P.Butler, M.Fowler
W1986	15 Feb	Fuhrer	M.Fowler, C.Watts
W1986	3-4Feb	Cold Sweat	M.E.Moran
W1986	22 Feb	Olfactory	B.Owen, D.Rubens, G.Macnair, G.Cohen
W1987	10 Jan	Cold Hole	M.Fowler, C.Watts
W1987	10 Jan	Pipped at the Post	M.Fowler, C.Watts
W1988	4 Mar	Evasion Grooves	S.Jenkins, M.E.Moran
W1989	23 Feb	The Ayatollah	I.Dring, M.E.Moran
W1989	3 Mar	Reach for the Sky	S.Jenkins, M.E.Moran
W1989	11 Mar	Mainline Connection	R.Anderson, R.Milne
W1991	16 Feb	Tubular Bells	D.Wills, M.Fowler
W1991	16 Feb	Investigator	M.Fowler, D.Wills
W1992	11 Mar	Newton's Law	M.Moran, J.Newton, J.Yates
W1992	13 Mar	Lair Wall	M.Moran, K.O'Neale, W.O'Neale
W1992	15 Mar	Luck Of The Irish	M.Moran, C.O'Callaghan, C.Swift

SGORR RUADH

S 1898	26 May	Robertson's Buttress	A.E.Robertson
S 1904	4 Apr	Raeburn's Buttress	H.Raeburn, E.B.Robertson
S 1948	Jun	Academy Ridge	Inverness Royal Academy C.C.
S 1955	Jul	Upper Buttress	I.H.Ogilvie, P.M.Francis
S 1961	8 Oct	Splintery Edge	T.W.Patey
W1967	20 Dec	Raeburn's Buttress Direct	W.D.Brooker, S.H.Wilkinson
W1969	Mar	Post Box Gully	A.Fyffe
W1969	Mar	Brown Gully	A.Fyffe
W1969		Steppin	A.Fyffe and party
W1969		The Slant	H.MacInnes and party
W1969		Croydon Chimney	H.MacInnes and party
W1969	Mar	Easy Gully	J.Cleare, P.Gillman
W1972	Feb	Upper Buttress	P.Nunn, A.Riley
W1976	31 Jan	Robertson's Gully	A.Nisbet, N.Spinks
W1976	1 Feb	High Gully	M.Hillman, A.Nisbet
W1978	Feb	Narrow Gully	G.Cohen, D.Rubens
W1983	4 Apr	Wildcat Gully	P.J.Biggar, I.Haig
W1987	6 Dec	Fox's Face	S.Jenkins, M.E.Moran
W1988	2 Apr	Ruadh Awakening	R.Anderson, R.Milne
W1988	21 Nov	First Blood	S.Jenkins, M.E.Moran
W1989	17 Feb	Raeburn's Superdirect	M.E.Moran, P.Potter
W1989		Tango In The Night	S.Aisthorpe, N.Forwood, P.Yardley

MAOL CHEAN-DEARG

W1968 22 Dec	Hidden Gully	H.M.Brown, R.J.Rankin, R.Aitken
W1969 29 Dec	Ketchil Buttress	H.M.Brown, D.Macnab
S 1971 1 Aug	No Birds	K.Schwartz
S 1971 1 Aug	But Midges	K.Schwartz, M.Horsburgh

AN RUADH-STAC

S 1960 Aug	North Face	C.J.S.Bonington, T.W.Patey
S 1967 21 Aug	Foxtrot	D.Stone, B.T.Hill

BEINN BHAN

S 1891 Jul	Upper Connecting Ridge of A'Chioch	L.W.Hinxman
S 1950 Jul	North Buttress of A'Chioch	S.Paterson, D.J.Bennet
S 1961 13 Oct	Upper Connecting Ridge of A'Phoite	T.W.Patey
1968	Upper Connecting Ridge of A'Chioch	J.Brown, T.W.Patey
W1969 1 Mar	March Hare's Gully	C.J.S.Bonington, T.W.Patey
W1969 2 Mar	North Gully, A'Chioch	A.Fyffe, C.MacInnes, M.Alburger
W1971 Feb	Upper Connecting Ridge of A'Phoite	B.Goodwin, J.Grieve, D.Tierney
W1971 Feb	Wall of the Early Morning Light	K.Spence, J.Horsfield, B.Jones, P.Thomas

The first route to breach the great back wall of Coire na Poite.

W1974 Apr	Gingerbread	A.C.Cain, C.Rowland
W1976 1 Feb	Mad Hatter's Gully	M.Freeman, G.Stephen
W1977 12 Feb	Silver Tear	N.Muir, A.Paul
W1978 11 Feb	Alice's Buttress	R.J.Archbold, J.C.Higham
W1978 19 Feb	Moonshine	D.M.Jenkins, C.Stead

This is thought to be only a slight variation on the earlier Wall of the Early Morning Light.

W1978 Feb	Deep Gully	D.M.Jenkins, P.F.Macdonald
W1979 17 Feb	The Chimney	A.Nisbet, B.Sprunt
W1980 26 Jan	Der Riesenwand	A.Nisbet, B.Sprunt

The first ascent involved a bivouac!

W1980 4 Feb	Dormouse Chimney	M.Freeman, J.Moreland
W1980 5 Feb	Hors d'Oeuvres	P.Anderson, K.Murphy
W1980 7 Feb	Donkey's Doobrie	P.Anderson, K.Murphy
W1980 7 Feb	Skidmark Buttress	R.Robb, S.Young
W1980	Crab Nebula	D.Dinwoodie, A.Williams
S 1981 4 Aug	Rory-Pory	D.Dinwoodie, R.A.Smith
W1981 30 Dec	Sheet Whitening	M.Fowler, S.Fenwick, M.Lynden

This is the same route as Guttersnipe (SMCJ 1983)

W	1983 24 Feb	The Cooler	D.Dinwoodie, A.Paul
W	1983 26 Feb	Adventures of Toad	D.Dinwoodie, A.Paul
W	1983 3 Apr	Gully of the Gods	M.Fowler, S.Fenwick
W	1983 3 Apr	Der Rise and Shine	A.Saunders, B.Simmonds
W	1984 8 Feb	The Acid Queen	D.Dinwoodie, C.Maclean
W	1984 17 Mar	Great Overhanging Gully	M.Fowler, P.Butler
W	1984 Mar	Threatening Behaviour	S.Fenwick, P.Thornhill

A similar climb was done by M.Geddes in the 1970s

W	1984 Mar	Breach of the Peace	P.Thornhill
W	1984 Mar	Indecent Exposure	S.Fenwick, N.Bankhead
W	1986 2 Feb	Harlequin Rib	H.M.A.Towler, G.S.Strange, J.C.Higham, B.S.Findlay, R.J.Archbold
W	1986 17 Feb	Sniper's Gully	J.Mothersele, A.Nisbet
W	1986 23 Feb	Unnamed	D.Gardiner, D.Hawthorn
W	1986 1 Mar	In X.S.	C.Downer, D.Scott
W	1986 1 Mar	Couldoran Gully	J.Lyall
W	1986 1 Mar	Grey Hair Gully	J.Lyall
W	1989 21 Feb	Flesheater	I.Dring, M.E.Moran
W	1989 17 Mar	Das Rheingold	M.E.Moran

SGURR A'CHAORACHAIN

A'Chioch

S	1908 6 Jun	Glover's Route	G.T.Glover, W.N.Ling
S	1952 28 Mar	Jupiter	J.M.Taylor, W.D.Brooker, T.W.Patey
S	1952 31 May	North Wall	T.W.Patey, G.B.Leslie, J.M.Taylor J.Morgan
S	1952 1 Jun	Turret Buttress	G.B.Leslie, T.W.Patey, J.M.Taylor
S	1953 30 Mar	Totem	T.W.Patey, J.M.Taylor
S	1953 2 May	Dexter	T.W.Patey, C.D.Thomson, R.P.U.Tait
S	1953 2 May	Sinister	J.M.Taylor, A.G.Nicol
S	1960 12 Aug	Cioch Nose	T.W.Patey, C.J.S.Bonington
S	1968 3 Jun	Cleavage	R.Hobbs, C.W.Dracup
S	1968 3 Jun	The Maxilla	R.Hobbs, C.W.Dracup
S	1968 9 Jun	Cioch Nose Direct	T.W.Patey, H.MacInnes
	1968	Sideburn	G.Anderson, A.Ewing
S	1969 May	Snothard	C.W.Dracup, R.Hobbs
S	1969 25 May	Cioch Corner	C.W.Dracup, R.Hobbs
S	1969 25 May	Lap of the Gods	R.How, J.R.Sutcliffe
S	1969 25 May	Gritstone Grooves	R.F.Allen, M.Allen
S	1970 May	Cioch Corner Superdirect	J.E.Howard, C.Rowland
S	1970 Jul	Parting	A.Ewing, F.Harper
S	1971	African Waltz	A.S.Macdonald, R.Popham
S	1975 May	Forgotten Corner	R.J.Archbold, G.Cohen

S 1975	Oct	Mantissa	R.J.Archbold, D.Dinwoodie
W1977	Feb	No.4 Gully	C.Rowland, A.C.Cain
W1979 14 Jan		South East Spur	A.Nisbet
W1980	Jan	Anonymous Gully	N.D.Keir, G.Muhlemann

Summit Buttress

S 1972	Jun	Big Daddy	G.Shields, R.Sharp
W1986 2 Feb		Excitable Boy	P.Long, B.Owen
W1986 2 Feb		Blade Runner	P.Long, B.Owen
S 1989 19 Jun		Synergy	P.Potter, M.Welch

South Face and South-East Cliff

S 1961 11 Oct	The Sword of Gideon	T.W.Patey
S 1968 11 Apr	Swordstick	T.W.Patey, J.Cleare
S 1969 25 May	Recess Rib	J.A.Austin, K.Wood
S 1970 18 Jun	Trundler	B.Beattie, T.McKenny, C.Brooker
S 1970 27 Jun	Bumblyone	T.Cardwell, B.Beattie, C.Brooker
S 1970 Jun	Bumblytwo	B.Beattie, K.Hiles, E.Gautier
S 1970 Jun	Broken Buttress	C.R.Brooker, P.Barroud, A.Bartholomew
S 1970 7 Jul	Anduril	B.Beattie, J.Napoleoni
S 1970 19 Jul	Broad Sword	J.Crawford, W.Skidmore
S 1971 25 Apr	Dougie's Climb	G.Anderson, P.F.Macdonald, D.B.Scott
S 1971 May	Swordthrust	W.March
S 1971 20 Aug	Ganglion	K.V.Crocket, C.Stead
S 1971 21 Aug	Gideon's Wrath	K.V.Crocket, C.Stead
S 1972 Jun	Big Daddy	G.Shields, R.Sharp
S 1973 20 Jun	North Circular	T.Doe, J.Duncan
S 1984 10 Jun	Rig Veda	G.Cohen, S.Brener
S 1984 Jul	Pommel	D.Rubens, D.Broadhead
W1987 22 Mar	Bee Gully	M.Fowler, A.Saunders
S 1988	Sanctuary	P.Potter, M.Welch
S 1991 5 Jul	Hotline	J.Lyall, A.Nisbet
W1984 15 Jan	Sinister	S.Allan, A.Nisbet
W1984 16 Jan	White Dwarf	S.Allan, A.Nisbet
S 1984 2 Jun	Lost Wall	D.Rubens, G.Cohen
W1986 2 Feb	Turret Buttress	M.Hamilton, G.Cohen
W1986 16 Feb	Voyager	A.Nisbet, J.Mothersele
W1990 30 Dec	Glover's Route	A.Tibbs, M.Shaw, A.Matthewson, C.Huntley
W1991 12 Jan	Dexter	G.Ettle, A.Nisbet
W1991 11 Feb	Jupiter	B.Davison, A.Nisbet

MEALL GORM

S 1953 2 May	Blue Pillar	A.G.Nicol, T.W.Patey
S 1953 2 May	Cobalt Buttress	J.M.Taylor, C.D.Thomson, R.P.U.Tait
S 1955 18 Aug	Blaeberry Corner	W.D.Brooker, A.J.R.A.Norton

W 1958	Feb	Blue Pillar	J.Brown, T.W.Patey
S 1965	15 May	Rattlesnake	P.Macdonald, A.R.M.Park
W 1970	10 Feb	Cobalt Buttress	I.Clough, G.Drayton, C.Young
W 1971	Feb	Blaeberry Corner	K.Spence, J.Horsfield, B.Jones, P.Thomas
S 1971	4 Sep	The Smooth Creep	S.J.Carroll, P.Macdonald
W 1978	25 Mar	The Six-track Mono Blues	M.G.Geddes, B.P.Hall, A.McIntyre, J.Porter
W 1980	Feb	Way Out	R.Robb, S.Young
W 1980	5 Feb	Stonner Falls	P.Anderson, K.Murphy
W 1986	15 Feb	Trident Gully, left branch	N.Eagers, P.Langhorne
W 1986	16 Feb	Spiral Terrace	P.Langhorne, N.Eagers
W 1986	21 Feb	Trident Gully, right branch	P.Langhorne, N.Eagers
W 1986	2 Mar	Wee Beastie	J.Douglas, P.Langhorne
W 1987	15 Mar	Lobster Gully	M.Fowler, A.Saunders
W 1991	8 Jan	Blue Moon	S Aisthorpe, J.Lyall

LIATHACH

S 1894	11 Jun	Northern Pinnacles	W.Douglas, L.Hinxman, W.Rennie W.MacDonald
S 1899	Easter	East Buttress	G.S.Lawson, W.N.Ling, G.T.Glover
W 1900	16 Apr	Northern Pinnacles	W.W.Naismith, A.M.Mackay, H.Raeburn
W 1928		Gully 1K	F.S.Goggs
W 1928		Left-Hand Trinity Gully	G.Sang, W.N.Ling, G.T.Glover
S 1939	Jun	P.C. Buttress	R.S.Horseman, H.K.Hartley
S 1947	30 Jun	Bell's Buttress	Dr. and Mrs. J.H.B.Bell
S 1952	4 Aug	Reflection Wall	W.J.Cole, J.R.Marshall
W 1955	29 Mar	Central Trinity Gully	D.Stevens, R.Urquhart
		Right-Hand Trinity Gully	D.Stevens, R.Urquhart
W 1955	31 Mar	3rd Pinnacle Gully	D.Stevens, R.Urquhart
		Twisting Gully	R.Urquhart, D.Stevens
		Left-Hand Trinity Gully	M.Robson, A.Delafield
S 1959	Easter	Dru	D.J.Temple, P.J.Crabb
W 1963		Gully 2A	R.Macdonald and party
W 1966		Hillwalk	unknown
W 1967	Feb	George	I.G.Rowe, M.Kelsey
W 1968		Chi Squared	C.Rowland, R.Toogood
		First recorded by D.Rubens and party in 1984	
S 1970	Aug	Triceratops	R.W.L. and D.G.Turnbull
W 1976	Dec	Stringless Gully	A.Barney, P.Nunn, C.Rowland, R.Toogood
W 1977		Left Gully	C.Rowland (solo)

W 1977		Spidean Way	C.Rowland, B.Griffiths
W 1977	Feb	Footless Gully	C. and A.S.Rowland

Originally recorded as Gloveless Gully after a glove was dropped en route!

W 1977	Feb	Pyramid Buttress	D.Jenkins, C.Rowland, M.Webster
W 1978		West Gully	C.Rowland, R.McHardy
W 1978 11 Feb		Poacher's Fall	R.McHardy, A.Nisbet

Eventually climbed after three attempts by C.Rowland over 1977/78 including one with McHardy in 1978.

W 1978 12 Feb		Sinister Prong	J.Grant, J.R.McKenzie
W 1979		Gully 1A	C.Rowland and party
W 1979 24 Feb		Vanadium Couloir	A.Paul, D.Sanderson
W 1980s		Pyramid Right Edge	B.Ledingham, C.Rowland
W 1980s		Gully 2A	C.Rowland and party
W 1984	Feb	Headless Gully	S.Kennedy, A.Nisbet
W 1984 21 Feb		Titanium Gully	D.Rubens, G.Macnair, G.Cohen
W 1984 1 Apr		Umbrella Fall	M.Fowler, P.Butler
W 1985		Hidden Buttress	C.Rowland, K.Hopper
W 1985 10 Mar		Jerbil	M.Fowler, B.Craig
W 1986 3 Jan		Terminal Buttress	G.Nicoll, J.Hotchkis

A similar line hereabouts was climbed in winter 1983 by C.Rowland, K.Hopper and B.Ledingham.

W 1986 15 Feb		The Executioner	A.Nisbet, J.Mothersele
W 1986 22 Feb		The Andes Couloir	A.Cunningham, A.Nisbet
		Bell's Gully	R.Anderson, M.Hamilton
W 1986 23 Feb		Salmon Leap	A.Cunningham, A.Nisbet
		Dru Couloir	R.Anderson, M.Hamilton
		Pyramid Left Icefall	K.Hopper, C.Rowland
W 1986 24 Feb		The Deerhunter	A.Cunningham, A.Nisbet
W 1986 25 Feb		Snow Goose	A.Cunningham, A.Nisbet
		The Snotter	A.Cunningham, A.Nisbet
W 1987		Pyramid Direct	C.Rowland, Mo Antoine
W 1987 2 Jan		Bannockburn	C.Forrest, W.Moir
W 1987 11 Jan		Test Department	M.Fowler, C.Watts (2 pts aid)
		Bell's Buttress, Left Chimney	G.Cohen, D.Broadhead
W 1987 13 Jan		Soul-Searcher	M.E.Moran
		Hooded Claw	A.Nisbet, A.Cunningham
		Brain Drain	A.Nisbet, A.Cunningham
W 1987 14 Jan		White Tiger	A.Cunningham, A.Nisbet
W 1987 15 Jan		Snow White	A.Nisbet, A.Cunningham
		Fairy Queen	A.Cunningham, A.Nisbet
W 1987 17 Jan		Salvation	M.E.Moran
		Toll Dubh Chimney	D.Rubens, D.Broadhead
W 1987 14 Feb		Valentine Buttress	D.Broadhead, W.Tring
W 1987 15 Feb		Rambler's Rib	D.Broadhead, S.Sillars
W 1988 16 Feb		The Temptress	A.Cunningham, A.Nisbet

W1989 25 Feb	Thumbscrew	I.Barron, S.Kennedy
	Thumbscrew Direct	G.Nicoll, S.Pearson
W1990 4 Jan	Holy Trinity	R. and C.Anderson
W1991 17 Feb	Brain Strain	D.Wills, M.Fowler

BEINN EIGHE

Far East Wall

S 1966 30 May	Kami-kaze	J.Brumfitt, W.Sproul
S 1966 16 Oct	Sidewinder	A.Fyffe, P.Williams
S 1973 7 Jul	Groovin' High	R.Archbold, J.Ingram, G.Strange
S 1974 5 May	Sting	J.Ingram, G.Strange
	FFA S.Blagborough A.Nisbet June 1988	
S 1974 5 May	Sundance	R.Archbold, G.Cohen
	FFA G.Cohen G.Nicoll June 1988	
S 1974 30 Jun	Birth of the Cool	R.Archbold, G.Cohen
	FFA M.Hamilton G.Cohen July 1978	
S 1976 21 Aug	Colgarra	R.Archbold, G.Cohen
	FFA S.Blagborough A.Nisbet 14 June 1988	
S 1980 17 May	Nightcap Groove	B.Sprunt, G.Strange
S 1980 17 May	The Reaper	B.Sprunt, G.Strange
S 1983 19 Jun	Morning Wall	R.Archbold, G.Strange
S 1986 22 Jun	The Rising Son	S.Pearson, D.Rubens
S 1987 20 Jun	Sumo	A.Cunningham, A.Nisbet
S 1987 Jul	Ling Dynasty	G.Livingstone, A.Nisbet
W1988 6 Feb	Kami-kaze	A.Cunningham, A.Nisbet
W1988 14 Feb	Vishnu	A.Cunningham, A.Nisbet
S 1988 1 Jun	Angel Face	C.Forrest, A.Nisbet
S 1988 9 Jun	Seeds of Destruction	A.Nisbet, W.Todd
S 1988 10 Jun	Moonshine	C.Forrest, A.Nisbet
W1990 12 Feb	Glow Worm	A.Nisbet, S.Dring
S 1991 Jun	Karaoke Crack	A.Fyffe, N.Ritchie
S 1992 11 Jun	Rudolf	B.Davison, J.Lyall, A.Nisbet
S 1992 12 Jun	King of the Swingers	B.Davison, J.Lyall, A.Nisbet
S 1992 13 Jun	Meccano	B.Davison, J.Lyall, A.Nisbet

Eastern Ramparts

S 1959 16 Aug	Gnome Wall	T.W.Patey
S 1961 Oct	Boggle	R.Smith, A.Wightman
S 1966 30 May	Samurai	J.Brumfitt, W.Sproul
S 1969 27 May	Rampart Wall	J.A.Austin, D.G.Roberts
S 1969 27 May	Cornice Groove	J.A.Austin, D.G.Roberts
S 1969 May	Eastern Promise	D.Millar, K.Wood
	Unwittingly renamed Forge by N.Muir, A.Paul in 1977	
S 1976 20 Aug	Shang-High	R.Archbold, G.Cohen
S 1977 18 Aug	Rampage	N.Muir, A.Paul
S 1978 12 Jul	Heavy Flak	M.Hamilton, G.Cohen
S 1980 17 May	Simpleton	A.Nisbet, N.Spinks

S 1980 18 May	Corniced Arete	A.Nisbet, N.Spinks
S 1980 18 May	Olympus	A.Nisbet, N.Spinks
S 1981 18 May	The Pale Diedre	B.Sprunt, G.Strange
S 1986 10 Aug	Pale Rider	A.Nisbet, B.Lawrie
S 1987 21 Jun	Turkish Delight	A.Cunningham, A.Nisbet
W1988 17 Feb	Gnome Wall	A.Cunningham, A.Nisbet
S 1988 1 Jun	Fairytale Groove	C.Forrest, A.Nisbet
S 1988 8 Jun	Tainted Galahad	J.Mothersele, A.Nisbet
S 1988 10 Jun	The Tower of Darkness	C.Forrest, A.Nisbet
S 1988 13 Jun	Claustrophobic Corner	S.Blagborough, A.Nisbet
S 1988 13 Jun	Fear of the Dark	S.Blagborough, A.Nisbet
S 1988 14 Jun	Paleface Wall	S.Blagborough, A.Nisbet
S 1988 15 Jun	The Ho Chi Minh Trail	S.Blagborough, A.Nisbet
W1991 12 Feb	Eastern Promise	B.Davison, A.Nisbet
W1992 18 Feb	Shang-High	B.Davison, A.Nisbet
S 1992 30 May	Feast of the East	A.Nisbet, G.Ollerhead
S 1992 12 Jun	The Trundler	B.Davison, J.Lyall, A.Nisbet
S 1992 12 Jun	The Modern Idiot	B.Davison, J.Lyall, A.Nisbet

The Triple Buttresses and Sail Mhor

1899 2 Apr	Lawson, Ling and Glover's Route	
S 1907 Jun	East Buttress Ordinary Route	G.B.Gibbs, E.Backhouse, W.A.Mounsey
W1910 26 Apr	White's Gully	S.White and party
S 1919 Jul	West Buttress Ordinary Route	G.S.Bower, J.B.Meldrum
1922	Piggott's Route	A.S.Piggott, M.Wood
S 1936 4 Jun	Hamilton's Route	J.F.Hamilton, W.Kerr
S 1954 9 Jun	East Central Ribs	L.S.Lovat, T.Weir
S 1954 12 Jun	Far West Buttress	L.S.Lovat, T.Weir
S 1954 12 Jun	East Wall	L.S.Lovat, T.Weir

Later guidebook writers were unable to identify this attractive sounding route

S 1957 2 Aug	Direct Route, Central Wall	T.W.Patey
S 1960 9 Aug	West Buttress, left-hand finish	C.J.S.Bonington, T.W.Patey
S 1960 11 Aug	The Upper Girdle	T.W.Patey, C.J.S.Bonington
S 1962 Jun	The Gash	T.W.Patey, A.G.Nicol, K.A.Grassick, J.M.Taylor
S 1962 Jun	Fuselage Wall	T.W.Patey, J.M.Taylor
S 1963 Jun	East Central Gully	W.Proudfoot, D.MacKenzie, D.Williamson, P.Acock
S 1968 Jun	Overkill	R.McHardy, P.Nunn, C.Rowland
S 1968 3 Jun	Readymix	M.Green, J.R.Sutcliffe

S 1970   Oct   Fulmar Chimneys   J.Hogan, D.Bell

W1971   Feb   Central Buttress   K.Spence, J.Rowayne, K.Urquhart
            Climbed over two days. A complete ascent by the line described was
            made by A.McIntyre and A.Rouse in Feb 1978.
S 1971   May   Direct Finish to West   W.March
                     Buttress
S 1972/3   Bloodstone Start   W.S.McKerrow, D.M.Nichols
S 1976 24 Apr   Assegai   P.Baines, D.M.Nichols
S 1976   Aug   Senior   D.M.Jenkins, P.F.Macdonald
S 1976   Aug   Junior   R.McHardy, J.McLean
S 1976   Aug   Sideshow   R.McHardy, B.J.Chislett
S 1976   Aug   Relayer   R.McHardy, B.J.Chislett
S 1976   Aug   Mistral   R.McHardy, B.J.Chislett
S 1976   Sep   Central Corner   A.Nisbet, N.Spinks
S 1977 17 Aug   Pelican   N.Muir, A.Paul
S 1977 17 Aug   Mango   N.Muir, A.Paul
S 1977 18 Aug   Twilight Zone   N.Muir, A.Paul
W1981 22 Dec   East Central Wall   P.Barrass, A.Nisbet
W1983 12 Feb   The Cool Cleft   R.Arnott, E.Clark, A.Nisbet,
                                           S.Thirgood
            The direct version was climbed by P.Thornhill, C.Watts, A.Saunders and
            M.Fowler on 9 April 1983. They called it Eighe and Spoon Race.
S 1985 15 Jun   Puddock   B.S.Findlay, G.Strange
W1986 1 Feb   Achilles   B.S.Findlay, G.Strange
W1986 1 Feb   West Buttress,   M.Hamilton, G.Cohen
                     right-hand finish
W1986 14 Feb   Smears for Fears   A.Cunningham, W.Todd
W1986 30 Mar   East Buttress, The   R.Anderson, G.Nicoll
                     Chimney
W1986 5 Apr   West Buttress   R.Anderson, R.Milne
                     Direttissima
            This was the name given to the winter combination of Senior on the
            lowest tier with the Bonington/Patey variation finish at the top.
S 1986 27 Jun   Condor Crack   D.Roberts, J.Scarborough
W1987 3 Jan   Fuselage Wall Direct R.Anderson, G.Nicoll
W1987 9 Jan   Pelican   A.Cunningham, A.Nisbet
W1987 21 Feb   The Upper Girdle,   M.Fowler, C.Watts
                     Part 1
W1987 14 Mar   The Upper Girdle,   M.Fowler, A.Saunders
                     Part 2
W1987 5 Apr   West Central Gully   M.Fowler, M.Morrison
W1988 21 Nov   Direct Route, Central A.Nisbet, P.Yardley
                     Wall
W1989 16 Feb   East Wall   B.Davison, A.Nisbet

W	1989 17 Feb	Flight of the Condor	B.Davison, A.Nisbet
S	1989 20 Jul	Flying Fortress	A.Tibbs, S.Steer
W	1990 3 Jan	Central Buttress, Right-Hand Finish	S.Allan, A.Nisbet
S	1990 15 Sep	Wall of the Winds	J.Lyall, A.Nisbet
W	1991 9 Jan	Far West Buttress	S.Aisthorpe, J.Lyall
W	1991 14 Feb	Mistral	B.Davison, A.Nisbet
S	1991 31 Aug	Earth, Wind and Fire	J.Lyall, A.Nisbet
W	1992 29 Mar	Maelstrom	A.Nisbet, S.Roberts
S	1992 26 May	Shoot the Breeze	A.Nisbet, G.Ollerhead
S	1992 28 May	Force Ten	A.Nisbet, G.Ollerhead
S	1992 29 Jun	Cyclonic Westerly	A.Nisbet, G.Ollerhead

Variation avoiding the crux climbed by the same party the same day.

S	1992 29 Jun	Chop Suey	A.Nisbet, G.Ollerhead
S	1992 2 Jun	Central Reservation	J.Lyall, A.Nisbet
S	1992 2 Jun	Swinging in the Rain	J.Lyall, A.Nisbet

Coire Rudha-Staca

S	1971 12 Jul	Thin Man's Ridge	D.Howard, C.S.Rose, R.W.L.Turnbull
S	1971 Sep	Spog aig Giomach	C.S.Rose, R.W.L.Turnbull
S	1972 Sep	Midge Ridge	C.S.Rose, S.Peterson
S	1977 Jul	The Independent Pineapple	C.S.Rose, D.Howard
S	1977 15 Oct	The Pineapple Chimney	Miss B.Clough, A.Nisbet, M.Thorp
S	1977 17 Oct	Autumn Rib	S.Ackerley, A.Nisbet
W	1984 7 Apr	Chockstone Gully	R.Archbold, G.Strange
W	1987 10 Jan	Midge Ridge	G.Nicoll, R.Anderson
W	1991 13 Jan	The Independent Pineapple	G.Ettle, A.Nisbet
W	1991 15 Feb	Three Tier Chimney	B.Davison, A.Nisbet
W	1991 21 Dec	Spog aig Giomach	J.Lyall, A.Nisbet

BEINN ALLIGIN

W	1973 Feb	West Coast Boomer	D.Gardner, N.Crawford, C.Ferguson
W	1981 Feb	Backfire Ridge	S.Chadwick, G.Powell
W	1984 15 Apr	Backyard Gully	S.Chadwick
W	1985 10 Feb	Diamond Fire	S.Chadwick, G.Livingstone, G.Strange
W	1986 1 Feb	Backyard Buttress	R.Archbold, J.C.Higham, H.M.A.Towler
W	1986 15 Feb	Koh-i-Noor	M.E.Moran, M.Hardwick
W	1986 18 Feb	Ice Gem	M.E.Moran, S.Chadwick
W	1986 2 Mar	Crown Jewel	M.E.Moran, N.Adey, M.Guest
W	1986 2 Mar	Moonstone	M.E.Moran
W	1987 18 Jan	Bilas	D.Rubens, D.Broadhead

W1987	Feb	Errors Cleft	S.Chadwick, I.Davidson
W1988	15 Mar	Diamond Cleft	C.Munro, S.Chadwick
W1989	26 Feb	Light of Bengal	I.Barron, S.Kennedy
W1989	26 Feb	Shezan	M.Macdonald, A.Scrase

DIABAIG

S 1975	3 Aug	Route One	J.A.Austin, E.Grindley
S 1975	4 Aug	Route Two	J.A.Austin, E.Grindley
S 1975	4 Aug	Route Three	J.A.Austin, E.Grindley
S 1976	9 Aug	The Black Streak	J.A.Austin, R.Valentine
S 1976	10 Aug	Gamhnachain's Crack	J.A.Austin, C.Rose, R.Valentine
S 1976	10 Aug	Charlie's Tower	J.A.Austin, C.Rose, R.Valentine
S 1982	24 Apr	Foil	C.Moody, R.Sharples
S 1982	24 Apr	Boab's Corner	C.Moody, R.Sharples
S 1982	23 May	Plunge	D.Hayter, C.Moody
S 1983		The Pillar	M.Hamilton
S 1984	May	Dire Wall	A.Nisbet, R.F.Allen
S 1984	May	Northumberland Wall	A.Nisbet, R.McHardy
S 1985	8 Jun	Dead Mouse Crack	J.Brown and partner
S 1987	16 Apr	An Eyeful	G.Latter, I.Griffiths, D.Griffiths
S 1987	27 May	Rubblesplitskin	K.Howett
S 1987	27 May	Edgewood Whymper	K.Howett, D.Cuthbertson
S 1987	28 May	Local Hero	K.Howett, D.Cuthbertson
S 1987	29 May	Condome	K.Howett, D.Cuthbertson
S 1987	10 Jun	Wall of Flame	K.Howett, C.Thomson
S 1988	4 Apr	Instant Muscle	D.Griffiths, I.Griffiths
S 1988		Final Demand	D.Griffiths
S 1988	30 Apr	Bromide	W.Hood, C.Moody, B.Williamson
S 1988	Aug	Going Home	G.Latter, K.Howett
S 1988	Aug	Afterglow	K.Howett, G.Latter
S 1990	May	An Offensive Man	K.Howett, A.Taylor, T.Prentice
S 1990	May	Animal Magic	K.Howett, A.Taylor, T.Prentice
S 1990	May	Porpoise Pun	K.Howett, A.Taylor, T.Prentice
S 1990		Batwing	B.Kerr, T.Prentice, A.Todd
S 1990	29 Jul	Evasion	S.Allan, D.Etherington
S 1990	29 Jul	Bogie	S.Allan, D.Etherington, A.Nisbet
S 1990	24 Oct	The Mynch	G.Fry, M.Moran, P.Mynch
S 1991	26 Mar	The Grunter	W.Hood, L.Skuodas
S 1991	15 Apr	Diabeg Corner	R.Lupton, C.Moody
S 1991	31 May	Dire Straits	S.Jenkins, M.Moran

BEINN DAMH

S 1967	Aug	Aquila	J.L.Cardy, G.Halleyard
W1979	12 Feb	Aquila Gully; Stag Gully	R.Butler, D.Howard, D.McCallum, C.Roylance
W1984	3 Mar	Aetos	I.Crofton, G.Caplan

BEINN A'MHUINIDH

S	1899 Easter	The West Climb	G.T.Glover, W.Inglis Clark
S	1910 Easter	Double Flake Route	C.W.Walker, W.Inglis Clark
	1946	Bell's Variation; Route I; Route II	J.H.B.Bell, Mrs Bell
S	1949 Aug	Zigzag Gully	F.F.Cunningham, A.B.Cunningham
S	1951 Jul	Prelude	J.D.Foster, D.Leaver
S	1952 9 Aug	Tuit	J.R.Lees, D.D.Stewart
S	1958 Jul	Staircase Ridge; Stepped Chimney; Silver Slab; Pinnacle Gully; Pinnacle Face	R.Harris, P.Bamfield
S	1959 4 Jun	Miscellany	A.Ellison, J.R.Harris
S	1959 4 Jun	Crypton Crack	
S	1959 6 Jun	Climax Slab	
S	1967 May	Centaur	W.March, D.Campbell
S	1967 30 May	Virus	P.Nunn, C.Rowland
S	1967 1 Jul	The Alley	I.G.Rowe, A.J.Trees
S	1967 2 Jul	Safari; A Walk on the Wild Side	I.G.Rowe, A.J.Trees
S	1968 Apr	The Rebound	B.Fuller, P.Nunn
S	1969 26 May	The Tallon; The Bow	J.A.Austin, D.G.Roberts
S	1970 4 May	Coloured Corner	A.Agnew, F.Jack, G.Skelton
S	1971 13 May	Stoater; Vertigo; The Creep	J.Cunningham, W.March
S	1971 30 May	Waterfall Corner	K.Baird, P.Macdonald
S	1971 5 Jul	The Tappit Hen	B.Dunn, J.R.Houston
S	1972 5 Aug	Linea Nigra	A.C.Cain, M.Gate
S	1975 31 Jul	Spider	K.Schwartz
S	1980 30 Sep	Aquila	N.Bielby, B.Nicolson
S	1982 25 Jul	Chiaroscuro; Rainbow's End	A.C.Cain, P.Davis
W	1984 27 Jan	The Waterfall	A.Nisbet, P.Thornhill
S	1984 16 Sep	Refuse Cruise	D.Rubens, S.Pearson

FURNACE CRAGS

S	1984 20 May	The Mad Fencer	A.C.Cain, J.Davies
S	1984 17 Jun	Skeleton Lum	A.C.Cain, B.Ledingham, B.Kennedy
S	1984 24 Jun	Caisteal Mor	A.C.Cain, B.Ledingham, B.Kennedy
S	1984 22 Jul	Soft Shoulder	A.C.Cain, B.Ledingham, B.Kennedy J.Cheesemond
S	1985 4 May	Norse Requiem	I.Davidson, S.Chadwick
S	1985 12 May	Riabhach Slab	A.C.Cain, J.Davies
S	1985 29 Sep	Indian Summer	J.Davies, A.C.Cain
S	1985 29 Sep	Phew	A.C.Cain, J.Davies

SLIOCH

S 1933 16 Apr		Stepped Ridge	Macdougall, Cram and W.Blackwood
S 1952		Main Buttress	A.Parker
W1981	Feb	Easy Gully	S.Chadwick
W1982	Feb	Starters Gully	S.Chadwick, A.Smailes
W1984	Mar	Surprise Gully	B.Findlay, S.Chadwick, G.Strange
S 1984	May	Pinnacle Surprise	I.Davidson, S.Chadwick

This is probably the same as Northern Pinnacles, climbed 19 April 1954 by D.J.Bennet and D.Mill.

S 1986 14 Jul		Skyline Highway	S.Chadwick, I.Davidson

RAVENS CRAG, GAIRLOCH

S 1981	Aug	Charlestone	S.Chadwick, H.Emerson
S 1982	Jul	Hydro Hek	G.Powell, S.Chadwick
S 1982	Aug	Badachro	G.Powell, S.Chadwick
S 1982	Sep	Ken's Joy	S.Chadwick, K.Anderson
S 1983	Jun	Lonmore	A.Smailes, S.Chadwick
S 1984	Sep	Lucy	S.Chadwick, I.Davidson
S 1985 Spring		Stage Fright	I.Davidson, S.Chadwick
S 1986 3 Apr		Entasis (Pitch 1) Leac McCac; Far Post	M. McKay, R.A.Napier
S 1986 6 Apr		Groove Climb	E.Simpson, G.Callander
		Entasis (Pitch 2)	D.Conway, R.A.Napier
S 1991		Flakes; Special K; Jutting Blocks; Two Guns; Mountain Ash	D.Lang (probably climbed before)

CREAG MHOR THOLLAIDH

S 1966 10 May		Knickerbocker Glory	B.Robertson, T.W.Patey, M.Galbraith
S 1966 11 May		Anti Gravity	B.Robertson, M.Galbraith
S 1966 15 May		The Hand Rail	T.W.Patey, M.Galbraith
S 1967 21 May		The Ugly Duckling	J.Renny, J.Porteous
S 1967	Jun	Hoax	W.Sproul, A.Ewing, J.Brumfitt
S 1967	Jun	Rumple Fyke	I.G.Rowe, A.J.Trees

FFA J.Lamb, P.Whillance 17 June 1975

S 1967 7 Sep		The Trip	C.Jackson, B.Andrews
S 1967 8 Sep		Teddy Bears Picnic	C.Jackson, B.Andrews

Variation: R.Anderson, C.Greaves 21 May 1988

S 1968 1 Jun		Cocaine	M.Curdy, A.McHardy, P.Nunn, A.Wright
S 1968	Jun	Siren	A.McHardy, P.Nunn, C.Rowland
S 1968	Jun	The Left Arete	M.Curdy, A.Wright
S 1968 1 Aug		Catastasis	B.Andrews, C.Jackson

S 1969		King Prawn; Shazam; Soft Option	Mr and Mrs F.W.Harper
S 1970	9 May	Stoney Broke	J.Cunningham, W.March
S 1970	18 Jul	Pokey Hat	D.C.Forrest, D.M.Jenkins
S 1971	2 Aug	Minute	M.Horsburgh, K.Schwartz
S 1971	17 Aug	Toady	C.Jackson, T.Proctor
S 1971	18 Aug	Gudgeon	C.Jackson, T.Proctor

FFA: R.Anderson, C.Greaves 22 May 1988

S 1974	11 Jun	The Bug	P.Botterill, J.Lamb
S 1975	17 Jun	Friday The Thirteenth	J.Lamb, P.Whillance
S 1975	31 Jul	Second	R.Morrow, K.Schwartz
S 1982	5 Jun	Stoney Broke Variation	P.Nunn, A.Livesey
S 1983	May	Decadent Days	R.Anderson, M.Hamilton
S 1983		Hamiltons Groove and Arete	M.Hamilton, D.Dinwoodie
S 1983		Murrays Arete	M.Hamilton
S 1987	18 Apr	Big Toe	R.Anderson, S.Pearson, A.Conkie
S 1987	9 May	Cloud Cuckoo Land	G.Nicoll, R.Anderson
S 1987	10 May	Second Coast	G.Nicoll, R.Anderson
S 1987	10 May	Loctite; Uhu; The Heretic	R.Anderson, G.Nicoll

Heresy variation to The Heretic climbed later by K.Howett.

S 1987		Spirit Air; Destitution Man; Blassad Den Iar;	K.Howett
S 1987		Jarldom Reach	K.Howett, A.Nelson
S 1987	27 Aug	Rain-In-The-Face; Each Uisge	D.Dinwoodie, A.Ross

Direct Start: Across the Lines R.Anderson, C.Greaves 8 July 1988

S 1988	22 May	Home Start	R.Anderson, C.Greaves
S 1988	3 Jul	Gulf Coast Highway	R.Anderson, C.Greaves
S 1988	4 Jul	Love Is The Drug	A.Tibbs, A.Milne
S 1991	12 May	North-West Orient	R. and C.Anderson
S 1992	30 May	Arial	K.Howett, G.Ridge, J.Horrocks
S 1992	6 Jun	Pagan Love Song	K.Howett, G.Ridge
S 1992	7 Jun	The Shimmer	K.Howett, J.Horrocks

BEINN AIRIGH CHARR

S 1909	May	Eastern Buttress	G.T.Glover, W.N.Ling
S 1910	Mar	Original Route	G.T.Glover, H.Walker, R.Corry, W.N.Ling

This name seems to ignore the 1909 climb, but for consistency with earlier guides it has been retained.

S 1951	4 Jul	Lower Buttress Direct	C.G.M.Slesser & party
S 1951	18 Jul	Square Buttress	J.C.Stewart, S.McPherson, W.D.Brooker, J.W.Morgan
W 1964	Mar	Staircase Gully	P.N.L.Tranter, N.Travers

S 1971	Oct	The Beanstalk	D.Bathgate, P.F.Macdonald
S 1974	Apr	The Roc	M.Boysen, P.Braithwaite, P.Nunn
S 1977	Jul	Lower Buttress	W.D.Brooker, A.G.Cousins
W1988	5 Feb	Comic Relief	D.Broadhead, I.Dalley

CREAG BEAG

S 1957	10 Aug	Temerity	D.Ashton, P.C.Machen
S 1972	Jun	Central Groove	P.Buckley, P.Gray
S 1988	26 May	Little Big-Horn	D.Dinwoodie, A.Nisbet

Aid was used to clean part of the top groove before free-climbing it.

CREAG NA GAORACH

S 1957	8 Apr	Jealousy	M.J.O'Hara, Miss M.Langmuir
S 1957	9 Apr	Zebra Slabs	M.J.O'Hara, Miss M.Langmuir
S 1967	22 May	Rainbow's End	P.J.Sugden, J.R.Sutcliffe
S 1978	30 May	Denizen	R.A.Croft, J.R.Sutcliffe

BEINN LAIR

S 1951	3 Jun	Angel Buttress Ordinary	Miss A.Hood, J.S.Orr
S 1951	6 Jun	The Ordinary variation	Miss A.Hood, J.S.Orr
S 1951	17 Aug	Wrangham's variation	E.A.Wrangham, F.Adams
S 1951	3 Jun	Pilgrim's Progress	J.S.Orr, Miss A.Hood
S 1951	3 Jun	Molar Buttress, Route I	D.C.Hutchinson, B.S.Smith
S 1951	3 Jun	Rose Route	J.Smith, N.A.Todd
S 1951	4 Jun	Cavity Chimney	D.C.Hutchinson, B.S.Smith
S 1951	4 Jun	Wisdom Wall	D.C.Hutchinson, B.S.Smith
S 1951	4 Jun	Wisdom Buttress	J.Smith, Miss A.Hood, J.S.Orr
S 1951	6 Jun	Bat's Gash	B.S.Smith, D.C.Hutchinson
S 1951	7 Jun	The Tooth	D.C.Hutchinson, B.S.Smith, Miss A.Hood, J.S.Orr
S 1951	5 Jul	West Chimney Route	C.G.M.Slesser, G.Dutton, J.Wight
S 1951	9 Jul	Marathon Ridge	W.D.Brooker, S.McPherson, J.W.Morgan, J.C.Stewart
S 1951	16 Aug	Left-hand Route	F.Adams, E.A.Wrangham
S 1951	20 Aug	Right-hand Route	E.A.Wrangham, F.Adams
S 1951	20 Aug	Y-Buttress	E.A.Wrangham, F.Adams
S 1951	Aug	Stag Buttress	J.D.Foster, D.Leaver
S 1951	Aug	Falstaff	D.Leaver, J.D.Foster
S 1951	Aug	Sesame Buttress	J.D.Foster, D.Leaver
S 1951	Aug	Rainbow Wall	D.Leaver, J.D.Foster
S 1951	Aug	Central Route	J.D.Foster, D.Leaver
W1952	Mar	Excalibur	E.A.Wrangham, A.B.Clegg
W1953	3 Dec	Right Wing	E.A.Wrangham, D.St.J.R.Wagstaff
W1953	5 Dec	Olympus	E.A.Wrangham, D.St.J.R.Wagstaff

S 1957	8 Apr	North Summit Buttress	Miss M.Langmuir, M.J.O'Hara
S 1967	6 Jul	Left Wing	I.G.Rowe
W1969 26 Feb		Easachan	Q.T.Crichton, G.N.Hunter
W1969 27 Feb		Geodha Ban	Q.T.Crichton, G.N.Hunter
W1978 18 Feb		Cabbage White	R.McHardy, A.Nisbet
W1978 19 Feb		North Summit Buttress	J.Anderson, R.McHardy, A.Nisbet, J.Unwin
W1978	Apr	Butterfly Gully	D.Dinwoodie, R.Renshaw
W1988	7 Feb	Left Wing	D.J.Broadhead, I.Dalley

HANGING CRAG

| S 1988 26 May | Causeway Corner | W.McCrae, N.Wilson |
| S 1988 26 May | Changing Face | N.Wilson, W.McCrae |

GHOST SLABS and CREAG DUBHDEARG

S 1958	Apr	Left-hand Route	E.A.Wrangham, P.Nelson
S 1958	Apr	Right-hand Route	G.T.Fraser, P.E.Evans, M.Fraser
S 1967	2 Aug	Doodle	R.Carrington, M.Shaw
S 1967	2 Aug	Leviathan	J.R.Jackson, I.Fulton
S 1988 23 May		Moby Dick	D.Dinwoodie, A.Nisbet
S 1988 23 May		Black Rain	D.Dinwoodie, A.Nisbet
		Probably climbed before	
S 1988 23 May		Tannasg Dubh	D.Dinwoodie, A.Nisbet

CARNMORE

| S 1952 31 Mar | Diagonal Route | E.A.Wrangham, A.B.Clegg |

Initiated Cambridge University's long association with the crag. Carnmore Corner was the lure.

S 1954		Poachers' Route	C.J.S.Bonington and party
S 1956	Mar	Thrutch	M.J.O'Hara, M.L.Langmuir
S 1956 29 Mar		Original Route	G.J.Fraser, M.J.O'Hara
S 1956 31 Mar		Happy Wanderer	M.J.O'Hara, M.L.Langmuir
S 1956 17 Jun		Botanist's Boulevard	J.H.Longland, M.J.Clay, H.B.Carslake, D.Rhodes
S 1956 17 Jun		Red Scar Entry	M.J.O'Hara, R.E.Kendell
S 1957 29 Mar		Needle	S.G.M.Clark, M.J.O'Hara
S 1957	2 Apr	Tinkerbell	M.J.O'Hara, M.L.Langmuir
S 1957	7 Apr	Fionn Buttress	M.J.O'Hara, W.D.Blackwood

A very fine discovery

| S 1957 20 Apr | Fionn Castle Variation | G.J.Fraser, J.D.C.Peacock, M.J.O'Hara |
| S 1957 22 Apr | Dragon | G.J.Fraser, M.J.O'Hara |

O'Hara took a cat's cradle belay on a leaf peg under the roof. A great ascent of an intimidating route.

S 1957   Jun   Grey Ridge   M.J.O'Hara, N.C.Peacock,
                                     R.G.Hargreaves
S 1957 24 Jun   Avoidance   G.Burns, D.Leaver
S 1957 8 Aug Initiation   D.Ashton, P.C.Machen, C.B.Harris
S 1960   Apr   Gob   D.Haston, R.Smith
S 1962   Apr   Yogi   D.Haston, A.Wightman
S 1966   May   Balaton   W.Gorman, C.Higgins
S 1966   May   Boo-Boo   W.Gorman, C.Higgins
S 1966   May   The Kady   W.Gorman, C.Higgins
S 1966 19 Jun   Black Mischief B.E.H.Maden, R.D.Sykes
S 1966 22 Jul   Abomination   J.McLean, A.Currey, J.Cunningham
S 1967   May   Green Corner A.G.Cram, R.Schipper, W.Young
      The main pitch had been climbed before in 1963 by P.Buckley and
      J.Budd.
S 1967 28 May St George   A.G.Cram, R.Schipper
S 1967   Jun   Kaleidoscope G.Macnair, R.Jones
S 1967   Jun   Connie-Onnie R.Jones, G.Macnair
S 1967   Jun   Strawberry Fields G.Macnair, R.Jones
S 1967   Jun   Penny Lane   R.J.Isherwood, E.Birch
S 1967   Jun   The Cracks   E.Birch, R.J.Isherwood
S 1967   Jun   Trampoline   R.Jones, G.MacNair
S 1967   Jun   The Sword   R.J.Isherwood, E.Birch
      Climbed late in the day after Penny Lane and The Cracks. About three
      aid points were used. A fine achievement on a very difficult route.
      FFA G.Duckworth and party, around 1980.
S 1968 19 Jun   Carnmore Corner R.Carrington, J.R.Jackson
      A long-standing problem. One aid point was used on the ramp below the
      roof.
      Probable FFA R.Perriment, A.Hodges 1975.
S 1974 15 Apr Purple Wall   P.Buckley, B.E.H.Maden, M.J.O'Hara
S 1974   Apr   Odyssey   P.Buckley, B.E.H.Maden, M.J.O'Hara
S 1974 16 Apr Ring of Bright Water A.Faller, M.Harris
S 1975 25 May Achilles   P.Buckley, C.Warnham
      Most pitches had been climbed on previous occasions by Buckley with
      O'Hara, Maden and Smith.
S 1975   May   Ulysses   P.Buckley, C.Warnham
S 1976 Spring   Claymore   S.B.Thomas, R.B.Evans
S 1980   May   Wilderness   M.Lawrence, D.Mullin
      Climbed on sight. A very bold ascent.
S 1981 1 Apr   Running Bear D.Dinwoodie, J.Wyness
      First pitch originally climbed with a detour into Boo-Boo.
      Direct ascent: D.Dinwoodie, A.Nisbet 20 May 1988.
S 1981 2 Apr   Naughty Alien D.Dinwoodie, J.Wyness
S 1982 20 May Black Magic   C.Dale, A.Dytch
      A similar line was climbed by P Buckley and B E H Maden in 1974
S 1982 21 May Dandelion Days C.Dale, A.Dytch
      Climbed earlier by M.Hamilton and P.Whillance, but unrecorded.

S 1984   1 Aug   Break In   A.Tibbs, A.Winton
S 1984   2 Aug   999   A.Tibbs, A.Winton
S 1985 15 Jun   Crackers   D.Hawthorn, C.Maclean
S 1985 16 Jun   The Orange Bow   D.Dinwoodie, D.Hawthorn
S 1985 16 Jun   Curare   D.Dinwoodie, D.Hawthorn
        Probably the first pre-cleaned routes at Carnmore.
        Left-hand start: D.Dinwoodie, A.Nisbet 22 May 1988
S 1986   8 Aug   Beastmaster   D.Dinwoodie, G.Livingston
S 1986   9 Aug   Lion Rampant   G.Livingston, D.Dinwoodie
S 1986   9 Aug   Death-Wolf   G.Livingston, D.Dinwoodie
        Climbed over two days, a nut being left in place overnight at the lip.
S 1986 10 Aug   Ride of the Valkyrie   D.Dinwoodie, G.Livingstone
S 1987 28 Apr   Jivaro Crack   D.Dinwoodie, D.Hawthorn
S 1987 21 Jun   It Was Twenty Years   D.Rubens, S.Pearson
                 Ago Today
        The Anniversary of Penny Lane etc.
S 1988 21 May   Red Crack   D.Dinwoodie, A.Nisbet
S 1988 22 May   Quagga   A.Nisbet, D.Dinwoodie

TORR NA H'IOLAIRE

S 1933 22 Jun   Baird's Route   P.D.Baird, J.W.Crofton, E.J.A.Leslie
S 1951   3 Jul   Skyline Route   C.G.M.Slesser, G.Dutton, J.Wight
S 1951   3 Jul   West Face Ledge   C.G.M.Slesser, G.Dutton, J.Wight
                 Route
S 1951   3 Jul   Tantivy Tower   C.G.M.Slesser, G.Dutton, J.Wight
S 1956 27 Mar   Ipswich Rib   G.J.Fraser, P.R.Steele
S 1956 29 Mar   Shark's Tooth   P.R.Steele, Miss M.M.Langmuir
S 1957 19 Apr   Red Admiral   G.J.Fraser, J.D.C.Peacock,
                                         M.J.O'Hara
S 1957 19 Apr   Hieroglyphics   M.J.O'Hara, J.D.C.Peacock,
                                         G.J.Fraser
S 1957 22 Apr   Wester   J.D.C.Peacock, A.Finlay
S 1957 22 Apr   Goat's Groove   J.D.C.Peacock, A.Finlay
S 1957 23 Jun   Sigma   M.J.O'Hara, D.Fagan, B.E.H.Maden
        The route described was climbed by D.J.Broadhead and G.Cohen while
        writing the guide.
S 1957 23 Jun   Sunday Climb   G.Burns, D.Leaver
S 1957 23 Jun   Rainbow Corner   B.E.H.Maden, M.J.O'Hara, D.Fagan
S 1957 25 Jun   Sarcophagus   D.Fagan, M.J.O'Hara
S 1957 25 Jun   Intimidation   M.J.O'Hara, D.Fagan
S 1957 25 Jun   Mica Rib   B.E.H.Maden
S 1957 25 Jun   Rose Rib   D.Fagan, M.J.O'Hara
S 1957 29 Jun   Frogmarch   G.G.Hargreaves, N.C.Peacock
S 1957 29 Jun   Juniper Groove   D.Fagan, M.J.O'Hara
S 1957 30 Jun   The Long Reach   D.Fagan, N.C.Peacock
S 1959   Apr   Suspension   G.McCallum, C.Pollock

S 1966	Mar	The Trees	G.Macnair, B.E.H.Maden
S 1966	20 Jun	Sickle; Sapros	B.E.H.Maden, R.D.Sykes
S 1967	1 Aug	Skeleton Corner	J.R.Jackson, M.Shaw
S 1967	3 Aug	Skull	J.R.Jackson, R.Carrington
S 1967	3 Aug	Wishbone Rib	J.R.Jackson, R.Carrington
S 1970	18 Jun	Eryr	C.L.Jones, C.F.Walmsley
S 1978	22 May	The Eyrie	G.Cohen, G.Macnair, R.J Archbold
S 1978	22 May	Holly Tree Wall	R.J.Archbold, G.Cohen, G.Macnair
S 1978	22 May	Cadaverous Crack	G.Macnair, G.Cohen

On the first ascent aid was used while gardening the top of the crack.

S 1988	20 May	Cleopatra	D.Dinwoodie, A.Nisbet
S 1988	20 May	Toad Hall	A.Nisbet, D.Dinwoodie
S 1988	22 May	Carnivorous Crack	D.Dinwoodie, A.Nisbet
S 1988	22 May	Hyena Corner	A.Nisbet, D.Dinwoodie

MAIDEN BUTTRESS AND CARNAN BAN

S 1955	10 Apr	Dishonour	M.J.O'Hara, M.Langmuir
S 1955	18 Aug	Tweedledee	M.J.O'Hara, R.E.Kendell
S 1955	19 Aug	Modesty	R.E.Kendell, M.J.O'Hara
S 1955	19 Aug	Strewth	M.J.O'Hara, R.E.Kendell
S 1955	19 Aug	Tweedledum	R.E.Kendell, M.J.O'Hara
S 1955	20 Aug	Cakewalk	R.E.Kendell, M.J.O'Hara
S 1955	20 Aug	Ecstasy	M.J.O'Hara, R.E.Kendell
S 1956	28 Mar	Barndance	M.J.O'Hara, M.Langmuir
S 1956	28 Mar	Doddle	G.J.Fraser, P.R.Steele
S 1956	31 Mar	Practice Precipice Climbs	G.J.Fraser, P.R.Steele
S 1967	17 Jul	Strider	D.T.McLennan, D.C.Forrest
S 1967	17 Jul	Balrog	D.T.McLennan, D.C.Forrest

A'MHAIGHDEAN

S 1933	23 Jun	Baird, Crofton and Leslie's Route.	P.D.Baird, J.W.Crofton, E.J.A.Leslie
S 1950		Pillar Buttress	Dr. and Mrs J.H.B.Bell
S 1951	2 Jul	West Face Climb	C.G.M.Slesser, G.Dutton, J.Wight

The lower part of this face is very indefinite and the account has not proved adequate for identification.

| S 1951 | Aug | Leeds Variation (direct start). | J.D.Foster, D.Leaver |
| S 1951 | | Triple Cracks Route | A.J.Bennet and party |

Possibly the same line as "The Slot", climbed (in descent) by M.J.O'Hara and R.G.Hargreaves, Jun 30 1957.

S 1954	17 Apr	Red Slab	D.J.Bennet, D.Mill
S 1957	31 Mar	Conglomerate Arete	M.J.O'Hara, M.M.Langmuir
S 1957	21 Apr	Doe Crack	M.J.O'Hara, G.J.Fraser
S 1957	21 Apr	Windslab	M.J.O'Hara, G.J.Fraser

S 1957 21 Apr   Whitbread's Aiguille   M.J.O'Hara, G.J.Fraser
S 1957 30 Jun   Vole Buttress   M.J.O'Hara, R.G.Hargreaves
S 1957 30 Jun   Eagle Grooves   M.J.O'Hara, R.G.Hargreaves
S 1959 1 Apr   Fahrenheit   F.Green, G.McCallum
S 1959 3 Apr   Soh What?   K.Torrance, A.Currie
S 1965 31 Mar   Kraken   W.D.Fraser, D.Martin
S 1966 15 Aug   Gladiator   J.R.Sutcliffe, D.Chapman
S 1966 15 Aug   Goats' Ridge   D.Chapman, J.R.Sutcliffe
S 1966 15 Aug   Hodge's Pinnacle   D.Chapman, J.R.Sutcliffe
S 1967 24 May   Trident Gully Buttress   J.R.Sutcliffe, P.J.Sugden
S 1967   Jun   Compensation   R.J.Isherwood, E.Birch
W 1978 29 Apr   Ermine Gully   R.F.Allen, M.G.Geddes
S 1988 24 May   The Cave Mouth   D.Dinwoodie, A.Nisbet
S 1988 24 May   The Cave   D.Dinwoodie
S 1988 24 May   Mossy Bower   D.Dinwoodie, A.Nisbet
S 1988 24 May   Gearradh   A.Nisbet, D.Dinwoodie
S 1988 24 May   Purity   D.Dinwoodie, A.Nisbet
        Probably climbed before

NA BEARTA BUTTRESS and CREAG TOLL A'MHADAIDH

S 1955 22 Aug   Ricepaper   R.E.Kendell, M.J.O'Hara
        One PA used on crux crack owing to vegetation.
S 1956 30 Mar   Wallflower   M.J.O'Hara, M.Langmuir
S 1956 30 Mar   Good Friday Climb   G.J.Fraser, P.R.Steele
        Several pitches near top avoided on lead and top-roped by second.
S 1957 3 Jul   Sanctuary Slabs   M.J.O'Hara

AN TEALLACH

Bidein a'Ghlas Thuill
W 1910 26 Mar   Hayfork Gully   G.Sang, W.A.Morrison
S 1945 10 Jun   Major Rib   E.C.Pyatt, K.C.King
W 1956 15 Apr   Minor Rib   R.Barclay, W.D.Brooker
S 1959 21 Sep   Minor Rib   F.Henderson, G.Sim, R.Sim
        An 'inviting crack' avoided on this ascent was climbed by T.W.Patey,
        N.Drasdo, C.M.Dixon May 1962
W 1959 15 Feb   Fourth Prong   T.M.Lawson, R.J.Tanton, J.Clarkson
W 1969 3 Mar   Checkmate Chimney   T.W.Patey, C.J.S.Bonington
W 1978 18 Dec   The Alley   R.Baker, A.McCord
W 1979   Feb   Major Rib   I.L.Dalley, J.Grant
W 1982   Dec   Intermediate Face   D.Butterfield, J.Elliot, P.Savill
        Route
W 1983   Feb   Stalemate   K.Schwartz, J.Mount
W 1986 23 Feb   White Knight   M.Fowler, C.Watts
W 1987 18 Jan   Pawn Cocktail   C.Forrest, W.Moir

Toll an Lochain

W 1923 Easter	Lord's Gully, right branch	J.H.B.Bell, E.E.Roberts
W 1945 5 Apr	Sulphur Gully	J.E.Q.Barford, F.A.Pullinger, M.P.Ward
S 1958 9 Aug	Lord's Gully, right branch	D.Robertson, F.Old
W 1973 17 Feb	Lord's Gully, left branch	A.Borthwick, F.Fotheringham
W 1974 30 Dec	Lady's Gully	F.Fotheringham, J.R.R.Fowler
W 1978 19 Feb	1978 Face Route	M.Freeman, N.Keir
W 1987 31 Jan	Potala Buttress	D.Rubens, D.Broadhead
W 1987 12 Apr	Bowling Alley	M.Fowler, C.Watts
W 1988 13 Mar	Bottomless Gully	M.Fowler, D.Wilkinson
W 1991 28 Jan	Lord Berkley's Seat	S.Jenkins, A.Nisbet

BEINN DEARG MOR

1899	South Peak	Sang and Morrison
S 1952 Easter	Flake Buttress	A.Parker, J.Derris, I.Richards
S 1953 5 Apr	Central Buttress	A.Parker and party
W 1963 Dec	Trident Gully, Central branch	P.N.L.Tranter, N.Travers
W 1966 Nov	Left Flank of Central Buttress	A.McKeith, I.G.Rowe
W 1980 19 Jan	Twisting Gully	M.G.Geddes, C.Higgins, A.Walne
W 1982 1 Jan	Deranged	J.Bennet, L.Bowie
W 1987 23 Mar	Fat Man's Folly	A.Todd, W.Curr
W 1987 2 Apr	Spring Maiden	G.Taylor, A.Todd

JUNCTION BUTTRESS and THE SIDINGS

S 1945	Pasture Gully	E.C.Pyatt, E.C.King
S 1952 Easter	Parker's Route	A.Parker, J.Derris, I.Richards
S 1952 30 Mar	Route 1	E.A.Wrangham, A.B.Clegg
S 1953 3 Apr	The Nose, Sapling Climb	H.G.Nicol, D.St.J.R.Wagstaff, E.A.Wrangham
S 1956	Rowell's Route	H.Rowell
S 1957 6 Dec	The Funnel	E.A.Wrangham, D.St.J.R.Wagstaff
S 1964 10 Apr	Rightward Slant	G.A.Watt, G.W.Jack

Proposed Extension to the Scottish Winter Grading System

Since the introduction of the numerical system for the grading of Scottish winter climbs more than two decades ago, several developments have taken place in equipment, technique and attitude. These developments have placed such a strain on the grading system that the leading activists have agreed that it must be extended to take these changes into account. In particular, the new modern mixed routes must be graded so as to indicate their high levels of technical difficulty, while taking into consideration the frequently greater seriousness of the older-style ice routes. The elements of this extended system can be summarised as follows:

(i) Nearly all grades up to and including grade IV will remain unaltered.

(ii) Climbs of grade V and above will have two grades, an overall grade in roman numerals, and a technical grade in arabic numerals. Some hard, technical mixed grade IV routes have also been given a technical grade. (iii) The overall grade will take into account all factors affecting the difficulty of reaching the top of the climb, including its technical difficulty, seriousness (frequency of protection and reliability of belays) and sustainedness (length of hard sections of climbing and number of hard pitches).

(iv) The technical grade will reflect the actual difficulty of the hardest section(s) of climbing, without reference to seriousness. It is not intended to be used as a technical pitch-by-pitch grading. A technical grade of 5 indicates relatively straightforward, steep ice climbing; a technical grade of 6 would generally indicate more technical mixed climbing; technical grades of 7 and 8 would indicate much more intricate and harder snowed-up rock moves.

(v) The technical grade will normally vary not more than two below or two above the overall grade. Thus V,5 can be taken as an average grade V route of the old system. A higher technical grade than the overall grade would indicate greater technical difficulty, offset by better protection (as frequently found on mixed routes); a lower technical grade would indicate greater seriousness. Thus the system has some parallels with the E-grade system for summer rock climbs.

(vi) The previous artificial ceiling of grade V (and reluctant VI) has been removed, so as to reflect more realistically the differences between the old classic climbs of grade V and the current state-of-the-art routes.

Some degree of variability will undoubtedly occur, but the grading has to take account of what is thought to be average conditions. These proposals should be a great improvement over the ridiculous cramming of the grades that had developed. It should also be noted that, while this list has been compiled after consultation with many of the leading figures in Scottish winter climbing, despite broad overall agreement it is possible that the use of this system in practice may lead to a revision of the boundaries between the overall grades. It is hoped that publication of this list will not only be useful to the higher grade winter climber, but that it will also lead to lively debate and exchange of information so that it can be progressively refined and improved. Where recent information has not been available, it has not been possible to give a technical grade; in the list that follows these climbs have been given only their existing overall grade.

A complete list of the suggested new grades for all the harder Scottish winter climbs (where information is available) has been published in the 1992 SMC Journal.

LADHAR BHEINN
Tir na Og	V, 5

FUAR THOLL
Cold Sweat	V, 6
Fuhrer	VI, 5
Tholl Gate	VI, 6
The Ayatollah	VII, 7
Evasion Grooves	V, 6
Pipped at the Post	V, 5
Cold Hole	VI, 6
Tubular Bells	VI, 7
Investigator	VI, 6
Reach for the Sky	VII, 6
Enigma	V
Mainline Connection	V

SGORR RUADH
Tango in the Night	VI, 6
Ruadh Awakening	V

BEINN BHAN
The Acid Queen	IV/V
Sheet Whitening	IV/V
In X.S.	V
Y Gully	IV/V
Mad Hatter's Gully	V, 5
Unnamed	V
Silver Tear	V
Wall of the Early Morning Light	IV/V
The Cooler	V
Moonshine	V
Meanderthal	V, 5
Die Riesenwand	VII, 6
Gully of the Gods	V, 6
Great Overhanging Gully	VI, 7
Threatening Behaviour	V

SGURR A'CHAORACHAIN
Voyager	V, 4
Jupiter	V, 5
Excitable Boy	V

LIATHACH		**Pelican**	VI, 6

LIATHACH

The Snotter	VII, 6
Thumbscrew	IV/V
Thumbscrew Direct	V
Headless Gully	IV, 5
The Executioner	IV, 5
Poacher's Fall	V, 5
The Salmon Leap	VI, 6
White Tiger	V, 5
The Deer Hunter	V, 6
Snow Goose	V, 5
Test Department	VII, 6
Brain Strain	V
Brain Drain	IV, 5
Dru Couloir	IV/V
Toll Dubh Chimney	V
Bell's Buttress Left Chimney	IV/V
Pyramid Direct	V
Salvation	VI, 6

BEINN EIGHE

Glow Worm	V, 6
Vishnu	VII, 6
Kami-Kaze	VI, 7
Eastern Promise	VI, 7
Shang-High	VII, 7
Gnome Wall	V, 6
The Chimney	V
East Wall	VI, 7
Patey's Direct Route	V, 6

Pelican	VI, 6
Flight of the Condor	VII, 7
Central Buttress, Piggott's Route	VI, 7
West Central Gully	VII, 8
West Buttress Direttissima	VII, 8
Maelstrom	VII, 7
Mistral	VII, 7
West Buttress Right-Hand Finish	V
Fuselage Wall	V, 7
The Upper Girdle	VI, 7
Achilles	IV/V
The Independent Pineapple	IV, 6
Spog aig Giomach	IV, 6

BEINN ALLIGIN

Ice Jem	IV, 5
Crown Jewel	IV, 5
The Moonstone	IV, 5

BEINN A'MHUINIDH

The Waterfall	V, 5

AN TEALLACH

Bottomless Gully	IV, 5
Lord Berkeley's Seat	V, 6

BEINN DEARG MOR

Spring Maiden	V

ADDENDUM

COIRE MHIC FHEARCHAIR

FAR EAST WALL

Nightcap Groove (see page 140) has received a winter ascent at Grade V, 7. The difficulties are short and well protected, suitable for early season conditions of deep powder and unfrozen ground. G.Ettle and A.Nisbet, 24 Oct 1992.

THE EASTERN RAMPARTS

The section of cliff around Samurai (see page 156) contains two parallel crack lines. Samurai takes the right-hand line, with a shallow cave on pitch one. The following route takes the left-hand line, leading directly to a square-cut notch in the cliff top.

Forgotten Warrior   120m   HVS
A.Nisbet and M.Sclater, 1 Oct 1992.
This climbs a right-slanting crack and chimney line, well seen from 30m below the start. From the start itself, only the final square-cut notch is obvious. The grade is uncertain, as the climb was done in the wet. Begin 5 metres left of Samurai.
1. 45m 4c Climb the crack line to a right-facing corner. At the Upper Girdle, traverse right back to the original line.
2. 20m 5a Climb the chimney, then the rib on its right and swing back left into the top of the chimney to gain the ledge above.
3. 20m 4c Continue up the chimney until forced out left to ledges.
4. 35m 4c Return to the chimney above its steep section, then gain the base of the square-cut notch either directly or by a spectacular loop out right on good rock. Climb the notch to the top.

WEST BUTTRESS, QUARTZITE TIER

The following route is between Chop Suey and Twilight Zone; see page 175.

Force Ten   95m   E2   (1992)
This gives sustained climbing in spectacular positions with only the occasional hollow block. Above the Upper Girdle it takes an undercut white-streaked and left-slanting ramp, which is well seen from the loch. Start as for Chop Suey.
1. 30m 5b Climb the sharp right arete of the huge groove to a ledge.
2. 20m 5c Continue just right of the arete to the Upper Girdle. Pull through the capping overhang and climb the ramp out leftwards to belay near its top.
3. 30m 5b Make a short traverse left round the arete, then climb steep cracks (just right of the long groove of Chop Suey) to blocky ground.
4. 15m 5a As for Chop Suey, climb a blocky step to the top.

Index

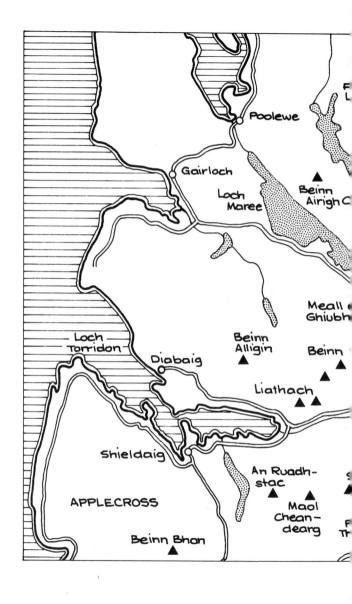